ROCK WALKS:

AN EXPLORER'S GUIDE TO AMAZING BOULDERS & ROCK FORMATIONS OF DOWNSTATE NEW YORK

RUSSELL DUNN

Rock Walks

Published by John Haywood Photography

Second Edition Paperback 2019

Copyright © 2019 by C. Russell Dunn

ISBN: 9798602007381
Imprint: Independently published

CAUTION: Outdoor recreational activities are by their very nature potentially hazardous and contain risk. See Caution: Safety Tips, p. 19.

Front cover: Rock on the Timp-Torne trail near its intersection with Timp Pass Road. Photograph by Dan Balogh.

Back cover: *Upper left*: Boulder on the Arden-Surebridge trail on Pine Swamp Mountain; *Upper right*: Hippo Rock; *Lower left*: View from the ridge of Ramapo Torne Mountain; *Lower right*: Fall blueberry bushes on the Ramapo-Dunderberg Trail on Black Rock Mountain. All photographs by Dan Balogh.

Printed in the USA

10 9 8 7 6 5 4 3 2 1

CONTENTS

Rock Walks

Rock Walks

Rock Walks

Rock Walks

Rock Walks

Chapel Rock
Lover's Rocking Stone
Giant's Slipper
Pic-nic Rock
Poised Rock
Natural Bridge
Hogencamp Mine Boulder
Pine Hill Boulder
Circle Mountain Boulder
Devil's Den
Buzzard's Cave
Finch's Rock House
Fishing Rock
Great Stone at Wading Place
Rock-shelter
Trinity Lake Balanced stone
Spindle Rock
Parson's Woods Tory Cave
Umbrella Point Rock
White Stone
Emmet's Cave
Balanced rocks
Large boulders
Devil's Stepping Stones
Jimmy-under-the-Rock
Kettle Hole Rock
Goldens Bridge Balanced rock
Upright rock
Stissing Mountain Meteor
Brogan's Rock
Seal Rocks
Nigger-head Rock
Strawberry Rock
Large boulder
Enormous boulder
Potholes
Glacial boulder
Indian Mill Pothole
Saddle Rock
Beach Rock
Joshua's Rock
Lionhead Rock
Large boulder

The Timp
A-mac-lea-sin Rock
Fort Skinnopck Boulder
Indian Rock
Sheepspen Rocks
Pidgeon Rock
Large erratic
Rock shelters
Talus caves
Bull's Hill Rock-Shelter
Talus caves
Rock-shelters
Boar's Den
Indian Cave
Balancing Turtle Rock
Robber Rocks
Glacial rock
Multiple rocks
Man-of-War Rock
Huge boulder
Lady's Chair/Lover's Leap/
    Devil's Toothpicks/Devil's Pulpits
Siwanay Indian Image Stone
Old Poker Hole
Ossining Rock Shelter
Leatherman Cave
Spook O Hole
Serpentine Cave
Prop Rock
Skedaddle Rock
Peddlers Rock
Spring House Rock Shelter
Hanging Boulder
Bear Mtn Balanced Rock
Bear's Den
Balanced Rock
Echo Rock Ridge Balanced Rock
Mine Hill Boulders
St. Anthony's Nose
Brundige Cave
Washington Rock
Chimney Rock

9

Let me start off by stating, unequivocally, that *Rock Walks* is an armchair explorer's guide to amazing boulders and rock formations of downstate New York, with *armchair* being the operative word here; for unlike my previous books showcasing boulders and natural rock formations, Rock Walks has not been constructed from on-site visits and field notes, but rather from extensive library and online research in combination with technological advances available through Google Earth, MapQuest, and Topo software; all which have allowed me to travel downstate, and into densely populated areas, without actually leaving my room and computer.

Sounds weird? Perhaps—but I believe that the concept of an armchair guide works, taking you to places that I would otherwise not have gotten to. Hopefully, you will agree as you begin to put this book to work.

Initially, my goal was a modest one—to write a book about downstate rocks and their varied histories, and to leave it at that. But as I delved deeper into the project, I came to realize that the book would be incomplete if I stopped short and didn't make an attempt to tell you how to get to the boulders and rock formation that I was writing about.

Although I believe my directions are pretty much spot-on thanks to MapQuest and Google Earth, there is always the chance I may have erred through misinformation or misunderstanding. For this reason, consider Rock Walks not only a hiker's guide, but an explorer's guidebook as well, an opportunity to go out and to explore on your own without always knowing with certainty what the outcome will be.

Why rocks?

I began thinking about writing a book on boulders and unusual rock formations of Eastern New York State over ten years ago. That thought, however, was momentarily set aside when I started working with Christy Butler, a Massachusetts photographer, on *Connecticut Waterfalls: A Guide*, which was released through Countryman Press/W. W. Norton in 2013. As it turned out, Christy and I had such fun working together on that book that we wanted to do another, and so was born *Rockachusetts: An Explorer's Guide to*

Boulders and Rock Formations of Massachusetts, which was published in 2016.

It was while working on Rockachusetts that we both came to realize that we were doing something special, perhaps something that had never been done before. Despite many books having been published on rock-climbing and bouldering, ours, we believed, was the first to feature boulders and rock formations as hiking destinations, each one unique in its own right. Since then, Christy has gone on to publish *Erratic Wandering: An Explorer's Hiking Guide to Vermont, New Hampshire & Maine* (an incredible undertaking by anyone's standards), and I, not being totally inactive, have gone on to publish *Rambles to Remarkable Rocks: An Explorer's Guide to Amazing Boulders and Rock Formations of the Greater Capital Region, Catskills & Shawangunks,* and *Boulders Beyond Belief: An Explorer's Hiking Guide to Boulders and Natural Rock Formations of the Adirondacks,* both in 2018.

The Hudson Highlands: From Breakneck Mountain.
Photograph 1990.

Rock Walks: An Explorer's Guide to Amazing Boulders and Natural Rock Formations of Downstate New York completes my trilogy of rock books of eastern New York State.

Rock Walks

The obvious question that inevitably comes to mind is: "Why write a book about rocks when everything around us is rock?" Truth be told, can there be anything more ordinary and commonplace than rock?

This argument would be unassailable if Earth was simply a mantle of unbroken, unvarying rock. It isn't—not by a long shot. The landscape before us has been immensely shaped and reshaped by plate tectonics, erosion, and repeating periods of glaciation.

Photograph (1907) by Sidney Benham.

Enormous boulders have been picked up and moved incredible distances. Talus slopes have formed where sections of rock have been ripped off from cliff faces by glaciers or collapsed on their own accord. Rivers have created enormous chasms that continue to deepen. Swirling whirlpools, seizing stones and spinning them endlessly around, have augered their way into streambeds to create potholes. Enterable fissures have formed where the bedrock has literally split asunder liken the shell of an egg cracking under pressure. Softer rock has been eroded out from under more durable rock to leave behind rock-shelters.

Yes, Nature has been at work, and, as an artist, has sculpted some pretty amazing natural rock formations.

When it comes to downstate New York, I have been particularly impressed by just how many of the countless number of rocks are historically significant. Thousands have been known about for centuries, many going back to the days when Native Americans used boulders and rock formations for meeting places and as refuges from the elements.

In the early days, large rocks served as natural points of navigation through a wilderness that was otherwise featureless.

They also served as boundary markers when lines of demarcation needed to be established through land cultivation.

Many downstate rocks were widely publicized during the lake nineteenth century and early twentieth century, their images reproduced through hundreds of thousands of postcards. You will see a number of these postcard reproductions scattered through the book.

Erratic behavior

Downstate New York possesses a great many small-to-large erratics. Erratics, by definition, are rocks that are not native or indigenous to their surroundings. They have traveled from other regional areas, often over great distances. Early scientists were perplexed by the presence of erratics, confounded over what kind of force was powerful enough to move rocks the size of houses and as massive as freight cars over tens to hundreds of miles.

Native Americans, of course, had their own theory about erratics. Out-of-place rocks simply fell from the sky, perhaps dropped by the Great Spirit himself. As it turns out, the notion of rocks falling from the sky is not as fanciful as it may have once sounded. Earth, as we now know, is

An odd-looking boulder along Pine Meadow Trail (Harriman State Park). Photograph by Dan Balogh.

constantly being bombarded by meteorites, with some making it to the ground as meteors. Fortunately, most are burned up and disintegrate before reaching terra firma, which is why you are unlikely to ever come across a meteor in your travels. For this reason, we can safely rule out meteors for being the source of the thousands upon thousands of erratics that lay about. Are there any other theories?

13

Rock Walks

The first scientific-sounding theory to explain the existence of erratics was called the Diluvial Theory. It drew inspiration from the Bible and postulated that it was the torrential deluge of waters from Noah's Great Flood that pushed and tumbled these huge rocks across the landscape. In this respect, the Diluvial Theory did make sense, for we all know the power of moving water and the tremendous force it can exert on objects encountered. The theory, however, only worked if you believed in a biblical, worldwide, great flood. It, blithely ignored the fact that millions of huge erratics were inexplicably not present in the southern hemisphere as you would expect if a worldwide flood once raged, and failed to answer how such rocks managed to get up to the top of high mountains given the fact that fast-moving waters would push boulders around obstacles, such as hills and mountains, as opposed to carrying them up to the top.

In 1833, the Diluvial Theory was made slightly more palatable by bringing into play the role of icebergs. It was called the Ice-Rafted Theory. Now, in addition to Noah's Great Flood, it was postulated that huge icebergs broke loose from the arctic ice circle and, like rafts, transported boulders south over great distances, dropping them as the ice slowly melted. This theory both explained how boulders ended up on top of mountains (the mountains were under water), and why few large boulders are found in the southern hemisphere (the melting icebergs dropped their load before they could get there). The problem with this theory, however, was that it couldn't explain how boulders began their journey on top of the icebergs. That went against the natural order that ice forms on rocks—not vice versa.

It was up to Swiss-born Louis Agassiz to come up with a satisfactory theory, which he advanced in 1837. It was called the Glaciation Theory, and asserted that erratics, or what we now call glacial erratics, were swept up by stupendous glaciers. These mile-high glaciers bulldozed the landscape, moving rocks and earth southward, and, in the process, depositing millions of large rocks in their wake as the Earth warmed and the glaciers began to retreat northward.

Since Agassiz's time, there has never been any further debate about the matter (except for Creationists who believe that the Earth is only 6,000 years old and that there has been insufficient time for such momentous events to have happened).

I find it somewhat ironic, however, that in the end, it *was* water after all that moved rocks across the landscape—only, in this case, water in its solid form as ice.

Downstate New York 10,000 years ago

It's important to understand that during the last Ice Age, North America looked a great deal different than it does today. At that time, a huge portion of the ocean was locked up as ice, causing sea levels to drop over 200 feet, and exposing vast tracts of land. Long Island was about twice as wide then as it is now. The Hudson River ran through a canyon whose walls were over 200 feet in height.

When the last Ice Age ended as glaciers retreated northward, a freshwater body of water called Lake Hudson momentarily formed. Its waters were temporarily dammed up by an earthen barrier that stretched between Brooklyn and Staten Island.

As far as Manhattan goes, there was little of it to see, just a portion of what we today call Midtown. Queens and the Bronx were essentially buried under Lake Flushing (where Flushing Meadow in Queens is now), and the East River (really just an arm of the Atlantic Ocean) that separated Manhattan from Brooklyn and Queens, had yet to come into existence.

It really was a different world back then as glaciers made their northward retreat!

How big is big?

You might wonder how big a boulder can get. As it turns out, you don't have to look very far. The largest freestanding boulder on the planet is reputedly located right here in the United States. It is the seven-story high Giant Rock (34°19.970'N 116°23.325'W) resting in the Mojave Desert near Landers, California. This is truly a humongous boulder. But large boulders aren't big just because of their size. They are massive—incredibly so. Double the size of a 4-foot boulder to 8 feet and its mass (weight) hasn't just changed by a factor of two. It has increased cubically, meaning that what started off at 10 tons now weighs 1,000 tons (10 x 10 x 10).

Largeness, then, really does matter when we talk about big boulders.

World's largest boulder—and it's right here in the USA!

GPS Coordinates – Virtually all GPS coordinates have been taken directly from Google Earth.

Some, by necessity, are estimates. But even such estimated GPS coordinates should get you to the general area where you want to be.

Delorme NYS Atlas & Gazetteer Coordinates – You will find that Delorme coordinates are ideal for giving you an overview of the area that you are traveling through to reach the parking area or trailhead.

Be aware, however, that Delorme recently updated their New York State Atlas & Gazetteer, completely reversing the numerical order of their maps. For this reason, two sets of Delorme Coordinates are provided to ensure that regardless of which Atlas & Gazetteer you are using, you will be able to find your way with maximum efficiency.

Directions – Most of the directions have been created using various combinations of Google Earth, MapQuest, and Topo Mapware.

In one or two instances where navigating by MapQuest through a quagmire of streets and expressways was too complicated for a simple set of directions, sufficient information has been provided to get you to the general area, leaving you to figure out the rest using local maps.

In almost all instances, the directions start from a major intersection, e.g., "junction of Routes 9 & 311", and from there, proceed to the trailhead parking.

In areas of high population density, like Manhattan, there are times when you may have to follow through on your own to find a parking space.

WOW Factor – A somewhat arbitrary Wow Factor number, ranging from 1 to 10, is given for each rock formation. The higher the number, the bigger the wow.

Photographing rocks – The ideal always is to include a person in the photograph where possible. Doing so not only humanizes the photograph, but provides important information regarding the size of the rock formation.

Secondly, most rocks tend to be in woodlands surrounded by trees. If possible, try to take as unobstructed a photograph of the boulder as possible. Trees and branches can get in the way and obscure the boulder or, minimally, act as a source of visual distraction.

Proper lighting also is a factor that cannot be disregarded. Since many boulders are located in deep woods, the light coming in can be severely restricted by trees, brush, and leaves. This fact needs to be taken into account when adjusting the setting on your camera.

On the other hand, if there is too much sunlight, the bright rays poking through branches and bushes can create a checkerboard pattern, once again making the image visually distracting. In this case, there may be little you can do to compensate except to wait for a momentary cloud to diffuse the sunlight.

This is an explorer's guidebook

This is not just a hiker's guidebook, but an explorer's guidebook as well. For this reason, some of the chapters cannot guarantee that you will necessarily find the geological formation that you are looking for, leaving you to your own ingenuity to locate the boulder or rock formation. However, what you are guaranteed to have is an adventure, and isn't half the fun just getting out into the great outdoors?

Regrettably, not all of the rocks described are accessible. In some cases, the boulder or rock formation may be on private land where visitors are not welcomed. I've included these rocks, not only for the sake of historical record (which is extremely important), but because there's always the possibility that the land may one day return to the public domain through the acquisition of lands from conservation-minded public and private agencies.

In other cases, the rock may simply no longer exist, destroyed either by man or by nature. This is particularly regretful when it is humans who are to blame.

Rocks that are nonexistent or currently inaccessible are listed as "historic."

Rocking Stone (Bronx Zoo). Old photograph.

Rock Walks

CAUTION: SAFETY TIPS

Nature is inherently wild, unpredictable, and uncompromising. Outdoor recreational activities are by their very nature potentially hazardous and involve risk. All participants in such activities must assume the responsibility for their own actions and safety. No book can replace good judgment. The outdoors is forever changing. The author and the publisher cannot be held responsible for inaccuracies, errors, or omissions; for any changes in the details of this publication; for the consequences of any reliance on the information contained herein; or for people's disregard for safety in the outdoors.

Remember: the destination is not the boulder, rock formation, or the mountain summit. The destination is home, and the goal is getting back there safely.

1. Always hike with two or more companions whenever possible.

2. Make it a practice of bringing along a day pack complete with emergency supplies, compass, whistle, flashlight, dry matches, raingear, power bars, extra layers, gorp, duct tape, lots of water (at least twenty-four ounces per person), mosquito repellent, emergency medical kit, sunblock, and a device for removing ticks.

3. Use sunblock when exposed to sunlight for extended periods of time, and apply insect repellents as needed.

4. Hike with ankle-high boots—always!

5. Be cognizant of hypothermia (overcooling) and hyperthermia (overheating). Bring along extra layers when the temperature is cold, and drink plenty of water when the weather is hot and muggy.

6. Stay out of the woods during hunting season in areas where hunters are present.

7. Stay on trails unless you are proficient in orienteering.

8. Be aware that trails described in this book can become altered by blowdown, beaver dams, avalanches, mudslides, forest fires, and so forth. Stay alert.

9. Always let someone know where you are going, when you will return, and what to do if you have not shown up by the designated time.

10. Leave early in the morning if you are undertaking a long hike, especially during the winter when daylight is at a premium.

11. Be mindful of ticks, which have become increasingly prevalent and virulent as their range expands. Check yourself thoroughly after every hike and remove any attached tick immediately.

So let's begin....

Downstate New York is huge, with many counties, boroughs, and islands. For this reason, particularly as a matter of convenience, we will use the Hudson River as a handy line of demarcation, and divide the book into two sections: rocks on the east side of the Hudson River, and rocks on the west side of the Hudson River.

With this said, we began our adventure, somewhat arbitrarily, starting with the east side of the Hudson River.

Indian Prayer Rock.

EAST SIDE OF HUDSON RIVER

This section of the book covers all of Dutchess, Putnam, Westchester, Nassau, and Suffolk Counties; the New York City boroughs, including Manhattan and Staten Island; and all of Long Island.

DUTCHESS COUNTY

Dutchess County encompasses 825 square miles of land and is named after Mary of Modena, the Dutchess of York. The terrain is mostly hilly, with the Taconic Range to the northeast, and the Hudson Highlands to the southwest.

1. STONE CHURCH CAVE

Type of Formation: Cave
WOW Factor: 8
Location: Dover Plains (Dutchess County)
Tenth Edition, NYS Atlas & Gazetteer: p. 104, C2; **Earlier Edition NYS Atlas & Gazetteer:** p. 37, BC7
Parking GPS Coordinates: 41º44.330′N 73º34.774′W
Stone Church Cave GPS Coordinates: 41º44.289′N 73º35.324′W
Accessibility: 0.4-mile hike
Degree of Difficulty: Moderately easy

Description: The Stone Church Cave is very impressive, and very much in keeping with what most people visualize when they bring to mind the image of a cave. Its vaulted entrance stands 30 feet high, and is nearly as wide. At first glance, the cave almost looks manmade, much like a railroad tunnel, except that no train will ever emerge from it. The cavern extends back for 75 feet and then ends, but not before a 20-foot-high waterfall crashes down onto the bedrock of the floor.

A stupendous rock inside the cave, reaching almost halfway to the ceiling and quite possibly a part of the ceiling that has dropped onto the floor, was reputedly named "The Pulpit" in 1908 by Richard Maher, author of *Historic Dover*, because of the rock's resemblance to

21

an old-fashioned New England pulpit. It's entirely possible that it was through "The Pulpit" that the cave came to be named Stone Church Cave. According to Virginia Palmer, in her article "The Stone Church," the rock's "base is approximately twenty-five feet wide, and its height about thirty feet." Palmer goes on to mention that "a large boulder, oblong-shaped, stands upright in the rear of the cave." She also writes, "In the interior of the Stone Church, rock formations which some years ago were likened to pews and alters are no longer in evidence, or only slightly."

The cave was created by Stone Church Brook, a tributary of Ten Mile River. Upstream from the cave, the river has cut out a fairly deep, narrow gorge with multiple cascades.

Hikers approach the entrance to Stone Church Cave.

History: Historical accounts tell us that Pequot Sachem Sassacus and a band of his warriors took refuge in the cave in the 1600s during King Philip's War, hoping to evade capture and execution by the British.

Stone Church Cave became a popular tourist Mecca in the 1830s. Droves of visitors from New York City and adjacent states would descend on Dover Plains to visit the cave. It was celebrated in much the same way that Howe Caverns in Schoharie County was. Weddings were even performed in the cave, which is another possible explanation for how the cave came to be named.

At one time, the waters from Stone Church Brook were impounded by a cement dam and used as a water supply for the residents of Dover Plains. By 1950, virtually all traces of the cement dam were gone.

Stone Church Cave's prominence rose to even greater heights after it was rendered onto canvass by several Hudson River School painters (one of them being Asher Durand) and featured by Benson Lossing in *Dover Stone Church and the History of Dutchess County*.

The land was acquired by the Dutchess County Open Space and Farmland Protection Fund, Friends of Dover Stone Church, and the Dutchess County Land Conservancy in 2002. This acquisition included not only the cave, but 58 acres of surrounding land as well as a conservation easement from Route 22 to the cave. Improvements were later made on the trail leading to the cave.

Dover Plains was named after the white, chalk cliffs of Dover, England.

Directions: From Amenia (junction of Routes 22, 343 & 44), drive south on Route 22 for ~9.0 miles to Dover Plains.

From Wingdale (junction of Routes 22 & 55), drive north on Route 22 for ~7.0 miles to Dover Plains.

Park at the Dover Elementary School or designated area if a new parking area has been created.

Look for a New York State historic sign for Stone Church Cave on the west side of Route 22, nearly opposite Mill Street. Follow the driveway uphill for 100 feet to reach the trailhead (41º44.383'N 73º34.924'W). Take note that parking here is reserved for homeowners in the adjacent houses.

From the trailhead, follow a flight of modern, railed, stone block steps down the side of a small hill to the valley floor, across an open field into the woods, through a grove of old trees, and then next to Stone Church Brook on your left.

By 0.3 mile, the path enters into a gorge. Slabs of rock provide ample footing. In another 0.1 mile or less you will reach the entrance to Stone Church Cave. If the stream is not running fast, there are sufficient slabs of rock to enable you to rock-hop into the interior of the cave.

.

Resources: Russell Dunn, *Hudson Valley Waterfall Guide* (Hensonville, NY: Black Dome Press Corp., 2005), 204–206.
townofdoverny.us/Stone_Church.cfm.
oblongland.org/pdf/stone_church_dover.pdf – This site contains the "Dover Stone Church Cave Visitor's Guide."
Wallace Bruce, *The Hudson: Three Centuries of History, Romance, and Invention. Centennial Edition* (New York: Walking News, Inc., 1982), 127.
Patricia Edwards Clyne, *Caves for Kids in Historic New York* (Monroe, NY: Library Research Associates, 1980), 55–62.
Thomas Sweet Lossing, *My Heart Goes Home: A Hudson Valley Memoir* (Fleischmanns, NY: Purple Mountain Press, 1997), 107 & 108.
Clay Perry, *Underground Empire: Wonders and Tales of New York Caves* (New York: Stephen Daye Press, 1948), 130 & 131. A spectacular photograph of the cave can be seen on an insert between pages 54/55.
Joyce C. Ghee & Joan Spence, *Harlem Valley Pathways: Images of America* (Charleston, SC: Arcadia Publishing, 1998). A photograph of the cave entrance is displayed on page 33. A caption accompanying the photograph reads, "Magnetite in the rock fools compasses and ancient petroglyphs confound archaeologists." Are there actually petroglyphs at Stone Church Cave?
Virginia Palmer, "The Stone Church" *Year Book: Dutchess County Historical Society. Vol. 33* (1948), 45–49.
Frank Hasbrouck, *The History of Dutchess County, New York* (Poughkeepsie, NY: S. A. Mattheu, 1909). A photo of the cave can be seen on an insert between pages 282/283.

2. INDIAN ROCK

Margaret Lewis Norrie State Park: Esopus Island

Type of Formation: Petroglyph/Megalith
WOW Factor: 2–3
Location: Staatsburg (Dutchess County)
Tenth Edition, NYS Atlas & Gazetteer: p. 103, A7; **Earlier Edition NYS Atlas & Gazetteer:** p. 36, B4
Parking GPS Coordinates: 41º49.946'N 73º56.459'W
Esopus Island GPS Coordinates: 41º49.506'N 73º56.858'W
Accessibility: 0.4-mile trek by water
Degree of Difficulty: Easy by boat
Additional Information: Norrie Point Environmental Center, 9 Old Post Road, Staatsburg, NY

Description: In *Hudson Valley Trails and Tales,* Patricia Edwards Clyne writes about a "...mysterious carved boulder in the [Hudson] river... known as Indian Rock." It is located on Esopus Island.

Esopus Island, accessible by water from Margaret Lewis Norrie State Park.

Esopus Island is a very narrow, 0.4-mile long island, 200 feet across at its widest. One writer has likened the island's shape to that of a "great stranded and petrified whale." Most of the island's shoreline is exposed bedrock, which would seem to make locating the petroglyphs/megaliths fairly difficult due to the island's extensive perimeter. Fortunately, one of my sources has narrowed the search down substantially, asserting that the Native American handiwork is on the east side of the island.

There is a small beach of sorts on the southeast side of the island, and shoals at its north end. I suspect most people dock at the beach area.

History: The Lenape Native Americans made use of Esopus Island and, while on it, fashioned carvings and a megalith of sorts.

According to legend, a Jesuit missionary was killed on the island by the Lenape, for reasons of which I am not clear, but which I can't help but wonder if it was due to religious zealotry.

During the nineteenth century, the island was part of Robert L. Pell's 1,200-acre estate and was then known as Pell Island.

By coincidence, there is also an Indian Rock (a cliff) in the same general area on the opposite side of the Hudson River, slightly northwest of Esopus Island. It can be seen clearly on mapcarta.com/22011990. I doubt, however, that confusion ever arises when people wish to delineate the two Indian Rocks.

Directions: From Staatsburg (junction of Routes 9 & 37/North Cross Road)), drive southwest on Route 9 for 0.5 mile and turn right onto Margaret Norrie State Park Road. At a fork, bear left to reach the Norrie Point Environmental Center, a distance of ~1.0 mile from Route 9.

Resources: Patricia Edwards Clyne, *Hudson Valley Trails and Tales* (Woodstock, NY: The Overlook Press, 1990), 258
en.wikipedia.org/wiki/Esopus_Island.
hudsonvalleyone.com/2015/07/20/retrace-steps-of-famed-mystic-aleister-crowley-on-esopus-island.
revolvy.com/page/Esopus-Island.
Capt. Stanley Wilcox & H. W. Van Loan, *The Hudson from Troy to the Battery* (Philmont, NY: Riverview Publishing, 2011), 60. The authors tell the tale of Aleister Crowley, an astrologer and occultist, who is said to have spent forty days and nights on the island in 1941 while exploring deeper levels of consciousness.

Rock Walks

3. WARYAS PARK ROCKS & KAAL ROCK
Waryas Park

Type of Formation: Strange Rock Sculpture; Historic Rock Bluff
WOW Factor: 2–3
Location: Poughkeepsie (Dutchess County)
Tenth Edition, NYS Atlas & Gazetteer: p. 103, C7; **Earlier Edition NYS Atlas & Gazetteer**: p. 36, C4
Parking GPS Coordinates: 41º42.333'N 73º56.405'W
Destination GPS Coordinates: *Rock Sculpture* -- 41º42.322'N 73º56.415'W; *Kaal Rock* -- 41º42.229'N 73º56.456'W
Accessibility: *Rock Sculpture* -- 20-foot walk; *Kaal Rock* – 0.2-mile trek
Degree of Difficulty: *Rock Sculpture* –Easy; *Kaal Rock* – Moderately easy

Description: Waryas Park Rocks consist of three moderately large, artificially-created rocks. Although it's not evident at first, these three, separated rocks actually form one large, extended piece of art work—the tail, back, and head of an enormous 80-foot-long sperm whale. The tail is about 7 feet in height; the head, 4 feet.

Harvey K. Flad & Clyde Griffin, in *Main Street to Mainframes: Landscape and Social Change in Poughkeepsie*, write that "The sculptures were built out of steel rebar and cement and covered by ceramic tile mosaics."

Just 0.3-mile upriver looms the 1.3-mile-long bridge, "Walkway Over the Hudson"—the centerpiece of the Walkway Over the Hudson State Historic Park. It is said to be the longest elevated pedestrian bridge in the world.

Just south of the park, >0.1 mile upriver from the 3,000-foot-long Mid-Hudson Bridge is Kaal Rock—a 50-foot-high *Strange rock sculpture at Waryas Park.* bluff that overlooks the Hudson River and that once served as a vital reference point for sailors navigating the river. Ernest Ingersoll, in *Handy Guide to the Hudson River and Catskill Mountains*, writes that

27

Rock Walks

"tradition says the early burghers of the town used to sit [on Kaal Rock], and hail the sloops for news as they drifted by..."

History: Waryas Park encompasses 9 acres of greenspace and was named after former Poughkeepsie major, Victor C. Waryas, who served from 1960–1964.

The sperm whale art piece was created by Cragsmoor-based artist Judy Sigunick in 2002. The subject chosen was not done haphazardly. Poughkeepsie at one time was a vibrant port, with two whaling companies operating from what is now Waryas Park.

Kaal Rock, aka Caul Rock and Call Rock, is Dutch for "Bald Rock."

Directions: Traveling north through Poughkeepsie along Route 9, get off at the Main Street Exit. When you come to Main Street, turn left and drive 0.3 mile west to reach Waryas Park.

Traveling south on Route 9, get off at the Laurel Street Exit, turn right onto Laurel Street, and head west for 0.05 mile to Rinaldi Boulevard. Turn right onto Rinaldi Boulevard and drive north for over 0.3 mile. Finally, turn left onto Main Street and proceed west for 0.1 mile to reach the park.

Park in the cul-de-sac. The cement sculptures are southwest of the cul-de-sac, a mere 50 feet away.

Kaal Rock is the wooded precipice beyond the south end of Waryas Park, lying between Waryas Park and Kaal Park. To reach Kaal Rock, walk uphill from the sculptures, first heading east, then south, as you follow along the edge of the woods for 0.1 mile. When the hill levels off, you will be at the cul-de-sac at the end of Long Street. A path from here to your right leads into the woods and up to the highest point of Kaal Rock in 0.1 mile. This vertical precipice is an impressive overlook by anyone's standards. To your left (south) is the Mid-Hudson Bridge and directly below, also south, is Kaal Park (which can be reached by following a rocky path downhill—a trek that is obviously not for everyone).

Rock Walks

Kaal Rock, overlooking the Hudson River. Old photograph.

Resources: Joyce C. Ghee & Joan Spence, *Poughkeepsie Halfway up the Hudson: Images of America* (Charleston, SC: Arcadia Publishing 1997), 29.
bing.com/images/search?q=kaal+rock+park+poughkeepsie+ny&qpvt=kaal+rock+park+poughkeepsie+ny&FORM=IGRE – This site contains a photograph of one of the rock sculptures.
Harvey K. Flad & Clyde Griffin, *Main Street to Mainframes: Landscape and Social Change in Poughkeepsie* (Albany, NY: New York State University Press, 2009), 227.
waymarking.com/waymarks/WM4KWZ_The_Whale_in_Waryas_Park_P oughkeepsie_NY.
hvmag.com/Hudson-Valley-Magazine/June-2014/Where-in-the-Hudson-Valley-Contest-Wayward-Whale-Park-Sculpture.
Ernest Ingersoll, *Handy Guide to the Hudson River and Catskill Mountains* (Astoria, NY: J. C. & A. L. Fawcett, Inc., 1989; reprint of 1910 book), 132.

4. LOVERS LEAP (Historic)
Poughkeepsie Rural Cemetery

Type of Formation: Bluff
WOW Factor: 3
Location: Poughkeepsie (Dutchess County)
Tenth Edition, NYS Atlas & Gazetteer: p. 103, C7; **Earlier Edition NYS Atlas & Gazetteer**: p. 36, C4
Estimated Lovers Leap GPS Coordinates: 41º40.818′N 73º56.320′W
Accessibility: Inaccessible

Additional Information: Poughkeepsie Rural Cemetery, 342 South Avenue, Poughkeepsie, NY 12601.

Description: Lovers Leap is a high bluff that overlooks the Hudson River and the Amtrak railroad. It is located along the west-most border of the Poughkeepsie Rural Cemetery — a 165-acre graveyard that dates back to 1853.

Rocky bedrock at Poughkeepsie Rural Cemetery. Photograph 2019.

History: A number of legends are associated with Lovers Leap, all involving one or two Native Americans or Victorians who commit suicide, generally out of unrequited or forbidden love. There is even one tale of a man pushing a woman off of the bluff, and then jumping to his own death.

These are very common stories, virtually all mythical, and associated with many high cliffs and vertical waterfalls in New York State.

In *Poughkeepsie Halfway up the Hudson: Images of America*, a photograph is shown of a well-dressed, Victorian man sitting in a summerhouse (gazebo) by Lovers Leap.

Directions: From Poughkeepsie (at the point where Route 9 passes under the Mid-Hudson River Bridge), drive south on Route 9 for >1.1 miles. Veer right onto Old South Road, which parallels Route 9, and then right into the entrance to the Poughkeepsie Rural Cemetery after 0.2 mile.

From here, make your way southwest across a landscape of rolling hills to the north end of a pretty, 0.1-mile-long, unnamed pond. Take note of an interesting 8–10-foot rock outcropping by the northeast corner of the pond.

From here, I thought I had it all figured out. Starting at the northwest corner of the pond, my plan was to follow a dirt road southwest through an isolated section of the cemetery for 0.3 mile to what look liked, using Google Earth, a mausoleum or a large vault. Then, from there, I was going to walk less than 200 feet to what I believed was the Lovers Leap precipice.

The problem, as it turns out, was one I could not have anticipated — the road leading to the mausoleum is private and not open to the public, even though it is located in the cemetery.

In the end, I never got to verify whether my hypothesis was correct; but I do believe that Lovers Leap is likely at the GPS Coordinates listed.

Resources: Joyce C. Ghee & Joan Spence, *Poughkeepsie Halfway up the Hudson: Images of America* (Charleston, SC: Arcadia Publishing 1997), 94.
riverletters.blogspot.com/2010/04/lovers-leap-from-poughkeepsie-rural.html.
poughkeepsieruralcemetery.com/history.php.

5. POUGHKEEPSIE STANDING STONE

WOW Factor: 2
Location: Wappinger Falls (Dutchess County)
Tenth Edition, NYS Atlas & Gazetteer: p. 103, D7–8; **Earlier Edition NYS Atlas & Gazetteer**: p. 36, CD4
Poughkeepsie Standing Stone GPS Coordinates: 41º36.620′N 73º55.896′W
Accessibility: Roadside
Degree of Difficulty: Easy

Rock Walks

Description: The Poughkeepsie Standing Stone is a rectangular, 4-foot-high slab of limestone jutting out of the ground at an inclined angle.

History: The Poughkeepsie Standing Stone is believed to have been shaped by human hands rather than by weathering. It is not a natural stone then. The rock is called a *menhirs*, which is a French term for a large, upright, standing stone of variable size, its shape, generally uneven, often tapering near the top.

The Poughkeepsie Standing Stone.

Laura M. Lane, who once lived across from the Standing Stone, never gave the rock much thought until her dad, an engineer, did some plotting, and figured out that 17 feet of the rock's length would have to be buried underground in order for the rock to sit as it does.

Whether seventeen feet of this rock actually lies buried underground or not, it serves to illustrate that the Standing Stone has been a point of curiosity for many years. Joyce C. Ghee & Joan Spence, in *Poughkeepsie Halfway up the Hudson: Images of America*, even go so far as to say that the stone has been here "since before recorded history."

David Beck, a Park Naturalist at Bowden Park, recounted to me a story he was told by a local historian who claimed that Native Americans used the stone to sight on a sacred, ceremonial site that lay uphill where the Mount Alvernia Retreat Center is now located.

Directions: From northwest of Spackenkill (junction of Routes 9 & 113/Spackenkill Road), drive south on Route 9 for ~1.7 miles. Turn right onto Sheafe Road and continue south for another ~2.0 miles. Finally, turn left onto Delavergne Avenue and drive east for 0.2 mile. The stone is at the intersection of Delavergne Avenue and Oakwood Drive, virtually opposite the road leading up to the Mount Alvernia Retreat Center.

Resources: Joyce C. Ghee & Joan Spence, *Poughkeepsie Halfway up the Hudson: Images of America* (Charleston, SC: Arcadia Publishing 1997), 86. grahamhancock.com/kreisbergg7.

6. BOWDOIN PARK ROCKLEDGE SHELTER
Bowdoin Park

Type of Formation: Rock-Shelter
WOW Factor: *North Rock-Shelter -- 4–5; South Rock-Shelter -- 5*
Location: Wappinger Falls (Dutchess County)
Tenth Edition, NYS Atlas & Gazetteer: p. 103, D7; **Earlier Edition NYS Atlas & Gazetteer**: p. 36, CD4
Main Parking GPS Coordinates: 41º36.144'N 73º56.452'W
Destination GPS Coordinates: *North Rock-Shelter* – Not determined; *South Rock-Shelter -- * 41º35.835'N 73º56.371'W (an estimate)
Accessibility: *North Rock-shelter* – 0.2 mile-walk, followed by a 100-foot uphill trek; *South Shelter* – 0.4-mile hike to top of bluff followed by 200-foot bushwhack to near base of escarpment
Degree of Difficulty: *North Rock-Shelter* – Moderately easy; *South Rock-Shelter* – Moderately easy to bluff overlook; moderately difficult to base of bluff
Additional Information: Dutchess County Bowdoin Park, 85 Sheafe Road, Wappingers Falls, NY 12590; (845) 298-4600
dutchesstourism.com/PDF/brochure-rack/Bowdoin_Trail_Map_Brochure_5_24_10.pdf -- Trail map.

Description: Bowdoin Park contains two historically significant rock-shelters. Both have formed at the base of rocky escarpments, and both have downslopes that lead from their base to the floor of the valley.

The *North Rock-Shelter*, roughly 6–7 feet high, is at the bottom of a 30-foot-high escarpment. Four feet of debris and earth had to be removed from the entrance in order to restore the shallow cavity to its original state when used by Native Americans thousands of years ago. It's possible that the rock-shelter may have been wider at one time. This can only be determined by further excavations in the future. Equally as possible is that the overhang may have extended out farther from the cliff, but no one really knows for sure.

By good fortune, David Beck, park naturalist, accompanied us to the rock-shelter and proved very helpful in translating what we were seeing into what the site was like centuries—even millenniums—ago. At that time, the land was not as devoid of sustenance as it is today. Game was more plentiful, and chestnut trees (which were literally everywhere until wiped out by the Chestnut blight in the early 1900s) provided plenty of nourishment.

It's very likely that Native Americans lived much closer to the river during the warmer months, retreating to the rock-shelter seasonally when conditions became less hospitable.

Part of the rock-shelter is presently covered with a wooden frame thatched with reed grass in order to show visitors how Native Americans created an enclosure to keep out the harsh weather.

Park naturalist, David Beck, stands next to the north rock-shelter.

The *South Rock-Shelter*, at the opposite end of Bowdoin Park, is located at the bottom of a 40-foot-high bluff, with considerably more rock-face showing, as well as more of an overhang than it northern counterpart. The rock-shelter evidently gets fewer visitors, for no discernable path leads down to it.

In their book, *Poughkeepsie Halfway up the Hudson: Images of America*, Joyce C. Ghee and Joan Spence mention that, historically, the rock-shelters were easily accessible from the Hudson River, and provided inhabitants with an unobstructed view of the river for defensive purposes. The view didn't look quite as unobstructed today on our visit.

History: Bowdoin Park encompasses 301 acres of lands and contains roughly five miles of trails. In the 1920s, the Children's Aid Society received the Bowdoin estate as a bequest. The land passed on to the county in the 1960s and opened to the public in 1975.

It is believed that a Native American village may have occupied the site where the soccer fields are located today.

Directions: From northwest of Spackenkill (junction of Routes 9 & 113/Spackenkill Road), drive south on Route 9 for ~1.7 miles. Turn right onto Sheafe Road and continue south for another ~2.6 miles. Then turn right into the entrance of Bowdoin Park and follow the main road downhill for 0.2 mile to a mid-level parking area.

North Rock-Shelter – From the parking area, walk north to the 4-way intersection you just turned left at. Cross the road and continue past a red-colored sign that says "Private. No Vehicles

South rock-shelter at Bowdoin Park.

Allowed," following a dirt road north for ~0.2 mile. At the time of year when trees are leafless, you will notice an old road to your right that gradually gets closer and closer to the dirt road until it merges.

35

At that point, you will see a faint path to your right that leads uphill in 150 feet to the rock-shelter.

South Rock-Shelter – Walk east uphill from the parking area for less than 100 feet to reach the trailhead. Follow the white-blazed trail south for 0.2 mile. At a fork (across from a bench), bear right and continue south on the now yellow-blazed trail for another 0.2 mile. When you come to a bare, rocky prominence overlooking the valley, you are directly above the rock-shelter. Backtrack a hundred feet or so, and then bushwhack southwest down the slope to reach the bottom of the escarpment and the rock-shelter. Expect a fairly demanding descent over blowdown and loose rock.

Resources: Joyce C. Ghee & Joan Spence, *Poughkeepsie Halfway up the Hudson: Images of America* (Charleston, SC: Arcadia Publishing 1997), 86.
co.dutchess.ny.us/CountyGov/Departments/DPW-Parks/PPbowdoin.htm.
hudsonrivervalley.com/lessons/print/native-peoples-of-the-hudson-valley.
Joyce C. Ghee & Joan Spence, *Poughkeepsie 1898–1998. A Century of Chang: Images of America* (Charleston, SC: Arcadia Publishing, 1999), 75.
Harvey K. Flad & Clyde Griffin, *Main Street to Mainframes: Landscape and Social Change in Poughkeepsie* (Albany, NY: New York State University Press, 2009), 166.
nynjctbotany.org/lgtofc/nybowdon.html.
Jeffrey Perls, *Paths along the Hudson: A Guide to Walking and Biking* (New Brunswick, NJ: Rutgers University Press, 2001), 324 & 325.

7. NUCLEAR LAKE ROCKS
Appalachian Trail

Type of Formation: Large Rock
WOW Factor: 5
Location: West Pawling (Dutchess County)
Tenth Edition, NYS Atlas & Gazetteer: p. 104, D1; **Earlier Edition NYS Atlas & Gazetteer**: p. 37, CD6–7
Parking GPS Coordinates: 41º35.388'N 73º39.551'W
Estimated Destination GPS Coordinates: Not determined
Accessibility: < 1.0-mile hike to the rocks; 1.2-mile hike to Nuclear Lake
Degree of Difficulty: Moderate

Description: Several large rock formations are encountered, one being 20–25 feet high and probably used, on occasion, for bouldering.

History: Nuclear Lake got its name when a nuclear research lab on the southwest shore of the lake exploded in 1972, scattering a significant amount of bomb-grade plutonium over the nearby woods and water. Fortunately, it was a chemical explosion, not a nuclear one.

Although hikers may jest in earnest about the risk of encountering traces of plutonium around the lake, the area has been tested and found to be perfectly safe.

Directions: From Poughquag (junction of Routes 55/Freedom Plains Road & 216), proceed southeast on Route 55/Freedom Plains Road for ~1.4 miles and park on your left in an unmarked, gravel, parking area for the Appalachian Trail. There is enough room for 6 cars.

Kris Klein makes his way up a large boulder while Jill Klein spots him. Photo by Mike Todd.

Follow the blue-blazed trail into the woods, and then, after going under powerlines, turn left onto the white-blazed Appalachian Trail (AT), heading northeast.

Rock Walks

In ~0.2–0.3 mile, stay to your right on the AT as the blue-blazed Beekman Uplands Loop Trail head off to your left.

Soon, you will begin passing by some large rock formations next to the trail as you descend towards the lake. Two small footbridges are also crossed. If you wish to hike around Nuclear Lake, after the second bridge crossing, turn right onto the yellow-marked Nuclear Lake Trail and follow it around the lake for 1.1 mile until you return to the Appalachian Trail. Turn left here, and take the trail back to your car.

Were you to continue east on the AT, you would eventually come to Cat Rock at ~3.0 miles, a panoramic, east-facing overlook. According to the *Guide to the Appalachian Trail in New York and New Jersey. Ninth Edition*, Cat Rock is "another conglomerate outcropping, with top leveled by glacial action."

Resources: hikethehudsonvalley.com/hikes/nuclear-lake.
hudsonvalleygeologist.blogspot.com/2014/12/nuclear-lake.html.
scoutigny.com/how-to-visit-new-yorks-nuclear-lake. This site provides additional history about the lab explosion.
gonehikin.blogspot.com/2018/06/appalachian-traill-ny-pawling-to.html.
pages.vassar.edu/historicenvironments/2017/04/05/a-world-renowned-trail-and-a-scenic-re-purposed-nuclear-lake.
cnyhiking.com/ATinNY-HammersleyRidge.htm.
New York-New Jersey Trail Conference, *Guide to the Appalachian Trail in New York and New Jersey. Ninth Edition* (Harpers Ferry, W. VI, The Appalachian Trail Conference, 1983), 93.

PUTNAM COUNTY
Putnam County encompasses 246 square miles of land, and is generally hilly. The county was named after Israel Putnam, a general in the American Revolutionary War who also fought in the French and Indian War.

8. SPLIT ROCK
Hudson Highlands State Park

Type of Formation: Split Rock; Large Boulder
WOW Factor: 6
Location: Nelsonville (Putnam County)
Tenth Edition, NYS Atlas & Gazetteer: p. 108, A2; **Earlier Edition NYS Atlas & Gazetteer**: p. 32, A4
Parking GPS Coordinates: 41º26.021'N 73º56.215'W
Destination GPS Coordinates: *Split Rock* – 41º26.318'N 73º56.250'W; *Large Boulder* -- 41º26.484'N 73º56.145'W
Accessibility: *Split Rock* -- 0.3-mile hike; *Large Boulder* – 0.2-mile bushwhack from Split Rock
Degree of Difficulty: Moderate
Additional Information: Trail map available at East Hudson Trails: Trail Map 102. Eleventh Edition
        parks.ny.gov/parks/attachments/HudsonHighlandsTrailMapNorth. pdf   dutchessny.gov/CountyGov/Departments/DPW-Parks/tmshudsonhighlands.pdf

Description: *Split Rock* is a large, 10-foot-high boulder that has fractured into two, 8–10-foot-long pieces that lay separated by a space of two feet or more.

The second, large boulder, most likely visited infrequently, requires a short bushwhack from the Lone Star Trail to reach. It is quite visible on Google Earth, which is where I first noticed it.

Rock Walks

History: The Hudson Highland State Park contains nearly 6,000 acres of wilderness, its major point of particular interest being Breakneck Ridge, which *Newsweek* rated as one of the ten best day hikes in America. Interestingly, Breakneck Mountain was earlier known by a different name. According to Ernest Ingersoll, in *Handy Guide to the Hudson River and Catskill Mountains*, "A century ago [that would be in the 1800s] it was known as *The Turk's Face*, owing to a remarkable image of a human countenance, formed by projecting rocks on the south side, where now a purplish wall of bare rock testifies to the ravages of stone-quarrying; but this was long ago tumbled down by the operations of blasting."

Ariel Schwartz at Split Rock. Photograph by Daniel Chazin.

The Split Rock Trail is a short connector trail between the Lone Star Trail and the Nelsonville Trail.

Directions: From McKeel Corners (junction of Routes 301 & 9), drive southwest on Route 301 for 1.5 miles. Turn sharply right onto Route 10/Fishkill Road and drive northeast for 0.4 mile. Park in a small area on your left.

Split Rock -- Head north on the blue-marked Lone Star Trail, an old woods road, for >0.3 mile. You will see the large split rock to your left at the point where the red-marked Split Rock Trail comes in on your left.

Large Boulder – From Split Rock, hike north, then slightly east for 0.2 mile, a comparatively short bushwhack.

Resources: New York-New Jersey Trail Conference, *New York Walk Book. Sixth Edition* (New York: New York-New Jersey Trail Conference, 1998), 148.
alltrails.com/parks/us/new-york/hudson-highlands-state-park.
nynjtc.org/hike/print/144.

Rock Walks

Ernest Ingersoll, *Handy Guide to the Hudson River and Catskill Mountains* (Astoria, NY: J. C. & A. L. Fawcett, Inc., 1989; reprint of 1910 book), 111.

9. GOOSE ROCKS
Oscawana Lake

Type of Formation: Large Boulder
WOW Factor: 4
Location: Fahnestock Corners (Putnam County)
Tenth Edition, NYS Atlas & Gazetteer: p. 108, A3–4; **Earlier Edition NYS Atlas & Gazetteer**: p. 33, A5
Parking GPS Coordinates: 41º27.158′N 73º50.278′W
Goose Rocks GPS Coordinates: 41º23.981′N 73º51.021′W
Accessibility: ~4.0-mile hike
Degree of Difficulty: Difficult due to distance
Additional Information: Trail map available at East Hudson Trails: Trail Map 103. Eleventh Edition.
    parks.ny.gov/parks/attachments/ClarenceFahnestockTrailMap.pdf
    Oscawana Lake Civic Association (LOCA) -- lakeoscawana.org

Description: Goose Rocks consist of a grouping of large boulders near the upper/middle section of 2.5-mile-long, 386-acre Oscawana Lake. Geologists believe that the rocks were dislodged and carried down by glaciers from the surrounding mountains. Two of the bigger rocks are roughly 30 feet long.

History: Most of Oscawana Lake is developed except for the northwest side which abuts the Clarence Fahnestock Memorial State Park. The park was given to New York State in 1929 by Dr. Alfred Fahnestock in memory of his dad, Dr. Clarence Fahnestock.

It seems probable that the rocks were named after flocks of geese who used the rocks for refuge.

Babe Ruth is reported to have spent time at the lake in the 1930s.

Rock Walks

Directions: From McKeel Corners (junction of Routes 301 & 9), drive northeast on Route 301 for ~4.8 miles. Park to your left in a pull-off near the southwest end of Canopus Lake.

Walk across Route 301 and follow the Appalachian Trail south for several miles. At a junction below Mud Pond, bear left onto the red-blazed Candlewood Hill Trail. When the Candlewood Hill Trail reaches its south-most point, continue straight ahead (south) on an informal path that soon parallels the west side of Oscawana Lake. After ~0.8 mile, turn left and bushwhack east for 0.1 mile to reach the shoreline of Oscawana Lake from where the rocks can be viewed, approximately 0.1 mile off-shore.

If you study the Fahnestock Memorial State Park map for a few minutes, these directions should begin to crystalize in your mind.

To be sure, the easiest way to access Goose Rocks is by boat, but this only works if you are friends with one of the lakefront residents.

Goose Rocks jutting out of Oscawana Lake. Postcard c. 1900.

Resources: New York-New Jersey Trail Conference, *New York Walk Book. Sixth Edition* (New York: New York-New Jersey Trail Conference, 1998). A line drawing showing the rocks can be seen on page 38.

en.wikipedia.org/wiki/Lake_Oscawana gives mention to a "peculiar rock formation" near the center of the lake.
tripadvisor.com/VacationRentalReview-g48458-d14078022-Spectacular_Lake_House-Putnam_Valley_New_York.html.
lakeoscawana.org.
Raymond H. Torrey, Frank Place, Jr. & Robert L. Dickinson, *New York Walk Book. Third Edition* (NY: The American Geographical Society, 1951), 120.Mention is made about how Fahnestock Memorial Park was named.

10. HAWK ROCK & BALANCED ROCK
New York City Environmental Protection land

Type of Formation: Large Boulder; Balanced Rock
WOW Factor: *Hawk Rock* -- 6–7; *Balanced Rock* – Not determined
Location: Kenwood Lake (Putnam County)
Tenth Edition, NYS Atlas & Gazetteer: p. 108, A5; **Earlier Edition NYS Atlas & Gazetteer**: p. 33, A6
Parking GPS Coordinates: 41º29.016′N 73º42.054′W
Destination GPS Coordinates: *Hawk Rock* -- 41º27.842′N 73º41.642′W (estimated); *Balanced Rock* – Not determined
Accessibility: *Balanced Rock* -- ~1.5-mile hike; *Hawk Rock* -- 1.7-mile hike
Degree of Difficulty: Moderate
Additional Information: Map of hike available at website kentcac.info/wp/wp-content/uploads/2015/07/Hawk-Rock-Brochure-v3.pdf.

Hawk Rock. Old photograph.

NOTE: An access permit from the Department of Environmental Protection is required in order to undertake this hike. A permit can be obtained from a826-web01.nyc.gov/recpermitapp.

Rock Walks

Description: *Balanced Rock* – The only description I have of the rock is from a website that calls it "a huge boulder that appears precariously balanced."

Hawk Rock – Some hikers refer to Hawk Rock as the "Stonehenge of Putnam County." The rock is 25-30 feet high, and is said to resemble a huge, perched bird, like a hawk, for instance.

History: According to Philip J. Imbrogno, a paranormal investigator, the wing on Hawk Rock's contains carvings of a turtle, long-tailed bird, and the sun. George Baum, chairman of the Kent Conservation Advisory Committee, believes that the carvings date back to the turn of the twentieth century, and may have been created by members of the Hunt family. The carvings are not considered to be the works of early Native Americans.

The trail to Hawk Rock was marked by Patrick LaFontaine as part of his 2015 Eagle Scout project. He also installed the information kiosk. In addition to LaFontaine, other hikers took part in the project as well.

Directions: From Carmel (junction of Routes 52 & 301), drive northwest on Route 52 for ~2.0 miles. Turn left onto Route 42/ Farmers Mills Road and head west for less than 1.0 mile. Then turn left onto Wangtown Road and proceed southwest for 0.8 mile. Park to your left in a small area near the end of the road.

Follow the red-marked trail south for 1.7 miles. Along the way, probably between 1.5 and 1.6 mile, you will encounter the Balanced Rock; then, at 1.7 miles, Hawk Rock.

Resources: kentcac.info/wp/hikes/hawk-rock.
greenwichtime.com/opinion/article/The-mysteries-of-Hawk-Rock-649692.php. – The site contains an article by Philip J. Imbrogno.
meetup.com/The-Hiking-Group-Ct-NY/events/247269648.
en.wikipedia.org/wiki/Rock_Hawk.
pages.vassar.edu/historicenvironments/2016/10/01/hiking-trail-from-mead-farm-to-hawk-rock. Balanced Rock is mentioned on this site.
nytimes.com/2010/10/15/nyregion/15hawk.html. – A photograph of Hawk Rock is included.

11. BREWSTER HIGH SCHOOL BOULDER

Type of Formation: Large Boulder
WOW Factor: 5–6
Location: Brewster Hill (Putnam County)
Tenth Edition, NYS Atlas & Gazetteer: p. 109, A6; **Earlier Edition NYS Atlas & Gazetteer**: p. 33, AB6–7
Parking GPS Coordinates: 41º26.454'N 73º36.073'W
Brewster High School Boulder GPS Coordinates: ~41º26.487'N 73º36.035'W
Accessibility: 0.1-mile hike or bushwhack
Degree of Difficulty: Easy
Additional Information: Brewster High School, 50 Foggintown Road, Brewster, NY 10509

Description: The Brewster High School Boulder is a 15-foot-high boulder that has broken into several pieces. It rests at the top of a small ridge overlooking a swamp.

History: The rock is named for its proximity to the Brewster High School—a proximity that has guaranteed an unwanted amount of graffiti on the boulder.

Brewster is named after Walter Brewster, a nineteenth-century land-owner.

Directions: From Brewster Hill (junction of Routes 62/"Farm to Market Road" & 312), drive north on Route 62/"Farm to Market Road" for 0.5 mile. Turn right onto Foggintown Road and proceed east for 0.3 mile, passing by the Brewster High School (to your left) along the way. Turn left into a small pull-off soon after the school.

From the pull-off, walk northeast for 0.1 mile into the woods to reach the boulder. I don't know if a path leads to the boulder, but I wouldn't be surprised if one existed.

The website I consulted mentioned that the boulder may be on property owned by the High School, but nothing was said with certainty.

Resources: adventuresaroundputnam.com/2014/04/26/glacial-erratic-on-brewster-high-school-property.

12. MARBLE BLOCKS
Patterson Environmental Park

Type of Formation: Large Quarried Block
WOW Factor: 4
Location: Patterson (Putnam County)
Tenth Edition, NYS Atlas & Gazetteer: p. 104, E1; **Earlier Edition NYS Atlas & Gazetteer**: p. 37, D7
Parking GPS Coordinates: *Patterson Recreation Center* -- 41º30.546′N 73º36.315′W; *End of dirt road* -- 41º30.468′N 73º35.827′W
Marble Blocks Coordinates: 41º30.468′N 73º35.906′W
Accessibility: *From Patterson Recreation Center* -- 0.3-mile walk; *from end of dirt road* – 0.1-mile walk
Degree of Difficulty: Easy

Description: A number of stacked, square-shaped blocks of marble are encountered as you walk along a short dirt road through the Patterson Environmental Park. The blocks are grouped in such a way as to form nooks and crannies that can be explored, for those who desire to do so.

History: The marble blocks are the residue of an old stone quarry whose stones were used in the construction of most of the house foundations in Patterson.

The blocks are located in the 23-acre town-owned nature preserve.

Directions: From east of Patterson (junction of Routes 311 & 22), drive west on Route 311 for 0.7 mile. Turn left onto Front Street and drive south for 0.3 mile. Park to your right at the Patterson Recreation Center.

From the Patterson Recreation Center walk east on Marble Quarry Road (a dirt road), immediately crossing over the active Metro North railroad tracks (Stay alert here!) At 0.3 mile, you will come to the stacked marble blocks, directly to your right. An informal loop path takes you behind the rocks and then back out.

The end of the dirt road is reached at 0.4 mile where a small parking area can be found. Driving in to this parking area and then walking back 0.1 mile to the stones is also an option, although not as much fun.

Resources: The Patterson Historical Society, *Vignettes of Patterson's Past* (Patterson, NY: Patterson Historical Society, 2007), 11. A photograph shows an area of large marble blocks.
pattersonny.org/TownPreserves.php.
nynjctbotany.org/lgtofc/grswppep.html.
historicpatterson.org/Exhibits/ExhIndustries.php.

13. MUDDY BROOK ROCK SHELTER & LAUREL LEDGES
Turtle Pond Preserve

Type of Formation: Rock-Shelter; High Ledge
WOW Factor: 7
Location: Patterson (Putnam County)
Tenth Edition, NYS Atlas & Gazetteer: p. 109, A6; **Earlier Edition NYS Atlas & Gazetteer**: p. 33, A7
Parking GPS Coordinates: 41º29.085'N 73º36.152'W
Estimated Destination GPS Coordinates: *Laurel Ledges* -- 41º28.989'N 73º36.103'W; *Muddy Brook Rock Shelter* -- 41º28.970'N 73º35.938'W (a guess)
Accessibility: *Laurel Ledges* – 0.1-mile hike; *Muddy Brook Rock-Shelter* -- ~0.4-mile hike (a guess)
Degree of Difficulty: Moderate

Description: The *Muddy Brook Rock Shelter* consists of an enormous, 20-foot-high rock overhang. Archaeologists have determined that the shelter was used by early Native Americans.

The *Laurel Ledges* is a 35–40-foot-high ridge line that extends for some distance. The Putnam County Land Trust website describes it as something unique and dramatic.

There may also be a boulder in the area. According to the Putnam County Land Trust website, while heading up to the top of the ledges "… the path curves left almost 180 degrees around a large boulder…." Exactly how large this boulder is remains to be seen.

Rock Walks

History: The 44-acre Turtle Pond Preserve property was acquired by the Putnam County Land Trust from Bill and Linda Hamilton in 2004. It is part of the Laurel Ledges Natural Area.

The trail was developed by Stephen Maddock in 2008 while doing his Eagle Scout project for Mahopac Troop 1.

Turtle Pond has also been known as Mendel Pond.

The Ice Pond Conservation website writes, "The earliest artifacts [from the rock-shelter] were projectile points which date back about 8000 years. Fragments of Indian pottery were found [at the rock-shelter] ….and along the ridges that formed travel routes above the tangled wetlands. The Woodland Period began here about 1000-2000 years ago and marked the beginning of the use of the bow and arrow, pottery, and the organized cultivation of corn, beans and squash. The Native Americans of this area were called the "River Indians" by Henry Hudson; we call them the Algonkian speaking people. The local groups probably consisted of 20 to 30 family members loosely known by the name of the area and joined in a larger assemblage or confederacy."

Directions: From Haines Corner (junction of Routes 164 & 22), drive west on Route 164 for 1.7 miles. At Turtle Pond, bear right onto Cornwall Hill Road and proceed north for 0.4 mile, turning into a pull-off on your right opposite Devon Road, where a sign says "Laurel Ledges."

The trail leading off from the parking area promptly turns right and heads south. It quickly takes you to views of high ledges that were not visible from Cornwall Hill Road. The path then leads down to a boardwalk at the edge of the Turtle Pond marshlands that follows along the base of towering cliffs. These are the Laurel Ledges.

At the end of the boardwalk, continue on until you come to a "Y".

Muddy Brook Rock-Shelter – Bear right at the fork, cross a small footbridge, and continue uphill. The Putnam County Land Trust website states that you will eventually reach a grassy area, where the trail seems to disappear. Somewhere in this area presumably is a large rock-shelter, but you may have to do some exploring to find it.

Rock Walks

Laurel Ledges – If you wish to climb up to the top of the ledges and see a "large boulder" along the way, bear left at the fork and follow a series of switchbacks that take you up to the top of the ledges.

Resources: The Patterson Historical Society, *Vignettes of Patterson's Past* (Patterson, NY: Patterson Historical Society, 2007), 14. The caption under the photograph of the rock-shelter reads, "Edie Keasbey stands in the Muddy Brook Rock Shelter." pclt.net/preserve-detail/ice-pond-conservation-area-historical. dec.ny.gov/docs/wildlife_pdf/greatswampwma.pdf. adventuresaroundputnam.com/places-to-go/laurel-ledges-turtle-pond.

Goose Rocks. Pen & ink sketch by Robert L. Dickinson.

WESTCHESTER COUNTY

Westchester County is named after the city of Chester, England. The county is bordered by the Hudson River to the west, and by the Long Island Sound and the county of Fairfield, Connecticut, to the east. It encompasses 450 square miles of land, and is the second-most populous county on the mainland of New York State.

14. BRINTON BROOK BALANCED ROCK

Brinton Brook Sanctuary

Type of Formation: Balanced Rock
WOW Factor: Unknown
Location: Croton-on-Hudson (Westchester County)
Tenth Edition, NYS Atlas & Gazetteer: p. 108, D3; **Earlier Edition NYS Atlas & Gazetteer**: p. 33, C4–5
Parking GPS Coordinates: 41º13.373'N 73º54.307'W
Balanced Rock GPS Coordinates: Unknown
Accessibility: ~0.3–0.4-mile trek (a guess)
Degree of Difficulty: Moderate
Additional Information: A map of the Brinton Brook Sanctuary is available at sawmillriveraudubon.org/maps/Brinton_Trails.pdf.

Description: In *Natural New York*, Bill & Phyllis Thomas write, "Rock ledges with glacial grooves and a boulder balanced atop smaller rocks attract students of geology." That's all the information I have about this geological formation.

History: The Brinton Brook Sanctuary is a 156-acre preserve offering up to three miles of hiking trails.

The sanctuary is named for Willard and Laura Brinton, who donated the first 112 acres to form the nucleus of the wildlife sanctuary. Additional parcels were acquired from the Brintons' niece, Ruth Brinton Perera, in 1975, and by the Saw Mill River Audubon in 1995.

The land is owned by the Village of Croton-on-Hudson, and managed by the Saw Mill River Audubon.

The Pond Loop Trail is marked by twenty interpretive signs that focus on the preserve's flora and bird inhabitants.

Directions: From Route 9 in Croton-on-Hudson get off at the Senasqua Road/9A exit. When you come to Route 9A, head north for ~1.1 miles (or <0.2 mile northwest of Arrowcrest Drive) When you see the sign for the sanctuary, turn right and drive east for >0.3 mile. Park in the area straight ahead at the point where the road turns sharply left as it heads towards a private residence.

A second entrance [41º13.276'N 73º54.062'W] is located along Arrowcrest Drive, ~0.5 mile from Route 9A, just before the entrance to the Hudson National Golf Club. A sanctuary sign is also present at this trailhead.

Finding the balanced rock mentioned by Bill & Phyllis Thomas may not prove to be easy. The sanctuary map makes no reference to a balanced rock, although a Split Rock Spring is indicated, possibly the site of something that may prove to be of interest.

To get to the Split Rock Spring area from the parking area, follow the yellow-marked Pond Loop Trail northeast for >0.1 mile. Bear right onto the red-marked Hemlock Spring Trail and head east for 0.05 mile. Finally, turn right onto the yellow-marked Laurel Rock Trail. You will immediately come to Split Rock Spring, where hopefully a geological formation or two await. If not, there are additional trails to explore, but I have no further suggestions to offer.

Resources: Bill & Phyllis Thomas, *Natural New York* (New York: Holt, Rinehart and Winston, 1983), 235.
sawmillriveraudubon.org/brinton.html.
sawmillriveraudubon.org/maps/Brinton_Brochure.pdf.
njurbanforest.com/2014/10/07/hiking-brinton-brook-sanctuary.

15. DEVIL'S STAIRS

Type of Formation: Rock Steps
WOW Factor: Unknown
Location: Ossining (Westchester County)
Tenth Edition, NYS Atlas & Gazetteer: p. 108, D3; **Earlier Edition NYS Atlas & Gazetteer**: p. 33, C5
Dale Cemetery Marble Place Entrance GPS Coordinates: 41º10.170'N 73º51.366'W
Devil's Stairs GPS Coordinates: Unknown
Accessibility: Unknown

Description: The Devil's Stairs is a natural rock formation formed on Sing Sing Brook.

History: Sing Sing Brook, aka Sint-sinck Brook and Kil Brook, is a small tributary to the Hudson River whose first 6,000 feet, as you head upstream, are tidal.

The Devil is no stranger to this part of the state, particularly to the Catskills where there is the Devil's Path, Devil's Kitchen, Devil's Pulpit, Devil's Hole, Devil's Chamber, and Devil's Tombstone, just to mention a few.

Directions: From Ossining (junction of Routes 133/Croton Avenue & 9/Highland Avenue), head northeast on Route 133/Croton Avenue for 0.3 mile. Bear left onto Dale Avenue and continue northeast for 0.2 mile. Then turn left onto Marble Place and proceed northeast until you reach the entrance to 40-acre Dale Cemetery.

The Devil's Stairs are located southwest of the Marble Place entrance to the cemetery, but that's about all I have been able to find out about where to look.

Sing Sing Brook makes a U-turn by the cemetery and then flows through a series of residential areas. The U-turn section of the stream can be observed from the southwest side of the cemetery, but it seems doubtful that the rock formation lies here.

Beyond the cemetery's reach, access is likely to be problematic due to houses and buildings lining the stream. Sing Sing Brook is essentially a non-navigational stream, so kayaking sections of it to access the rock formation is undoubtedly impractical. It will have to be done by foot if a public way to it exists.

One place where I see a stretch of whitewater on Sing Sing Brook is by Ossining Recreation & Park [41º09.804'N 73º51.772'W] at 95 Broadway in Ossining (off of North Highland Avenue). There is a walkway leading down to the river from the recreation center, and I also notice that another walkway extends south from here, following along the bank of the creek for >0.2 mile, and even crossing it twice. Who knows what you might see along this section of the Sing Sing Kill. It may be a longshot, but at least it does meet the requirement of being southwest of the cemetery.

Resources: Richard M. Lederer, Jr., *The Place-Names of Westchester County, New York: Expanded Version* (Harrison, NY: Harbor Hill Books, 1980), 40.

Arthur G. Adams, *The Hudson River Guidebook* (NY: Fordham University Press, 1996), 145.

16. DEVIL'S ROCK & DEVIL'S FOOTPRINTS

Type of Formation: Large Boulder
WOW Factor: Unknown
Location: Croton-on-Hudson (Westchester County)
Tenth Edition, NYS Atlas & Gazetteer: p. 108, D3; **Earlier Edition NYS Atlas & Gazetteer**: p. 33, BC4–5
Hessian Hill GPS Coordinates: 41º13.366'N 73º52.715'W (Google Earth)
Devil's Rock GPS Coordinates: Unknown
Accessibility: Presumably near roadside

Alfred P. Gardiner's estate on Hessian Hill.

53

Rock Walks

Description: The Devil's Rock is a large boulder that bears the imprint of a pair of human feet. In an article that appeared in the *Syracuse Journal* in 1913, the author writes, "On the east shore, along the old Albany postroad (sic) and at the bottom of a steep hill belonging to the A. P. Gardiner estate, lies a huge boulder shadowed by tall trees . . . Its smooth surface bears the imprint of a pair of human feet placed side by side, as if a barefooted man had walked down the hill and stood on the spot while the stone was still soft and yielding from nature's crucible. Every toe is clearly defined, and judging from the mold he left in the granite, the foot of this ancient man was both large and shapely. Behind the footprints, all the way to the top of the rock, are a series of peculiar indentations such as the links of a heavy chain would make in soft earth."

FOOTPRINTS IN ROCK PUZZLING BIG SCIENTISTS

Huge Boulder at Croton, N. Y., Bears Imprint of Pair of Human Feet.

WEIRD LEGENDS TOLD

One Attributes Mysterious Footprints to His Satanic Majesty.

CROTON, N. Y., May 2.—Mysterious footprints in the solid rock on the east and west banks of the Hudson here have puzzled the scientists, who be—

Such a strange rock, it should be pointed out, is not as unique as you might think at first. There are a number of Devil's Rocks and Devil's Footprints in the United States, one of the most famous being the Devil's Rock (with Satan's footprint imbedded in it) in North Carolina.

History: The Devil's Rock has also been referred to as the Devil's Track, presumably because of the footprints.

The rock is what scientist call a *petrosomatoglyph*, a representative part of a human or animal that has formed naturally in rock—in this case the impression of a footprint.

The rock is located on the former Alfred P. Gardiner estate which extended east uphill from the Hudson River for over a mile.

The only other Devil's Rock in New York State that I am familiar with is the Devil's Rock [42º59.306'N 78º07.408'W] along Route 5 in Batavia where, rumor has it, the Devil was temporarily chained until, trying to escape by madly running around and around the boulder, he finally broke lose, leaving behind a deep groove he had worn into the rock, which is why the boulder is mushroom shaped.

Directions: When the article about the Devil's Rock was written in 1906, the exact location of the boulder was already gone from memory.

It's possible that during the last hundred years this fascinating boulder has been rediscovered. If so, I can find no mention of it in the current literature.

To look for the Devil's Rock, I would start at the base of Hessian Hill along Route 9 which, I believe, is the Old Albany Post Road mentioned in the *Syracuse Journal* article. The problem is, there is a considerable amount of terrain to cover, and no specific clues to serve as a guide.

Resources: *Syracuse Journal* (May 2, 1913) – The digitalized version is crotonhistory.org/2013/11/12/the-mystery-of-the-devils-footprints. crotonhistory.org/category/mysteries.

17. POTATO ROCK (Historic)
Croton Point Park

Type of Formation: Large Rock
WOW Factor: Unknown
Location: Croton Point (Westchester County)
Tenth Edition, NYS Atlas & Gazetteer: p. 108, D3; **Earlier Edition NYS Atlas & Gazetteer**: p. 33, C4–5
Parking GPS Coordinates: 41º11.024'N 73º53.962'W
Potato Rock GPS Coordinates: 41º11.156'N 73º54.226'W (Google Earth)
Fee: Modest charge to enter park
Additional Information: Croton Point Park, 1 Croton Point Avenue, Croton-on-Hudson, NY 10520

Rock Walks

parks.westchestergov.com/images/stories/pdfs/Croton.pdf -- Croton Point Park map

Not to be used for navigation. Use NOAA Charts #12343 and 12347.

Description: Potato Rock, before its destruction, was a large, oblong-shaped rock located slightly offshore. Its oblong shape and perhaps rough, knobby surface is undoubtedly what gave rise to the name Potato Rock.

Google Earth and a couple of websites continue to list the rock's GPS coordinates even though Potato Rock has not existed for some time now.

Raymond H. Torrey, Frank Place, Jr. and Robert L. Dickinson, in *New York Walk Book. Third Edition*, write, "Along the shores of both sides of the tip are great quantities of ice- and water-born boulders deposited in the moraine." On the west side of the tip, facing the Hudson River, are small-to-medium-sized rocks to be seen, but none that will excite the imagination.

History: Potato Rock was blasted to bits sometime in the late 1900s for being a navigational hazard.

Croton Point Park was established ~1924. The 508-acre park is the site of an old Native American village described by James Owen in "The Fortified Indian Village at Croton Point." According to Ann B. Silverman in "Guarding County's Archaeological Past," the site was occupied by Native Americans as far back as 6,300 years ago.

Directions: From Route 9, get off at the exit for Croton Point Avenue/Croton Harmon Station. When you come to Croton Point Avenue, drive southwest for ~1.2 miles to reach the Croton Point Park parking area.

Rock Walks

From the northwest end of the parking area, walk north for >0.1 mile and look out to your left across the Hudson River. There is nothing to see of Potato Rock except to know that you are one of the few people who know both of its existence, and where it was located.

Resources: Richard M. Lederer, Jr., *The Place-Names of Westchester County, New York: Expanded Version* (Harrison, NY: Harbor Hill Books, 1980), 115.
boatered.com/forum/topic.asp?TOPIC_ID=108211.
parks.westchestergov.com/croton-point-park.
placekeeper.com/New_York/Potato_Rock-973884.html.
James Owen, "The Fortified Indian Village at Croton Point." *The Westchester Historian. The Quarterly Bulletin of the Westchester County Historical Society* (April, 1925), 3.
Ann B. Silverman, "Guarding County's Archaeological Past," *The Times* (November 17, 1985).
Raymond H. Torrey, Frank Place, Jr. & Robert L. Dickinson, *New York Walk Book. Third Edition* (NY: The American Geographical Society, 1951), 74.

18. FRANK'S ROCK

Type of Formation: Rock Outcrop
WOW Factor: Unknown
Location: Ossining (Westchester County)
Tenth Edition, NYS Atlas & Gazetteer: p. 108, D3; **Earlier Edition NYS Atlas & Gazetteer**: p. 33, C5
Parking GPS Coordinates: 41º11.076'N 73º52.449'W
Estimated Frank Rock's GPS Coordinates: 41º11.195'N 73º52.538'W
Accessibility: 0.1-mile walk

Description: There is little specific information about Frank's Rock other than what is listed in the history section. My suspicion is that Frank's Rock is not a boulder, but rather a rock outcropping. This hunch seems to be borne out by a photograph taken of the rock in 1965 by Renoda Hoffman. Still, it's entirely possible that there may be a rock or small boulder associated with the rock outcropping.

Rock Walks

History: Frank's Rock, aka Frans Besley's Rock, is named after Frans Besley who was born in 1686, and who fished from the rock at the mouth of the Croton River below the former Mary Immaculate School.

FRANK'S ROCK   — *Renoda Hoffman*

Directions: From Crotonville (junction of Ogden Road and Old Albany Post Road), drive southwest on Old Albany Post Road for >0.1 mile. As soon as you pass under the Route 9 overpass, turn right at a stop sign onto Eagle Park and proceed >0.2 mile to St. Augustine's Roman Catholic Church & School to park.

Walk north, if permitted, to reach the south bank of the Croton River near its confluence with the Hudson River. It's hard to know what you are going to find here. I have provided a GPS coordinate to flag a possible candidate for Frank's Rock. However, it's important to bear in mind that nearly 350 years have transpired since Besley fished from the rock. A lot could have happened and probably has since then.

Resources: Richard M. Lederer, Jr., *The Place-Names of Westchester County, New York: Expanded Version* (Harrison, NY: Harbor Hill Books, 1980), 53.
notorc.blogspot.com/2009/03/no-longer-on-map-forgotten-names-in.html – Forgotten Place Names in Northwestern Westchester County.
Greta Cornell, "Frank's Rock." *Westchester Historian. Quarterly of the Westchester County Historical Society* Vol. 41, no. 1 (1965), 11. A photograph of the rock taken by Renoda Hoffman can be seen on page 11.

19. TEATOWN BOULDERS
Teatown Lake Reservation Nature Preserve

Type of Formation: Large Boulder
WOW Factor: 5–6
Location: Ossining (Westchester County)
Tenth Edition, NYS Atlas & Gazetteer: p. 108, D3–4; **Earlier Edition NYS Atlas & Gazetteer**: p. 33, C5
Teatown Nature Center Parking GPS Coordinates: 41º12.676'N 73º49.626'W
Blinn Road Parking GPS Coordinates: 41º12.817'N 73º49.602'W
Tea Town Boulders GPS Coordinates: 41º12.841'N 73º49.616'W (per rock climbing website); *large rock near alternate parking area* -- 41º12.816'N 73º49.607'W
Accessibility: Variable distances
Degree of Difficulty: Easy to moderately easy
Additional Information: Teatown Nature Center 1600 Spring Valley Road, Ossining, NY 10562
    Trail map -- teatown.org/wp-content/uploads/2018/06/Teatown-trail-map-1.pdf

Visitor Center. Photograph from teatown.org.

Description: A number of large boulders can be found along the Lake Trail, particularly as you head into the woods from Teatown Lake.
    Boulders are also mentioned near Vernay Lake.

59

Rock Walks

History: The Teatown Lake Reservation Nature Preserve encompasses 1,000 acres of land, including 42-acre Teatown Lake. It contains fifteen miles of hiking trails.

The name Teatown dates back to 1776 Revolutionary War days when a group of local women who called themselves "Daughters of Eve" boycotted an entrepreneur named John Arthur who wanted to sell his supply of tea at exorbitant prices. They won out, and the area, as a result, became known as Teatown.

The property subsequently passed through several owners, including Arthur Vernay, who built "The Croft," and then later, Dan Hanna, whose horse stable eventually became the Nature Center. In 1923, Gerard Swope, Sr. purchased the land, created the lake by damming up Bailey Brook, devised a system of trails, and used the land for horseback riding. Six years after Swope's death, his family donated 194 acres of land to the Brooklyn Botanical Garden to establish an outreach station in Ossining. In 1971, Teatown become incorporated, and eventually the tie with the Botanical Garden was broken.

There may also be boulders in nearby Ossining and Sing Sing, although I have not been able to find any references to large rocks through my library research. I mention Ossining and Sing Sing because an online magazine called the *Postscripts* (notorc.blogspot.com/2010/05/whats-in-name-catalog-of-indian-place.html) reminds us that the name Ossining is Native American for "a place of stones" (presumably dolomitic limestone outcroppings) and Sing Sing, for the "place of rocks."

Directions: *Visitor Center parking* -- From Glendale (junction of Spring Valley Road & Glendale Road), drive northeast on Spring Valley Road for ~1.4 miles to reach the Teatown Lake Reservation Nature Preserve Visitor Center, on your left.

Blinn Road Parking -- From the Visitor Center, continue southeast on Spring Valley Road for over 0.1 mile and turn left onto Blinn Road, Go northwest on Blinn Road for less than 0.2 mile, and turn left onto a dirt road that leads promptly to a parking area.

Many of the rocks can be found along the Lake Trail on the east side of Teatown Lake, and into the woods.

Vernay Lake – To reach 9-acre Vernay Lake from the Visitor Center, walk across the road and up to a gate in the stone wall that leads to a kiosk. From there, follow the orange-blazed Twin Lakes Trail south, initially following a gravel road, and then down a stone-step path to the lake. Expect to do some bushwhacking and reconnoitering to find the boulders once you reach the lake. Most are on the opposite side of the lake.

Resources: Lincoln Diamant, *Teatown Lake Reservation: Images of America* (Charleston, SC: Arcadia Publishing, 2003). The book provides extensive information about the reservation, but no information on the boulders.
teatown.org/about/history.
mountainproject.com/area/107.
mountainproject.com/forum/topic/107492270/tea-to   497338/tea-town-boulders.
mountainproject.com/area/107497338/tea-town-boulders.
wn-westchester-county-boulders.
climbingandbouldering.com/new-york/teatown-reservation-bouldering.
New York-New Jersey Trail Conference, *Day Walker: 32 Hikes in the New York Metropolitan Area. Second Edition* (Mahwah, NJ: New York-New Jersey Trail Conference, 2002), 148–153.

20. NATURAL BRIDGE (Historic)

Type of Formation: Natural Bridge
WOW Factor: Unknown
Location: Salem Center (Westchester County)
Tenth Edition, NYS Atlas & Gazetteer: p. 109, BC6; **Earlier Edition NYS Atlas & Gazetteer**: p. 33, B6–7
Natural Bridge GPS Coordinates: Unknown

Description: Richard M. Lederer, Jr., in *The Place-Names of Westchester County, New York*, makes mention of a natural bridge that once existed near Salem Center but, unfortunately, cites no specifics other than that Titicus Road crossed over it near the intersection of Titicus Road and Delancy Road.

Rock Walks

In her article, "A Natural Bridge in Westchester," Allison Albee writes, "Many years ago the bridge was a featured attraction in the area and all traffic between Salem and Purdy's passed over it." When the natural bridge was visited in 1940, it was supposedly almost indistinguishable due to the accumulation of growth. The north side of the bridge was completely filled in, and the south side had a 2-foot-wide opening, with a tiny stream emerging from it. "We are at a loss," wrote Albee, "to reconcile the present approximate twelve foot height of the rock face with the twenty-five foot height given in Bolton's 1848 description of the spot."

I can only imagine what the spot must look like now, 60 years later.

Natural Bridge. Photograph c. mid-1960s.

History: The 681-acre Titicus Reservoir, which flooded the valley and forced the rerouting of Titicus Road in 1893, obviously changed the topography of the area, as well as causing the natural bridge to fade from memory.

The reservoir is one of twelve in New York City's Croton system.

Directions: From North Salem (junction of Routes 116/Titicus Road & 121/Grant Road), head west on Route 116/Titicus Road for ~1.5

miles to reach the intersection of Titicus Road and Delancey Road. This is not the original location of the intersection, which was shifted northward when the reservoir was created. Allison Albee writes that the natural bridge "is located in the Town of North Salem close beside the north shore of Titicus Reservoir."

To be honest, my first assumption was that the natural bridge had been engulfed by waters when the reservoir was created. It was a surprise, then, to learn that although it became part of the watershed, the natural bridge remained above water level.

It is unknown to me whether the natural bridge, or what remains of it, can still be visited. I do see a stream coming down into the reservoir at 41º20.099'N 73º36.768'W along Titicus Road and can't help but wonder if that might lead to the natural bridge. Whether permission to enter watershed land has to first be obtained could be a factor, however.

Resources: Richard M. Lederer, Jr., *The Place-Names of Westchester County, New York: Expanded Version* (Harrison, NY: Harbor Hill Books, 1980), 99.
en.wikipedia.org/wiki/Titicus_Reservoir.
Allison Albee, "A Natural Bridge in Westchester," *Westchester Historian. Quarterly of the Westchester County Historical Society* Vol. 33, no. 4 (November, December, 1957), 114 & 115.
gov/html/dep/html/watershed_protection/titicus.shtml.

21. GREAT BOULDER

Type of Formation: Perched Rock
WOW Factor: 7
Location: North Salem (Westchester County)
Tenth Edition, NYS Atlas & Gazetteer: p. 109, BC7; **Earlier Edition NYS Atlas & Gazetteer**: p. 33, B7
Destination GPS Coordinates: *Great Boulder* -- 41º20.044'N 73º34.298'W; *Old Academy Boulder* -- 41º19.739'N 73º35.878'W
Accessibility: Roadside
Degree of Difficulty: Easy

Rock Walks

Description: The *Great Boulder*, aka Big Rock, Balanced Rock, and the North Salem Dolmen, weighs about 69 tons according to a sign next to the rock, and is supported on five native limestone rocks. Boulders that are supported by smaller, underlying, peg-like rocks are typically called Dolmens.

The Great Boulder measures 16'x14'x10' feet. Steve Schimmrich, a contemporary geologist, estimates its weight to be ~178 tons (almost three times the weight that is indicated on the sign accompanying the rock). Whatever the actual weight is, there is no doubt about one thing—this is truly a big rock.

In *History of Westchester County, New York*, Frederic Schonnard and W. W. Spooner write, "It is a prodigious rock of red granite, said to be the solitary one of its kind in the country."

Old Academy Boulder is a medium-sized, 3–4-foot high boulder that rests in front of the Old Academy at Salem Center. I mention it for its historic value.

Great Boulder. Postcard c. 1910.

History: The *Great Boulder* is believed to have been carried by glaciers from New Hampshire to its present location and then unceremoniously dropped on top of several small stones.

64

Others, however, contend that the boulder was propped up by Celts for religious ceremonies long before Christopher Columbus set sail to the New World. Patricia Edwards Clyne in *Hudson Valley Trails and Tales*, for one, writes, "...the boulder's seven support stones form an isosceles triangle, the legs of which are in units of a measurement known as the megalithic yard (2.72 feet). The megalithic yard has been cited by various researchers—including Alexander "Sandy" Thom, who studied structures in the British Isles—as the basic measurement used in laying out dolmens and other Old World megaliths."

This may be one of those instances where it's impossible to prove with certainty whether the boulder came to rest naturally in its present position, or whether it was artificially propped up by an ancient tribe many centuries ago.

The Town took possession of the great rock sometime around 1959.

Old Academy Boulder – According to the July 1941 issue of *The Quarterly Bulletin of the Westchester County Historical Society*, Charles J. F. Decker "was instrumental in erecting the natural boulder weighing twenty tons and brought one mile and placed in front of the old

Old Academy Boulder. Old photograph.

Academy in memory of the boys of the town who died in the World War."

The historic Town Hall/former North Salem Academy was built ~1770. From 1790 to 1884 it served as the North Salem Academy; after 1886, it became the Town Hall.

Directions: *Great Boulder* -- From North Salem (junction of Routes 116/Titicus Road & 121/Peach Lake Road), head southwest on Route 116/ Titicus Road for 0.5 mile (or 0.1 mile past Keeler Lane). The rock is on your left, next to the historic Cable Barn that was erected in 1869.

Rock Walks

Old Academy Boulder – From the Great Boulder, continue on Route 116/Titicus Road for another 0.5 mile. Bear right at a fork (where Route 121/Grant Road goes left), and continue now west on Route 116/Titicus Road for another 0.9 mile. Then turn right onto a dead-end road shared by several buildings, including the North Salem Town Police and the Ruth Keeler Memorial Library. The first building on the left is the Old Academy. A boulder, 60 feet south of the building, is visible.

Resources: Patricia Edwards Clyne, *Hudson Valley Trails and Tales* (Woodstock, NY: The Overlook Press, 1990), 13 & 14.
hudsonvalleygeologist.blogspot.com/2013/07/north-salem-balanced-rock.html.
adventuresaroundputnam.com/day-trips-outside-putnam/balanced-rocknorth-salem-ny – This site contains some excellent photographs of the rock.
Chris Gethard, *Weird New York: Your Travel Guide to New York's Local Legends and Best Kept Secrets* (New York: Sterling Publishing Co., Inc., 2005), 31.
Frederic Shonnard & W. W. Spooner, *History of Westchester County, New York* (New York: The New York History Company, 1900), 15.
The Quarterly Bulletin of the Westchester County Historical Society Vol. 17, no. 3 (July 1941). On the cover is a photograph of the Great Rock. On page 61 is a photograph of a medium-sized boulder in front of the Old Academy.
Susan Cochran Swanson & Elizabeth Green Fuller, *Westchester County. A Pictorial History* (Norfolk, VA: The Donning Company, 1982). On page 14 is a lateral shot of the Great Boulder. On page 77 is the Old Academy Boulder.
Frances Eichner & Helen Ferris Tibbets (editors), *When our Town was Young: Stories of North Salem's Yesterday* (North Salem, NY: Town of North Salem, 1945). Page 17 includes a photograph of the Great Rock and commentary: "The Boulder, which is estimated to weigh about sixty tons, rests on five smaller stones of limestone and stands about four feet from the surface of the hill on which it is situated."
en.wikipedia.org/wiki/North_Salem_Town_Hall.
C. R. Roseberry, *From Niagara to Montauk: The Scenic Pleasures of New York State* (Albany, NY: State University of New York Press, 1982), 334 & 335.
The Westchester Historian. Quarterly of the Westchester County Historical Society Vol. 17, no. 3. (July, 1941). A photo of the Great Boulder adorns

the cover of the bulletin. On page 61 is a photograph of the Academy Boulder, with further information provided on page 63. *Westchester Historian. Quarterly of the Westchester County Historical Society* Vol. 32, no. 1 (January 1956). On page 29 is a photograph of the great rock by Fred C. Warner in an article entitled "North Salem's Great Boulder."

"North Salem Great Granite Boulder" *Westchester Historian. Quarterly of the Westchester County Historical Society* Vol. 3, no 1 (January, February, March, 1959). A photograph of the boulder is shown on page 22.

22. SARAH BISHOP'S CAVE (Historic)

Type of Formation: Shelter Cave
WOW Factor: 5
Location: Grant Corner (Westchester County)
Tenth Edition, NYS Atlas & Gazetteer: p. 109, C7; **Earlier Edition NYS Atlas & Gazetteer**: p. 33, B7
Estimated Sarah Bishop's Cave GPS Coordinates: 41º18.198'N 73º33.644'W (a pure guess, but definitely in the general vicinity)
Accessibility: The shelter cave is on private land
Degree of Difficulty: Unknown
Additional Information: Nearby is Sal J. Prezioso Mountain Lakes Park, 201 Hawley Road, North Salem 10560. In the past, it may have been possible to access the cave from one of the park's trails.

Description: Sarah Bishop's Cave, aka Sarah Bishop's Rock, is a substantial-sized rock-shelter located on a boulder-strewn cliff on West Mountain above the north shore of 35-acre Lake Rippowam.

According to the Discovery Center at Ridgefield, Sarah Bishop's Cave "… was a natural hollow in the rock about 6' square with bark for a door. " The cave was occupied by Sarah Bishop. "Except for a few rags and an old basin, it was unfurnished. Her bed was the floor of the cave and her pillow a projecting point of rock. In a nearby cleft she kept a supply of roots and nuts that she gathered or were given to her by the local townspeople, as she was never a beggar. In the summer, she grew a patch of beans, cucumbers and potatoes. Nearby were some poor peach trees and numerous highly productive grapevines."

History: Sarah Bishop was a real life hermitess who lived during the Revolutionary War days and is said to have spent thirty years, more or less, living in the cave. No one knows for sure why she withdrew from the world-at-large, but undoubtedly she experienced some kind of emotional or physical trauma when she was a young woman. Bishop died from either sickness

Sarah Bishop's Cave. Old photograph.

or exposure around 1810. She was buried at the June Road Cemetery [41°19.825'N 73°35.401'W] in North Salem, where her gravesite is marked by a small plaque.

From accounts, the cave was somewhat of a tourist attraction during the nineteenth century.

Directions: From east of Salem Center (junction of Routes 116/June Road & 124), drive south on Route 116/June Road for 0.6 mile until you come to Grant Corner. Turn left onto Hawley Road and proceed southeast for ~1.5 miles. Then turn left onto Mountain Lakes Camp Road. This is as far as I can take you.

I have not been able to find any specific directions regarding how to get to the cave, which is not surprising since it appears to be located on private property. In the past, hikers probably made their way over to the cave from the Sal J. Prezioso Mountain Lakes Park on Mountain Lakes Camp Road.

One website indicates that the Westchester County Parks Commission occasionally leads hikes to the cave, with the landowner's permission, of course.

When Patricia Edwards Clyne wrote *Caves for Kids in Historic New York* forty years ago, it was possible to access the cave with permission from Mountain Lakes Camp (as she called it back then), but a lot has changed in forty years.

Resources: Maureen Koehl, *Lewisboro: Images of America* (Charleston, SC: Arcadia Publishing, 1997). On page 72 is a photograph taken in 1890 of the cave.
parks.westchestergov.com/sal-j-prezioso-mountain-lakes.
en.wikipedia.org/wiki/Lewisboro,_New_York.
Patricia Edwards Clyne, *Caves for Kids in Historic New York* (Monroe, NY: Library Research Associates, 1980), 53 & 54. A photograph of the cave is shown on page 46.
chs.org/2013/11/sarah-bishops-cave.
ridgefielddiscovery.org/page/sarahbishop.
sarahbishop.org/about-sarah-bishop.
greensleeves.typepad.com/berkshires/2006/10/the_lonesome_de.html –
This site contains a great deal of information about Sarah Bishop's history.
Fred C. Warner, "Lady of the Cave." *Westchester Historian. Quarterly of the Westchester County Historical Society* Vol. 40, no. 3 (1964). Someone even wrote a poem about Sarah Bishop.
"The Hermitess of Salem." *The Westchester Historian. Quarterly of the Westchester County Historical Society* Vol. 19, no. 1 & 2. (January-April, 1943), 14–18.

23. SPLIT ROCK
Blue Mountain Reservation

Type of Formation: Split Rock
WOW Factor: 4
Location: Peekskill (Westchester County)
Tenth Edition, NYS Atlas & Gazetteer: p. 108, C2–3; **Earlier Edition NYS Atlas & Gazetteer**: p. 33, BC4–5
Parking GPS Coordinates: 41º16.199'N 73º55.305'W
Estimated Split Rock GPS Coordinates: 41º15.893'N 73º54.948'W
Accessibility: >0.5-mile hike (estimated)
Degree of Difficulty: Moderate
Additional Information: Blue Mountain Reservation, Welcher Avenue, Peekskill, NY 10566
-parks.westchestergov.com/images/stories/pdfs/BlueMtn_map_2015.pdf
– trail map.

Rock Walks

Description: In *Day Walker: 32 Hikes in the New York Metropolitan Area. Second Edition*, the boulder is described as "a very large split rock..." That really is all I have to go on.

History: The original 1,538 acres of the Blue Mountain Reservation were once farmlands owned by several families. Later, to take advantage of the growing need for keeping produce refrigerated, two artificial ponds—Loundsbury and New—were created by the Loundsbury family, and ice-harvesting became a bustling business. With the advent of modern refrigeration, however, the ice-harvesting industry waned, and the property, having lost its value, was acquired by the county in 1926.

The reservation has become a popular Mecca for mountain bikers due to its elaborate trail system.

Directions: From Peekskill (junction of Routes 9/Croton Expressway & 6), drive south on Route 9/Croton Expressway for ~1.4 miles. Turn left onto Welcher Avenue and drive east for 0.2 mile to the park entrance. From here, continue east on Welcher Avenue, then south, for another >0.6 mile and park in a pull-off to your left.

From the parking area, follow the blue/white-colored Blue Mountain Summit Trail southeast, in the process passing by the yellow-marked Dickey Brook Trail, to your left, and then the yellow/orange-colored Hip Hop Trail to your right. When you come to the next junction, take the white-colored trail to the right as the blue-colored Blue Mountain Summit Trail veers left.

The white-colored trail now passes by the west side of the New Pond. Near the south end of the pond, look for post #13 by a station where an orange-colored trail goes off to your right. The split rock is to your right here.

The directions sound complicated but really aren't once you are on the trails.

Resources: New York-New Jersey Trail Conference, *Day Walker: 32 Hikes in the New York Metropolitan Area. Second Edition* (Mahwah, NJ: New York-New Jersey Trail Conference, 2002), 147
parks.westchestergov.com/blue-mountain-reservation.
traverseoutfitters.com/blue-mountain-reservation.

Rock Walks

24. HUNTER BROOK ROCK SHELTER

Type of Formation: Rock-Shelter
WOW Factor: 4
Location: Croton Reservoir (Westchester County)
Tenth Edition, NYS Atlas & Gazetteer: p. 108, C3; **Earlier Edition NYS Atlas & Gazetteer**: p. 33, BC5
Parking GPS Coordinates: 41º'N 74º'W
Estimated Hunter Brook Rock Shelter GPS Coordinates: 41º15.584'N 73º50.499'W
Accessibility: Near roadside; may be on private land
Degree of Difficulty: Unknown

Description: According to Roberta Wingerson (a professional archaeologist), in her article "The Hunter Brook Rockshelter," "The shelter was formed by the overlap of several large rock slabs probably torn from the ridge above as the glacier moved across it in a southerly direction." The rock shelter is located at the extreme northwestern end of the 2,182-acre Croton Reservoir.

The Hunter Brook Rock Shelter, restored through excavation, is 6–8 feet wide and 10 feet long, with adequate headroom for occupants.

It should be noted that due to the creation of the New Croton Reservoir in 1904–1905, waters flowing through the Hunter Brook Valley have been backed up to within 50 feet of the rock-shelter. The immediate surroundings are now much different than they were for early Native Americans.

History: Archaeological digs have revealed that the rock-shelter was used by bands of Native American hunters or small families moving through the valley.

Directions: From the Taconic Parkway, get off at the Underhill Avenue Exit. Drive southwest on Underhill Avenue for ~0.2–0.4 mile (depending upon which direction you exited). Turn right onto Baldwin Road and head north for 0.3 mile.

Then turn left onto Baptist Church Road and drive west for 1.8 miles. If the GPS coordinates that I borrowed from Roberta

71

Wingerson's article are correct [adjustments had to be made], then the rockshelter will be directly to your right, just before crossing over a short bridge that spans Hunter Brook.

It's quite possible that the rock-shelter may be on private land, but I can't tell for sure using Google Earth.

Resources: Roberta Wingerson, "The Hunter Brook Rockshelter" *The Bulletin. New York Archaeological Association #68* (November, 1976), 19–26.
tapinto.net/towns/yorktown/events/the-hunterbrook-rock-shelter.

25. BAPTIST CHURCH ROAD ROCK CAVE

Type of Formation: Rock Cave
WOW Factor: 3
Location: Yorktown (Westchester County)
Tenth Edition, NYS Atlas & Gazetteer: p. 108, C4; **Earlier Edition NYS Atlas & Gazetteer**: p. 33, BC5
Estimated Baptist Church Road Rock Cave GPS Coordinates: 41º15.514'N 73º49.965'W
Accessibility: Near roadside
Degree of Difficulty: Easy

Description: This rock shelter is a grouping of large boulders that have come together to create a small cave.

Directions: From the Taconic Parkway, get off at the Underhill Avenue Exit. Drive southwest on Underhill Avenue for ~0.2–0.4 mile (depending upon which direction you exited). Turn right onto Baldwin Road and head north for 0.3 mile.

When you come to Baptist Church Road, turn left and drive west for ~1.2 miles. Somewhere in this general area you will see the rock-shelter.

Resources: ossininghistoryontherun.com/2017/06/07/the-hunterbrook-rock-shelter.

26. GIANT BOULDER
Granite Knolls Park

Type of Formation: Large Boulder
WOW Factor: 6
Location: Yorktown (Westchester County)
Tenth Edition, NYS Atlas & Gazetteer: p. 108, C4; **Earlier Edition NYS Atlas & Gazetteer**: p. 33, B5
Parking GPS Coordinates: 41º18.571'N 73º49.249'W
Destination GPS Coordinates – *Giant Boulder* -- 41º18.693'N 73º49.826'W; *Second rock site* -- 41º18.681'N 73º49.754'W
Accessibility: ~1.0-mile hike
Degree of Difficulty: Moderate
Additional Information: A trail map of Granite Knolls Park can be obtained at leathermansloop.org/download/trailmap/granite-knolls-park-trail-map.pdf nynjtc.org/map/granite-knolls-park ride914.com/local-trails-rides/granite-knolls-park.

Description: Giant Boulder is a large, near house-sized glacial erratic that lies within a small-scale quarry.

A number of other large boulders also populate the area.

History: Granite Knolls Park was purchased by the Town of Yorktown in 2010.

The area was originally owned by the Jesuits, who farmed the land. The property was also actively quarried.

It's said that some of the quarrymen etched their names into the top of Giant Boulder. This would definitely be worth checking out when visiting the rock.

Directions: From the Taconic State Parkway, get off at Exit 17A. Head east on Route 202 for ~0.7 mile and turn left onto Old Yorktown Road. Proceed north for 1.5 miles. Then turn left onto Strang

73

Rock Walks

Boulevard (on some maps listed as Hunters Brook), head west for 0.5 mile, and park at Woodlands Legacy Field Park.

From the parking area at Woodlands Legacy Field Park, walk west on the pink-marked Taconic Bridge Trail for 0.2 mile to reach the start of the Granite Knolls Park trails. In doing so, you will cross over the Taconic State Parkway via the Taconic State Parkway Overpass, a footbridge that was constructed in 2007.

Once across the bridge, proceed north on the pink-marked Taconic Bridge Trail/green-marked Yorktown Trailway for 0.05 mile. Along the way, the Taconic State Parkway will be to your right. Stay left at a junction as the Taconic Bridge Trail separates from the green-marked Yorktown Trailway, and heads southwest. You will pass by the Lavender-marked Dynamite Run Trail (to your right); then the white-marked Circolara Trail as it comes in on your right and joins with the Taconic Bridge Trail.

Stay on the white-marked Circolara Trail when the pink-marked Taconic Bridge Trail goes off to your left. Several more junctions are passed. The Circolara Trail is then joined by the blue-marked Giant Boulder Trail, entering on your left.

The joint trails now head north. When the two divide at a junction, follow the Giant Boulder Trail to your right. In 400 feet, it crosses the green-marked Granite Knolls Trail and quickly reaches the quarry and boulder.

The directions given here sound impossibly complicated. However, essentially all you need to remember to do is to take the Taconic Bridge Trail to the Circolara Trail to the Giant Boulder Trail. I would highly recommend using a trail map to clear up any points of uncertainty along the way.

Resources: yorktownny.org/community/granite-knolls-park. geocaching.com/geocache/GC2XQBM_erratic-behaviour-at-granite-knolls. nynjtc.org/hike/granite-knolls-easy-loop.

27. KATONAH WOODS BOULDERS & ROCKING STONE

Type of Formation: Large Boulder
WOW Factor: 4
Location: Katonah (Westchester County)
Tenth Edition, NYS Atlas & Gazetteer: p. 108, C5; **Earlier Edition NYS Atlas & Gazetteer**: p. 33, BC6
Katonah Boulders -- General Area GPS Coordinates: 41º14.666'N 73º39.517'W
Estimated Katonah Boulders GPS Coordinates -- 41º14.627'N 73º39.527'W
Accessibility: 200-foot trek (a guess)
Degree of Difficulty: Moderately easy

Description: *Katonah Woods Boulders* – These two large boulders supposedly mark the burial site of Chief Katonah and his wife.

Rocking Stone -- According to Frances R. Duncombe & etc. in *Katonah: The History of a New York Village and its People,* "In the woods

north of Old Katonah and of great interest to children of the late eighteen hundreds was a 'rocking stone' which they believed had been used by Indians to call one another. According to Margery Van Tassel, it 'could be made to teeter back and forth and make a deliciously thrilling thud of a noise as it hit the underlying rock bed.'"

Boulders: Katonah Woods. Old photo.

History: Katonah is named for Chief Katonah, a Native American. Katonah's wife was occasionally called Cantitoe; at other times, Mustato, according to an online magazine called *Postscripts,* (notorc.blogspot.com/2010/05/whats-in-name-catalog-of-indian-place.html), Katonah is a shortened form of *Ketatonah*, meaning "great mountain."

At first I thought it likely that Katonah Woods and its boulders may no longer be accessible. After all, in 1897 the valley was flooded to create the Cross River Reservoir, and the original 50-building hamlet of Katonah (called Old Katonah) was relocated to its present site. By good fortune, however, I came across an article that was written long after the valley was flooded, and gives directions on how to reach the rocks.

Directions: From I-686/Saw Mill Parkway at Katonah, get off at Exit 6 and head east on Route 35/Cross River Road for ~0.4 mile. Turn right onto Golden Bridge Road (which quickly becomes Jay Street) and head southeast for ~2.5 miles. Then turn right onto Katonah Woods Road, just before the John Jay Homestead Historic Site is reached (which is also on the right).

From here, I must turn to Arthur I. Bernhard's "Katonah and Bedford: A Do-It-Yourself Historical Tour" for guidance on how to proceed. Start by following Katonah Road south. "Where the road turns left downgrade. Stop. Park and walk the narrow branch at right a short distance. On left side – Two large rocks – Legend says Indian Chief Katonah and his wife are buried here."

Here's my interpretation of what to do -- Drive south on Katonah Road for <0.4 mile and stop just after the road bears noticeably left. I have given the GPS Coordinates for this spot. Bernhard's directions from here sound obtuse, but may make total sense when you are at the spot.

Walk south from where you parked on Katonah Woods Road for ~230 feet. Here, Google Earth seems to show two boulders at the GPS reading I have given. But perhaps my imagination is overactive here. If so, explore the woods more closely around this spot and, if this fails, drive farther south along Katonah Woods Road to see if anything else matches Bernhard's directions. Fortunately, Katonah Woods Road is short, and there really aren't that many other possibilities to consider.

Should the land next to the road be posted, however, be respectful of private property and act accordingly.

Rock Walks

Resources: Frances R. Duncombe & the Historical Committee, Katonah Village Improvement Society, *Katonah: The History of a New York Village and its People* (Katonah, NY: The Society, 1961). On page 15 is a photograph of two medium-to large-sized boulders in the Katonah Woods that supposedly mark the graves of Chief Katonah and his squaw. On page 7, reference is made to the "rocking stone."
en.wikipedia.org/wiki/Katonah,_New_York.
Arthur I. Bernhard, "Katonah and Bedford: A Do-It-Yourself Historical Tour." *The Westchester Historian. Quarterly of the Westchester County Historical Society* Vol. 43, no. 2 (Spring, 1967), 32. The cover of this issue shows a photograph of the Katonah Woods boulders that was taken by Renoda Hoffman.

28. COBBLING-STONE (Historic?)

Type of Formation: Large Boulder; Rock Profile
WOW Factor: Unknown
Location: Katonah (Westchester County)
Tenth Edition, NYS Atlas & Gazetteer: p. 108, C5; **Earlier Edition NYS Atlas & Gazetteer**: p. 33, B5–6
Parking GPS Coordinates: *Cobbling Rock Drive* -- 41º16.783'N 73º43.679'W; *Lasdon Park & Arboretum* -- 41º16.589'N 73º44.253'W
Cobbling Rock GPS Coordinates: Unknown
Accessibility: Unknown
Degree of Difficulty: Unknown

Description: In J. Thomas Scharf's *History of Westchester County, New York*, the *Cobbling-Stone* is described as "A remarkable boulder...found in Somers. It stands on the hill directly northeast of Muscoot Mountain in the southwestern part of Somers, and from its top can be seen the blue hills of Long Island across the sound,...One side of this curious rock has the appearance of an Indian face. It is an immense mass of red granite, said to be the only specimen in the county, and is perched upon three lime-stone points, two or more feet above the surface of the ground."

Sounds a bit like the Great Boulder in North Salem, doesn't it?—Except for the setting, which doesn't fit at all.

77

History: In geology, a cobbling is defined as a rock fragment larger than a pebble and smaller than a boulder. If Cobbling-Stone meets this definition, then it cannot be a terribly large rock.

Muscoot is Native American for "something swampy," which, to me, suggests that Muscoot Mountain was named for the swamp.

Cobbling Rock. Old photograph.

Directions: I have no idea where this rock is located or if it even still exists. However, I have come up with several possible leads to explore:

First, it's entirely possible that the rock may be close to Cobbling Rock Drive in Katonah, a street that adopted the rock's namesake. My rationale here is that street names are often a dead giveaway if you're out exploring.

Rock Walks

To get to Cobbling Rock Drive, start from Whitehall Corners (junction of Routes 35 & 100/Somerstown Turnpike), and head northwest on Route 35 for 1.2 miles. Turn left onto Cobbling Rock Drive, which is only 0.4 mile long. It's doubtful that you will see anything from the road. However, if homeowners are working outdoors by their houses, I wouldn't hesitate to ask if they know the whereabouts of this boulder.

Another possible lead, a longshot I would imagine, is to look for the rock at the Lasdon Park & Arboretum in Katonah, which originally was called Cobbling Rock Farm. Acquired by William and Mildred Lasdon in 1939, it was modeled after George Washington's home in Virginia. Westchester County purchased the estate in 1986.

To get to the park, start at Whitehall Corners (junction of Routes 35 & 100/Somerstown Turnpike), and proceed west on Route 35 for 1.9 miles. Turn left into the park entrance.

What's interesting when you study a map closely is that only 0.5 mile of land separates Cobbling Rock Drive from the former Cobbling Rock Farm. Surely there must be something between these two points.

One last clue to follow-up on is based upon the Somers Historical Society's assertion, in *Somers: Its People and Places*, that the rock is on land owned by the New York City Water Department. This would seem to narrow down the search even further.

Resources: John Thomas Scharf, *History of Westchester County. Volume II* (New York: L. E. Preston & Company, 1886), 499. The author describes the rock as a "genuine natural curiosity."
John Thomas Scharf, *History of Westchester County, New York Vol. 1* (Philadelphia: L. E. Preston & Company, 1886), 9. A photograph of the Cobbling-Stone is shown on page 8.
Somers Historical Society, *Somers: Its People and Places:1788–1988* (Somers, NY: Somers Historical Society, 1989). On page 48 the authors write "On a hill northeast of Muscoot Mountain in southwestern Somers on land owned by the New York City Water District lies Cobbling Rock, an immense mass of red granite."
hudsonrivervalley.org/learning/pdfs/lasdonparkandarboretum.pdf.

29. GREAT STONE FACE ROCK SHELTER

Type of Formation: Rock-Shelter
WOW Factor: 6
Location: Bedford (Westchester County)
Tenth Edition, NYS Atlas & Gazetteer: p. 109, D6; **Earlier Edition NYS Atlas & Gazetteer**: p. 33, C6
Bedford Center Coordinates: 41º12.234'N 73º38.625'W
Tiny lake 1.2 miles southwest of Bedford Center GPS Coordinates: 41º12.229'N 73º38.623'W
Accessibility: Unknown
Degree of Difficulty: Unknown

Great Stone Face visible at upper right corner. Old photograph.

Description: The Great Stone Face Rock Shelter's main feature (and namesake), according to an article that appeared in the *Quarterly Bulletin. Westchester County Historical Society*, is a "massive gargoyle like head which protruded above the shelter and formed a part of it and which fancy could liken to a frowning stone giant."

History: Native American artifacts have been found at the site, which makes it historically significant.

Directions: The article on the Great Stone Face Rock Shelter mentions that the geological formation is ~1.25 miles southwest of the old court house in Bedford. The 1787 Old Court House, now occupied by the Bedford Museum and Bedford Historical Society,

(615 Old Post Road), is at a GPS reading of 41°12.234'N 73°38.625'W. If we draw a straight line southwest for ~1.2 miles from the Bedford Museum, we end up near the south end of a small, unnamed lake, at a GPS reading of 41°12.229'N 73°38.623'W. Hopefully, this bit of geometry has put us in the general area.

To the west of the lake, 0.1-mile distant, is a small quarry; to the east, within 0.1 mile, are some residential homes. To my way of thinking, the best way to explore the area is to head uphill from the southwest side of the lake. In doing so, you will find that the elevation changes rapidly from 343 feet to 422 feet—a 99-foot gain in just 120 feet. I make no guarantees, but I can't help but wonder just what might be here to find.

To reach this small lake from Bedford Center (junction of Old Post Road & Pound Ridge Road), drive southwest on Old Post Road for 1.1 miles. Turn left onto Crusher Road and go less than 0.3 mile. Perhaps, before the quarry, there is an off-road place to park, or even at the Town of Bedford Highway Department Facility, from where you can go east for 0.1 mile, down to the small lake, and then have an opportunity to check out what looks to be a very steep slope (assuming, of course, that the land isn't posted).

Resources: "Great Stone Face Rock Shelter." *Quarterly Bulletin. Westchester County Historical Society* Vol. 7, no. 1 (January, 1931). On page 39 is a photo of the rock-shelter taken by Leslie Verne Case.

30. WARD POUND RIDGE RESERVATION ROCKS
Ward Pound Ridge Reservation

Type of Formation: Rock-Shelter; Boulder: Petroglyph
WOW Factor: *Leatherman's Cave* – 5; *Bear Rock Petroglyph* – 3; *Shelter Cave* -- 3–4
Location: Cross River (Westchester County)
Tenth Edition, NYS Atlas & Gazetteer: p. 109, D6; **Earlier Edition NYS Atlas & Gazetteer**: p. 33, BC7
Parking GPS Coordinates: 41°14.886'N 73°35.689'W

Rock Walks

Estimated Destination GPS Coordinates: *Leatherman's Cave* -- ~41º14.518'N 73º36.172'W; *Indian Rock-Shelter* – ~41º14.632'N 73º34.586'W; *Bear Rock Petroglyph* -- ~41º13.735'N 73º35.591'W
Fee: Modest entry fee
Accessibility (these are guesstimates): *Leatherman Cave* – ~1.3-mile hike; *Indian Rock-Shelter* – ~1.5-mile hike; *Bear Rock Petroglyph* – ~1.4-mile hike
Additional Information: Ward Pound Ridge Reservation, Routes 35 & 121 South, Cross River, NY 10518

Park map -- parks.westchestergov.com/images/stories/pdfs/WPRsm_2012.pdf

wcgis.maps.arcgis.com/apps/MapTour/index.html?appid=eb6a2bbf59b74b289dd05baa843cc3f6.

Description: *Leatherman Cave* lies on the south shoulder of Overlook Hill not far below its summit. The cave consists of a jumble of boulders that have fallen together to form a small enclosure.

This is one of the shelter caves reputedly used by the legendary Leatherman during the late 1800s.

Indian Rock-Shelter consists of an overhanging ledge that archaeologists have determined was used by Native Americans as a hunting camp.

Bear Rock Petroglyph is a gumdrop-shaped boulder that contains a series of squiggles carved into its rock face. The squiggles, which are believed to date back many hundreds of years, depict the shape of a bear, turkey, and deer—all which were plentiful at the time Native Americans hunted the woods. Interestingly, the petroglyphs were not "discovered" until the park's curator came upon them in 1971.

In *50 Hikes in the Lower Hudson Valley*, Stella Green and H. Neil Zimmerman sound a cautionary note about the petroglyphs. Jim Swager, author of *Petroglyphs in America*, examined Bear Rock and found the authenticity of the petroglyphs questionable.

Additional Boulders -- Near the Michigan Road entrance are two large rocks that Katherine S. Anderson & Peggy Turco's write about in their book *Walks and Rambles in Westchester & Fairfax Counties*. "The big boulders on top [of either a drumlin or a recessional moraine], to the right of the shelter, are glacial erratics, likewise dumped."

In addition, there are also rock destinations called *Castle Rock* (a rock outcropping), *Magie Stairs, Spy Rock,* and *Raven Rocks,* but I don't have any specific information on these geological features other than that below Raven Rocks is a cavern called the *Devil's Den.*

Bear Rock. Photograph by Daniel Chazin.

A *Dancing Rock* is also contained in the preserve. According to Richard M. Lederer, Jr., in *The Place-Names of Westchester County, New York: Expanded Version,* "To keep harvest workers warm on cold autumn evenings, a fire was built on a large flat rock. When the work was done there was dancing on the rock."

History: The Ward Pound Ridge Reservation encompasses 4,315 acres of land, and is the largest park in Westchester County. Raymond H. Torrey, Frank Place, Jr. and Robert L. Dickinson, in *New York Walk Book. Third Edition* describe it as elliptically-shaped, 3.5 miles by 4.5 miles with a circumference of fifteen miles. It was first occupied by Native Americans who used "pounds" (or enclosures) to confine captured game. It was undoubtedly this word that later gave rise to the area being called Poundridge.

83

Rock Walks

In 1938, "Ward" was added on to Poundridge to honor a twentieth-century Westchester County Republican leader named William Lukens Ward.

The part of the park that is of most interest to us is found in the southern section

Ariel Schwartz poses inside the Indian Rock-Shelter.
Photograph by Daniel Chazin.

Directions: From Cross River (junction of Routes 121/Cross River Road & 35), drive south on Route 121/Cross River Road for 0.1 mile, crossing over the Cross River. Turn left onto Reservation Road and proceed east for 0.7 mile until you reach the park's entrance. Once passing through, continue east for another 0.1 mile. Then turn right onto Michigan Road and follow it south for over 0.8 mile to a parking area just before a cul-de-sac.

Near the kiosk is a colored map of the area.

Leatherman's Cave -- From the Michigan Road parking area, follow the red-blazed/green-blazed trail southwest. When you come to the Leatherman Trail (LT), head northwest; then, south (avoiding going over the summit of 665-foot-high Overlook Hill), and then west again. In a short while, you will come to the spur path on your right that leads quickly up to Leatherman's Cave.

The park's map also shows what looks like a much shorter path to the cave from Honey Hollow Road. I am not clear as to the accessibility of this approach, however.

Indian Rock-Shelter -- From the Michigan Road parking area, follow the red-blazed/yellow-blazed trail east, and then south. When you come to the Rock Trail (RT), turn left and continue south for a short distance until you reach the Indian Rock-Shelter, which will be on your left.

Bear Rock Petroglyph -- From the Michigan Road parking area, pick up the yellow-blazed trail and head south, staying right at a fork where the yellow-blazed trail divides. When you come to the junction with the Rock Trail (RT), continue south for over an additional 0.8 mile, now on the Rock Trail (RT). The Bear Rock Petroglyphs will be to your right, not far from a powerline corridor.

Dancing Rock – This flat rock formation is off of the Rock Trail (RT), northeast of the Bear Rock Petroglyphs.

All of these interesting sites are indicated by name on the trail map -- parks.westchestergov.com/images/stories/pdfs/WPRsm_2012.pdf

Resources: parks.westchestergov.com/ward-pound-ridge-reservation.
New York-New Jersey Trail Conference, *Day Walker: 32 Hikes in the New York Metropolitan Area. Second Edition* (Mahwah, NJ: New York-New Jersey Trail Conference, 2002), 133.
New York-New Jersey Trail Conference, *New York Walk Book. Sixth Edition* (New York: New York-New Jersey Trail Conference, 1998), 111.
Patricia Edwards Clyne, *Caves for Kids in Historic New York* (Monroe, NY: Library Research Associates, 1980), 29.
Katherine S. Anderson & Peggy Turco (reviser & expander), *Walks and Rambles in Westchester & Fairfax Counties* (Woodstock, VT: Backcountry Publications, 1993), 108.
Richard M. Lederer, Jr., *The Place-Names of Westchester County, New York: Expanded Version* (Harrison, NY: Harbor Hill Books, 1980), 37 & 49.
Patricia Edwards Clyne, *Hudson Valley Trails and Tales* (Woodstock, NY: The Overlook Press, 1990), 34.
Beth Herr & Maureen Koehl, *Ward Pound Ridge Reservation: Images of America* (Charleston, SC: Arcadia Press, 213). The entire book is devoted to images of the park.

scenesfromthetrail.com/2017/11/23/leathermans-loop-and-rocks-trail-ward-pound-ridge-reservation. This site includes many photographs of the preserve.
Stella Green and H. Neil Zimmerman, *50 Hikes in the Lower Hudson Valley* (Woodstock, VT: Backcountry Guides, 2002), 39. The story of the Leatherman is described in some detail. On page 34 is a rather striking photograph of Leatherman's Cave, complete with a hiker sitting on a rock at the entrance.
Daniel Case, *AMC's Best Day Hikes Near New York City* (Boston: Appalachian Mountain Club Book, 2010), 84.
Raymond H. Torrey, Frank Place, Jr. & Robert L. Dickinson, *New York Walk Book. Third Edition* (NY: The American Geographical Society, 1951), 76–79.

31. HENRY MORGENTHAU PRESERVE BOULDER
Henry Morgenthau Preserve

Type of Formation: Large Boulder
WOW Factor: 4
Location: Pound Ridge (Westchester County)
Tenth Edition, NYS Atlas & Gazetteer: p. 109, D6–7; **Earlier Edition NYS Atlas & Gazetteer**: p. 33, C6–7
Parking GPS Coordinates: 41º12.085′N 73º35.279′W
Estimated Boulder GPS Coordinates: 41º12.018′N 73º35.313′W
Accessibility: 0.1–0.2-mile hike
Degree of Difficulty: Moderately easy
Additional Information: Henry Morgenthau Preserve, Route 172, Pound Ridge, NY 10576

Description: In the *Eastern New York Chapter Preserve Guide: Lower Hudson Region*, the authors describe the 6-foot-high boulder as "a large glacial erratic (boulder) perched on a ridge."

History: The boulder is contained in a 36-acre preserve that abuts Blue Heron Lake. The initial land that served as a nucleus for the preserve was donated by Ruth M. Knight in memory of her father Henry Morgenthau (a U.S. diplomat, attorney, and real estate investor).

Rock Walks

Directions: From Bedford (junction of Routes 172/Pound Ridge Road & 22), drive east on Route 172/Pound Ridge Road for ~3.0 miles and turn right into a small parking area 0.1 mile after passing by Tatomuck Road, on your left. Look for a preserve sign at the park entrance, just after the guardrail ends.

The 6-foot-high boulder is found at the junction of the Blue Trail and White Trail (the latter, possibly being unmarked).

Resources: Chris Harmon, Matt Levy & Gabrielle Antoniadis, *Eastern New York Chapter Preserve Guide: Lower Hudson Region.* (Mt. Kisco, NY: The Nature Conservancy, 2000), 32 & 33.
henrymorgenthaupreserve.org.
americantowns.com/place/henry-morgenthau-preserve-katonah-ny.html – "The largest boulder in the preserve, located at the split of the Blue and White Trails, is over six feet in diameter. It was carried by glacial action thousands of years ago."
woodlandwalks.org/henry-morgenthau-preserve.

32. CHOATE SANCTUARY BOULDER
Choate Audubon Sanctuary

Type of Formation: Large Boulder
WOW Factor: Not determined
Location: Mt. Kisco (Westchester County)
Tenth Edition, NYS Atlas & Gazetteer: p. 108, D4–5; **Earlier Edition NYS Atlas & Gazetteer**: p. 33, C5–6
Parking GPS Coordinates: 41º12.537′N 73º44.797′W
Trailhead GPS Coordinates: 41º12.482′N 73º44.815′W
Choate Sanctuary Boulders GPS Coordinates: *Main boulder* - Not determined; *Mini-car-sized boulder* -- 41º12.436′N 73º45.020′W
Accessibility: <0.5-mile walk
Degree of Difficulty: Moderately easy
Additional Information: Trail map -- sawmillriveraudubon.org/maps/Choate_Trails.pdf

87

Rock Walks

Description: Katherine S. Anderson and Peggy Turco, in *Walks and Rambles in Westchester & Fairfax Counties*, mention "...a huge erratic — a boulder that stands alone dropped here by a glacier..."

Several sources mention unusual rock outcroppings which are formed out of Fordham Gneiss. I have not been able to obtain any specific descriptions of the boulder(s), however.

History: The 32-acere sanctuary began with a 23-acre bequest from the heirs of Joseph H. Choate, Jr. In 1972, three additional acres were acquired from Geoffrey Platt in memory of his wife, Helen; and then, in 1997, an additional four acres were added under a ninety-nine year lease from the Town of New Castle.

The sanctuary has been owned and operated by the Saw Mill River Audubon since 1975.

Directions: From Mt. Kisco (junction of Routes 133/West Main Street & 117), drive west on Route 133/West Main Street/Millwood Road for 1.1 miles. Turn right onto Crow Hill Road and head north for 0.1 mile. Then turn right and park along Red Oak Lane, being sure not to block any of the homeowner's driveways.

Walk carefully down Crow Hill Road to reach the sanctuary's entrance, which you passed on the way up to Red Oak Lane. Follow the 0.5-mile-long, white-marked White Oaks Trail that begins at the park's entrance. The boulder is encountered at some point along the trail.

The mini-car-sized boulder is located near the south end of the preserve, about 100 feet up from the highway. A bushwhack is probably required to get to it.

Resources: Katherine S. Anderson & Peggy Turco (reviser & expander), *Walks and Rambles in Westchester & Fairfax Counties* (Woodstock, VT: Backcountry Publications, 1993), 66.
sawmillriveraudubon.org/choate.html.

33. KIDD'S ROCK
Kingsland Point Park

Type of Formation: Historic Rock
WOW Factor: Unknown; likely, 1–2
Location: Sleepy Hollow (Westchester County)
Tenth Edition, NYS Atlas & Gazetteer: p. 108, E3; **Earlier Edition NYS Atlas & Gazetteer**: p. 33, CD4–5
Parking GPS Coordinates: 41º05.331'N 73º52.241'W
Estimated Kidd's Rock GPS Coordinates: 41º05.050'N 73º52.417'W
Fee: Modest entry fee per car charged
Accessibility: 0.4-mile walk
Degree of Difficulty: Moderately easy
Additional Information: Kingsland Point Park, 299 Palmer Ave, Sleepy Hollow, NY 10591

Description: Kidd's Rock is most likely a rock outcropping on the bank of the Hudson River at a spot where it was once possible for a pirate's ship to make landing.

History: Kidd's Rock is supposedly where Captain William Kidd landed while conspiring with Frederick Philipse I to smuggle illicit goods inland. Philipse I's role was to light a fire on the rock to guide Kidd's ship in.

Kingsland Point Park is an 18-acre riverfront park at the mouth of the Pocantico River named after Ambrose Kingsland who erected a summerhouse (gazebo) on the rock in the

William Kidd.

nineteenth century. Kingsland Point is formed at the confluence of the Pocantico River and Hudson River. Because the point proved hazardous to navigation, a lighthouse was erected near it in 1883.

The park is owned by Westchester County and is operated and maintained by the village of Sleepy Hollow.

Rock Walks

Captain Kidd seems to have been everywhere. In *Rock Walks*, I recount a number of caves and rocks in downstate New York that are identified with the pirate. One of the citations, however, has eluded me. In *A Guide to New Rochelle and Lower Westchester*, Robert Bolton writes "On the opposite shore of Long Island is a small jutting promontory, which runs into the entrance of Hempstead Bay, called to this day 'Kidd Rock.'" I can't seem to find any modern references to this promontory. Perhaps it has become part of the Bar Beach Town Park on the west side of the harbor.

There also happens to be a Kidd's Point on the west side of the Hudson River across from the Highlands. It has gone by other names as well, including Caldwell's Point, Donder Berg Point, and Jones Point. Nothing, however, is as colorful as invoking the name of Captain Kidd.

Directions: From Sleepy Hollow (junction of Routes 9/North Broadway & 448/Bedford Road), drive north on Route 9/North Broadway for >0.5 mile. Turn left onto Palmer Avenue and proceed west for 0.4 mile, crossing over the Amtrack rail line just before the Hudson River. Turn right and drive south for 0.3 mile to reach the parking area.

From the parking area walk southwest to the end of the park. From what I've read, Kidd's Rock is located not far from the south end of Kingsland Point Park, near the Sleepy Hollow Lighthouse (41º05.043'N 73º52.455'W). I don't believe that there is actually anything to see, other than to have an interesting walk with a sense of history about it.

Resources: Henry Steiner, *The Place Names of Historic Sleepy Hollow & Tarrytown* (Bowie, MD: Heritage Books, Inc., 1998), 70 & 71.
sleepyhollowny.gov/recreation-parks-department/pages/kingsland-point-park.
explore-hudson-valley.com/kingsland-point-park.html.
explore-hudson-valley.com/tarrytown-new-york-10-outdoor-escapes-35-minutes-from-grand-central.html.
Richard M. Lederer, Jr., *The Place-Names of Westchester County, New York: Expanded Version* (Harrison, NY: Harbor Hill Books, 1980), 77. According to Lederer, the story about Kidd landing at the point has never been confirmed. Oh well, so much for a good story.

Rock Walks

Robert Bolton, *A Guide to New Rochelle and Lower Westchester* (Harrison, NY: Harbor Hill Books, 1976 facsimile of a 1842 book), 27.
Wallace Bruce, *The Hudson: Three Centuries of History, Romance and Invention* (NY: Walking News, Inc., 1982. Centennial edition reprint), 80 & 81. Bruce relates the story of Captain Kidd.

34. ROCKEFELLER STATE PARK PRESERVE ROCKS
Rockefeller State Park Preserve

Type of Formation: Large Rock
WOW Factor: 5
Location: Sleepy Hollow (Westchester County)
Tenth Edition, NYS Atlas & Gazetteer: p. 108, E3–4; **Earlier Edition NYS Atlas & Gazetteer**: p. 33, CD5
Parking GPS Coordinates: 41º06.693'N 73º50.222'W
Estimated Destination GPS Coordinates: *Glacial Erratic* -- 41º06.511'N 73º50.562'W; *Spook Rock* -- ~41º06.476'N 73º51.211'W; *Raven Rock* -- ~41º05.800'N 73º48.966'W
Fee: Entrance fee charged
Accessibility: *Glacial erratic* – 0.5-mile hike
    Spook Rock -- ~1.5-mile hike
    Raven Rock – Probably >2.0-mile hike. Bring along a trail map in order to navigate the complexity of the trail system.
Degree of Difficulty: *Glacial Erratic* – Moderate
    Spook Rock – Moderate
    Raven Rock – Moderately difficult
Additional Information: Rockefeller State Park Preserve, 125 Phelps Way, Pleasantville, NY 10570
    Trail map for the Rockefeller State Park Preserve available at"
    parks.ny.gov/parks/attachments/RockefellerTrailMap.pdf,
    friendsrock.org/wp-content/uploads/2014/06/2014-05-29-RSPP-Trail-Map-Brochure.pdf

Description: *Spook Rock* is described by one source as a "large rock." I suspect that it is associated with a bluff that may also be called Spook Rock. In *The Place Names of Historic Sleepy Hollow & Tarrytown*, Henry Steiner describes Spook Rock as an "… unmarked…large flat rock…"

Rock Walks

Glacial Erratic is just as the name suggests—a large rock that is not indigenous to the immediate area. It obviously is of decent size in order for its position to be noted on the trail map. The rock is squarish in shape and probably a minimum of 8–10 feet in height. Benches are lined up in front of the rock to accommodate those who come to hear nature talks or to meditate.

In *Day Walker: 32 Hikes in the New York Metropolitan Area. Second Edition*, the authors write, "Reputedly, this stone is the largest such boulder deposited in this part of the country by the receding glacier." Given the fact that there are some really big glacial boulders in this part of the country, I am assuming that the writers meant to say "county" instead of "country."

Glacial Rock. Photograph by Carlos Gonzalez

Raven Rock is a massive rock or group of rocks that were detached from the cliffs on the east side of Pocantico Hills east of

Rock Walks

Ferguson Lake. According to a quote from the *Westchester Historian* in Henry Steiner's *The Place Names of Historic Sleepy Hollow & Tarrytown*, "It is an unusual arrangement of rocks with perpendicular walls, deep crevices and an old cave that has almost completely disappeared."

The rock has also been known as Crow's Rock.

History: The Rockefeller State Park Preserve is a 1,552-acre park established as a state park in the 1970s. It was donated to New York State by the William Rockefeller family in 1963. For those who are interested in media information, the park's entrance on Route 117 was used briefly in the 2002 movie, *Super Troopers*.

Spook Rock -- According to Native American folklore, a young man spied twelve beautiful, young girls dancing by Spook Rock. He kidnapped the loveliest of the twelve and took her home to be his bride. They had a baby together, but all was not to be well. Within three years, the baby had died, and then the mother. It is said that the wandering ghost of this young mother still returns to the rock, looking for her husband and baby.

I have read that strange lights have been reported in the vicinity, presumably caused by the spirit of the young mother. A nice Halloween story for Spook Rock, if you believe in this kind of thing.

The name Spook Rock is not as uncommon as you might at first think. Just in Eastern New York State alone there are spook rocks in Montebello, Suffern, and Greenport Center.

Raven's Rock – A legend accompanies this rock. An unfortunate woman became lost in a snowstorm and sought shelter between the rock and the hillside. She ended up dying from exposure. It is rumored that her ghost now rises up whenever someone approaches in the winter so that she might warn them of impending danger.

Directions: From Philipse Manor (junction of Routes 117 & 9/Albany Post Road), drive northeast on Route 117 for ~1.4 miles and turn right into the park's entrance, parking by the Visitor Center.

Glacial Erratic – From the parking lot, follow the Old Sleepy Hollow Road Trail (an old, colonial road) southwest. By 0.4 mile, you will come to Nature's Way Path on your right. Follow it north for a short distance, and then turn left onto a spur path that takes you quickly to the glacial boulder.

Spook Rock – From Nature's Way Path, continue southwest on Old Sleepy Hollow Road. You will soon cross over the paved Sleepy Hollow Road at >0.5 mile; then a footbridge, after which the trail quickly comes to a "T." Turn left onto the Pocantico River Trail, and then promptly right onto the Eagle Hill Summit Trail. When you come to the 13 Bridges Trail junction, bear left; then right onto the Witch's Spring Trail. Finally, turn right onto the Spook Rock Trail and follow it up to and around Spook Rock. The total distance hiked is less than 1.5 miles.

Raven Rock – There are so many paths and turns to negotiate that bringing along a copy of the trail map to refer to constantly is virtually a necessity.

However, there is an easier way to get to Raven's Rock, and I have devoted an entire chapter to it [see next chapter].

By good fortune, all three sites are shown on the trail map, *parks.ny.gov/parks/attachments/RockefellerTrailMap.pdf*, which, to me, means that they are worthy points of interest, and can be gotten to by paying close attention to the trail map.

Resources: New York-New Jersey Trail Conference, *Day Walker: 32 Hikes in the New York Metropolitan Area. Second Edition* (Mahwah, NJ: New York-New Jersey Trail Conference, 2002), 139 & 141. A trail map is contained on page 136.
parks.ny.gov/parks/59/details.aspx.
gothichorrorstories.com/behind-urban-legends/hiking-rockefeller-state-park-preserve-looking-for-spook-rock-hulda-the-witch-and-the-non-headless-horseman-origins-of-the-legend-of-sleepy-hollow.
Richard M. Lederer, Jr., *The Place-Names of Westchester County, New York: Expanded Version* (Harrison, NY: Harbor Hill Books, 1980), 118.
scenesfromthetrail.com/2017/03/18/eagle-hill-area-rockefeller-state-park-preserve. – This site contains photographs of the glacial erratic.
Henry Steiner, *The Place Names of Historic Sleepy Hollow & Tarrytown* (Bowie, MD: Heritage Books, Inc., 1998), 132. Steiner also recounts the legend behind Spook Rock.
gonehikin.blogspot.com/2017/01/rockefeller-state-park-preserve-ny.html.

35. RAVEN ROCK
Rockefeller State Park Preserve

Type of Formation: Large Rock
WOW Factor: 5
Location: Sleepy Hollow (Westchester County)
Tenth Edition, NYS Atlas & Gazetteer: p. 108, E4; **Earlier Edition NYS Atlas & Gazetteer**: p. 33, CD5
Parking GPS Coordinates: 41º06.196'N 73º49.448'W
Raven Rock GPS Coordinates: Not determined
Accessibility: 1.8-mile hike
Degree of Difficulty: Moderately difficult
Additional Information: Rockefeller State Park Preserve, 125 Phelps Way, Pleasantville, NY 10570
parks.ny.gov/parks/attachments/RockefellerTrailMap.pdf – trail map

Description: Raven Rock is a large rock outcropping with historical and mythical significance.

Raven Rock. Old photograph.

History: As it turns out, Raven Rock is an actual landmark that ties in with Washington Irving's tale of Ichabod Crane and the "Legend of Sleepy Hollow," and a woman in white who haunted the rock, often shrieking at night before a winter's storm because she had perished in one.

Pocantico is the Native American word, *Po-can-tee-co,* for "a swift dark stream running between the hills."

Directions: From Graham (junction of Routes 448/Bedford Road & 117), head south on Route 448/Bedford Road for ~1.5 miles.

These following directions are taken, with modification, from Lucas Buresch's *Archive Sleuth's* website:

95

Rock Walks

Park off-road along the east side of Bedford Road, opposite the entrance to "Blue Hill at Stone Barns." Walk east along a carriage road across a cow pasture and into the woods. After <0.4 mile, an intersection is reached. Turn right and walk south for >400 feet. When you come to a 3-way intersection, bear left and proceed east for 400 feet.

Then turn right onto the Laurence's Ridge Trail and head south for ~1.1 miles (staying to your left when you come to a 3-way intersection along the way).

At the Raven Rock Trail intersection, bear left and follow the trail north as it makes a sharp U-turn and descends steeply. After 0.4 mile, the trail dead-ends at Raven Rock.

Resources: William Owens, *Pocantico Hills 1609–1959* (Sleepy Hollow, NY: Sleepy Hollow Restorations, 1960), 2. A photograph of Raven Rock is shown along with a caption narrating the rock's legend. findery.com/MadameSpooky/notes/legend-of-sleepy-hollow-raven-rock. archivesleuth.wordpress.com/2011/04/10/raven-rock.

36. HELICKER'S CAVE & BIG BOULDERS
Betsy Sluder Preserve

Type of Formation: Rock-Shelter; Boulder
WOW Factor: 6
Location: Armonk (Westchester County)
Tenth Edition, NYS Atlas & Gazetteer: p. 108, E5; **Earlier Edition NYS Atlas & Gazetteer**: p. 33, CD6
Parking GPS Coordinates: 41º07.239'N 73º43.025'W
Estimated Destination GPS Coordinates: *Helicker's Cave* -- 41º07.020'N 73º43.493'W; *Big Boulders* -- 41º07.407'N 73º43.484'W
Accessibility: 0.2–0.3-mile hike
Degree of Difficulty: Moderately easy
Additional Information: A map of the Betsy Sluder Preserve is at leathermansloop.org/2009/02/how-do-you-train-betsy-sluder-preserve.

Description: *Helicker's Cave* is a small-to-medium-sized rock-shelter located on a hillside.

Rock Walks

Big Boulders -- One website (alltrails.com/trail/us/new-york/betsy-sluder-nature-trail) has this to say about the boulders: "In the middle of the park there are big boulders that *are* great fun to climb on." They must be of fairly good size if you can scramble around on them.

The exact location of the boulders is not depicted on the park map, but these rocks are definitely worth making an effort to locate. I have come up with a possible GPS reading using Google Earth. I suspect that there will be no difficulty locating these rocks once you are on the trail and fully involved in the hunt.

History: Helicker's Cave is historically significant, for not only was it occupied by early Native Americans, but later by Anne Hutchinson and her children, who lived at the site temporarily sometime after the Revolutionary War; then by Old Bet Helicker, a hermit who resided at the rock-shelter from 1783–1802 (although one site suggests that Bet Helicker was a "li'l ol' lady" who lived in a

Glacial erratic. Photograph by Alex Smoller.

shack near the cave); and lastly by the mysterious Leatherman, who used it as one of his stopovers while making his regular 365-mile, near-monthly circuit.

The Betsy Sluder Preserve is a 70-acre parcel of land in a forested area completely surrounded by homes and businesses. The preserve is named for Betsy C. Sluder.

Google Earth identifies the preserve by a different name, Whippoorwill Ridge Park, which perhaps was the park's earlier name.

According to Richard M. Lederer, Jr. in *The Place-Names of Westchester County, New York: Expanded Version*, there is also a Little Bet Helicker's Cave, south of Helicker's Cave. More to look for, I guess.

Rock Walks

Directions: From I-684 east of Armonk, take Exit 3 and head southwest on Armonk-Bedford Road/Route 22 for ~0.6 mile. At the traffic light, turn right onto Main Street, which takes you north towards the center of Armonk. Within 0.1 mile, turn left onto Old Route 22, and proceed southwest for 0.2 mile.

Park to your right immediately after Birdsall Farm Drive (and just before Tutor Time of Armonk) in a small area for the preserve. Check the kiosk for pertinent information.

A 1.5 mile-long trail leads around the perimeter of the preserve. From the parking area, take the red-marked path clockwise west (left), then south, for ~0.2 mile. The Leatherman Cave is located just off the trail at the south-most part of the preserve. A faint path leads to it, I presume.

The moss-covered boulders are located near the middle of the park on a fairly steep hillside.

Resources: Patricia Edwards Clyne, *Caves for Kids in Historic New York* (Monroe, NY: Library Research Associates, 1980), 9–16.
leathermansloop.org/2009/02/the-legend-of-the-leatherman.
Richard M. Lederer, Jr., *The Place-Names of Westchester County, New York: Expanded Version* (Harrison, NY: Harbor Hill Books, 1980), 17.
Patricia Edwards Clyne, *Hudson Valley Trails and Tales* (Woodstock, NY: The Overlook Press, 1990), 82 & 162.
leathermansloop.org/2009/02/how-do-you-train-betsy-sluder-preserve.
nynjctbotany.org/lgtofc/whippoor.html.
alltrails.com/trail/us/new-york/betsy-sluder-nature-trail.
woodlandwalks.org/whippoorwill-park.
The Westchester Historian. Quarterly of the Westchester County Historical Society Vol. 4, no. 2 (April, 1925). On page 40 is a photograph of Bet Helicker's Cave.

37. HORACE SARLES ROCK & SHELTER CAVES
Wampus Pond County Park

Type of Formation: Large Rock or Rock Outcropping; Rock-Shelter
WOW Factor: Unknown
Location: Armonk (Westchester County)

Rock Walks

Tenth Edition, NYS Atlas & Gazetteer: p. 108, E5; **Earlier Edition NYS Atlas & Gazetteer**: p. 33, CD6
Parking GPS Coordinates: 41º08.836'N 73º43.678'W
Estimated Destination GPS Coordinates: *Horace Sarles Rock* -- 41º08.864'N 73º43.885'W (a guess); *Shelter Cave(s)* -- Unknown, but probably in the same general area as Horace Sarles Rock
Accessibility: <0.6 mile if walking clockwise around perimeter of pond, or >0.1 mile if padding across pond
Additional Information: Wampus Pond County Park, 1 Wampus Lake Drive, Armonk, NY 10504

Description: *Horace Sarles Rock* is a fairly nondescript rock or rock outcropping that juts out into Wampus Pond.

Rock-Shelter(s) -- I do not have any specific descriptions about the shelter caves, but assume that they are fairly small in size and likely formed by overhanging ledges.

History: *Horace Sarles Rock* acquired its name when Horace Sarles (most likely a local resident) was killed by a nearby tree that fell and struck him while he was fishing from the rock.

Rock-Shelters -- Parker Harrington, doing a cultural resources inventory of the pond area, found several early twentieth-century rock-shelters in or near the park. I have not been able to find any further information regarding this matter.

In *New York Walk Book. Third Edition*, however, Raymond H. Torrey, Frank Place. Jr. and Robert L. Dickinson do write that "The scenery [along the west shore] is picturesque with high ledges frowning under hemlock forest." This sounds like the ideal spot, if any, to find rock-shelters.

Wampus is Native American for "opossum."

Wampus Pond was earlier known as Wampus Lake Reservoir when it was part of the New York City water supply. This ended in 1963 when the pond, including 93 acres, was purchased by the county from New York City.

Directions: From Armonk (junction of Routes 128/Armonk Road & 22), drive north, then northwest, on Route 128/Armonk Road for ~2.5 miles and turn left into a small parking area by the pond.

The perimeter of the lake is roughly 1.0 mile long, but not all of it needs to be explored.

Horace Sarles Rock -- I suspect that the rock is on the west side of the lake, probably somewhere along ~0.4 mile of shoreline.

Rock Shelter – Topo maps show that the land along the west side of the pond rises up steeply, gaining nearly 250 feet of elevation in 0.1 mile. You couldn't hope for better conditions than this to look for rock-shelters in the park.

Resources: Richard M. Lederer, Jr., *The Place-Names of Westchester County, New York: Expanded Version* (Harrison, NY: Harbor Hill Books, 1980), 69.
parks.westchestergov.com/wampus-pond.
Raymond H. Torrey, Frank Place, Jr. and Robert L. Dickinson, *New York Walk Book. Third Edition* (NY: The American Geographical Society, 1951), 106 & 107.

38. IRVINGTON WOODS ROCKS
Irvington Woods

Type of Formation: Split Rock
WOW Factor: 5–6
Location: Irvington (Westchester County)
Tenth Edition, NYS Atlas & Gazetteer: p. 111, A6; **Earlier Edition NYS Atlas & Gazetteer**: p. 33, D4–5
Parking GPS Coordinates: 41º02.519'N 73º50.781'W
Destination GPS Coordinates: *Split Rock* -- 41º02.309'N 73º50.883'W; *Kiosk Boulder* -- 41º02.519'N 73º50.793'W (a guess); *Irving Rock* -- 41º02.214'N 73º51.109'W
Accessibility: *Kiosk Boulder* – 0.0-mile walk; *Split Rock* -- >0.5-mile hike
Degree of Difficulty: Moderate
Additional Information: The Irvington Woods Trail map is available at theirvingtonwoods.org/peter-k-oley-trail-network/peter-k-oley-trail-maps

O'Hara Nature Center, 170 Mountain Road, Irvington, NY 10533 (914)

Rock Walks

Split Rock. Photograph by Carlos Gonzalez

Description: *Kiosk Boulder* -- A big 6-foot-high boulder is visible next to the kiosk at the start of the trail.

Split Rock is a large glacial erratic that, many years ago, broke into two pieces that now lie apart on a slightly rounded mound of bedrock. Both pieces are over 6 feet in height. The larger of the two of is ~10 feet in length. The smaller, more compact half, lies tilted on the bedrock, propped up by a smaller rock.

Sunset Rock is a rocky section of bedrock with views of the Saw Mill River valley during the winter when the trees are bereft of leaves. It is not a boulder.

Jenkins Rock is located on the northwestern shore of the Irvington Reservoir and dedicated in 1984 to Rev. Dr. Frederick Jenkins who, while Pastor of the Irvington Presbyterian church, conducted Easter Sunday sunrise services overlooking the reservoir.

History: The Irvington Woods contain 400 acres of land. Historical rumor has it that Washington Irving composed some of his works here.

The O'Hara Nature Center is a recent addition to the woods, having opened in 2012.

Rock Walks

The Irvington Reservoir dates back to 1900 and was initially used as a source of uncontaminated, household water for residents of Irvington.

Interestingly, MapQuest shows the name of the woods as Fieldpoint Park.

Directions: Heading southwest on the Saw Mill River Parkway, turn sharply right onto Mountain Road as soon as you go under the New York State Thruway (I-87). Watch out for incoming traffic, just before the turn, coming off of the Thruway. Head southwest on Mountain Road for ~0.8 mile and turn left into the parking area for the O'Hara Nature Center.

Kiosk Boulder – Look for the boulder near the kiosk close to the Nature Center's parking area.

Split Rock -- From the Nature Center, follow the North-South (NS) trail west, then south. When you come to the junction with the Split Rock Trail (SR), turn right and go west. Look for Split Rock on your right.

Sunset Rock -- continue south on the North-South Trail (NS) until you come to the Sunset Rock Trail (SN). Turn left and head east. Look for Sunset Rock on your left. Just remember—this is an overlook, not a boulder.

Jenkins Rock – This historic rock is located at the northwest end of the Irving Reservoir along the Hermit's Grave Trail

Alternate Parking -- At the southeast end of the Irvington Reservoir, off of Cyrus Field Road, is a small parking area [41º02.068'N 73º50.916'W].

Resources: theirvingtonwoods.org.
irvingtonny.gov/DocumentCenter/Home/View/4305.
scenesfromthetrail.com/2017/06/17/irvington-woods – This site contains a photograph of Split Rock.
theirvingtonwoods.org/peter-k-oley-trail-network/suggested-hikes.
bing.com/search?q=irvington%20woods%20ny&qs=n&form=QBRE&sp=
-1&pq=irvington%20woods%20ny&sc=2-http://theirvingtonwoods.org.

39. AQUEHUNG BOULDER

Type of Formation: Large Boulder
WOW Factor: 5
Location: Bronxville (Westchester County)
Tenth Edition, NYS Atlas & Gazetteer: p. 111, B6; **Earlier Edition NYS Atlas & Gazetteer**: p. 25, A5
Aquehung Boulder GPS Coordinates: 40º55.915′N 73º50.991′W
Accessibility: Roadside. On private property.
Degree of Difficulty: Easy

Description: An old-time photograph shows a big rock tilted at a 45-degree angle. Unfortunately, nothing of known size is in the photograph, which makes it difficult to estimate the boulder's actual size. My suspicion, however, is that the rock is at least 15 feet high.

Aquehung Boulder. Old photograph.

History: According to Frank L. Walton, in *Pillars of Yonkers*, the "history [of the rock] is unknown but probably dates back to the Glacial Age. At least one of the oldest objects in Yonkers."

The word *Aguehung* is Mohican for "River of High Bluffs," a nod to the Bronx River and one section where the banks rise up to as high as 75 feet.

Directions: From the junction of Midland Avenue and Wrexham Road, drive northwest on Midland Avenue for 0.1 mile. Look to your right to see the boulder between two apartment complexes, 50 feet from the road. A sign near the road says "Judge Arthur J. Doran Townhouses."

You will probably need a map to find your way to the junction of Midland Avenue & Wrexham Road. It looks like if you get off at

Rock Walks

Exit 5 of the Cross County Parkway as you travel west, it will get you to Midland Avenue. The junction with Wrexham Road, then, is immediately to your left. But you may need to figure this one out on your own.

Resources: Frank L. Walton, *Pillars of Yonkers* (NY: Stratford House, 1951), 237. A photograph of the rock can be seen on an insert between pages 274 & 275.
nycgovparks.org/parks/X004.
tripadvisor.com/ShowTopic-g60763-i5-k1974928-
The_Broncs_and_Harlem-New_York_City_New_York.html.
Anita Inman Comstock, *Wondrous Westchester: Its History, Landmarks, and Special Events* (Mount Vernon, NY: Effective Learning, Inc., 1984), 43.

40. FARCUS HOTT CAVE

Type of Formation: Rock-Shelter
WOW Factor: 3
Location: Elmsford (Westchester County)
Tenth Edition, NYS Atlas & Gazetteer: p. 111, A6–7; **Earlier Edition NYS Atlas & Gazetteer**: p. 33, D5
Parking GPS Coordinates: 41º03.454'N 73º49.477'W
Estimated Farcus Hott Cave GPS Coordinates: 41º03.010'N 73º49.717'W (a guess)
Accessibility: 0.7-mile hike
Degree of Difficulty: Moderate

Description: According to Rob Yasinsac on his website, hudsonvalleyruins.org/rob/?p=541, this historic cave "appears to be a pile of boulders massed together in some great natural calamity, all tossed about in disarray around a small mouth-shaped opening under a ledge."

History: Farcus Hott Cave, also known as Kathy's Cave, was recently rediscovered by Lucas Buresch.

Rock Walks

Legend has it that the cave was used as a hideout by colonial farmers to avoid capture from invading British soldiers.

Directions: From Elmsford (junction of Routes 119/West Main Street & 9A/Central Avenue), drive northwest on Route 119/West Main Street for ~0.3 mile and park to your right in a large paved area crossed

Farcus Hott Cave. Old photograph.

over by power lines (currently next to the Elmsford Diner).

Walk carefully across West Main Street and then follow an old dirt road for 0.7 mile along a powerline corridor as you ascend Beaver Hill.

When you begin descending Beaver Hill, still following the powerline corridor, look for the rock-shelter next to the left side of the corridor. (I know this because in a photograph taken from inside the rock-shelter, the power lines are visible to your right.)

You are not that far from the Saw Mill River Parkway, which lies directly downhill from the cave.

The entire area is circumscribed by the Saw Mill River Parkway (to your east and south), I-87 (to your west), and I-287 (to your north).

It's worth keeping in mind that there are housing apartments (Avalon Green Apartments and Ridgeview Apartments) nearby, which means it might be possible, with permission from a homeowner, to reach the powerline corridor with only minimal effort if you start from near the top of the hill.

Resources: hudsonvalleyruins.org/rob/?p=541 – This website tells the story about how a group of modern day explorers sleuthed out the location of this cave.
Lucille and Ted Hutchinson, *Storm's Bridge, a History of Elmsford, N.Y. 1700-1976*, (), 33.

41. SIGGHES ROCK & AMACKASSIN ROCK (Historic)

Type of Formation: Large Rock
WOW Factor: Sigghes Rock – 4; Amackassin Rock -- Unknown
Location: Yonkers (Westchester County)
Tenth Edition, NYS Atlas & Gazetteer: p. 111, B6; **Earlier Edition NYS Atlas & Gazetteer**: p. 25, A4–5
Andrus Foundation GPS Coordinates: 40º59.032′N 73º52.790′W
Street Addresses associated with Amackassin Rock -- GPS Coordinates: *Amackassin Terrace* -- ~40º57.239′N 73º53.108′W; *Warburton Avenue* -- ~40º57.405′N 73º53.691′W

Description: Many years ago, two rocks that were located near opposite ends of Amackassin Creek, aka Meccackassin Creek, achieved a modicum of notoriety. One was called Sigghes Rock; the other was known as Amackassin Rock.

Sigghes Rock. Old photograph.

Sigghes Rock marked the Yonkers-Hastings line, and earlier was a significant Indian boundary stone. Judging from a photograph in George L. McNew's article, "The Paradise World of the Red Man in Westchester County," the rock may be at least 8 feet high and many times as long.

According to *Postscripts,* an online magazine, "Sigghes [rock] stands on the Andrus Foundation property and marks the boundary between Greenburgh and Yonkers."

The *Amackassin Rock* marked the extreme northwestern corner of Yonkers. It was a large rock, but old photographs don't give a clue as to its actual size. According to Frank L. Walton, the glaciers carried "...a great Copper Colored Rock [Amackassin Rock] which it deposited in the waters of the Hudson River, some 25 feet from the shore. This rock was worshipped by the Indians because it sparkled in the sun and glowed in the moonlight."

106

The online magazine *Postscripts* states that "Amackassin [is a] large rock on the shore of the Hudson River. It marked the northern boundary of Van der Donck's purchase."

Frank L. Walton gives two different accounts of what may have happened to Amackassin Rock. The first contends that the rock was destroyed in 1848 when the Hudson River Railroad was built along the edge of the river. The second advances the notion that the rock was never actually destroyed, but merely buried under rubble when the railroad line was built. If so, then this historic rock still exists, albeit now underground.

Amackassin Rock. Old photograph.

History: Amackassin Creek is (or was) a small, 0.5-mile-long brook that flowed from the North Broadway hillside to the Hudson River.

Sigghes Rock is a Native American rock that marked the boundary of Philipse's purchase from Adriaen van der Donck (a lawyer and landowner, and from whom his honorific, *Jonkheer*, Yonkers took its name).

According to an article called "The Amackassin Stone," "the name of the rock is probably derived from two Delaware Indian words, *'mackaak'* (great), and *'acksin'* (stone)."

107

Rock Walks

Directions: As far as I can tell, Amackassin Creek no longer exists, or else is so insignificant that it doesn't show up on local maps. Perhaps the creek was incorporated into an underground sewer/water drainage line like so many of the creeks have been in Albany, where I live.

The lack of recognizable landmarks makes finding the site of Amackassin Rock a virtual impossibility.

Sigghes Rock, on the other hand, at least seems to be within the realm of possibility to find. According to the January 1967 issue of the *Yonkers Historical Bulletin*, Sigghes Rock is on the east side of North Broadway. Richard M. Lederer, Jr., in *The Place-Names of Westchester County, New York: Expanded Version* states that the rock is on the Andrus Foundation property, marking the Greenburg-Yonkers boundary.

If you want to look for Sigghes Rock, the parking area for Andrus-on-Hudson (assuming that this is the Andrus Foundation property mentioned) is between Old Broadway (a one-way road heading north) and New Broadway (a one-way road heading south) at a GPS reading of 40º59.032′N 73º52.790′W.

I tried to figure out where the Yonkers/Hasting-on-Hudson border crosses Andrus property, and it seems to be somewhere around 0.3 mile south of the main building. The rock's exact location, however, remains a mystery to me.

Resources: George L. McNew, "The Paradise World of the Red Man in Westchester County," *Yonkers Historical Bulletin* Vol. XV. No. 1 (January 1965), 11.
"Legendary Amackassin Rock Shown in Photograph," *Yonkers Historical Bulletin* Vol. IX, no. 1 (April 1962), 16.
The Herold Statesman, Yonkers, NY, Monday June 6, 1960.
Yonkers Historical Bulletin Vol. XV, no.1 (January 1968). On page 11 is a photograph of Sigghes Rock.
Yonkers Historical Bulletin Vol. IX, no. 1 (April 1962). On page 16 is a photograph of Amackassin Rock.
Frank L. Walton, "Sigghes Rock." *The Westchester Historian. Quarterly of the Westchester County Historical Society* Vol. 42, no. 3 (Summer, 1966), 47.
"The Amackassin Stone," *Quarterly Bulletin. Westchester County Historical Society* Vol. 5, no. 1 (January, 1924), 6 & 7.

Rock Walks

Edward Martin (photographer), *Yonkers Historical Bulletin* Vol. IX, no. 1 (April, 1962). On page 16 is a photograph of Amackassin Rock. *Yonkers Historical Bulletin* Vol. XV, no. 1 (January, 1968). On page 11 is a photograph of Sigghes Rock.

Richard M. Lederer, Jr., *The Place-Names of Westchester County, New York: Expanded Version* (Harrison, NY: Harbor Hill Books, 1980).

Postscript (online magazine) -- notorc.blogspot.com/2010/05/whats-in-name-catalog-of-indian-place.html.

42. BENZIGER BOULDER

Type of Formation: Large Rock
WOW Factor: 4–5
Location: Bronxville (Westchester County)
Tenth Edition, NYS Atlas & Gazetteer: p. 111, B6–7; **Earlier Edition NYS Atlas & Gazetteer**: p. 25, A5
Parking GPS Coordinates: 40º56.704′N 73º49.963′W
Benziger Boulder GPS Coordinates: 40º56.739′N 73º50.001′W (per bouldering website)
Accessibility: 0.1-mile hike
Degree of Difficulty: Moderately easy

Description: Benziger Boulder is a 15-foot-high rock.

Presumably, the rock was named for a rock climber or boulderer named Benziger. As for me, I'm most familiar with the name being associated with a California winery.

Directions: From Bronxville (junction of Sagamore Road and Avon Road), drive southwest on Sagamore Road for over 0.1 mile and park to your right, just down the road from the Sagamore Road Playground.

You will probably need to consult a map to hone in on the exact spot.

Two hours of free parking is available along the road.

Follow a path that leads downhill through the park to the northwest quadrant. The rock is located near Kensington Road. It is hidden a bit from view, so you will need to look for it.

Rock Walks

Resources: rockclimbing.com/routes/North_America/
United_States/New_York/Westchester_County/Benziger_Boulder.

43. INDIAN ROCK SHELTER

Type of Formation: Rock-Shelter
WOW Factor: 7–8
Location: Larchmont (Westchester County)
Tenth Edition, NYS Atlas & Gazetteer: p. 111, B8; **Earlier Edition NYS Atlas
& Gazetteer**: p. 25, A5–6
Parking GPS Coordinates: Unknown
Indian Rock Shelter GPS Coordinates: 40º55.741'N 73º45.752'W
Accessibility: Near roadside; on private property
Degree of Difficulty: Easy

Description: In a photograph of the Indian Rock Shelter, a huge slab of rock appears to be leaning against the side of a hill or slope, forming a tall, enterable shelter.

Judith Doolin Spikes, in *Larchmont, NY: People and Places*, writes that the rock shelter has "a deep recess under it that could easily be made into a large and well-sheltered living room."

Quite frankly, I can't tell using Google Earth if the rock I found is the historic Indian Rock Shelter, but the rock does look big, and it is just south of Palmer Avenue.

If this isn't the Indian Rock-Shelter, then it is still a natural rock feature in Larchmont that warrants some mention.

History: The rock-shelter was first identified on a tract of land sold in 1794 by John Bailey.

Some imaginative folks were able to see the face of a Native American in the rocks, but by the 1960s this profile had apparently disappeared or been obscured.

Directions: Here's what the 1962 issue of the *Westchester Historian* had to say about the rock's location. It is "located a few yards south of Palmer Avenue, a short distance west of the last of the series of

110

stores on that street. It adjoins a dry bed of Gravely Brook" (which now goes under a culvert).

Indian Rock Shelter. Photograph by Officer Dix Bruggese c. 1960.

Much has changed over the last 50 years. Larchmont is now heavily populated and Palmer Avenue particularly so. The rock-shelter may no longer exist, or could be squirreled away behind someone's house.

However, I did notice in a photograph taken at Pine Brook Park, a huge rock mound, 15–20 feet high, which is either within the park or immediately next to it.

To get to Pine Brook Park – From near the center of Larchmont (junction of Chatsworth Avenue & Route 1/Boston Post Road), drive northwest on Chatsworth Avenue for 0.5 mile. Turn left onto Palmer Avenue and head southwest for 0.3 mile. Pine Brook Park is directly to your left at the intersection of Palmer Avenue and Pine Brook Drive. Park along the south side of Palmer Avenue just east of Pine Brook Drive.

The large rock is next to Pine Brook Park, behind a tall wooden fence, and very close to a private landowner's house.

Resources: "The Indian Rock Shelter." *The Westchester Historian. Quarterly of the Westchester County Historical Society* Vol. 38, no. 2

(April, May, June, 1962), 49 & 50. Officer Dix Bruggese's photograph of the rock shelter rock is on page 48.

patch.com/new-york/larchmont/pine-brook-park-renovation-underway-in-larchmont.

Judith Doolin Spikes, *Larchmont, NY: People and Places* (Larchmont, NY: Fountain Square Books, 1991), 0.

44. ROCKING STONE

Type of Formation: Large Rock
WOW Factor: 5–6
Location: Larchmont (Westchester County)
Tenth Edition, NYS Atlas & Gazetteer: p. 111, B7–8; **Earlier Edition NYS Atlas & Gazetteer**: p. 25, A5–6
Rocking Stone GPS Coordinates: 40º56.412'N 73º46.067'W
Accessibility: Roadside
Degree of Difficulty: Easy

Ken Jacobs & Lisa Nissenbaum stand in front of the Rocking Stone. Photograph by Alex Helfand.

Description: Rocking Stone is an 11-foot-high, 150-ton glacial erratic. Reputedly, the boulder was so perfectly balanced at one time that it behaved like a seesaw, and could be rocked back and forth. In 1842, Robert Bolton, in *A Guide to New Rochelle and Lower Westchester*, wrote that "This natural curiosity is a mass of solid rock, weighing, perhaps, more than twenty tons, which can be moved to and fro, at pleasure, by a child." Unfortunately, nearby blasting by workers in the 1920s to put in a sewer line destabilized the rock sufficiently to make it inert.

History: The curious engravings visible on the rock are explained in Judith Doolin Spikes' *Larchmont, NY: People and Places*. "In 1854, the Chatsworth Land Company hired a New Rochelle engineer, William Bryson, to survey their land and draw a map. When Bryson finished the survey, he carved his name, the name of the company, and the date into the Rockingstone...."

In 2012, a filmmaker who wanted to use the boulder in a forthcoming movie walked into the Mamaroneck Town Administrator's office and asked if he could obtain a temporary permit to destabilize the boulder and return it to its original function again. The request was promptly denied. Apparently, it's just not in the cards for the Rocking Stone to rock and roll again—ever. This is probably just as well since the rock, due to its prominent location, would prove dangerously irresistible to locals wishing to do mischief.

Rocking Stone. Postcard c. 1940.

Rock Walks

Directions: The Rocking Stone is located at the center of the intersection of Rockingstone Avenue, Spruce Road, Poplar Road, and Springdale Road.

To get there from Route 1/Boston Post Road, take Chatsworth Avenue northwest for 1.0 mile. As Chatsworth Avenue veers right, continue straight ahead on Rockingstone Avenue for 0.2 mile to reach the boulder.

Resources: Judith Doolin Spikes, *Larchmont, NY: People and Places* (Larch-mont, NY: Fountain Square Books, 1991), 57.
Robert Bolton, *A Guide to New Rochelle and Lower Westchester* (Harrison, NY: Harbor Hill Books, 1976 facsimile of a 1842 book), 40 & 41.
theloopny.com/he-wants-to-rock-the-rocking-stone-a-larchmont-landmark.
Herbert B. Nichols, *Historic New Rochelle* (New Rochelle, NY: Board of Education, 1938), 112.
en.wikipedia.org/wiki/Rocking_stone.

45. MANOR PARK ROCKS
Larchmont Manor Park

Type of Formation: Large Rocks
WOW Factor: 3
Location: Larchmont (Westchester County)
Tenth Edition, NYS Atlas & Gazetteer: p. 111, B8; **Earlier Edition NYS Atlas & Gazetteer**: p. 25, A5–6
General GPS Coordinates for Manor Park: 40º55.048'N 73º44.904'W
Estimated Dinosaur Egg GPS Coordinates: 40º55.052'N 73º44.680'W
Accessibility: ~1.0-mile walk along path at top of rocky shoreline
Degree of Difficulty: Moderately easy

Description: A number of medium-to-large-sized rocks can be seen along the pathway overlooking the Long Island Sound. I suspect several of these rocks are actually outcroppings and protrusions of bedrock.

Sliding Rock -- "The 'Sliding Rock' near the pumping station is a granite erratic, whose side was rasped by the dropping of the glacier."

Rock Walks

Whale-Back -- "The 'Whale-Back' near the flag pole got its rounded hump as it rolled and tumbled along."

Death's Head -- "Opposite the flag pole, near the shore, the alien 'Death's Head' balanced on native rock."

Dinosaur Egg – located roughly midway between the South and North Gazebos.

History: Manor Park encompasses ~13 acres of land, with nearly one mile along the Long Island Sound and Larchmont Harbor. It is privately owned, but open to the public.

Land ownership goes back to the 1600s. The initial 6.0 acres for Manor Park was established by land developer Thomas J. S. Flint in the 1870s.

The Larchmont Manor Park Society was established in 1892 to preserve and protect the park. The park is presently owned by ~280 residents of the Larchmont Manor neighborhood, who generously allow public access to what otherwise would be a private domain.

Directions: From South of New Rochelle, get off at Exit 15 from I-95/New England Thruway. Head northeast on Route 1/Main Street for >2.5 miles. Then turn right onto Beach Avenue and proceed south for 0.7 mile. When you come to the end of Beach Avenue, follow it as it now turns around and heads north as Park Avenue. You will see Manor Park to your right.

I suspect that parking is not allowed in the Larchmont Manor neighborhood, which means that you may need to park along Boston Post Road/Route 1 and walk 0.8 mile along either Larchmont Avenue or Beach Avenue to access the park.

Manor Park Association can be contacted at larchmontmanorpark.org.

Resources: Judith Doolin Spikes, *Larchmont, NY: People and Places* (Larchmont, NY: Fountain Square Books, 1991), 1.
en.wikipedia.org/wiki/Manor_Park,_Larchmont.
fifiandhop.com/2015/05/29/when-we-cant-get-away-our-local-get-away.
larchmontmanorpark.org/geographic-history.html -- This site talks about not only the geology of the park, but specifically mentions a rounded boulder called Dinosaur Egg.
larchmontmanorpark.org/the-park.html.

46. WASHINGTON ROCK

Type of Formation: Rock Profile
WOW Factor: 3
Location: Mamaroneck (Westchester County)
Tenth Edition, NYS Atlas & Gazetteer: p. 111, B8; **Earlier Edition NYS Atlas & Gazetteer**: p. 25, A5–6
Parking GPS Coordinates: 40º56.944'N 73º43.885'W
Washington Rock GPS Coordinates: 40º56.620'N 73º44.312'W
Accessibility: Roadside
Degree of Difficulty: Easy

Description: The Washington Rock is a medium-sized rock profile that either formed naturally or, as some believe, was intentionally sandblasted onto the rock face by a construction crew around 1890.

Washington Rock. Postcard c. 1910.

History: The Washington Rock property has exchanged hands a number of times. Originally, it was owned by the titleholders of the 1677 Henry Disbrow House; then later, by proprietors of the Washington Arms Restaurant. It wasn't until 1901, however, that the rock's amazing likeness to George Washington's face was noticed by one of the town folks. I'm not sure if an answer was ever obtained as to why it took so long for the rock's unusual likeness to be noticed. In any case, Washington Rock immediately became the rage, and postcards of it were reproduced in great numbers.

Then, as the years turned into decades, the rock gradually fell into obscurity until no one alive even knew its exact location any longer. In 2007, efforts to locate the lost rock paid off when it was rediscovered behind a thick growth of sumac and vines near roadside at the Liberty Montessori School.

Directions: From Mamaroneck (at the junction of Routes 1/Boston Post Road & 127/Harrison Avenue), drive south- west on Route 1/Boston Post Road for 0.8 mile and turn left (south) onto Orienta Avenue. The rock will be immediately on your right, located on the slope adjacent to the Liberty Montessori School, directly across from Mamaroneck Harbor.

Resources: theloopny.com/george-washington-rocked-mamaroneck. foursquare.com/v/washington-rock/54b7eb98498eaedcbc134bdd. theloopny.com/george-washington-returns-to-mamaroneck-after-a-lo-o-o-o-ong-absence. facebook.com/MamaroneckHistory/posts/925987910771410.

47. STEPHENSON BOULDER
Stephenson Park

Type of Formation: Large Boulder
WOW Factor: Unknown
Location: New Rochelle (Westchester County)
Tenth Edition, NYS Atlas & Gazetteer: p. 111, BC7; **Earlier Edition NYS Atlas & Gazetteer**: p. 25, A5
Parking GPS Coordinates: 40º55.057'N 73º46.441'W
Stephenson Park GPS Coordinates: 40º55.106'N 73º46.434'W
Stephenson Boulder GPS Coordinates: 40º55.121'N 73º46.436'W
Accessibility: Near roadside
Degree of Difficulty: Easy

Description: I have not been able to find any specific information about the Stephenson Boulder. A distant picture of the rock shows a boulder around 7–8 feet high and over 12 feet long, resting at the base of a tiny hillock.

117

History: Stephenson Park is a recreational area containing mainly an athletic field and playground.

Somehow fittingly, the Rock Club & Climbing Gym [40º55.061'N 73º46.594'W] is literally only a block away on 130 Rhodes Street.

Stephenson Boulder has its own park and namesake.

Directions: Stephenson Park lies between Palmer Avenue and Lispenard Avenue almost exactly in the middle of the park. A walkway from Lispenard Avenue leads past the boulder.

From Main Street/Route 1 in New Rochelle, drive northwest on Stephenson Avenue for 0.2 mile to reach the park. The park can be accessed from any of the streets around it.

Stephenson Park is named after Stephenson Boulevard, a divided highway that runs along the west side of the park.

Resources:
rockclimbing.com/routes/North_America/United_States/New_York/Westchester_County/stephenson_boulder

THE BRONX

The Bronx encompasses 57 square miles of land and water, and is named after Jonas Bronx, a Dutch landowner. It is the northernmost of New York City's five boroughs, and the only part of New York City (except for a minor sliver) that is located on the mainland. It is defined by the Hudson River to the west, Harlem River to the southwest, East River to the southeast, Long Island Sound to the east, and Westchester County to the north.

48. FORT NUMBER 8 BOULDER
University Woods

Type of Formation: Medium-sized Boulder
WOW Factor: 3–4
Location: University Heights (The Bronx)
Tenth Edition, NYS Atlas & Gazetteer: p. 110, CD5; **Earlier Edition NYS Atlas & Gazetteer**: p. 24, A2
Estimated Parking GPS Coordinates: 40º51.550'N 73º54.870'W
University Woods GPS Coordinates: 40º51.553'N 73º54.900'W
Fort Number 8 Boulder GPS Coordinates: Not determined
Accessibility: Variable depending where you parked
Degree of Difficulty: Moderately easy

Description: This medium-sized boulder marks the site of Fort Number 8, a small, four-pointed star British redoubt that commanded a view of the *Fort Number 8 Boulder. Old photograph.* Harlem River from Fordham Heights.

119

Rock Walks

History: Words have been chiseled into the boulder's surface, but a photograph that I have seen of the rock is too indistinct and the words too distant to be legible. No doubt, the words convey an account of the site's history.

Fort Number 8 was built by the British in 1776 on one of the highest points in the Bronx. The fort endured until 1782, when it was abandoned by the redcoats.

In 1857, Justus Schwab built a mansion on the site.

Fort Number 8 Boulder is located in University Woods, aka Cedar Park—a section of the University Heights neighborhood between Sedgwick Avenue and Cedar Avenue.

University Heights was formerly known as Fordham Heights. The name of the community changed due to its association with the former New York University campus.

Directions: From the Major Deegan Expressway (I-87) following along the east side of the Harlem River, get off at Exit 9 for "West Fordham Road & University Heights Blvd." Go east on West Fordham Road for >0.2 mile and then turn right onto Sedgwick Avenue. Proceed southwest for over 0.3 mile and park along the street as best as you can. The park is directly to your right, located near the west side of the Bronx Community College.

I assume that the boulder should be easy to locate once you get there. It's quite possible, however, that for all your effort, the boulder's size may be underwhelming.

Resources: Stephen Jenkins, *The Story of the Bronx: From the Purchase made by the Dutch from the Indians in 1639 to the Present Day* (New York: G. P. Putnam's Sons, 1912), 346/347. A photograph of the boulder at Fort Number 8 is shown in the insert.
fortnumber8restoration.org/?page_id=67.
fortwiki.com/Fort_No._8_-_NYC.
nycgovparks.org/parks/university-woods/history.

49. INDIAN ROCK
Crotona Park

Type of Formation: Large Boulder
WOW Factor: 6
Location: Claremont (The Bronx)
Tenth Edition, NYS Atlas & Gazetteer: p. 111, CD6; **Earlier Edition NYS Atlas & Gazetteer**: p. 25, B4–5
Crotona Park GPS Coordinates: 40º50.284'N 73º53.757'W
Indian Rock GPS Coordinates: 40º50.257'N 73º53.715'W
Accessibility: 0.1-mile walk from Crotona Avenue
Degree of Difficulty: Easy

Description: In *South Bronx Rising: The Rise, Fall, and Resurrection of an American City*, Jill Jonnes writes, "Indian Rock, a tall boulder, was a favorite destination for clambering and adventure." It still is today.

According to John McNamara, in *History in Asphalt: The Origin of Bronx Street and Place Names*, the rock measures 6 feet by 8 feet with a height of 10 feet and "has four deeply-cut steps on its north face. These steps are evenly spaced, and resemble stirrups."

History: The 127-acre Crotona Park is named after the Greek colony of Croton. The land was acquired by the city in 1888. By 1914, the perimeter of 3.3-acre Indian Lake was fortified with concrete walls, and pathways were established around the lake and through sections of the park.

Like many bodies of water, ice was harvested from Indian Lake during the winter for summer refrigeration.

The rock is believed to have been named by local youths in the late 1800s who, engaging in play by the rock, would conjure up images of Indians and war council meetings.

The rock has also been used for political gatherings. In "The History of Indian Lake – Crotona Park," Harvey Lubar writes that "Socialist rallies were occasionally held at the lake and their fiery speakers tried to excite the crowds from the top of Indian Rock."

The land was originally part of the extensive, 140-acre Alexander Bathgate farm during the nineteenth century.

Rock Walks

Directions: There really is no easy way to get to Crotona Park, and you may need to plot out your own course.

Indian Rock.

However, I did find one relatively easy route. If you are traveling east on the busy Cross Bronx Expressway, get off at Exit 2B for Webster Avenue. When you come to Webster Avenue, turn right and drive south for 0.3 mile. At Claremont Parkway, turn left and proceed southeast for 0.3 mile. This highway takes you right into the park, where roadside parking may be available here and there. Or, you could turn left onto Fulton Avenue (a one-way street) and head around the two-mile perimeter of the park, from Crotona Park North to Crotona Park East to Crotona Park South, all one-way, so that you will be continually traveling clockwise. There are many places to park around the park.

Indian Rock can be found on a small hill overlooking the southwest end of Indian Lake, 75 feet uphill from the walkway that circles around the lake.

Resources: Jill Jonnes, *South Bronx Rising: The Rise, Fall, and Resurrection of an American City* (NY: Fordham University Press, 2002), 212.

Harvey Lubar, "The History of Indian Lake," *The Bronx County Historical Society* Vol. XXII, no. 2 (Fall 1985), 54. "A large boulder on the southwest corner of the lake was named 'Indian Rock' as the boys named the rock the chief's seat."

nycgovparks.org/parks/crotona-park/highlights/11612.

bronxboard.com/diary/diary.php?f=Crotona%20Park – Daniel Wolfe writes about his time spent at Crotona Park and Indian Rock.

nytimes.com/1999/11/21/nyregion/in-crotona-park-signs-of-new-season.html.

parkodyssey.blogspot.com/2014/03/crotona-park.html – This site shows a photograph of Indian Rock.

nycgovparks.org/parks/crotona-park.

John McNamara, *History in Asphalt: The Origin of Bronx Street and Place Names* (The Bronx, NY: Bronx County Historical Society, 1996), 381.

Harry T. Cook, *The Borough of the Bronx. 1639–1913* (NY: Author, 1913), 68.

Harvey Lubar, "The History of Indian Lake – Crotona Park," *The Bronx County Historical Society Journal* Vol. XXII, no. 2 (Fall, 2988), 50–58. On page 54, Lubar writes, "A large boulder on the southwest corner of the lake was named 'Indian Rock' as the boys named the rock the chief's seat."

50. CAT ROCK CAVE (Historic)

Type of Formation: Cave
WOW Factor: Unknown
Location: Rochelle Heights (Westchester County)
Tenth Edition, NYS Atlas & Gazetteer: p. 111, C7; **Earlier Edition NYS Atlas & Gazetteer**: p. 25, A5
Junction of Rockland Place and Lemke Place GPS Coordinates: 40º55.469'N 73º46.418'W
Accessibility: Undoubtedly on private land that was terraformed by developers

Description: According to Morgan Secord in his article, "Cat Rock Cave", Cat Rock was a true cave, and not just a rock-shelter. It originally extended into a rocky ridge. However, when the land around Rockland Place (the street) underwent further development, a considerable volume of the ridge was sliced off.

In the April 1955 issue of the *Westchester Historian. Quarterly of the Westchester County Historical Society,* "A field trip to the area revealed a high shattered rock mass facing Rockland Place about three hundred feet west of Lemke Place. Its natural, shattered appearance had been made even more so by other blasting which destroyed a small natural cave during the improvement of Rockland Place some years ago."

It would seem that nothing is left of the cave now except for a memory.

Of particular interest, however, is what Secord went on to say. "Originally, there existed in front of Cat Rock Cave a thickly strewn area of dozens of large boulders, dropped during the ice age covering over half an acre. These stones varied in size, many larger than half a barrel."

Directions: In his article on Cat Rock, Secord places the location of the cave "to the east or rear of Rochelle Heights, a subdivision adjoining the east side of Rockland Place, north of Lemke Place." The GPS I have given is the junction of Rockland Place and Lemke Place. I suspect the cave is/was only several hundred feet from this spot where there is a wooded area between houses.

To get there: From Rochelle Heights (junction of 5th Avenue & North Avenue), go northeast on 5th Avenue for 0.8 mile. Turn right onto Rockland Place (a one-way street until Pierce Street) and head southeast for 0.3 mile to reach the junction with Lemke Place.

Cat Rock Cave. Old photograph.

Resources: Morgan Secord, "Cat Rock Cave," *The Westchester Historian. Quarterly of the Westchester County Historical Society.* Vol. 41, no.4 (Autumn, 1965), 68.

"Elastic Cave." *Westchester Historian. Quarterly of the Westchester County Historical Society.* Vol. 31, no. 2 (April, 1955), 54. A field trip to Cat Rock Cave is described.

Herbert B. Nichols, *Historic New Rochelle* (New Rochelle, NY: Board of Education, 1938), 170.

51. SPLIT ROCK & LINCOLN ROCK
Bronx Park: New York Botanical Garden

Type of Formation: Split Rock
WOW Factor: 3
Location: Bronx (The Bronx)
Tenth Edition, NYS Atlas & Gazetteer: p. 111, C6; **Earlier Edition NYS Atlas & Gazetteer**: p. 25, AB4–5
Parking GPS Coordinates: 40º51.627'N 73º52.887'W
Split Rock GPS Coordinates: 40º51.833'N 73º52.721'W
Lincoln Rock GPS Coordinates: Unknown
Fee: Admission charged
Accessibility: *Split Rock* -- 0.2-mile walk
Degree of Difficulty: Easy
Additional Information: New York Botanical Garden, 2900 Southern Boulevard, Bronx, NY 10458
　　　　Map of the Botanical Garden is available at mappery.com/map-of/The-New-York-Botanical-Garden-Map
　　　　Days & Hours – Tuesday – Sunday, 10 a.m. – 6 p.m.

New York Botanical Garden: Bronx Park. Postcard c. 1910.

Description: The New York Botanical Garden *Split Rock* is a 6-foot-high, 8-foot-long boulder made of Fordham gneiss that was broken into two uneven pieces by the roots of a long-vanished tree. The larger half is about two-thirds of the rock's total length.

　　A second point of interest is called *Lincoln Rock*. In *History in Asphalt: The Origin of Bronx Street and Place Names*, John McNamara describes it as a high point at the gardens west of the Bronx River

Rock Walks

where "a likeness of the president [was] cut into the rock sometime in the 1940s." I have not been able to find any current information about this profile, however.

History: The 250-acre Botanical Garden was created in 1891; the 2.5-acre rock garden, in the 1930s.

The Bronx River—New York City's only freshwater stream—runs through the park. More is said about it in the next chapter.

Directions: From the Bronx River Parkway, get off at Exit 8 and take the Southern Boulevard/Dr. Theodore Kazimiroff Boulevard southwest for ~1.0 mile. Get off for the Botanical Garden and park in parking area A.

You may also wish to consult the New York Botanical Garden website for more specific directions depending upon where you are heading from.

Split Rock is located inside the Botanical Garden almost equidistant along a walkway between the Native Plant and Rock Garden areas.

I don't know exactly where Lincoln Rock is or whether it still exists, but John McNamara's description suggests that you want to look for a high point in the gardens.

Resources: 3dparks.wr.usgs.gov/nyc/parks/loc5.htm – This site includes a photograph of Split Rock.
nybg.org – Main site for the New York Botancial Garden.
en.wikipedia.org/wiki/New_York_Botanical_Garden.
geologycafe.com/nyc/parks/loc5.htm.
nycmanhattan.org/p/new-york-botanical-garden.html.
Allen Rokach, "History Underfoot: A Short Geological History of the Bronx," *The Bronx County Historical Society Journal* Vol. XI, no. 2 (Fall 1974), 71–80.
Randall Comfort (compiler), *History of Bronx Borough. City of New York* (New York: North Side News Press, 1906). 2. Mention is made of Indian Well and Bear's Den.
Herbert B. Nichols, *Historic New Rochelle* (New Rochelle, NY: Board of Education, 1938), 112. "In Bronx Park a big stone can still be seen in the bottom of a large pothole."
John McNamara, *History in Asphalt: The Origin of Bronx Street and Place Names* (The Bronx, NY: Bronx County Historical Society, 1996), 398.

Rock Walks

Andrew S. Dolkart, *Guide to New York City Landmarks* (NY: John Wiley & Sons, Inc., 1998), 260.
city-data.com/forum/new-york-city/113048-st-james-park-bronx-late-1960s-4.html – Mention is made of Lincoln Rock in the forum exchange.

52. BRONX RIVER GORGE POTHOLES
Bronx Park

Type of Formation: Pothole
WOW Factor: 4
Location: Bronx (The Bronx)
Tenth Edition, NYS Atlas & Gazetteer: p. 111, C6; **Earlier Edition NYS Atlas & Gazetteer**: p. 25, AB4–5
Parking GPS Coordinates: 40º51.709'N 73º52.846'W
Estimated Destination GPS Coordinates: Not determined
Fee: Admission charged
Accessibility: Not determined
Degree of Difficulty: Moderate
Additional information: New York Botanical Garden, 2900 Southern Boulevard, Bronx, NY 10458
   Map of the Botanical Garden is available at mappery.com/map-of/The-New-York-Botanical-Garden-Map
   Days & Hours – Tuesday – Sunday, 10 a.m. – 6 p.m.

Description: A number of potholes have formed in the bedrock of the Bronx River Gorge. In *The Borough of the Bronx, 1639–1913*, Harry T. Cook writes, "The Bronx River runs directly thru part of the park from north to south varying in width from 50 to 400 feet."
   There are other geological features also worthy of note that are located, I believe, in the area of the Bronx River. *Indian Well*, aka Indian Bath, is described as "…a rocky basin perhaps used by the red men as a place to grind their corn that is located inside a cliff." I suspect that this is one of the potholes. In addition, there is *Bear's Den*, "a romantic spot where the rocks were piled perpendicularly by some immense force, between them being a natural cave…"

History: Geologist believe that during the last Ice Age, the Bronx River emptied into the Hudson River before a huge ice mass blocked

127

the river's flow west, forcing it to cut its present channel into the East River and Long Island Sound. It is for this reason that the gorge is so deeply cut in the area by the New York Botanical Garden. Native Americans called the river Aquehung, or "River of High Bluffs," due to its 75-foot-high walls. Early on, it served as a major border between the Wappinger and Siwanoy tribes.

The gorge starts half a mile or so downriver from the Williams Bridge and ends before a rocky waterfall at Bronxdale.

Like many industrialized rivers, the Bronx River had become an open sewer by the early 1900s. Fortunately, during the years that followed, a number of advocacy groups began working to clean up the river, culminating with the Bronx River Alliance in 2001.

Directions: See previous chapter for directions.

The Bronx River is ~0.3–0.4 linear miles east of the parking area. The best route to take to get to the river seems to be to follow the Forest Path, which approaches the river in at least two spots. I suspect that there is an informal trail right next to the river.

Other entry points to the river are from the Hester Bridge or Snuff Mill Bridge, both within the park. The Snuff Mill Bridge was named for a mill built in 1840 that ground tobacco into snuff. It was acquired by the Botanical Garden in 1915. The mill now houses a café.

It is even possible to explore the Bronx River by kayak or canoe, putting in at Shoelace Park [40º53.359'N 73º51.891'W off of East 233rd Street] and debarking at Hunts Point Riverside Park [40º49.063'N 73º52.901'W off of Lafayette Avenue]. It will require three short portages, and you are not permitted to enter the grounds of either the botanical garden or Bronx from this river journey. For more details, consult Kevin Stiegelmaier's *Canoeing & Kayaking New York*.

I have no idea exactly where along the river the potholes or the Bear's Den are, but that's what makes the exploration part of this book so much fun. Take heart. You will be in good company, for Edgar Allan Poe and Joseph Rodman Drake (an early nineteenth-century poet) once walked along the same pathways and riverbed.

Rock Walks

Resources: Lloyd Ultan, *The Northern Borough: A History of the Bronx* (The Bronx, NY: The Bronx Historical Society, 2009), 3. "Many [potholes] can be found in the Bronx River Gorge at the northeast end of the forest in New York Botanical Garden." nycgovparks.org/parks/X004/highlights/11583. C. R. Roseberry, *From Niagara to Montauk: The Scenic Pleasures of New York State* (Albany, NY: State University of New York Press, 1982), 278 & 279. researchgate.net/publication/267552855_DIVERSION_OF_THE_BRON X_RIVER_IN_NEW_YORK_CITY_- EVIDENCE_FOR_POSTGLACIAL_SURFACE_FAULTING bronxriver.org/?pg=content&p=abouttheriver&m1=13&m2=78&m3=71. nybg.org/content/uploads/2017/03/BronxRiverSelf- GuidedVisitTeacherGuide.pdf. Christopher J. Schuberth, *The Geology of New York City and Environs* (Garden City, NY: The National History Press, 1968), 88. The author mentions that the river's course was altered when it eroded "a new, narrow gorge along this fault through the mica schist, thereby abandoning the lower part of its original way." Schuberth believes this occurred some 20–30 million years ago. Harry T. Cook, *The Borough of the Bronx. 1639–1913* (NY: Author, 1913), 67. Kevin Stiegelmaier's *Canoeing & Kayaking New York* (Birmingham, AL: Menasha Ridge Press, 2009), 176–180.

53. ROCKING STONE
Bronx Park: Bronx Zoo

Type of Formation: Rocking Stone
WOW Factor: 4
Location: Bronx (The Bronx)
Tenth Edition, NYS Atlas & Gazetteer: p. 111, C6; **Earlier Edition NYS Atlas & Gazetteer**: p. 25, AB4–5
Parking GPS Coordinates: 40º51.179'N 73º52.373'W
Rocking Stone GPS Coordinates: 40º50.876'N 73º52.674'W
Fee: Admission charged
Accessibility: 0.4-mile walk
Degree of Difficulty: Easy
Additional Information: Bronx Zoo, 2300 Southern Boulevard, Bronx, NY 10460

Rock Walks

Map of the Bronx Zoo is available at bronxzoo.com/map.
Open daily, 10 a.m. - ~5 p.m.

Description: The Bronx Zoo Rocking Stone is a pink, granite rock that measures 7 feet high by 10 feet wide. It rests on top of a bedrock outcrop. Some estimate its weight to be up to 30 tons. John McNamara, in *McNamara's Old Bronx*, describes it as "A rough cube of pinkish granite..." that could be tilted a scant 2 inches. So much for the boulder moving like a rocking horse."

The bedrock upon which the boulder rests shows very defined groove marks that were caused by stones being rubbed together as they were pushed forward by glaciers.

The rock has been a major attraction at the zoo since 1895 when it was featured on postcards and frequently used as a backdrop for family photographs.

Because visitors were always trying to dislodge the boulder by rocking it, the Zoo officials decided to play it safe, eventually shoring up the boulder's base to prevent it from rocking at all.

History: According to legend, a team of twenty-four oxen once tried to dislodge the rock without success. Whether this is true or not is debatable.

Like many large boulders or rocks with unusual properties, the Rocking Stone served as a convenient landmark for colonial surveyors, thereby fixing the northern boundary that made up the original twelve West Farms.

The Rocking Stone Restaurant, which often shows up in the background on postcards featuring the Rocking Stone, operated until 1942.

In his book, *History of Bronx Borough. City of New York*, Randall Comfort includes a brief poem about the rock:

A rock, chance poised and balanced lay,
So that a stripling arm might sway,
A mass no host could raise.

In nature's rage at random thrown
Yet trembling like the Druid's stone
On its precious base.

Rock Walks

The Bronx Zoo, aka New York Zoological Park, encompasses 265 acres of land, and is partially bisected by the Bronx River. It opened in 1898.

Rocking Stone Bronx Zoo. Old photograph.

Directions: Driving along the Bronx River Parkway, get off at Exit 6, which leads immediately to the east side (Gate B) parking area for the Bronx Zoo.

The boulder is located next to the former House (World) of Darkness that opened in 1969 and closed in 2009. The House of Darkness was built on the site of the former Rocking Stone Restaurant.

Using Google Earth, I was able to locate a building called the "Nocturnal House," 0.4-linear mile southwest of the parking area, and saw what looked like a large boulder on the walkway leading to it. Hopefully, what my GPS reading indicates is the Rocking Stone.

Rock Walks

Resources: John Scheier, *New York City Zoos and Aquarium: Images of America* (Charleston, SC: Arcadia Publishing, 2005). A photograph of the rock is shown on page 27.

bronxriver.org/?pg=content&p=abouttheriver&m1=13&m2=78&m3=59 – An article by Stephen Paul Devillo gives pertinent information about the rock and its history.

3dparks.wr.usgs.gov/nyc/parks/loc5.htm.

mentalfloss.com/article/502750/9-facts-about-the-bronx-zoo.

boweryboyshistory.com/wp-content/uploads/2010/04/zoo1.jpg – This site shows a postcard image of the Rocking Stone.

richardcassaro.com/tag/rocking-stone

Randall Comfort (compiler), *History of Bronx Borough. City of New York* (New York: North Side News Press, 1906). On page 2 is a photograph of the Rocking Stone, with tiny girls posed at each end as if trying to rock it back and forth.

John McNamara, *McNamara's Old Bronx* (The Bronx, NY: The Bronx County Historical Society, 1989), 102.

Diana Farkas, "The Zoological Park, Bronx, N.Y." *The Bronx County Historical Society Journal* Vol. XI, no. 1 (Spring 1974). On page 2 is a 1908 photograph of the Rocking Stone.

Stephen Jenkins, *The Story of the Bronx* (New York: G. P. Putnam's Sons, 1912), 308. "The 'Rocking-stone' is an immense boulder weighing several tons, left here by some melting glacier, whose course is plainly marked by the scratche [sic] on the exposed rock surface. The boulder is so nicely balanced that a slight force will set it rocking."

Lloyd Ultan, *The Northern Borough: A History of the Bronx* (The Bronx, NY: The Bronx Historical Society, 2009), 3. "When it dropped, it was delicately perched atop a Fordham gneiss outcropping in such a way that it could be tipped back and forward, giving it its name."

Harry T. Cook, *The Borough of the Bronx. 1639–1913* (NY: Author, 1913), 2. "…a colossal cube of pinkish granite." On page 66, Cook also calls it a "100-ton Rocking Stone."

bronxriver.org/?pg=content&p=abouttheriver&m1=13&m2=78&m3=59.

C. R. Roseberry, *From Niagara to Montauk: The Scenic Pleasures of New York State* (Albany, NY: State University of New York Press, 1982), 278.

Allen Rokach, "History Underfoot: A Short Geologic History of the Bronx," *Yonkers Historical Bulletin* Vol. XI, no. 2 (Fall, 1974), 71–80. Rokach mentions that "The two most prominent erratics are located in the Botanical Garden and the Zoological Park."

Raymond H. Torrey, Frank Place, Jr. and Robert L. Dickinson, *New York Walk Book. Third Edition* (NY: The American Geographical Society, 1951), 11. "In the northern part of the park is the Rocking Stone—a boulder seven feet high with a two-inch swing."

54. BLACK ROCK
Soundview Park

Type of Formation: Large Rock
WOW Factor: Unknown
Location: Bronx (The Bronx)
Tenth Edition, NYS Atlas & Gazetteer: p. 111, D6; **Earlier Edition NYS Atlas & Gazetteer**: p. 25, B4–5
Parking GPS Coordinates: 40º49.196′N 73º52.403′W
Soundview Park GPS Coordinates: 40º48.728′N 73º51.936′W
Black Rock GPS Coordinates: Not determined
Accessibility: Could be up to 0.5-mile walk depending on exactly where the boulder is located
Degree of Difficulty: Moderately easy

Description: In *History in Asphalt: The Origin of Bronx Street and Place Names,* John McNamara writes, "This great boulder imbedded in the salt marshes near the junction of Ludlow's Creek and the Bronx River was thought by the early inhabitants of Clason Point to be a meteorite."

Randall Comfort, in *History of Bronx Borough. City of New York,* writes that Black Rock is a great boulder that lies "...partially imbedded in the salt marshes to the south of Westchester Turnpike, not far from Pugsley's Causeway."

In the 1830s, Black Rock became part of Ludlow's Black Rock Farm on Clason Point.

The boulder is said to be formed of gneiss, a coarse-grained, imperfectly layered metamorphic rock.

History: Ludlow Creek, mentioned by McNamara, doesn't appear on current maps except for Ludlow Creek (not the same one) in Suffolk County.

It's possible that Pugley's Causeway, which is not identified by name today, may be the causeway at the southeast end of Soundview Park. If that is so, then why does MapQuest place Pugsley Creek on the east side of Clason Point? It can get confusing when you try to reconcile the past with the present, for land features have changed significantly over the last couple of hundred years. Complicating matters further, there is also a Blackrock Playground

133

Rock Walks

[40º49.709'N 73º51.477'W] bounded by Watson Avenue, Blackrock Avenue, and Pugsley Avenue, and this site may have played a role in Black Rock's history..

Fortunately, we know exactly where the boulder is today. According to the New York City Department of Parks and Recreation's excellent website, nycgovparks.org/parks/black-rock-playground/history, after being "mistaken for a meteorite by early settlers, the boulder was moved to Soundview Park, where it can be seen today."

The 205-acre Soundview Park, the so-called "gateway to the Bronx River," opened in 1937. At that time, the entire area was composed of marshland, with three streams running through it. Landfill operations lasted forty years, bringing the height of the shoreline up to 30 feet above its starting level. To be sure, the park looks nothing like it did in the 1930s.

Directions: Approaching the south terminus of the Bronx River Parkway, get off at the last exit, which is for Morrison Avenue. Drive south on Morrison Avenue for less than 0.2 mile. Then bear right (west) onto Lafayette Avenue and park on either side of the road. The entrance to Soundview Park, which you just passed by, is at the corner of Morrison Avenue and Lafayette Avenue.

I have not been able to determine where the large rock is located in Soundview Park, but I suspect it's on full display, since the park obviously went to some trouble to preserve it.

Resources: John McNamara, *History in Asphalt: The Origin of Bronx Street and Place Names* (The Bronx, NY: Bronx County Historical Society, 1996), 287.
nycgovparks.org/parks/soundview-park/history.
bronx.com/Local/Attractions/Parks/370.html – The *Bronx Times*.
Randall Comfort (compiler), *History of Bronx Borough. City of New York* (New York: North Side News Press, 1906), 2.
Harry T. Cook, *The Borough of the Bronx. 1639–1913* (NY: Author, 1913). Cook mentions that Black Rock is on Westchester Avenue just above the old Watson Estate and the Westchester Golf Club." One should bear in mind that this account was written over 100 years ago.
Stephen Jenkins, *The Story of the Bronx* (NY: G. P. Putnam's Sons, 1912), 402.

Rock Walks

55. KILLY'S ROCK
Edgewater Park

Type of Formation: Large Rock
WOW Factor: Unknown
Location: Schuylerville (The Bronx)
Tenth Edition, NYS Atlas & Gazetteer: p. 111, D7; **Earlier Edition NYS Atlas & Gazetteer**: p. 25, B5
Parking GPS Coordinates: 40º49.379'N 73º48.621'W
Edgewater Park GPS Coordinates: 40º49.461'N 73º48.495'W
Killy's Rock GPS Coordinates: 40º49.459'N 73º48.402'W (a guess)
Accessibility: Unknown; hopefully, access to the beach is not restricted.

Description: There are several rocks along the beach, and one that lies along the shoreline, but whether these qualify for Killy's Rock is a matter I leave for others to determine. In John McNamara's *History in Asphalt: The Origin of Bronx Street and Place Names*, the author writes, "This flattish boulder on the shoreline of Eastchester Bay at the Park of Edgewater was known to generations of children."

History: "Park of Edgewater," today called Edgewater Park, is a heavily developed private waterfront community. The name of the park comes from George Townsend Adee's mid-1850's estate, which was known as Edgewater.

While at Eastchester Bay, it's worth noting that there is also a large rock called *Big Tom* [40º50.141'N 73º47.379'W] in Eastchester Bay (1.2 miles northeast of Edgewater) that lies underwater, but is well-known known to navigators and has probably been struck by numerous ships in the past. It is seldom visible but clearly marked by Google Earth. I mention this to you just as a point of curiosity.

Directions: From Throgs Neck (junction of Lawton Avenue & Pennyfield Avenue), head north on Lawton Avenue for 0.1 mile (which crosses over the Throgs Neck Expressway – the superhighway). Turn left onto Throgs Neck Expressway (the regular road) and proceed northwest for <0.2 mile. When you come to Meagher Avenue/Adee Drive (look for the Edgewater Park Sign), bear right and head northeast for <0.2 mile to reach the main parking area, which is just beyond a tiny, triangle-shaped greenery.

From the parking area, walk east on Edge Street to reach the beach, which is just beyond a barrier at the end of Edge Street. Walk north up the beach for ~0.1 mile. The rock that I have given a GPS reading to may be Killy's Rock, but I'm just guessing. There are other rocks to check out, and you may draw a different conclusion.

Resources: John McNamara, *History in Asphalt: The Origin of Bronx Street and Place Names* (The Bronx, NY: Bronx County Historical Society, 1996), 390.
facebook.com/pages/Killy-Rock-Edgewater-Beach/416841278346817.

56. INWOOD HILL PARK ROCK FORMATIONS
Inwood Hill Park

Type of Formation: Pothole; Rock-Shelter
WOW Factor: 5–6
Location: Inwood (The Bronx)
Tenth Edition, NYS Atlas & Gazetteer: p. 110, C5; **Earlier Edition NYS Atlas & Gazetteer**: p. 24, A2
Parking GPS Coordinates: Park where you can
Estimated Destination GPS Coordinates: *Potholes* -- 40º52.225'N 73º55.580'W; 40º52.287'N 73º55.525'W; *Rock- Shelter* -- 40º52.390'N 73º55.502'W; *Shorakapok Rock* -- 40º52.395'N 73º55.420'W
Accessibility: 0.2–0.9-mile walk
Degree of Difficulty: Easy
Additional Information: Trail map of the park can be obtained at nycgovparks.org/pagefiles/82/Inwood-Hill-Park-map_2014.pdf

Description: *Potholes* – A number of potholes can be found at the park. Of these, the Inwood Hill Park Pothole is the largest, and allegedly the largest of its kind in New York City. The pothole's overlying mica schist has been worn away to expose the underlying Inwood marble.

In *The Geology of New York City and environs*, Christopher J. Schuberth mentions that these series of subglacial potholes were

Rock Walks

formed by an "eddy in water of a stream flowing beneath the melting ice of the Wisconsin Glacier." They are found in an area of the park called The Clove, and were first "discovered" in 1931 by Patrick Coghlan, an Inwood resident.

I have seen some estimates of the potholes' sizes as being as large as 5 feet deep and 3.5 to 8 feet in diameter.

Rock-Shelters – The rock-shelters are formed from configurations of slabs of Manhattan schist that were literally torn out of the bedrock by glaciers. The main rock-shelter was "discovered" by Alexander Chenoweth in 1890, who opened up the cave by digging through mounds of earth that had washed into the mouth of the cave over the previous two centuries.

One of the formations, called the Inwood Hill Tunnels, was bricked over in the 1920s out of concerns for public safety due to illicit activities taking place (this was similarly done in the Rambles section of Central Park).

Reginald Pelham Bolton, in *Washington Heights, Manhattan: Its Eventful Past*, mentions an "overhanging rock-shelter in which were found layers of ashes that had formed in the household fires..."

Shorakapkok Rock, also spelled *Shorakkopoch Rock* is a small boulder that marks the general area where Peter Minuit bought Manhattan Island from Native Americans for what amounted to sixty guilders (the equivalent of $24 today). The concrete circle around the boulder represents the circumference of a great Tulip tree that once occupied this spot.

Bolton, in *Washington Heights, Manhattan: Its Eventful Past*, also mentions 'Spouting Spring' where, "above this ancient outlet, a great slab of rock is exposed, in which are formed by a freak of nature, aided perhaps by some human labor, three depressions which take the form of eyes and a beak or nose." Bolton goes on to speculate that the name of the Spuyten Duyvil Creek may have originated from this spring, since a 1672 document describes it as "Spuyten Duyvil alias the Fresh Spring."

History: Inwood Hill, formerly called Cock Hill and, before that, New Haarlem in 1677, was earlier the site of a Native American village called *Shorakapkok* (meaning "as far as the Sitting-Down place"). The hill, sheltered from icy winds that made Manhattan's rocky ridge less hospitable, proved to be an ideal spot for a village.

Inwood Hill Park officially opened in 1917, but land purchases continued to increase the size of the park until 1941. It contains 196 acres.

The Hudson River Bike Trail and secondary hiking trails provide ready access to the park's interior. The trails were constructed in the 1930s by the Work Projects Administration.

Directions: Inwood Hill Park is located at the northwest corner of Manhattan near Route 9, north of Fort Tryon Park.

From I-87 (called here the Major Deegan Expressway), get off at Exit 9 for West Fordham Road and University Heights Blvd. Head northwest (in the opposite direction from West Fordham Road), crossing over

Glacial pothole.

University Bridge and continuing on West 207th Street for 0.6 mile until you come to Inwood Hill Park.

Parking, of course, is always problematic when there are no designated parking areas. Nearby streets, such as Dyckman Street or Payson Avenue (a one-way street with parking on both sides), may afford spaces to park.

To reach the glacial potholes, follow the ravine down the east side of the ridge. The Indian Rock Shelters are encountered further down, through a grove of spicebush.

I have no idea where Spouting Spring is located, or whether it is even in the park.

Resources: Christopher J. Schuberth, *The Geology of New York City and environs* (Garden City, N.J: The Natural History Press, 1968), 224.

nycgovparks.org/park-features/hiking/inwood-hill-park#map_canvas – The website includes a 17 minute video about the geology of the park, featuring Ranger Teddy Bailey.

geocaching.com/geocache/GC2RWPQ_glacial-pothole-in-the-city.

nycgovparks.org/parks/inwood-hill-park.

en.wikipedia.org/wiki/Inwood_Hill_Park.

myinwood.net/glacial-potholes-of-inwood-hill-park.

Lisa Montanarelli, *New York City Curiosities: Quirky Characters, Roadside Oddities & Other Different Stuf* (Guilford, CT: Morris Book Publishing, LLC, 2011), 54 & 55. A photograph of one of the boulders is shown on page 54.

nycgovparks.org/park-features/hiking/inwood-hill-park – This site also includes a map that shows the relative positions of the glacial potholes and rocks.

myinwood.net/glacial-potholes-of-inwood-hill-park – The website includes photographs of the glacial potholes. They are located in a part of the park called "The Clove." The potholes are said to be 5 feet deep and 3–4 feet in diameter."

Reginald Pelham Bolton, *Washington Heights, Manhattan: Its Eventful Past* (NY: Dyckman Institute, 1924), 13. On page 15 is a photograph of one of the park's rock-shelters. Bolton devotes an entire chapter to the park, 179–173, and to Tubby Hook, 172–178.

Reginald Pelham Bolton, *Indian Life of Long Ago in the City of New York* (NY: Bolton Books, 1924). Between pages 123 and 135 is an insert containing an illustration of how Native Americans used the rock overhangs for shelter by draping poles in front of the overhangs, and then closing them off using skins or sheets of bark.

C. R. Roseberry, *From Niagara to Montauk: The Scenic Pleasures of New York State* (Albany, NY: State University of New York Press, 1982), 275. "Huge, fallen wedges of rock from the Inwood Heights form a disorderly cluster locally known as the Indian Caves."

Sanna Feirstein, *Naming New York Manhattan Places & How They Got Their Names* (NY: New York University Press, 2001), 176 & 178.

Lee Ann Levinson, *East Side, West Side: A Guide to New York City Parks in all five Boroughs* (Darien, CT: Two Bytes Publishing, Ltd., 1997), 60. "Still today, caves in the park have Indian relics."

Charles Merguerian and Charles A. Baskerville, *Geology of the Manhattan Island and the Bronx, New York City, New York*, 138. Published in *Northeast Section of the Geological Society of America: Centennial Field Guide Vol. 5*. Editor, David C. Roy. (Boulder, CO: The Geological Society of America, Inc., 1987).

Christopher J. Schuberth, *The Geology of New York City and Environs* (Garden City, NY: The National History Press, 1968), 224.

Rock Walks

Lisa Montanarelli, *New York City Curiosities: Quirky Characters, Roadside Oddities & Other Different Stuff* (Guilford, CT: Morris Book Publishing, LLC, 2011). On page 40 is a photograph taken while looking out from inside the shelter cave.
myinwood.net/the-indian-caves-of-inwood-hill-park.
Jeffrey Perls, *Paths along the Hudson: A Guide to Walking and Biking* (New Brunswick, NJ: Rutgers University Press, 2001), 148.
Raymond H. Torrey, Frank Place, Jr. & Robert L. Dickinson, *New York Walk Book. Third Edition* (NY: The American Geographical Society, 1951), 8. "From the top of Inwood Hill, follow the ravine down the east side of the ridge, by the great potholes in the exposed rock."

57. FORT TRYON ROCKS
Fort Tryon Park

Type of Formation: Large Boulder
WOW Factor: 4–5
Location: Fort Tryon (The Bronx)
Tenth Edition, NYS Atlas & Gazetteer: p. 110, C5; **Earlier Edition NYS Atlas & Gazetteer**: p. 24, B4
Parking GPS Coordinates (Cloisters Museum & Gardens): 40º51.903′N 73º55.849′W
Destination GPS Coordinates: *Fort Tryon* -- 40º51.758′N 73º55.993′W; *Zombie Rock* -- 40º51.931′N 73º55.803′W; *Glacial Boulder* -- 40º51.746′N 73º56.000′W
Accessibility: All are within a 0.5-mile walk
Degree of Difficulty: Moderately easy
Additional Information: nycgovparks.org/parks/M029/map/ft-tryon-park-map.pdf – park map.

Description: It is entirely possible that many of the rocks in the park are rock buttresses or cliff-faces, for you can never tell for certain from the name provided until you are actually at the site. Boulderers have given the rocks such quaint names as *Zombie Rock, Bulging Boulder, Ivy Rock, Guns, Cars Boulder, Life is Beautiful Boulder, Sherman Boulders,* and *Pathway Boulder* (obviously next to the pathway).

One notable fact is that at a height of 267 feet, Fort Tryon Park is the highest point of land in Manhattan.

Rock Walks

History: Fort Tryon Park is named for a Revolutionary War redoubt constructed by the Americans that fell to British forces in 1776. That redoubt, in turn, was named for William Tryon, a Loyalist and last colonial governor of New York.

The property was later owned by Cornelius Kingsley Garrison Billings, a wealthy industrialist tycoon, from 1907 to 1916.

The Cloister: Fort Tryon Park. Old Postcard.

John D. Rockefeller Jr. began acquiring land that would eventually become the park in 1917. In 1931, Rockefeller gifted the property to the public and then, from 1931 to 1935, the Olmstead Brothers firm, led by Frederick Law Olmstead, Jr., created the 67-acre park that we see today.

The large erratics are believed to have been carried down by the Wisconsin Glacier from the Palisades. The bedrock that forms the outcroppings is made out of Manhattan schist.

The park offers commanding views of the New Jersey Palisades, Hudson River, and George Washington Bridge.

The area, known by the Lanape as *Chquaesgeck*, was first called *Lange Bergh* (Long Hill) by Dutch settlers.

Fort Tryon Park was added to the National Register of Historic Places in 1978, and to the New York City Scenic Landmark registry in 1983. It serves as a memorial to Revolutionary War soldiers from Maryland and Virginia who fought against Hessian troops in 1776.

141

Rock Walks

Directions: Fort Tryon Park lies just south of Inwood Hill Park.

From I-87/Major Deegan Expressway, get off at Exit 9 for West Fordham Road & University Heights Blvd. Head northwest (in the opposite direction from West Fordham Road), crossing over University Bridge and continuing on West 207th Street for >0.4 mile. Turn left onto Broadway and head southeast for ~1.4 miles. When you come to West 181st Street, turn right and proceed west for 0.1 mile. Then turn right onto Fort Washington Avenue and head north for ~0.6 mile until you come to Margaret Corbin Circle, the park's entrance.

The Fort Tryon Park Trust website, which is forttryonparktrust.org/visit-and-park-map/getting-here, also provides directions, and from different approaches. You may find the following helpful --

"From Manhattan and Brooklyn, Queens, or Long Island via the Triborough (RFK) Bridge or 59th Street (Edward Koch Queensboro) Bridges and the Midtown Tunnel, take the FDR/Harlem River Drive north to the Amsterdam Avenue/George Washington Bridge exit. At the light, make a right onto Amsterdam Avenue. Proceed north to 179th Street. Make a left onto 179th Street and proceed west to Fort Washington Avenue. At Fort Washington Avenue, turn right and proceed north to Margaret Corbin Circle. This is the southern entrance to Fort Tryon Park.

From Westchester County and parts of Connecticut, take the Henry Hudson Parkway South to the exit for Riverside Drive. Stay to the left in the exit lane. At the stop sign, make a left onto Riverside Drive. Stay in the left lane on Riverside Drive, which turns back into the Henry Hudson Parkway northbound. Take Fort Tryon Park Exit, the next exit off of the highway. From Long Island, Queens (via the Whitestone or Throgs Neck Bridges) or Connecticut, take the Cross-Bronx Expressway to the last exit in New York (Henry Hudson Parkway South–181st Street, Exit 1). Stay to the right in the exit lane until you come to the stoplight. At the light, take a right onto 181st Street. Make the first left off of 181st Street onto Cabrini Boulevard. Follow Cabrini Boulevard to its northern terminus, which is Margaret Corbin Circle."

Rock Walks

Limited, free parking is available at the New Leaf Restaurant and the Metropolitan Cloisters.

The vehicle entrance to the park is from Margaret Corbin Circle at the intersection of Fort Washington Avenue and Cabrini Boulevard.

Zombie Rock is located near the north end of the park, northeast of the Cloisters Museum & Gardens.

Many of the rocks are located near the bike path.

Resources: Christopher J. Schuberth, *The Geology of New York City and environs* (Garden City, N.J: The Natural History Press, 1968), 220.

nycgovparks.org/parks/fort-tryon-park.

en.wikipedia.org/wiki/Fort_Tryon_Park.

rockclimbing.com/photos/Topo/Zombie_Rock_119944.html.

rockclimbing.com/routes/North_America/United_States/New_York/New_York_City/Fort_Tryon_Park.

thecrag.com/climbing/united-states/new-york-city/area/12665821.

thecrag.com/climbing/united-states/new-york-city/area/766566459.

forttryonparktrust.org/geology-and-topography.

forttryonparktrust.org/visit-and-park-map/getting-here.

C. R. Roseberry, *From Niagara to Montauk: The Scenic Pleasures of New York State* (Albany, NY: State University of New York Press, 1982), 269.

Sanna Feirstein, *Naming New York Manhattan Places & How They Got Their Names* (NY: New York University Press, 2001), 171.

Lee Ann Levinson, *East Side, West Side: A Guide to New York City Parks in all five Boroughs* (Darien, CT: Two Bytes Publishing, Ltd., 1997), 43–45.

Christopher J. Schuberth, *The Geology of New York City and Environs* (Garden City, NY: The National History Press, 1968), 220. A map shows the location of a glacial erratic in the park that the author has discerned was carried there from the Palisades.

Reginald Pelham Bolton, *Washington Heights, Manhattan: Its Eventful Past* (NY: Dyckman Institute, 1924), 158–162.

Jeffrey Perls, *Paths along the Hudson: A Guide to Walking and Biking* (New Brunswick, NJ: Rutgers University Press, 2001), 145–147.

143

Rock Walks

58. SETON FALLS CAVE (Historic)
Seton Falls Park

Type of Formation: Cave
WOW Factor: 6–7
Location: Edenwald (The Bronx)
Tenth Edition, NYS Atlas & Gazetteer: p. 111, B7; **Earlier Edition NYS Atlas & Gazetteer**: p. 25, AB5
Park GPS Coordinates: 40º53.197′N 73º50.248′W
Estimated Cave GPS Coordinates: Not determined
Accessibility: Unknown, but probably no longer accessible

Description: According to Randall Comfort, in *History of Bronx Borough. City of New York*, Seton Falls Park contains "...an immense cavern in a precipitous ledge of rock, large enough to form a whole room..."

History: The 30-acre Seton Falls Park is named after William Seton. The waterfall is an artificial one, created when Seton dammed up Rattlesnake Creek.

Some have called Seton Falls Park the "Grand Canyon of the Bronx." The park was acquired by the city in 1914.

Directions: Traveling south on the New England Thruway/I-95, get off at Exit 13 for Conner Street and Baychester Avenue. The exit ramp takes you onto Hollers Avenue, which is a one-way street. When you come to Conner Street, turn right, and head north for 0.1 mile to the Boston Road/Route 1.

Traveling north on the New England Thruway, get off at Exit 13 for Conner Street. When you come to Tillotson Avenue, turn left and head northeast for >0.1 mile. Then turn left onto Conner Avenue and proceed north for 0.2 mile to the Boston Road/Route 1.

Turn left onto Boston Road/Route 1 and then head southwest for <0.4 mile. As soon as you go under a railroad bridge, turn right onto Marolla Place and drive northwest for >0.1 mile to the junction of Marolla Place and Pratt Avenue, which is at the south end of Seton Falls Park. Parking is available along either of the streets.

From here on, you are on your own. I can find no references to the cave nor its location in modern literature. Yet, there it is in

Former cave at Seton Falls Park?

Comfort's book, including not only an actual photograph of the cave, but a description of it being located at the bottom of a cliff, and large enough to be easily entered, but shallow in depth.

Today, who knows what remains of the cave? My guess is that it was permanently sealed up some time ago, perhaps because of its proximity to the Seton Falls (Elementary) School.

Resources: Randall Comfort (compiler), *History of Bronx Borough. City of New York* (New York: North Side News Press, 1906), 51. nycgovparks.org/parks/seton-falls-park/history. bchnhealth.org/bronx-park-guide/Seton-Falls-Park-Bronx-Guide.pdf. Stephen Jenkins, *The Story of the Bronx* (NY: G. P. Putnam's Sons, 1912), 422. "Here is the old Seton estate, through which runs Rattlesnake Brook, upon which were was formerly a mill." Jenkins goes on to describe "...a narrow and picturesque gorge where the water has a descent of about thirty feet in two falls..." No mention is made of a cave, however. bchnhealth.org/bronx-park-guide/Seton-Falls-Park-Bronx-Guide.pdf. John McNamara, *History in Asphalt: The Origin of Bronx Street Names and Place Names* (Harrison, NY: The Bronx Historical Society, 1978), 210. Robert Loeb, "The Story of Seton Falls Park." *The Westchester Historian. Quarterly of the West County Historical Society* Vol. 57, no. 3 (Summer, 1981), 69–72. Once again, I find it a bit unsettling that no reference is made to the cave in this article.

59. RICHMOND (ECHO) PARK ROCKS
Richmond (Echo) Park

Type of Formation: Medium-sized Rock
WOW Factor: 4
Location: Mount Hope (The Bronx)
Tenth Edition, NYS Atlas & Gazetteer: p. 111, C6; **Earlier Edition NYS Atlas & Gazetteer**: p. 25, B4–5
Parking GPS Coordinates: 40º50.955′N 73º54.058′W
Richmond (Echo) Park GPS Coordinates: 40º50.988′N 73º54.069′W
Accessibility: <0.1-mile walk
Degree of Difficulty: Easy

Description: Some interesting rocks can be found in the park, particularly huge upthrusts of bedrock. Hopefully, there will also be a boulder or two.

The park is <0.2 mile long and 0.1 mile across at its widest.

History: Richmond Park, aka Julius Richmond Park, was a favorite outing for early New Yorkers. Visitors would come to the park, cup their hands in front of their mouths, and shout loudly just to hear their voices echo between the park's two rocky ridges. It was for this reason that the city named it Echo Park when they acquired the property in 1888. Politics won out in 1973, however, and the name changed to Richmond Park in honor of a deceased civic leader, Julius J. Richmond, who was chairman of the Twin Parks Association and the Urban Action Task Force, as well as Assistant Administrator of the City's Finance Committee.

Richmond Park is defined by Valentine Avenue to the east, East Tremont Avenue to the south, East Burnside Avenue to the north, and partly by Ryer Avenue to the west.

Directions: From Fordham Manor (junction of Grand Concourse & Route 1/East Fordham Road), drive southwest on Grand Concourse for 0.8 mile. Turn left onto East Burnside Avenue and proceed southeast for 0.2 mile until you reach Valentine Avenue.
Park along one of the streets next to Richmond Park.

Resources: John McNamara, *History in Asphalt: The Origin of Bronx Street Names and Place Names* (Harrison, NY: The Bronx Historical Society, 1978), 85
nycgovparks.org/parks/richman-echo-park.
yelp.com/biz/richmond-echo-park-bronx.

60. INDIAN CAVE

Type of Formation: Rock-Shelter
WOW Factor: Unknown
Location: Spuyten Duyvil (The Bronx)
Tenth Edition, NYS Atlas & Gazetteer: p. 111, C6; **Earlier Edition NYS Atlas & Gazetteer**: p. 25, AB4–5
Parking GPS Coordinates: 40º53.144'N 73º54.896'W
Seton Park GPS Coordinates: 40º53.159'N 73º54.977'W
Raoul Wallenberg Forest GPS Coordinates: 40º53.159'N 73º54.977'W
Indian Cave GPS Coordinates: Not determined
Accessibility: 0.1–0.3mile hike/bushwhack
Degree of Difficulty: Moderate
Additional Information: Seton Park, W 235th St & Independence Ave, New York, NY 10463

Description: In *History in Asphalt: The Origin of Bronx Street and Place Names*, John McNamara writes, "Several gorges lead from the steep hillside of the former Seton Hospital grounds atop Spuyten Duyvil. In one of the gorges, some overhanging rocks form a natural cave known locally as 'Indian Cave'."

History: According to Native American legend, the shelter was occupied by two of Nimham's bands of Stockbridge warriors, taking refuge there after being defeated in a battle near Woodlawn Heights in 1778.

The Raoul Wallenberg Forest is named after Raoul Gustaf Wallenberg, a Swedish

Former Seton Hospital. Old photo.

diplomat who is credited with saving the lives of thousands of Hungarian Jews during WWII.

Directions: I have done my best to track down the location of this cave site. Although the Seton Hospital was demolished in 1955, I was able to learn that its GPS coordinates were 40º53.100′N 73º54.933′W, which places the hospital's site 0.1 mile above Seton Park (a small park at an elevation of 184 feet, overlooking the Hudson River, named after Saint Elizabeth Ann Seton).

Downhill from Seton Park is the Raoul Wallenberg Forest, which is my best guess as to where the gorge and shelter cave are likely to be. It should be an easy buswhack over a very small, defined area to see what can be seen. There may even be paths.

If you turn up nothing in the Wallenberg Forest, keep in mind that the forest continues on the other side of Palisade Avenue, all the way down to the Hudson River, now as Riverdale Park. This park might also be worth exploring.

To get there: Going south on the Henry Hudson Parkway, after crossing over the Harlem River, get off at Exit 19 for West 232rd Street. Turn left onto West 232nd Street and head west for one block. Then turn right onto Independence Avenue and park immediately on the left side of road, which faces Seton Park.

Going north on the Henry Hudson Parkway, get off at Exit 19. When you come to West 232rd Street, turn right and, in one block, turn right onto Independence Avenue and park.

From Seton Park, head west, downhill, towards the Hudson River. Some exploring on your own will be required to find the location of this rock-shelter.

Resources: John McNamara, *History in Asphalt: The Origin of Bronx Street and Place Names* (The Bronx, NY: Bronx County Historical Society, 1996), 380.
nycgovparks.org/parks/raoul-wallenberg-forest/history.

61. BASS ROCK
Huntington Woods: Pelham Bay Park

Type of Formation: Large Boulder
WOW Factor: 3
Location: Schuylerville (The Bronx)
Tenth Edition, NYS Atlas & Gazetteer: p. 111, CD7; **Earlier Edition NYS Atlas & Gazetteer**: p. 25, AB5
Parking GPS Coordinates: 40º50.922′N 73º49.283′W
Bass Rock GPS Coordinates: 40º50.897′N 73º48.965′W
Accessibility: <0.3-mile walk from parking area
Degree of Difficulty: Moderately easy

Description: Bass Rock is a modest-sized rock, but I can find no reference to it other than an historical one. Its physical appearance remains unknown to me.

History: The rock was mentioned in an 1835 deed as the boundary marker for William Bayard's farm, which is now part of Pelham Bay Park. In earlier deeds, the rock was called Bess Rock.

Directions: Driving south on the Buckner Expressway/I-695, get off at Exit 8A for Westchester Avenue. Continue south on Buckner Boulevard for 0.8 mile. When you come to Country Club Road, turn left and drive southeast for 0.1 mile. Then turn left onto Macdonough Place and head north for >0.1 mile. At a fork, continue north on Macdonough Avenue for another 0.1 mile. Finally, turn right onto

Middletown Road and drive northeast for 0.3 mile. When you come to Stadium Avenue, turn left and proceed to the parking area.

Going north on the Buckner Expressway/I-695, get off at Exit 7C for County Club Road and Pelham Bay Park. From County Club Road, continue north on Macdonough Place for >0.1 mile. At a fork, continue north on Macdonough Avenue for another 0.1 mile. Finally, turn right onto Middletown Road and drive northeast for 0.3 mile. When you come to Stadium Avenue, turn left and proceed to the parking area.

From the parking area, walk southeast on Stadium Avenue for 0.05 mile. Then turn left onto Watt Avenue and head east for 0.2 mile. At the end of the street, where Bay Shore Avenue goes right, continue down onto the beach, if possible, where the chain-link fence ends. Head south for 150 feet to a rock that I hope (fingers crossed) is Bass Rock.

Resources: John McNamara, *History in Asphalt: The Origin of Bronx Street and Place Names* (The Bronx, NY: Bronx County Historical Society, 1996), 280.

62. PUDDING ROCK (Historic)

Type of Formation: Large Rock
WOW Factor: 7
Location: Bronx (The Bronx)
Tenth Edition, NYS Atlas & Gazetteer: p. 111. D6; **Earlier Edition NYS Atlas & Gazetteer**: p. 25, B4–5
Exact Pudding Rock GPS Coordinates: 40º49.603′N 73º54.336′W

Description: Pudding Rock, aka Puddling Rock, was a prominent landmark until officials determined that it stood in the way of the city's expansion and destroyed it in the early 1900s.

Stephen Paul Devillo, in an article called "Puddling Rock," describes the rock as "An immense loaf-shaped boulder of sandstone and gravel conglomerate…"

Rock Walks

History: According to Randall Comfort, in *History of Bronx Borough. City of New York*, "Many are the tales recounted about this huge mass of rock. Rising 'not unlike a puddling in a bag,' it was gracefully ornamented at the top by an attractive group of cedar trees, its dimensions being twenty-five feet high and thirty-five feet in diameter—truly a gigantic boulder in every sense of the word. The Indians of old were not slow in discovering that on one side possessed a natural fire-place, where they cooked their oysters and clams and held their 'corn feasts'."

Pudding Rock. Old photograph c. 1900. Note girl on top.

Mention is made that the rock was named Pudding Rock because the big, purplish rock was peppered with gravel and small stones, making it look like Christmas plum pudding.

The rock was later used by Huguenots, fleeing France, as a rest stop along the Old Boston Road.

Puddling—the rock's alternate spelling— conjures up a word not commonly used, and refers to the process of converting pig iron into wrought iron, subjecting it to intense heat in a furnace. I can't help but wonder if Puddling Rock was possibly a misspelling of

Rock Walks

Pudding Rock, and yet the name also seems to strangely fit the description of the rock.

According to John McNamara, in *History in Asphalt: The Origin of Bronx Street Names and Place Names*, it's possible that the boulder may also have been known as *Tramps' Rock*, serving as a refuge for vagabonds. It's also said that the decomposed body of bank robber George Leonidas Leslie, aka "Western George," was found at the rock (or one very similar to it).

Directions: Until Pudding Rock was destroyed, it could be seen at the intersection of the Boston Post Road and 166th Street, about a mile west of the Bronx River.

Today, what is visible at the intersection of these two streets, are tall buildings and relentless traffic. Still, you can use your imagination to envision what the area might have once looked like when the rock, not the tall buildings, was the highest object in the area.

For matter of historical record, the rock was located at what is now 1074 Boston Road, which are the exact GPS coordinates I have provided.

Resources: Randall Comfort (compiler), *History of Bronx Borough. City of New York* (New York: North Side News Press, 1906), 1.
bronxriver.org/?pg=content&p=abouttheriver&m1=13&m2=78&m3=58 – This website contains an article called "Puddling Rock" that was written by Stephen Paul DeVillo and published by the Bronx River Alliance.
Harry T. Cook, *The Borough of the Bronx. 1639–1913* (NY: Author, 1913), 2. A photograph of the rock can be seen on page 3.
John McNamara, *History in Asphalt: The Origin of Bronx Street Names and Place Names* (Harrison, NY: The Bronx Historical Society, 1978), 447.

152

PELHAM BAY PARK

Pelham Bay Park, now consisting of 2,772 acres of land, was created in 1888 when New York City bought Hunter Island and Twin Island and some nearby pieces of land, and began to combine them into one landmass.

63. PELHAM BAY NAVAL CAMP BOULDER

Type of Formation: Large Rock
WOW Factor: 5
Location: City Island (Pelham Manor)
Tenth Edition, NYS Atlas & Gazetteer: p. 111, C7; **Earlier Edition NYS Atlas & Gazetteer:** p. 25, AB5
Parking GPS Coordinates: 40º52.174'N 73º47.749'W
City Island Circle GPS Coordinates: 40º51.598'N 73º48.114'W
Naval Camp Boulder GPS Coordinates: 40º51.678'N 73º47.935'W (a guess)
Accessibility: 0.3-mile bushwhack from south end of Old Orchard Beach
Degree of Difficulty: Moderate
Additional Information: Pelham Bay map available at pelhambaypark.org/wp-content/uploads/2014/02/F-of-PBP-map.pdf.

Description: The Naval Camp Boulder is a fairly broad rock some 6–7 feet high.

Old photograph of sailors posed in front of boulder.

History: The boulder is one of the surface features on the grounds of the former Pelham Bay Naval Camp (which operated from 1917 to 1919). The naval camp was essentially dismantled after WWI.

The rock's existence was brought to the forefront again recently thanks to local history buff Charlie Krieg who, coming across an old photograph of the rock, induced Jorge Santiago to join him in a search for the boulder. They succeeded, coming across the boulder just northeast of the traffic circle.

Directions: From the Hutchinson River Parkway, get off at Exit 5 for Pelham Bay Park. Drive southeast for 1.1 miles, passing through the Bartow-Pell Traffic Circle midway. When you come to Park Drive/Orchard Beach Road, turn left and proceed northeast on Orchard Beach Road for 0.4 mile. Turn right into the enormous parking area for Orchard Beach. The parking lot encompasses 4.5 acres of pavement and can accommodate up to 6,800 cars.

From the Orchard Beach pavilion, follow a white-marked trail west for 0.3 mile to reach the bike path that parallels Orchard Beach Road. Walk south for 0.3 mile to reach the City Island Traffic Circle (whose GPS I have listed). Follow a white-marked trail northeast into a wooded area bounded by Park Drive to the west, Orchard Beach to the north, Long Island Sound to the east, and City Island Avenue to the south. This is an area on the Pelham Bay map listed as The Meadow. There are trails in the woods that you can follow, but it may be necessary to bushwhack to locate the boulder. It makes sense that you visit when the trees are devoid of leaves, thereby increasing your range of vision dramatically. The GPS reading I have given for the boulder is a guesstimate, but I bet I'm not too far off the mark.

Resources: pelhambaypark.org/?page_id=73 (under "Friends of Pelham Bay Park).

64. JACK'S ROCK & MISHOW ROCK
Orchard Beach

Type of Formation: Large Boulder; Historic Rock
WOW Factor: 2
Location: Pelham Manor (The Bronx)
Tenth Edition, NYS Atlas & Gazetteer: p. 111, C7; **Earlier Edition NYS Atlas & Gazetteer**: p. 25, B5
Parking GPS Coordinates: 40º52.174′N 73º47.749′W

Estimated Destination GPS Coordinates: *Jack's Rock* -- 40º51.748'N 73º47.614'W; *Mishow Rock* -- 40º52.230'N 73º47.309'W (Both of these are guesstimates)
Accessibility: *Jack's Rock & Mishow Rock* – Distances depend upon where you enter the beach; could be up to a 0.5-mile walk to each
Degree of Difficulty: Easy
Additional Information: Pelham Bay map available at pelhambaypark.org/wp-content/uploads/2014/02/F-of-PBP-map.pdf.

Description: *Jack's Rock* is a large, glacial boulder that lies partially buried on the sandy beach at Orchard Beach. Only its top two feet are exposed.

Mishow Rock, aka Wedding Rock, is a large, glacial boulder also in the Orchard Beach area that was nearly buried when Hunter Island was joined to the mainland to create Orchard Beach. According to the City of New York Parks & Recreation's *Pelham Bay Park History*, "…only twin points [of the boulder] project from the ground…" Reputedly, the rock measured 8 feet high and 12 feet long before its full size was obscured,

Old photograph of Mishow Rock prior to the creation of Orchard Beach.

In Stephen Jenkins' *The Story of the Bronx*, an old photograph shows the rock and a couple of men standing next to it. The rock, with the words "Loreley Point, 1902" painted on it, appears to be 6–7 feet high.

History: Prior to the creation of the 1.0-mile long, 300–400 feet wide, crescent-shaped Orchard Beach, *Jack's Rock* could be seen offshore, a large portion of its bulk rising above the water line. According to Randall Comfort, in the *History of Bronx Borough. City of New York*, "Jack's Rock [was] one of the best fishing resorts in the area." When Orchard Beach was extended farther out into the ocean. Jack's Rock virtually disappeared except for what shows today.

If Jack's Rock served as the centerpiece for a fishing resort, *Moshaw Rock*, anthropologists believe, earlier served as both a meeting place and ceremonial site for Native Americans. With the construction of Orchard Beach, Mishow Rock would have been completely buried were it not for the efforts of Bronx historian Theodore Kazimiroff, who persuaded developers to leave a portion of the rock exposed for historical preservation.

Directions: From the Hutchinson River Parkway, get off at Exit 5 for Pelham Bay Park. Drive southeast for 1.1 miles, passing through the Bartow-Pell Traffic Circle midway. When you come to Park Drive/Orchard Beach Road, turn left and proceed northeast on Orchard Beach Road for 0.4 mile. Turn right into the enormous parking area for Orchard Beach.

Jack's Rock – From the parking lot, walk east to Orchard Beach, turn right, and head south. Look for the boulder near the southeast end of the beach. Keep your eyes open, for the rock will not be a prominent feature of the landscape.

Mishow Rock – From the parking lot, walk east to Orchard Beach, turn left, and head towards the northeast end of the beach. When you come to the Kazimiroff Nature Trail, turn left and begin looking for the rock which, from what I've read, lies at the northwest end of the promenade in deep grass.

Resources: New York-New Jersey Trail Conference, *Day Walker: 32 Hikes in the New York Metropolitan Area. Second Edition* (Mahwah, NJ: New York-New Jersey Trail Conference, 2002), 54. nycgovparks.org/parks/pelham-bay-park/highlights/11658.

pelhambaypark.org/?page_id=73.
historicpelham.blogspot.com/2005/05/grey-mare-and-mishow-boulders-part-of.html.
Randall Comfort (compiler), *History of Bronx Borough. City of New York* (New York: North Side News Press, 1906), 2.
City of New York Parks & Recreation, *Pelham Bay Park History* (New York: Administrator's Office, City of New York Parks & Recreation, 1986), 2.
Bill Twomey, *East Bronx. East of the Bronx River: Images of America* (Charleston, SC: Arcadia Publishing, 1999). On page 128 is a photograph of Jack's Rock with Bill Twomey standing behind it. The caption mentions that Skipps Lane goes by the rock.
nypost.com/2010/07/05/do-you-remember – An article by Bill Twomey provides further details about Jack Rock's history.
Stephen Jenkins, *The Story of the Bronx: From the Purchase made by the Dutch from the Indians in 1639 to the Present Day* (New York: G. P. Putnam's Sons, 1912), An old photograph of the rock, with two men next to it, is shown on page 316/317.
Raymond H. Torrey, Frank Place, Jr. & Robert L. Dickinson, *New York Walk Book. Third Edition* (NY: The American Geographical Society, 1951), 11. The writers claim that no one knows for sure which rock is Mishow Rock.

65. GREY MARE ROCK
Hunter Island

Type of Formation: Large Rock
WOW Factor: 4
Location: Hunter Island (The Bronx)
Tenth Edition, NYS Atlas & Gazetteer: p. 117, C7; **Earlier Edition NYS Atlas & Gazetteer**: p. 25, B5
Parking GPS Coordinates: 40º52.174'N 73º47.749'W
Gray Mare Rock GPS Coordinates: 40º52.857'N 73º47.371'W
Accessibility: ~1.0-mile hike
Degree of Difficulty: Moderate
Additional Information: A map of the Kazimirorff Nature Trail is at nycgovparks.org/sub_about/parks_divisions/nrg/documents/NRG_Public ation_The_Kazimiroff_Nature_Trail_Pelham_Bay_Park_Bronx.pdf
pelhambaypark.org/wp-content/uploads/2014/02/Kazimiroff-Nature-Trail.pdf.

Rock Walks

pelhambaypark.org/wp-content/uploads/2014/02/F-of-PBP-map.pdf.

Description: Grey Mare Rock is a large, grayish, moss-covered boulder that was brought to its present position by glaciers during the last Ice Age. It has also been spelled "Gray Mare Rock" at various times.

In *Field Guide to the Natural World of New York City*, Leslie Day writes, "You will see a large boulder, or glacial erratic protruding from the water. The Siwanoy Indians called this sacred ceremonial site the Grey Mare."

Interestingly, the term Grey Mare (as applied to a rock) originated in Northumberland, England, where locals used the word to describe boulders that tapered at the top. Such rocks attracted children, who would climb up and straddle them, and then pretend to be riding a horse.

History: According to Sharon Seitz & Stuart Miller in *The Other Islands of New York City*, "Hunter was called *Laap-Ha-Wach-King*, or 'place of Stringing Beads' by the Siwanoy, who held religious rituals

Grey Mare Rock. Old photograph.

on the island's odd rock formations." The island has gone by many names over time, including Pells Island (1654), Pelican Island, Appleby's Island (during the Revolutionary War), Blagge's Island, and Henderson Island.

The name Hunter Island stuck after John Hunter purchased the property in 1804 and built his grand mansion on it in 1813. The house survived through multiple owners until it was destroyed in 1937 when Orchard Beach was created.

Rock Walks

The Kazimirorff Nature Trail, which opened in 1986, was named for past noted Bronx Naturalist, Dr. Theodore Kazimirorff. It takes you to various sections of 189-acre Hunter Island.

Directions: From the Hutchinson River Parkway, get off at Exit 5 for Pelham Bay Park. Drive southeast for 1.1 miles, passing through the Bartow-Pell Traffic Circle midway. When you come to Park Drive/Orchard Beach Road, turn left and proceed northeast on Orchard Beach Road for 0.4 mile. Turn right into the enormous parking area for Orchard Beach.

Both the red-marked and blue-marked Kazimiroff Trails can be accessed from the northeast end of the Orchard Beach Promenade. The blue-marked trail will get you closest to the northwest end of the island. From there, you will need to continue walking towards the island's northern tip via secondary trails, where *Grey Mare Rock* can be found on marshy lands, facing the Long Island Sound.

Resources: New York-New Jersey Trail Conference, *New York Walk Book. Sixth Edition* (New York: New York-New Jersey Trail Conference, 1998), 53.
nycgovparks.org/sub_about/parks_divisions/nrg/documents/NRG_Publicat ion_The_Kazimiroff_Nature_Trail_Pelham_Bay_Park_Bronx.pdf
nycgovparks.org/parks/pelham-bay-park/highlights/11658
pelhambaypark.org/?page_id=73 – This site contains a photograph of the rock by Tom Casey.
New York-New Jersey Trail Conference, *Day Walker: 32 Hikes in the New York Metropolitan Area. Second Edition* (Mahwah, NJ: New York-New Jersey Trail Conference, 2002), 50–52.
historicpelham.blogspot.com/2005/05/grey-mare-and-mishow-boulders-part-of.html.
heddonhistory.weebly.com/blog/the-named-stones-of-northumberland-revisited.
Stephen Jenkins, *The Story of the Bronx* (New York: G. P. Putnam's Sons, 1912), 316.
Sharon Seitz & Stuart Miller, *The Other Islands of New York City: A History and Guide. Third Edition* (Woodstock, VT: Countryman Press, 2011), 120 & 130–135.
Leslie Day, *Field Guide to the Natural World of New York City* (Baltimore, MD: The Johns Hopkins University Press, 2007), 31.

66. TILLIE'S ROCK
Hunter Island

Type of Formation: Large Boulder
WOW Factor: 4
Location: Hunter Island (The Bronx County)
Tenth Edition, NYS Atlas & Gazetteer: p. 117, C7; **Earlier Edition NYS Atlas & Gazetteer:** p. 25, B5
Parking GPS Coordinates: 40º52.174'N 73º47.749'W
Tillie's Rock GPS Coordinates: 40º52.645'N 73º47.062'W and 40º52.614'N 73º47.025'W
Accessibility: 0.5-mile hike from north end of Orchard Beach
Degree of Difficulty: Moderate
Additional Information: Pelham Bay map available at pelhambaypark.org/wp-content/uploads/2014/02/F-of-PBP-map.pdf.

Tillie's Rock. Pen & ink sketch by Robert L. Dickinson.

Description: Tillie's Rock, aka Tilly's Rock, is the last rock in a series of medium-sized boulders along a narrow strip of land extending out from the northeast tip of Hunter Island.

History: Years ago, the Tillie's Rock area grew to be a favorite bathing site for men and boys since, due to its inaccessibility, it provided seclusion for nude bathing (which is why, obviously women chose not to go there). This privacy ended when Orchard Beach was created and Hunter Island was joined to the mainland.

No one knows for sure how the rock was named. One theory contends that the rock may have originally been known as Tiller Rock, named by seamen who used it as a navigational marker to take tiller and change their course. A second theory suggests that the name came from a woman named Matilda.

Siwanoy Native Americans called the island *Laap-Ha-Wach-King*, meaning "the place of stringing beads." While most have taken this to mean the stringing together of shells for wampum, I can't help but wonder if it actually refers to the bead-like string of boulders at Tillie's Rock.

Directions: From the Hutchinson River Parkway, get off at Exit 5 for Pelham Bay Park. Drive southeast for 1.1 miles, passing through the Bartow-Pell Traffic Circle midway. When you come to Park Drive/Orchard Beach Road, turn left and proceed northeast on Orchard Beach Road for 0.4 mile. Turn right into the enormous parking area for Orchard Beach.

From the northeast end of the Orchard Beach Promenade, follow the red-marked Kazimiroff Trail and spur paths northeast until you come to the northeast end of the island where sizeable boulders can be seen both along the ridge line and along a 0.1-mile long spit of land attached to the island. During high tide, however, this 120-foot-long stretch of land that attaches the two points of land goes slightly underwater.

Undoubtedly, the bathing area that attracted so many swimmers prior to modern times was in this section of Tillie's Rock.

Resources: John McNamara, *History in Asphalt: The Origin of Bronx Street and Place Names* (The Bronx, NY: Bronx County Historical Society, 1996), 126 & 127 & 487.
historicpelham.blogspot.com/2015/07/tillies-rock-swimming-hole-paradise-for.html.

67. INDIAN PRAYER ROCK
Athletic Field

Type of Formation: Large Rock
WOW Factor: 5–6
Location: Pelham Manor (The Bronx)
Tenth Edition, NYS Atlas & Gazetteer: p. 117, C7; **Earlier Edition NYS Atlas & Gazetteer**: p. 25, B5
Parking GPS Coordinates: 40º50.922′N 73º49.287′W
Estimated Indian Prayer Rock GPS Coordinates: 40º51.123′N 73º49.197′W
Accessibility: 0.2–0.3-mile walk
Degree of Difficulty: Easy

Description: *Indian Prayer Rock,* aka Indian Rock, is a large, black-colored rock formation that may have initially been one huge, intact boulder before geological forces shattered it into smaller, but still, large pieces. The rock formation, made out of gneiss and schist, rises up 25 feet at its highest point. Look closely and you will see igneous intrusions of quartz and feldspar in the rock.

In 1913, a bronze plaque was affixed to the rock to celebrate the 30th anniversary of the creation of the Bronx parks system, but vandals pried it off and stole it many decades ago.

Indian Prayer Rock. Postcard c. 1900.

History: Indian Prayer Rock was named for its past association with the Siwanoy and the Lenape who frequented the boulder for religious ceremonies. Unlike the Incas and Mayas, these northeast Native Americans never used rocks to construct massive stone structures; rather, they simply used what was at hand and were satisfied to leave it the way it was found.

Indian Prayer Rock has been utilized in different ways during the twentieth century. In 1904, to celebrate the opening of the new athletic field and parade grounds, the rock was used as a backdrop for archery practice, thus ensuring that errant arrows, missing their mark, would hit the boulder and be harmlessly deflected.

Later, a grandstand was placed next to Indian Prayer Rock, which provided an enclosure or side wall for one of the bleachers. The rock was so close, in fact, that it is said that spectators could reach out and touch it.

Directions: Driving south on the Buckner Expressway/I-695, get off at Exit 8A for Westchester Avenue. Continue south on Buckner Boulevard for 0.8 mile. When you come to Country Club Road, turn left and drive southeast for 0.1 mile. Then turn left onto Macdonough Place and head north for >0.1 mile. At a fork, continue north on Macdonough Avenue for another 0.1 mile. Finally, turn right onto Middletown Road and drive northeast for 0.3 mile. When you come to Stadium Avenue, turn left and proceed to the parking area.

Going north on the Buckner Expressway/I-695, get off at Exit 7C for Country Club Road and Pelham Bay Park. From County Club Road, proceed north on Macdonough Place for >0.1 mile. At a fork, continue north on Macdonough Avenue for another 0.1 mile. Finally, turn right onto Middletown Road and drive northeast for 0.3 mile. When you come to Stadium Avenue, turn left and proceed to the parking area.

According to directions from Blake A. Bell, Pelham historian, Indian Rock is "…located in a wooded area just behind the baseball diamond after you pass the dog run. To find the site, walk into the woods from center field." Another source says of the rock's location, "Its site is located in the southwestern section of Pelham Bay Park beyond Pelham Bridge and the reclaimed and rehabilitated Bronx-Pelham Landfill. It is in a wooded area that can be entered from center field of the baseball diamond near the dog run." I suspect these directions will make sense once you are at the park.

My best guess is to walk north from the Aileen B. Ryan Recreation Complex parking area for over 0.1 mile, passing by the Aileen B. Ryan Recreational Center to your left. Turn right onto a road (Dog Run) and head northeast for over 0.1 mile. You will see a baseball diamond to your left.

Go out to center field, and begin looking for the rock near or back from the edge of the forest.

Resources: historicpelham.blogspot.com/2017/05/indian-prayer-rock-in-pelham-bay-park.html.
theislandcurrent.com/Island_Currents/May%20IC%202011.pdf – The May 2011 issue of *The Island Current* contains Jane Rothman's article "A Rock Tour of Pelham Bay Park", p. 7.
pelhambaypark.org/?page_id=73 – This site contains a photograph of the rock by Jorge Santiago.
thebronxchronicle.com/2014/09/30/indian-prayer-rock.
pelhamplus.com/opinion/blogs/article_2e3b5f40-3bcd-11e7-aa30-9b0a7e9b764e.html.
thebronxfreepress.com/i-love-the-bronx-boulders-amo-el-bronx-rocas – Site contains a photograph of the rock.

68. GLOVER'S ROCK
Pelham Bay Park

Type of Formation: Large Boulder
WOW Factor: 3–4
Location: Pelham Manor (The Bronx)
Tenth Edition, NYS Atlas & Gazetteer: p. 111, C7; **Earlier Edition NYS Atlas & Gazetteer**: p. 25, B5
Parking GPS Coordinates: *Split Rock Golf Course* -- 40º52.319'N 73º48.617'W; *Orchard Beach* -- 40º52.103'N 73º47.860'W
Destination GPS Coordinates: *Glover's Rock* -- 40º51.902'N 73º48.202'W; *Boulder beyond Glover's Rock* -- 40º51.895'N 73º48.202'W
Accessibility: 0.6- mile walk
Degree of Difficulty: Moderately easy
Additional Information: Map available at pelhambaypark.org/wp-content/uploads/2014/02/F-of-PBP-map.pdf.

Rock Walks

Description: *Glover's Rock* is an 8-foot-high, granite boulder of historical significance.

A second, sizeable erratic lies 30 feet behind Glover's Rock.

History: *Glover's Rock* designates the site of the Battle of Pell's Point when Colonel John Glover in October of 1776 led a small brigade of 750 Americans against British General William Howe's force of 4,000 redcoats and Hessians. Glover's forces didn't win the battle, but strategically delayed the British's advancement just long enough to allow General George Washington and his men to escape to White Plains where they were able to rest and regroup.

There is an old account that suggests that Colonel Glover stood on top of the rock to track the British forces as they landed. This, undoubtedly, is apocryphal, but remains a lively story today.

A plaque was installed on the rock in 1901 by the Daughters of the American Revolution to honor the 125th Anniversary of the Battle at Pell's Point and Colonel Glover's victory. Vandals ripped it off, but a new, larger bronze tablet that was installed in 1960 still remains in place. A sign next to the rock provides valuable historical information as well.

Glover's Rock and early members of the Bronx Historical Society.

Directions: *Glover's Rock* can be found on Orchard Beach Road, less than 0.5 mile southeast of the Bartow-Pell Traffic Circle.

Get off at Exit 5 of the Hutchinson River Parkway. When you come to the Bartow-Pell Traffic Circle, head north on Shore Road for 0.3 mile to reach the Split Rock Golf Course, on your left.

Starting from the Golf Course's parking area, pick up the yellow-marked Siwanoy Trail and follow it southeast. The path initially follows along Shore Road and then, after going under Orchard Beach Road, takes you southeast, paralleling Orchard Beach Road. In ~0.7 mile, you will reach Glover's Rock, on a white-marked spur path to your left.

The rock can also be accessed from the Siwanoy Trail, starting at a wooded area called The Meadows by Orchard Beach.

Best of all, however, is that appears likely that you can simply pull over off the road next to the rock if you are traveling on the east-bound lane.

Resources: nycgovparks.org/parks/pelham-bay-park/monuments/590. historicalmarkerproject.com/markers/HM1UZ3_glovers-rock-historical_NY.html.
Catherine A. Scott, *City Island and Orchard Beach* (Charleston, SC: Arcadia Publishing, 1999). On page 11 is a photograph of Glover's Rock.
forgotten-ny.com/2000/08/bronx-rocks-revolutionary-war-remains-in-pelham-bay-park.
pelhambaypark.org/?page_id=73 – This site contains a photograph of the rock.by Deborah Wye.
New York-New Jersey Trail Conference, *Day Walker: 32 Hikes in the New York Metropolitan Area. Second Edition* (Mahwah, NJ: New York-New Jersey Trail Conference, 2002), 50–52.
bridgeandtunnelclub.com/bigmap/bronx/pelhambaypark/gloversrock/index.htm – This site contains several photographs of Glover's Rock.
youtube.com/watch?v=xxFZcGpgh18 –This site contains a 1 minute video of the rock.
pelhambaypark.org/?page_id=805 – The Battle of Pell's Point is described.
Randall Comfort (compiler), *History of Bronx Borough. City of New York* (New York: North Side News Press, 1906), 1–2.
Paul G. Brown, "The Battle of Pell's Point," *The Bronx County Historical Society Journal* Vol. X, no. 2 (July 1973), 66–73.
Robert F. Ryan, "John Glover and the Battle of Pell's Point," *The Bronx County Historical Society Journal* Vol. II, no. 2 (July 1965), 65–85. A full account is given on page 67 concerning the Glover's Rock plaque.
John McNamara, *History in Asphalt: The Origin of Bronx Street and Place Names* (Harrison, NY: Harbor Hill Books, 1978), 105.
John McNamara, *McNamara's Old Bronx* (The Bronx, NY: The Bronx County Historical Society, 1989), 241. A photograph can be seen of the rock, along with some early members of the Bronx Historical Society.
Stephen Jenkins, *The Story of the Bronx: From the Purchase made by the Dutch from the Indians in 1639 to the Present Day* (New York: G. P. Putnam's Sons, 1912), 144/145. An insert photo shows Glover's Rock,

including a large boulder nearby in the background. On page 311 are the words contained on an old plaque on Glover's Rock.
The Bronx County Historical Society Journal, Vol. II, no. 2 (July 1965). Information on the rock is provided on pages 67 & 68.
Lee Ann Levinson, *East Side, West Side: A Guide to New York City Parks in all five Boroughs* (Darien, CT: Two Bytes Publishing, Ltd., 1997), 179.
Harry T. Cook, *The Borough of the Bronx. 1639–1913* (NY: Author, 1913), 58.

69. SPHINX ROCK
Twin Island

Type of Formation: Medium-sized Rock
WOW Factor: 3
Location: Twin Island (The Bronx)
Tenth Edition, NYS Atlas & Gazetteer: p. 111, C7; **Earlier Edition NYS Atlas & Gazetteer**: p. 25, B5
Parking GPS Coordinates: 40º52.174'N 73º47.749'W
Destination GPS Coordinates: *Sphinx Rock* – Not determined; *Several Large Rocks* -- 40º52.422'N 73º47.005'W
Accessibility: <0.4-mile hike from northeast end of Orchard Beach
Degree of Difficulty: Moderate
Additional Information: Pelham Bay map available at pelhambaypark.org/wp-content/uploads/2014/02/F-of-PBP-map.pdf.

Description: In *The Other Islands of New York City*, Sharon Seitz & Stuart Miller write, "There are several massive boulders, including a glacial erratic known as Sphinx Rock just before the informal trail bends [from Twin Island] west toward Hunter Island."

Catherine Scott, in "Twin Island: A Bronx Secret" that appeared in the Spring 1998 issue of *The Bronx County Historical Society Journal,* writes, "The rock remained here for over 10,000 years with a precariously balanced boulder on top. Within the last several years, however, the top half broke away and now lies near the larger piece. Early colonists noted that the Indians revered this boulder as they did other erratics" It was probably the smaller boulder balanced on top of the larger rock that gave rise to the name "Sphinx Rock."

Rock Walks

Recent photographs of Sphinx Rock show a highly irregularly-shaped rock with both ends off the ground.

Sphinx Rock is perched on the northeastern edge of Twin Island. It is just one of a number of medium-sized boulders that populate the area.

History: In the past, Sphinx Rock has also been called Lion Rock, probably because the boulder resembled the Great Sphinx of Egypt, whose body was that of a recumbent lion.

Twin Island (which, until recently, consisted of cigar-shaped East Twin Island and cigar-shaped West Twin Island) became linked with Hunter Island in 1947, just as Hunter Island was connected to Rodman's Neck when Orchard Beach was created in the 1930s.

Directions: From the Hutchinson River Parkway, get off at Exit 5 for Pelham Bay Park. Drive southeast for 1.1 miles, passing through the Bartow-Pell Traffic Circle midway. When you come to Park Drive/Orchard Beach Road, turn left and proceed northeast on Orchard Beach Road for 0.4 mile. Turn right into the enormous parking area for Orchard Beach.

From the northeast end of the parking area, walk east along a paved walkway and then the Beach Promenade for >0.3 mile to reach the Orchard Beach Nature Center near the northeast end of Orchard Beach. From the Nature Center, follow a white-marked trail northeast that leads to the tip of Twin Island, a hike of 0.4 mile. Twin Island, once an island, today is simply a grassy extension of the northeast tip of Orchard Beach.

Resources: Sharon Seitz & Stuart Miller, *The Other Islands of New York City: A History and Guide* (Woodstock, VT: The Countryman Press, 2001), 125.
pelhambaypark.org/?page_id=71 – The website contains a photograph by John Grayley of Sphinx Rock.
Catherine Scott, "Twin Island: A Bronx Secret," *The Bronx County Historical Society Journal* Vol. XXXV, no. 1 (Spring 1998), 31.
Leslie Day, *Field Guide to the Natural World of New York City* (Baltimore, MD: The Johns Hopkins University Press, 2007), 27 & 28.

70. SPLIT ROCK
Pelham Bay Park

Type of Formation: Split Rock; Historic Rock
WOW Factor: 6
Location: Pelham Manor (The Bronx)
Tenth Edition, NYS Atlas & Gazetteer: p. 111, C7; **Earlier Edition NYS Atlas & Gazetteer**: p. 25, AB5
Parking GPS Coordinates: 40°52.319′N 73°48.617′W
Bartow Circle GPS Coordinates: 40°52.133′N 73°48.642′W
Split Rock GPS Coordinates: 40°53.187′N 73°48.893′W
Accessibility: >1.0-mile hike
Degree of Difficulty: Moderate
Additional Information: Pelham Bay map available at website pelhambaypark.org/wp-content/uploads/2014/02/F-of-PBP-map.pdf.

Description: Split Rock, as suggested by the name, is a 12–15-foot-high, 25-foot-long glacial boulder that has cracked into two halves. The gap would be wide enough to conceal a person except for the fact that a tree has claimed first dibs on the space today.

Randall Comfort, in *History of Bronx Borough, City of New York*, says of the Split Rock, "Cleft directly in the middle with a good-sized tree growing in the fissure, this great boulder is one of the sights of the neighborhood...." Or at least it was one of the neighborhood sights during Randall Comfort's time. Today, the rock is partially isolated by superhighways—the Hutchinson River Parkway and New England Thruway—that pass close by next to it.

To be sure, most people driving along the Hutchinson River Parkway today have absolutely no idea how the highway came to be named after Anne Hutchinson, or how her history is intimately associated with Split Rock.

It is fortunate indeed that this historic rock has survived into modern times. In the 1960s, Split Rock was almost destroyed by engineers while clearing the way for Interstate 95. Fortunately, community activism initiated by the Bronx Historical Society prevented the boulder from being demolished, and the Hutchinson River Parkway was subsequently moved 50 feet to the north.

Rock Walks

History: In 1643, Anne Hutchinson [see chapter on Helicker's Cave for additional information] and members of her family hid in the crevice at Split Rock to avoid being captured by Siwanoy Indians. Apparently, this ruse didn't work for long, for Ann and the others in her party were captured and subsequently massacred—the one possible exception being Ann's daughter, Susanna, whose fate is not entirely known for certain.

Split Rock at Pelham Bay. Old photograph.

A tablet was affixed to the boulder in 1911 by the Colonial Dames of the State of New York to honor Anne Hutchinson. By 1914 it was stolen by vandals.

We know, however, that the plaque read: "Anne Hutchinson. Banished from the Massachusetts Bay Colony in 1638 because of her devotion to religious liberty. This courageous woman sought freedom from persecution in New Netherland. Near this rock in 1643 she and her household were massacred by Indians. This tablet is placed here by the Colonial Dames of the State of New York. Anno Domini MCMXI [1911] Virtutes Majorum Filiae Conservant."

Anne Hutchinson may have been more significant than I first realized as I did further research on this book. In *The Shaping of North*

America, Isaac Asimov contends that she "was the first woman of note in American history."

Recent concerns have been raised about the rock losing its purchase on the supporting cliff base and falling onto the highway below. Presumably, action can be (or has been) taken to prevent this from happening.

Eagle Rock – Although not a boulder, but rather a bluff, Eagle Rock is mentioned by John McNamara in his book *History in Asphalt: The Origin of Bronx Street Names and Place Names,* and is described as "a prominent bluff on east bank of the Hutchinson River 200 yards north of the Hudson River Parkway." I have no idea if the bluff still exists today.

Directions: Get off at Exit 5 of the Hutchinson River Parkway. When you come to the Bartow-Pell Traffic Circle, head north on Shore Road for 0.3 mile to reach the Split Rock Golf Course. Turn left to park. If you enjoy golf, you may want to play a round while there.

From the golf course parking lot, walk south along the bike path to the Bartow-Pell Traffic Circle, and then follow the Split Rock Trail as it meadows through Goose Creek Marsh and then the 50-acre Thomas Pell Sanctuary. The Split Rock Trail was restored in 1985 by the Park and the Mayor's City Volunteer Corps, and hopefully remains serviceable today.

The Pelham Bay Map also shows that Split Rock can also be reached by taking a bridle path that leads from the west side of the parking area, and goes north to the northwest corner of Pelham Bay Park, across from Split Rock, before circling back.

Split Rock can be seen from both the Split Rock Trail and bridle path, which are enjoined at this point. The problem, however, is this. Split Rock is on a tiny triangle of land walled off by two super-highways— the Hutchinson River Parkway and the New England Thruway. The only way to physically get to the rock is to cross over a busy exit ramp from the Hutchinson River Parkway. Doing this is not something that is recommended. For this reason, you may have to content yourself with a view of the rock from the east side of the exit ramp.

Rock Walks

Resources: placematters.net/node/1802.

historicpelham.blogspot.com/2005/03/split-rock-pelham-landmark-for.html.

pelhamplus.com/opinion/blogs/article_a5e87662-73e9-11e4-acbc-97371de60fa7.html.

Catherine A. Scott, *City Island and Orchard Beach* (Charleston, SC: Arcadia Publishing, 1999). On page 10 is a photograph of the boulder with four men standing on top of it.

New York-New Jersey Trail Conference, *New York Walk Book. Sixth Edition* (New York: New York-New Jersey Trail Conference, 1998), 47.

patch.com/new-york/larchmont/who-was-anne-hutchinson-2.

Randall Comfort (compiler), *History of Bronx Borough. City of New York* (New York: North Side News Press, 1906), 1.

pelhambaypark.org/?page_id=73 – This site contains a photograph of the rock taken by Jorge Santiago.

City of New York Park & Recreation, *Pelham Bay Park History* (New York: Administrator's Office, City of New York Park & Recreation, 1986). A photograph of Split Rock is shown on page 4.

Westchester Historical Society, *Anne Hutchinson and Other Papers* (White Plains, NY: Westchester County Historical Society, 1929). The rock is described as "...a great cloven boulder." A photograph of the rock atop a hill as seen from a great distance is shown on an insert between pages 12 and 13.

John McNamara, *History in Asphalt: The Origin of Bronx Street and Place Names* (Harrison, NY: Harbor Hill Books, 1978), 216.

Stephen Jenkins, *The Story of the Bronx* (New York: G. P. Putnam's Sons, 1912). On an insert between pages 310 and 311 is a photograph of Split Rock.

Harry Hansen, *North of Manhattan: Persons and Places of Old Westchester* (NY: Hastings House Publisher, 1950). Detailed information about Anne Hutchinson is provided on pages 137–165. On page 150, specifically, the author writes, "Across the river and on the eastern slope, directly above the new parkway, stands an immense double boulder, the split rock that became the first landmark for supervisors in this area."

Anonymous, *Pelham Bay Park History* (NY: Administrator's Office, Van Cortlandt and Pelham Bay Parks, 1986), 4. A photograph of Split Rock is shown on the page, including additional history.

Harry T. Cook, *The Borough of the Bronx. 1639–1913* (NY: Author, 1913). 3. On pages 58 and 123 are photographs of Split Rock.

forgotten-ny.com/2000/08/bronx-rocks-revolutionary-war-remains-in-pelham-bay-park.

John McNamara, *History in Asphalt: The Origin of Bronx Street Names and Place Names* (Harrison, NY: The Bronx Historical Society, 1978), 329.

Rock Walks

Lee Ann Levinson, *East Side, West Side: A Guide to New York City Parks in all five Boroughs* (Darien, CT: Two Bytes Publishing, Ltd., 1997), 179 & 180.

Isaac Asimov, *The Shaping of North America* (London: Dobson Books, LTD, 1973), 105.

Raymond H. Torrey, Frank Place, Jr. & Robert L. Dickinson, *New York Walk Book. Third Edition* (NY: The American Geographical Society, 1951), 12. Split Rock and the story of Anne Hathaway are discussed.

71. ROOSEVELT ROCK
Pelham Bay Park

Type of Formation: Medium-sized Boulder; Historic Rock
WOW Factor: 3
Location: Pelham Manor (The Bronx/Westchester County)
Tenth Edition, NYS Atlas & Gazetteer: p. 111, C7; **Earlier Edition NYS Atlas & Gazetteer**: p. 25, AB5
Shore Road & Pelhamdale Ave Junction GPS Coordinates: 40º53.218'N 73º47.469'W
Parking GPS Coordinates: 40º52.890'N 73º47.718'W
Roosevelt Rock GPS Coordinates: 40º52.955'N 73º47.605'W (my best guess)
Accessibility: 0.1 mile walk
Degree of Difficulty: Easy

Description: Roosevelt Rock is a medium-sized, fairly nondescript rock with historic significance that lies near the seashore.

History: The boulder is located on the former grounds of the Elbert Roosevelt estate. Roosevelt was a New York City merchant and distantly related to the famous Roosevelts. One of Elbert's sons, Isaac, made a carving in the rock in 1833 that read "Isaac Roosevelt. 1833." Apparently, the words are still legible nearly two centuries later.

Readers may be interested to know that this is not the first Roosevelt Rock that I have encountered or written about. In *Boulders Beyond Belief: An Explorer's Hiking Guide to Amazing Boulders and Natural Rock Formations of the Adirondacks* (Chapter 97), I describe an

173

Rock Walks

historic rock associated with John Ellis Roosevelt, cousin of Theodore Roosevelt.

Directions: The Historic Pelham Website, dated November 13th, 2006 (historicpelham.blogspot.com/2006/11/) provides fairly clear directions to accessing Roosevelt Rock. "As you leave Pelham on Shore Road [heading south] you will pass Shore Park on the left and a number of homes on the east side of Shore Road. Shortly after you leave Pelham and enter Pelham Bay Park, there is a small parking area on the left (east side) of the roadway. Its entrance usually is blocked with boulders. Several footpaths are accessible from that parking area. They lead down to the shoreline."

"At low tide it is easy to walk along the shoreline back toward the Pelham Town Boundary (northward). You will reach the "end" of the shoreline where a fence blocks your continued progress along portions of the shore owned by private home owners. The last large boulder lying on the shore at that spot contains the carving, although it is difficult to see."

My interpretation of these directions, starting from the junction of Shore Road and Pelhamdale Ave (which is 0.2 mile north of Shore Park), is to drive southwest on Shore Road for < 0.5 mile. Then turn left and park in a small area where boulders block a more substantial parking area off in the woods.

I would suggest, however, approaching from Pelham Bay Park. Get off from the Hutchinson River Parkway at Exit 5. At the Bartow-Pell Traffic Circle, head north on Shore Road for ~1.3 miles, and park to your right.

Follow a path southeast for 200 feet to reach the shoreline. From here, walk north along the beach for < 0.1 mile until you come to the rock.

Resources: pelhambaypark.org/?page_id=73.
historicpelham.blogspot.com/2014/05/elbert-roosevelt-early-settler-of-manor.html.
historicpelham.blogspot.com/2015/04/the-beginnings-of-todays-shore-park-in.html.
historicpelham.blogspot.com/2006/11/isaac-roosevelt-stone-carved-in-1833.html.

Rock Walks

72. HUTCHINSON RIVER POTHOLES
Pelham Bay Park

Type of Formation: Pothole
WOW Factor: *Old Bartow Station* -- 1–2; *Potholes* – Unknown; *Middle Rock* -- 1
Location: Pelham Bay Park (The Bronx)
Tenth Edition, NYS Atlas & Gazetteer: p. 111, C7; **Earlier Edition NYS Atlas & Gazetteer**: p. 25, AB5
Bronx Equestrian Center Parking GPS Coordinates: 40º51.956′N 73º48.830′W
Destination GPS Coordinates: *Old Bartow Station* --40º52.154′N 73º48.776′W; *Potholes* -- 40º52.091′N 73º48.854′W (a guess); *Middle Rock* -- 40º51.650′N 73º48.778′W
Accessibility: *Potholes* -- 0.3–0.4-mile hike/bushwhack; *Middle Rock* – 0.2-mile walk
Degree of Difficulty: Moderate
Additional Information: Pelham Bay map available at pelhambaypark.org/wp-content/uploads/2014/02/F-of-PBP-map.pdf.

Description: According to Lloyd Ultan, in *The Northern Borough: A History of the Bronx*, "Other pot holes can be seen near the old Bartow Station and near the bridge at Shore Road in Pelham Bay Park."

History: The potholes are most likely along the bank of the Hutchinson River—a medium-sized stream that rises in Scarsdale and, ten miles later, flows into Eastchester Bay.

The Bartow Station, which provided a line into City Island, stopped service in 1919, and has remained abandoned since the 1930s.

Directions: Get off at Exit 5 from the Hutchinson River Parkway. When you come to the Bartow-Pell Circle, drive southwest on Shore Road for 0.3 mile and turn right into the Bronx Equestrian Center.

From the center, follow the bike path north for ~0.2 mile. A white-colored spur path leads to the area of the old Bartow Station, which will be in the woods off to your left, 40 feet east of the Amtrak Railroad line.

175

Return to the bike path and continue north, carefully crossing over the west side of the Bartow-Pell Traffic Circle. Immediately, bear left onto the Split Rock Trail. On the other side of the Amtrak line, turn left onto a spur path that takes you south towards the Hutchinson River. You will probably have to bushwhack along the Hutchinson River shoreline, where hopefully surviving potholes can be found. I make no guarantees on this one.

Resources: Lloyd Ultan, *The Northern Borough: A History of the Bronx* (The Bronx, NY: The Bronx Historical Society, 2009), 3
atlasobscura.com/places/bartow-station.
scenesfromthetrail.com/2017/04/14/bartow-station-ruins-bronx-ny.
John McNamara, *History in Asphalt: The Origin of Bronx Street Names and Place Names* (Harrison, NY: The Bronx Historical Society, 1978), 160.

Hutchinson River Parkway. Old postcard.

NASSAU COUNTY

73. EXECUTION ROCK

Type of Formation: Historic Rock
WOW Factor: 2–3
Location: Larchmont (Nassau County/Westchester County)
Tenth Edition, NYS Atlas & Gazetteer: p. 111, C8; **Earlier Edition NYS Atlas & Gazetteer**: p. 25, AB6
Execution Rock GPS Coordinates: 40º52.681'N 73º44.261'W
Evers Marina GPS Coordinates: 40º50.688'N 73º48.895'W
Accessibility: >6.0-mile boat trip from Eastchester Bay
Degree of Difficulty: Easy by boat
Additional Information: Evers Marina, 1470 Outlook Avenue, Bronx 10465; (718) 863-9111

Description: A field of small-to-medium-sized rocks and boulders virtually surrounds Execution Rock and its lighthouse. The boulders would undoubtedly go unnoticed were it not for the fact that legend and myth also surround the rocks, just as the rocks, in turn, surround the lighthouse.

History: According to legend, the boulders along the island achieved notoriety when the British would chain condemned prisoners to the rocks during low tide, and drown them as the tide came in.

It's more likely, however, that the island and its submerged rocks got its name from posing a serious hazard to passing ships, doing more than its share to drown those unfortunate enough to run into the low-lying rocks. Folks at nearby Sands Point (then known as Cow Neck) called the island Executioner's Rock.

The granite, 55-foot-high lighthouse on Execution Rock was constructed in 1849, followed by the light-keeper's house in 1867. The lighthouse was automated in 1979, no longer requiring personnel living on the island to maintain it.

I have read that Execution Rock is now a Bed & Breakfast for tourists looking for a once-in-a-lifetime experience. My wife, Barbara Delaney, and I stayed overnight at the Saugerties Lighthouse on the

Hudson River years ago, and this kind of experience is one that is well worth trying.

Execution Rock Lighthouse. Old postcard.

Directions: Execution Rock lies ~1.0 mile across the water from the Sands Point shoreline. It is visible from the shore, but obviously at some distance away.

Water route – Realistically, the only way to access Execution Rock is by water. One way of doing so is to take a 6.0-mile boat trek from Evers Marina, which is located in Eastchester Bay.

To get to the marina -- From Eastchester (junction of Griswold Road and Macdonough Place), drive east on Griswold Road for 0.5 mile, and then turn right onto Outlook Avenue. Evers Marina will be immediately on your left.

Additional Offshore Rocks – There are many named rocks in the waters around New York City, Long Island, and Staten Island. The following represent a mere sample of possibilities if you wish to get out and visit them by boat: *Jones Rocks* (40º59.301'N 73º38.092'W), *Grassy Rocks* (40º59.438'N 73º38.851'W), *Channel Rocks* (40º59.125'N 73º39.235'W), *Great Captain Rocks* (40º59.030'N 73º39.025'W), *Red Rocks* (41º00.391'N 73º36.746'W), *Pecks Rocks* (41º00.818'N 73º36.201'W), *Hitchcock Rocks* (41º00.632'N 73º36.259'W), *Salt Rock* (41º00.617'N 73º35.817'W), *Cove Rock* (41º00.528'N 73º35.331'W),

178

Woolsey Rock (41º00.031'N 73º33.912'W), *Highwater Rock* (41º01.116'N 73º32.518'W), *Flathead Rock* (41º01.396'N 73º32.772'W), *Bold Rock* (41º01.833'N 73º29.584'W), *Yellow Rock* (41º02.960'N 73º24.872'W), *Old Baldy* (41º02.698'N 73º25.544'W), *Copps Rocks* (41º03.558'N 73º22.855'W), *Beers Rocks* (41º03.857'N 73º22.760'W), *Chimon Rock* (41º04.015'N 73º22.921'W), *Dunder Rock* (41º04.626'N 73º20.942'W), *Haycock Rock* (41º04.834'N 73º21.498'W), *Big Boil* (41º14.115'N 72º54.148'W), and *The Chimney* (41º14.186'N 72º53.755'W).

Resources: scoutingny.com/a-trip-to-execution-rocks.
knowledgenuts.com/2014/02/22/the-creepy-bloody-history-of-execution-rocks.
lighthousefriends.com/light.asp?ID=749.
Richard M. Lederer, Jr., *The Place-Names of Westchester County, New York: Expanded Version* (Harrison, NY: Harbor Hill Books, 1980), 47.
Frances Meyer Lawrence, "The Story of a Rock," *The Nassau County Historical Journal* Vol. XV, no. 1 (Spring, 1954), 21–24.

74. SANDS POINT PRESERVE BOULDERS
Sands Point Preserve

Type of Formation: Medium-sized Boulder
WOW Factor: 5
Location: Manorhaven (Nassau County)
Tenth Edition, NYS Atlas & Gazetteer: p. 111, C8; **Earlier Edition NYS Atlas & Gazetteer**: p. 25, B6
Parking at Castle Gould GPS Coordinates: 40º51.693'N 73º41.908'W
Destinations GPS Coordinates: *Boulders in general* -- 40º51.822'N 73º41.824'W and 40º51.622'N 73º41.147'W; *Pond Boulder* -- 40º51.740'N 73º41.810'W*; Hen Boulder with 6 Chicks* -- 40º51.623'N 73º41.048'W (a guesstimate)
Fee: Modest admission fee charged
Accessibility: 1.0-mile trek along beach
Degree of Difficulty: Moderately easy
Additional Information: Sands Point Preserve Conservancy, 127 Middle Neck Road, Sands Point, NY 11050; (516) 571-7901.
sandspointpreserveconservancy.org/wp-content/uploads/2017/06/
Sands-Point-Preserve-Map.pdf – map of preserve

Rock Walks

Description: *Sands Point Preserve Boulders*– Dozens of large, 20-foot-high boulders are contained in the 216-acre Sands Point Preserve.

Sands Point Giant is a large, 17-foot-high, 20-40-foot-long boulder that is located on a private estate at Sands Point. It was first reported by Samuel L. Mitchill in 1800.

Hen Boulder (49x39x8) with 6 chicks (12–16 feet) – These rocks are located just offshore southeast of "Falaise" (the historic Guggenheim mansion), lying in shallow water. Unfortunately, they are only visible at low tide. Geologists believe that the rocks were at one time one large supergiant until the boulder broke up.

History: Sands Point is named after Captain John Sands, who visited the area in 1695.

The preserve is the former estate of railroad magnate Jay Gould, who purchased the land in 1900–1901. He subsequently built two enormous mansions on the property in an effort to please his wife, Katherine Clemmons. In this he was not successful, for the two divorced after Clemmons allegedly had an affair with William F. Cody, better known as Buffalo Bill.

The land was subsequently purchased in 1917 by mining tycoon Daniel Guggenheim. His son, Harry, built a mansion on a bluff overlooking Long Island Sound and called his estate Falaise (French for "cliff").

When Daniel Guggenheim died in 1930, his wife, Florence, built a smaller mansion on the property and called it Mille Fleurs.

It seems fair to say that this was a family of mansion builders.

The story of ownership and usage gets somewhat complicated from here (as if it wasn't already), so we'll just skip to the part where Nassau County acquired 127 acres of prime land in 1971, including the former Gould/Guggenheim estate, which became as a museum. All of this, today, is the Sands Point Preserve.

Directions: Driving west along the Long Island Expressway (I-495), get off at Exit 36 for Searingtown Road & Rock Shelter Road and at a traffic light, turn right onto Searingtown Road/Route 101.

Rock Walks

Driving east along the Long Island Expressway (I-495), get off at Exit 36 for Searingtown Road and Port Washington, and then turn left onto Searingtown Road/Route 101.

Head north on Searingtown Road/Route 101 (which changes along the way to Port Washington Boulevard, and then Middle Neck Road) for ~6.0 miles. Eventually, you will see signs for the preserve. Turn right and park in the area for Castle Gould.

To reach the Pond Boulder, walk east from the parking lot. You will quickly come to the pond, where a good-sized boulder can be seen along the east side.

From here, a road leads northwest down to the beach, where you can walk southeast along the shoreline for ~1.0 mile to see a number of medium-to- large-sized boulders. What I'm guessing to be the location of the Hen Boulder with 6 Chicks is ~0.7 mile along the beach.

Resources: sandspointpreserveconservancy.org. alltrails.com/trail/us/new-york/sands-point-preserve-loop-trail. sandspointpreserveconservancy.org/about/mission-history. geo.sunysb.edu/lig/Conferences/abstracts17/Mills.pdf – Herbert C. Mills, Allan J. Lindberg, Lois A. Lindberg, "Distribution of Large Glacial Erratic Boulders on the North Shore of Nassau County, New York" (Nassau County Division of Museums & Preserves (Ret).

75. COUNCIL ROCK

Type of Formation: Large Boulder
WOW Factor: 3
Location: Oyster Bay (Nassau County)
Tenth Edition, NYS Atlas & Gazetteer: p. 111, C10; **Earlier Edition NYS Atlas & Gazetteer**: p. 25, AB7
Council Rock GPS Coordinates: 40º52.427'N 73º32.480'W
Accessibility: Roadside
Degree of Difficulty: Easy

Description: Council Rock is a medium-to-large-sized boulder that lies across from 0.2-mile long Mill Pond, just uphill from Lake

Avenue. An historic marker, erected next to the rock in 1939, tells the story of the boulder's history.

History: Council Rock was the location of a sacred council fire and a gathering site for the Matinecock (a tribe of skilled hunters and fishermen).

George Fox, who was the founder of the "Society of Friends," is said to have used this huge rock in 1672 to preach at a four-day-long meeting.

An inscription on the rock reads: Council Rock/ Here George Fox 1672 met with/ Wrights, Underhill and Feeke/ at a Quaker Meeting."

Directions: At the village of Oyster Bay (junction of Route 106/South Street and West Main Street), turn left onto West Main Street and drive west for 0.6 mile. Then turn left onto Lake Avenue and head south for 300 feet. Council Rock is on the right side of the road.

Council Rock (Wikipedia).

Resources: Raymond E. Spinzia, Judith A. Spinzia & Kathryn E. Spinzia, *Long Island: A Guide to New York's Suffolk and Nassau Counties* (NY: Hippocrene Books, 1991), 393.
en.wikipedia.org/wiki/Council_Rock_(Oyster_Bay,_New_York).
en.advisor.travel/poi/Council-Rock-Oyster-Bay-New-York-16199.
dictionary.sensagent.com/Council_Rock_(Oyster_Bay,_New_York)/en-en
– This site contains a fair amount of history about George Fox.
Mary K. Peters, "Address at the unveiling of a tablet to George Fox at Council Rock" *The Nassau County Historical Journal* Vol. V, no. 1 (March, 1942), 26 & 27. Background information is provided on George Fox.

76. SHELTER ROCK

Type of Formation: Large Boulder
WOW Factor: 5
Location: Manhasset (Nassau County)
Tenth Edition, NYS Atlas & Gazetteer: p. 111, D8; **Earlier Edition NYS Atlas & Gazetteer**: p. 25, B6
Estimated Shelter Rock GPS Coordinates: 40º47.350'N 73º41.463'W
Accessibility: Roadside. A limited view of the boulder can be obtained through a chain-link fence; otherwise, the rock is inaccessible.
Degree of Difficulty: Easy

Description: Shelter Rock, aka Manhasset Rock and Milestone Rock, is a massive, granite boulder, with a 30-foot overhang, reputedly weighing up to 1,800 tons. It is roughly 55 feet high and 35 feet wide.

History: A roadside sign near the boulder states that Shelter Rock was used for shelter by Native Americans (this was particularly true of the Matinecock tribe), as far back as 1,000 BC.

The site was excavated in 1946 by Carlyle S. Smith and Ralph Solecki for the American Museum of Natural History. Numerous artifacts were found, indicating a long-standing Native American presence.

In an article that appeared in the *Manhasset Press*, Steve Mosco states that for a period of time following World War I, Shelter Rock was the most photographed rock in the United States. Tales grew up about the rock—one even hinting that Captain Kidd may have hidden some treasure by the rock.

Today, the boulder is on land managed by the Greentree Foundation—a continuation of the 438-acre John Hay Whitney

Rock Walks

family estate founded in 1903. Whitney was a publisher, and also served as ambassador to England.

Directions: From Manhasset (junction of Route 25A and Shelter Rock Road), drive south on Shelter Rock Road for ~0.3 mile until you come to an intersection. Look for an historical marker about the rock on the right side of the road virtually across from Old Shelter Rock Road. Here, next to the sign, can be seen the boulder behind a chain-link fence, 10 feet from the road.

The fact that the boulder lies close to what became the border line between Manhasset and North Hills is not accidental. Like many big rocks in its day, Shelter Rock proved to be a convenient marker for a boundary line.

It should be noted that the Greentree Foundation occasionally leads tours to the boulder for special groups.

Resources: scoutingny.com/stumbling-on-the-largest-boulder-on-long-island.
nytimes.com/1999/02/28/nyregion/shelter-rock-facing-an-uncertain-future.html.
suffolkgem.com/shelter-rock.html.
Steve Mosco, "What is Shelter Rock?" *Manhasset Press* September 20, 2015. Website version is at manhassetpress.com/what-is-shelter-rock.
suffolkgem.com/shelter-rock.html – This website contains an article by Amanda Bielskas entitled "Shelter Rock."
Carlyle S. Smith, "Manhasset Rock." An unpublished paper on file with the Department of Anthropology Archives at the American Museum of Natural History (June 10, 1946).
Margaret M. Voelbel, *The Story of an Island: The Geology and Geography of Long Island* (Point Washington, Long Island, NY: Ira J. Friedman, Inc., 1965), 39. A drawing of the rock can be seen on page 39. The author writes, "...there is a tremendous rock lying near the edge of the road...Years ago, when the road was a narrow dirt path, farmers driving cows along it would seek shelter under the overhang part of the rocks during storms. It has also been said that Indians used it for protection."
Paul Bailey (editor), *Long Island. A History of Two Great Counties: Nassau and Suffolk*, "The Geology of Long Island" by Jay T. Fox (NY: Lewis Historical Publishing Company, Inc., 1949), 11.

184

77. BIG ROCK & LITTLE ROCK

Type of Formation: Large Boulder
WOW Factor: 7–8
Location: Plandome Heights (Nassau County)
Tenth Edition, NYS Atlas & Gazetteer: p. 111, D8; **Earlier Edition NYS Atlas & Gazetteer**: p. 25, B6
Junction of The Terrace & Plandome Road GPS Coordinates: 40º48.218′N 73º42.582′W
Big Rock and Little Rock GPS Coordinates (General area): 40º48.280′N 73º42.374′W
Accessibility: Roadside or near roadside.
Degree of Difficulty: Unknown

Description: In Arlene Hinkemeyer's *A History of the Incorporated Village of Plandome Heights*, Big Rock is described as "…a large glacial deposit up on the hill above what was then the end of Shore Road." In an old photograph, the rock appears to be 20–25 feet high. Hinkemeyer writes, "We would walk down The Terrace from Plandome Rd, and when the road made a right turn there was a path that went into the woods and right to Big Rock, and right across from it was another large rock called "Little Rock." The woods are essentially gone, replaced by entire neighborhoods today.

History: The name Plandome is from the Latin words *planus* (plain) and *domus* (home) or "plain home."

Another rock was discovered in the Plandome/Manhasset area, although I suspect that it no longer exists. Margaret M. Voelbel, in *The Story of an Island: The Geology and Geography of Long Island* writes, "When some new stores were being built on Plandome Road (in Manhasset) the workmen dug up a boulder that weighed 168 tons. It was just like the rock in the Palisades of New Jersey…"

Directions: From Manhasset (junction of Plandome Road & Northern Boulevard), drive northwest on Plandome Road for ~1.0 mile. Turn left onto The Terrace, a 0.2-mile-long road in the general area where the rocks are located. Likely, the path that led off from the road is gone, undoubtedly obliterated by the construction of new

185

houses. You may have to ask around for the exact location of the rock since the area seems to be very residential.

Big Rock. Old photograph.

Resources: Arlene Hinkemeyer, *A History of the Incorporated Village of Plandome Heights* (Manhasset, NY: Incorporated Village of Plandome Heights, 1997). A photograph of *Big Rock* is shown on page 8.
plandomeheights-
ny.gov/Attachments/A%20History%20of%20the%20Incorporated%20Vill age.htm.
Margaret M. Voelbel. T*he Story of an Island: The Geology and Geography of Long Island* (Port Washington, NY: Ira J. Friedman, Inc., 1965), 37.

Rock Walks

78. TARGET ROCK
Target Rock National Wildlife Refuge

Type of Formation: Large Boulder
WOW Factor: 5
Location: Huntington (Nassau County)
Tenth Edition, NYS Atlas & Gazetteer: p. 112, A1; **Earlier Edition NYS Atlas & Gazetteer**: p. 26, B1
Parking GPS Coordinates: 40º55.630'N 73º26.303'W
Target Rock GPS Coordinates: 40º55.778'N 73º25.822'W
Fee: Modest admission charged
Accessibility: 0.4 mile
Degree of Difficulty: Moderate
Additional Information: Target Rock National Wildlife Refuge, Target Rock Road, Lloyd Neck, Huntington, NY; (516) 271-2409 in order to visit the site.
Special Use Permits are required for any activity that requires accessing closed areas of the refuge, commercial activities, research and other miscellaneous events.
Map of site -- fws.gov/refuge/Target_Rock/map.html.

Description: Target Rock is a 14-foot-high boulder jutting out of Huntington Bay, whose flat sidewall proved to be an inviting target for sharpshooters.

History: The 80-acre Target Rock National Wildlife Refuge was donated in 1967 by the family of Ferdinand and Mary Eberstadt under the Migratory Bird Conservation Act. It is managed by the U.S. Fish & Wildlife Service.

The preserve and rock's unusual name comes from the belief (probably true) that the British Navy used the rock for target practice during the Revolutionary War and War of 1812.

Directions: From Huntington (junction of West Neck Road & Route 25A/Main Street), take West Neck Road northwest for ~3.5 miles. At the end of the causeway between the main land and Lloyd Neck, head east on Lloyd Harbor Road for ~2.7 miles. As the road turns left it becomes Target Rock Road. Continue north for ~0.3 mile. As soon as you pass by Hawk Drive (to your right), you will come to the wildlife refuge's entrance, also on the right.

187

Rock Walks

A 8062 Target Rock, Huntington, L. I.

Target Rock. Old postcard.

From the parking area, walk northeast for ~0.4 mile to reach the beach, staying on trails. Follow the shoreline north for less than 0.1 mile. Target Rock is directly offshore, roughly 150 feet from the beach.

Another, smaller, offshore boulder can be seen 0.1 mile southeast from Target Rock at 40º55.711′N 73º25.797′W, as well as a variety of smaller boulders scattered along the beach.

Resources: fws.gov/refuge/Target_Rock/about.html. discoverlongisland.com/member/target-rock-national-wildlife-refuge. recplanet.com/ny/huntington/target-rock-national-wildlife-refuge. Raymond E. Spinzia, Judith A. Spinzia & Kathryn E. Spinzia, *Long Island: A Guide to New York's Suffolk and Nassau Counties* (NY: Hippocrence Books, 1991), 118.
New York-New Jersey Trail Conference, *Day Walker: 32 Hikes in the New York Metropolitan Area. Second Edition* (Mahwah, NJ: New York-New Jersey Trail Conference, 2002), 79.
fws.gov/refuge/Target_Rock/map.html.

79. CAUMSETT STATE HISTORIC PARK BOULDERS
Caumsett State Historic Park Preserve

Type of Formation: Large Boulder
WOW Factor: 4–5
Location: Lloyd Neck (Suffolk County)
Tenth Edition, NYS Atlas & Gazetteer: p. 112, A1; **Earlier Edition NYS Atlas & Gazetteer**: p. 26, A1
Parking GPS Coordinates: 40º55.046′N 73º28.377′W
Seashore Boulder GPS Coordinates: 40º56.332′N 73º28.131′W
Fee: Admission charged
Accessibility: 1.8-mile walk to shoreline
Degree of Difficulty: *Walking* -- Moderately difficult due to length; *Biking* – Moderately easy
Additional Information: Caumsett State Historic Park Preserve, 25 Lloyd Harbor Rd, Huntington, NY 11743

parks.ny.gov/parks/attachments/CaumsettTrailMap.pdf – trail map
The most efficient way of exploring the park is by bike.

Description: A number of medium-sized to large-sized boulders can be seen along the shoreline.

History: The site is the former 1,750-acre estate of Marshall Field III which he purchased in 1921. The property was acquired by New York State in 1961.

Caumsett is Matinecock for "place by a sharp rock."

The Caumsett State Historic Park Preserve is located on Lloyd Neck, a small body of land measuring 3.5 miles long by 2.0 miles wide, and connected to the mainland by only the tiniest sliver of land.

Directions: From Huntington (junction of West Neck Road & Route 25A/Main Street), take West Neck Road northwest for ~3.5 miles. At the end of the causeway between the main land and Lloyd Neck, head east on Lloyd Harbor Road for 0.7 mile and then turn left into the entrance to Caumsett State Historic Park Preserve. Drive north for 0.2 mile to the parking area, which is to the right of the contact station.

189

Rock Walks

Walk along Fishing Drive Road for ~1.8 miles to reach the Fisherman's parking area and the shoreline. Only permit-holders are allowed to park in the Fisherman's parking area.

From the parking area, walk to the beach where a couple of medium-sized boulders can be seen directly in front of the parking area. From here, head southeast for ~0.5 mile to reach the main boulder. Along the way, impressive, 100-foot-high bluffs are passed.

Resources: C. R. Roseberry, *From Niagara to Montauk: The Scenic Pleasures of New York State* (Albany, NY: State University of New York Press, 1982), 299–303.
New York-New Jersey Trail Conference, *Day Walker: 32 Hikes in the New York Metropolitan Area. Second Edition* (Mahwah, NJ: New York-New Jersey Trail Conference, 2002), 83.
geologycafe.com/nyc/parks/loc64.htm.
parks.ny.gov/parks/23/details.aspx.

Manhattan skyline. Old postcard.

MANHATTAN

Manhattan is a 12.5-mile-long, 2.5-mile-wide (at its widest) island that is delineated by the Hudson River to the west, the Spuyten Duyvil Creek to the north, the Harlem River, Hell Gate, and East River (really an arm of the sea) to the east, and the East River and Upper New York Bay to the south. Perhaps not so strangely, fourteen percent of Manhattan is built on a landfill.

The name Manhattan is a corruption of the Mohican word *Menohanet*, meaning "people of the islands." The island's main natural feature is Central Park.

80. CENTRAL PARK ROCKS

Central Park

Type of Formation: Large Rock Mound; Medium-to-large-sized Boulder; Historic Cave
WOW Factor: 5
Location: Central Park (Manhattan)
Tenth Edition, NYS Atlas & Gazetteer: p. 110, D5; **Earlier Edition NYS Atlas & Gazetteer**: p. 24, B1–2
Destination GPS Coordinates: *Umpire Rock* -- 40º46.149'N 73º58.672'W; *Cat Rock* -- 40º46.099'N 73º58.417'W; *Tooth Rock* -- 40º46.020'N 73º58.440'W; *Split Rock* -- 40º46.563'N 73º58.115'W; *Arch Rock* -- 40º46.706'N 73º58.277'W; *Blockhouse Boulder* -- 40°47.890'N 73°57.382'W (a guesstimate); *Worthless Rock* -- 40°47.898'N 73°57.271'W; *Sheep Meadow Boulders* -- 40°46.235'N 73°58.471'W (primary); 40°46.380'N 73°58.552'W (secondary #1); 40°46.302'N 73°58.563'W (secondary #2)
Accessibility: Variable depending upon where you enter the park, and which rocks you are visiting
Degree of Difficulty: Easy-Moderate
Additional Information: Map of Central Park available at centralparknyc.org/assets/pdfs/maps/CPC_Map_2014_V2.pdf
This particular map -- centralpark.com/locations/umpire-rock – shows the location of Umpire Rock.

Description: *Umpire Rock*, aka Rat Rock, is a stupendous mound of exposed schist bedrock. It stands approximately 15 feet high, and

191

extends outward to form a crude circle approximately 55 feet wide. The rock has been a favorite gathering place for crowds of people for centuries. Like *Drip Rock* in another area of New York City, it is a major outcropping of bedrock.

Close by, to the north and east of Wollman Rink, are *Cat Rock* (perhaps named in response to Rat Rock), *Chess Rock* (named for its proximity to the Chess & Checkers House at 40°46.140′N 73°58.550′W), and *Tooth Rock*. By coincidence, there also happens to be a Cats Rock in Yonkers between Sprain Road and Grassy Sprain Road. However, it is more of a bluff than a defined rock and, more to the point, is not located in Central Park.

Down to the cave entrance. Old illustration.

Blockhouse Boulder is a rock of significant size, but I know nothing more about its height or width.

Split Rock is a large boulder that has split into two halves with an appreciable gap between the two pieces.

Worthless Rock is a 12–15-foot-high boulder near roadside. A small slab has fractured off from the main body of the rock and lies close at hand.

Sheep Meadow Boulder is a large glacial erratic associated with the 33-acre Sheep Meadow, its namesake. A photograph of the rock can be seen in *The Conservationist* on page 13. Several medium-sized boulders resting on mounds of bedrock are also found in Sheep Meadow.

Arch Rock – This rock is located next to a 13-foot-high stone arch that helps form a 9-foot-high passageway. I don't have any description of the rock's size or shape.

Ramble Cave – During the early nineteenth century, a flight of steps led down from the stone arch mentioned above to an artificially created underground cave. Unfortunately, the cave was closed up in the 1920s, a victim of unintended consequences. According to M. M. Graff in *Central Park. Prospect Park: A New Perspective*, "The cave [was] sealed at both ends because of misuse by tramps. However, you can reach the steps, chiseled out of solid rock, by going south over the bridge and walking a few paces to the right; the treads pitch downward … until you stand under the immense looming rock that juts like a giant visor over the former boat landing…"

History: Bill Thomas & Phyllis Thomas, in *Natural New York*, write, "The park offers much to those interested in rocks and geology. Boulders more than a billion years old are found here, as well as some of the finest ice-polished rock anywhere. Layers of bedrock under the park, known as the Manhattan foundation, were formed 480 million years ago. It's that same rock that makes it possible to

Sheep Meadow. Old photograph.

build huge skyscrapers without their foundations giving way."

According to C. R. Roseberry in *From Niagara to Montauk: The Scenic Pleasures of New York State*, most of the boulders came from the Hudson Highlands and Palisades.

For more details about boulders and rocks in this area, consult the *NYC Bouldering Guide* by Gareth "Gaz" Leah, and *A Climber's Guide to Popular Manhattan Boulder Problems* by Nicholas Falacci.

Rock Walks

One of Central Park's glacial erratics even made it into the 2008 science-fiction thriller movie, *Jumper*. You will see a big glacial erratic near the beginning of the film.

Central Park was designed by Frederick Law Olmstead and Calvin Vaux. It remains a byproduct of the Romantic Revolution which, in turn, was a reaction to the Industrial Revolution and its despoiling of nature. The 840-acre park is rectangular in shape, 2.5 miles long, and over 0.5 mile wide. It contains 57 miles of pedestrian paths.

The northerly section of the park at the Harlem end is considerably more rugged than the southern section, rising up in places to as much as 100 feet above the rest of the landscape. The park is big!

Umpire Rock was named for its close proximity to the Heckscher Ballfields, northwest of Umpire Rock's rocky mound. Umpire Rock's alternate name, Rat Rock, came about from swarms of rats that would emerge at night and engulf the rock. I believe this is no longer the case.

Blockhouse Boulder is named for its location near the Block House, a historic fortress that overlooks the flat surrounding areas north of Central Park. The fort was used in 1812 for defensive purposes.

Split Rock in The Rambles.

Sheep Meadow Boulder – This boulder and others nearby are named for their proximity to Sheep Meadow. Initially, this tract of land was meant to serve as a parade ground. In 1864, however, it was put to more practical use when 200 sheep were brought into the park and housed in a Victorian building on the meadow. This

194

practice lasted until 1934, when the sheep were relocated to Prospect Park in Brooklyn, and then later to the Catskills.

In more recent times, Sheep Meadow has been used for outdoor concerts and protests.

Arch Rock – This rock is named for its location next to the Ramble Arch, east of the northeast end of The Lake.

Ramble Cave, aka Indian Cave, is another natural feature in Central Park, or should I say *was*, for it no longer exists. The cave (an artificial chamber) was created by the careful placement of large rocks to add diversity to the landscape. This was done after the original Olmsted and Vaux's "Greensward Plan" was implemented. Unfortunately, the enclosure began to attract unsavory characters and, as a result, was sealed up in the 1930s. Today, only the steps leading down to the former entrance are visible, and they are hard to find unless you know exactly where to look.

Directions: Central Park occupies a considerable portion of the lower half of Manhattan delineated by Central Park South to the south, Central Park West to the west, 5th Avenue to the east, and Central Park North, to the north.

It is probably best to consult a map to guide you to Central Park. My guess is that your initial approach would be either from the Henry Hudson Parkway (west side of Manhattan) or the Franklin D. Roosevelt East River Drive (along the east side of Manhattan).

Umpire Rock is located near the southwest end of Central Park. From Central Park West and West 63rd Street, walk into the park and head southeast towards the south side of the Heckscher Ballfields. You will see the huge mound of bedrock between the Heckscher Ballfields and the Heckscher Playground.

Cat Rock is just a short distance northeast of the Victorian Gardens Amusement Park and Wollman Rink Skating School.

Split Rock is 200 feet northeast of the east end of The Lake. From the Boathouse Restaurant, follow a path west to the Rambles. Look for a large boulder up on a small slope next to some benches.

Blockhouse Boulder is located not far from the north end of the North Woods section of Central Park, along a path behind the Block House.

195

Rock Walks

Central Park Cave. Postcard c.1910.

Worthless Rock is 0.1 mile northwest of Harlem Meer, a small pond, and 200 feet of West 110th Street. *Meer* is a Dutch word for "small sea." The boulder lies next to a paved walking path that parallels the road.

Tooth Rock can be found near the northeast end of "The Pond."

Sheep Meadow Boulders are located in the large, grassy, Sheep Meadow Field not far from the south end of Central Park

Resources: Christopher J. Schuberth, *The Geology of New York City and environs* (Garden City, N.J.: The Natural History Press, 1968). On page 188 is a photograph of an unidentified glacial erratic in Central Park taken by Schuberth that is believed to have come from the Hudson Highlands.
rockclimbing.com/routes/North_America/United_States/New_York/New_York_City/Central_Park/Tito___Tanya_Cave.
rootsrated.com/new-york-city-ny/climbing/central-park-bouldering.
nytimes.com/2005/09/14/nyregion/the-very-cold-case-of-the-glacier.html.
centralparknyc.org/things-to-see-and-do/attractions/umpire-rock.html.
hudsonvalleygeologist.blogspot.com/2011/03/umpire-rat-rock-in-central-park.html.
en.wikipedia.org/wiki/Rat_Rock.
atlasobscura.com/places/the-ramble-cave.
untappedcities.com/2013/05/20/secrets-central-park-waterfalls-caves-prehistoric-rocks.

Rock Walks

viewing.nyc/there-is-a-hidden-cave-in-the-middle-of-central-parks-ramble.
bookwormhistory.com/2015/10/01/central-park-and-the-long-lost-ramble-cave.
Bill & Phyllis Thomas, *Natural New York* (New York: Holt, Rinehart and Winston, 1983), 154.
James Freund, *Central Park: A Photographic Excursion* (New York: Fordham University Press, 2001). On page 62 is an unidentified photograph of a huge rock mound, presumably Umpire Rock.
    On page 99 is a photograph of jumbo-sized rocks with The Dakota in the background. This, then, would place this grouping of unnamed rocks near the intersection of Central Park West and 72nd Street.
climberism.com/wp-content/uploads/2013/05/med_NYCBG_SamplePagesFromCentralPark-2.jpg.
Edward J. Levine, *Central Park: Postcard History Series* (Charleston, SC: Arcadia Publishing, 2006), 43. A photograph of the Rambles cave is shown before it was sealed up in 1929.
dec.ny.gov/permits/56387.html – Website shows a photograph of a large, unnamed glacial erratic with people standing next to it.
landforms.eu/Central%20Park/glacial%20erratics.htm. – Interesting photos are provided.
M. M. Graff, *Central Park. Prospect Park: A New Perspective* (NY: Greensward Foundation, Inc., 1985), 97 & 98.
"A Special Section: Central Park," *The Conservationist* Vol. 28, no. 4 (February-March, 1974), 8–29.
geo.hunter.cuny.edu/research/archive/tcarboni_2016.pdf.
C. R. Roseberry, *From Niagara to Montauk: The Scenic Pleasures of New York State* (Albany, NY: State University of New York Press, 1982), 265.
Roy Rosenzweig & Elizabeth Blackman, *The Park and the People: A History of Central Park* (Ithaca, NY: Cornell University Press, 1992). The authors include an 1870 map of Central Park (pages 206 & 207) and then a modern map of the park (pages 464 & 465), revealing interesting changes.
Christopher Gray, "Central Park Indian Cave," *Northeastern Caver* XLII, no. 3 (September 2011), 89. This is a piece taken from an article that appeared in the May 26, 2011 *New York Times*.
Lee Ann Levinson, *East Side, West Side: A Guide to New York City Parks in all five Boroughs* (Darien, CT: Two Bytes Publishing, Ltd., 1997), 81–91.
Christopher J. Schuberth, *The Geology of New York City and Environs* (Garden City, NY: The National History Press, 1968). On page 188 is a photograph of an upright glacial erratic in Central Park.
Elizabeth Barlow Rogers (principal author), *Rebuilding Central Park: A Management and Restoration Plan* (Cambridge, MA: The MIT Press, 1987). A photograph of Umpire Rock is shown on Page 45 and 143.

197

81. FLOOD ROCK (Historic)

Type of Formation: Destroyed Rock Island
WOW Factor: Unknown
Location: East River (Manhattan)
Tenth Edition, NYS Atlas & Gazetteer: p. 110, D5; **Earlier Edition NYS Atlas & Gazetteer**: p. 24, BC4
Flood Rock GPS Coordinates: 40º46.769′N 73º56.246′W

Description: Flood Rock is not really a rock, but rather a tiny island, nor can it be seen today, for it is long gone. I bring it to your attention for the fact that the largest, man-made, non-nuclear explosion in the world up to that time took place on the island.

Mill Island, aka Great Mill Rock, and a smaller island called Little Mill Rock, were located in Hell's Gate on the East River, and contributed greatly to Hell Gate's notorious reputation for being a deadly channel for ships to navigate through.

History: Flood Rock (Island) was originally called Mill Rock (Island) after John Marsh constructed a saw mill on the island in 1701.

Years later, in anticipation of the upcoming War of 1812, a U.S. Army fort was constructed on Mill Rock (Island), complete with a blockhouse and two cannons.

When both the War of 1812 and the Civil War had ended, government officials determined that it was time to deal with Mill Rock, now called Flood Rock. Thousands of ships had been damaged, lost, or run aground trying to get through Hell Gate, the threat increased manifold by the presence of a giant whirlpool that frequently formed at the gateway. The U.S. Army Corps of Engineers were assigned the task of destroying the island. To accomplish this mission, they dug a tunnel under the East River from Queens to underneath Flood Rock. A subterranean chamber was loaded with ~300,000 pounds of high explosives and detonated it on October 10, 1885.

Flood Rock was instantaneously obliterated. What remained of the rubble was used to fill in around Little Mill Island, which became Mill Island Park today.

All that remains of Flood Island today, except for what's on Mill Island, lies on the bottom of the East River, a scattered pile of rocks.

Mill Rock Park has not been open to the public since the 1960s, despite a dock being present on the island's southern shore. It is presently home to nesting colonies of various birds.

Directions: Although Flood Rock no longer exists, the spot it occupied is about 0.1 mile southeast of Mill Rock Park.

The general area can be easily seen from 255-acre Ward Island Park (40°46.991'N 73°56.100'W), northeast of Mill Rock, Hellgate Field, aka Astoria Athletic Field (40°46.663'N 73°56.095'W), southwest of Mill Rock, and 15-acre Carl Schurz Park (40°46.614'N 73°56.537'W), southwest of Mill Park.

Spectacular underground detonation of explosives at Flood Rock.

Resources: Henry Collins Brown (editor), *Valentine's Manuel of Old New York* (NY: Valentine's Manuel Inc., 1927). On page 307 is a photograph of Floor Rock being blown up.
wikimapia.org/9312630/Flood-Rock-Former-Site-of-Flood-Rock-Great-Mill-Island.
en.wikipedia.org/wiki/Mill_Rock.
nygeschichte.blogspot.com/2010/06/blasting-of-flood-rock-1885.html.

82. PIER 63 ROCKS
Hudson River Park: Stonefield

Type of Formation: Large Rock
WOW Factor: 3
Location: Chelsea (Manhattan)
Tenth Edition, NYS Atlas & Gazetteer: p. 110, DE4; **Earlier Edition NYS Atlas & Gazetteer**: p. 24, BC3–4
Parking GPS Coordinates: None given. Park whatever you can
Stonefield Boulder GPS Coordinates: 40º45.009′N 74º00.539′W
Accessibility: Between Pier 64 to north and Pier 62 to south
Degree of Difficulty: Easy
Additional Information: Chelsea Waterside Park, 185 11th Avenue, NYC

Rock Walks

Description: A number of large, quarried rocks have been placed in Stonefield for artistic purposes, the tallest stone being at least 10 feet in height.

History: Stonefield is part of the 550-acre Hudson River Park which includes the Chelsea Waterside Park.

The stones used for Stonefield were taken from quarries in New York State and at northeast Pennsylvania, and chosen for their shape, size, and color.

The landscape was created by artist Meg Webster. Piers 62, 63, and 64 were designed by Michael Van Valkenburgh.

All of these artistic renderings were made possible through the Hudson River Park Trust, a state-created entity that oversees the planning, design, construction, and maintenance of the waterfront park.

Chelsea was given its name by British Major Thomas Clarke, who brought the land in 1750. Interestingly, Clarke was the grandfather of Clement Clarke Moore, author of the famous "'Twas the Night Before Christmas."

The Chelsea piers were used extensively as ports for ocean liners, particularly so during the 1920s up to the mid-1940s.

Directions: The stones are part of the Chelsea Waterside Park by the junction of 11th Avenue and W 23rd Street. Park wherever you can – This is Manhattan after all.

Resources: hudsonriverpark.org/explore-the-park/art/stonefield.
offbeatnewyork.com/tji-hudson-river-park-chelsea-piers-expands.html.
Sanna Feirstein, *Naming New York Manhattan Places & How They Got Their Names* (NY: New York University Press, 2001), 95.
Capt. Stanley Wilcox & H. W. Van Loan, *The Hudson from Troy to the Battery* (Philmont, NY: Riverview Publishing, 2011), 138.

Rock Walks

83. THE POINT OF ROCKS

St. Nicholas Park

Type of Formation: Historic Rock Bluff
WOW Factor: 3
Location: Central Harlem (Manhattan)
Tenth Edition, NYS Atlas & Gazetteer: p. 110, D5; **Earlier Edition NYS Atlas & Gazetteer**: p. 24, AB2
St. Nicholas Park GPS Coordinates: 40º49.011'N 73º56.950'W
Estimated Point of Rocks GPS Coordinates: 40º48.776'N 73º57.059'W
Accessibility: Roadside
Degree of Difficulty: Easy
Additional Information: A general map of the park is can be found at stnicholaspark.wordpress.com/history/parkmap/

Description: The Point of Rocks is a small rocky bluff, fairly undistinguished except for its history. I don't know if it exists in its original form. Possibly it has been modified structurally over the last two hundred years.

History: It was while standing on top of The Point of Rocks that General George Washington successfully directed his forces to outmaneuver Lord Howe's British forces at the Battle of Harlem Heights.

The 23-acre St. Nicholas Park, which is what some might call a "ribbon park" due to its narrow length, was designed by Samuel Parsons, Jr. to preserve "the rugged qualities of the natural landscape," and built in 1895.

Directions: St. Nicholas Park goes from West 128th Street to West 141st Street. It lies somewhat midway between the Henry Hudson Parkway and the Harlem River Drive, around seventeen blocks north of Central Park. Because there's no simple way to get to the park, I would suggest using a map of Manhattan or MapQuest to guide you there.

The Point of Rocks is located near the southeastern corner of the park by the junction of St. Nicholas Avenue and 129th Street.

Rock Walks

The Point of Rocks. Old photograph.

Resources: William Pennington Toler and Harmon De Pau Nutting, *New Harlem Past and Present* (NY: New Harlem Publishing Company, 1903). nycgovparks.org/parks/st-nicholas-park/history. stnicholasparknyc.org/about-the-park. nyc.gov/html/edc/pdf/greenway_mapside.pdf. Sanna Feirstein, *Naming New York Manhattan Places & How They Got Their Names* (NY: New York University Press, 2001), 165. Erik K. Washington, *Manhattanville Old Heart of West Harlem: Images of America* (Charleston, SC: Arcadia Publishing, 2002). A photograph of Point of Rocks is shown on page 74. Andrew S. Dolkart & Gretchen S. Sorin, *Touring Historic Harlem: Four Walks in Northern Manhattan* (NY: New York Landmark Conservancy, 1997), 97. A photograph of the park can be seen on page 98. Carl Horton Pierce, *New Harlem Past and Present* (NY: New Harlem Publishing Company, 19030. A photo of the rocks is shown on an insert between pages 258 and 259.

QUEENS

Queens is the easternmost and largest of the five boroughs of New York City. Its northern portion consists of a rolling landscape, but with no hills of any particularly height. The boulders found are mostly granite.

In the southern portion of the borough, there are virtually no rocks of any significant size.

84. GIANT ROCK

Type of Formation: Large Boulder
WOW Factor: 7
Location: East Elmhurst (Queens)
Tenth Edition, NYS Atlas & Gazetteer: p. 111, D6; **Earlier Edition NYS Atlas & Gazetteer:** p. 25, BC4–5
Estimated Parking GPS Coordinates: 40º46.074'N 73º52.039'W
Giant Rock GPS Coordinates: 40º46.068'N 73º52.047'W
Accessibility: Roadside
Degree of Difficulty: Easy
Additional Information

Description: The Giant Rock, aka Big Boulder, Pet Rock, and Ditmars Boulevard Crowne Plaza Pet Rock is a 1,000-ton, 15–20-foot high boulder primarily made up of granite pegmatite.

History: One writer has said that if there were a New York City version of the Seven Wonders of the World, Giant Rock would be on the list.

Some years ago, a competition between hotel employees at the Crowne Plaza Hotel and the Hampton Inn was held to name the rock, and Pet Rock won out. Apparently, the name Pet Rock had arisen after some children started burying their pets near the rock.

Hearing about this, the Corona-East Elmhurst Historic Society promptly notified both hotels that the boulder already had an official name, and that Pet Rock just would not do. The boulder became Giant Rock again to all concerned.

Rock Walks

Although Giant Rock has been in its current location for 10-12,000 years, it was almost destroyed by overeager developers. The first to target the rock was the Crowne Plaza Hotel. This was in 1980. Fortunately, citizens who wanted this historic rock preserved won out. Then, 19 years later, it was the Hampton Inn's turn. In the end, they also relented. Giant Rock, however, bears scars from the initial attempts that were made to obliterate it.

Today, the rock displays a plaque that reads (in part): "This

Giant Rock.

1000-ton boulder was brought to its present location (probably from southern Westchester) by an ice sheet about 10,000 or 12,000 years ago. Although the boulder is impressive, it is only a small part of the ice sheet's load. Long Island is built almost entirely of materials (boulders, sand, gravel, and clay) that were brought here by ice."

Directions: The boulder is located between the Hampton Inn and Crowne Plaza Hotel off of Ditsmar Boulevard, southwest of the Grand Central Parkway, and very close to the LaGuardia Airport.

Precise directions to this general location can be obtained from the website of either hotel.

Resources: placematters.net/node/1039.
gothamist.com/2018/05/10/photos_laguardia_airports_giant_rock.php#photo-2.
timesledger.com/stories/2017/44/bigboulder_2017_11_03_q.html.
ipetitions.com/petition/about-that-giant-rock.

85. WHITE STONE

Type of Formation: Large Boulder
WOW Factor: 6
Location: Whitestone (Queens)
Tenth Edition, NYS Atlas & Gazetteer: p. 111, D7; **Earlier Edition NYS Atlas & Gazetteer**: p. 25, B5
Francis Lewis Park Parking GPS Coordinates: 40º47.761'N 73º49.451'W
White Stone/Rock Point GPS Coordinates: 40º48.059'N 73º49.191'W
Accessibility: 0.4-mile paddle by water
Degree of Difficulty: Easy
Additional Information: In order to launch a kayak, canoe, or boat, it is necessary to first obtain a permit. For more information, consult the following website -- nycgovparks.org/pagefiles/127/Kayak-Canoe-Boat-Launch-Permit__5ade12c252c6c
.pdf.

Description: *White Stone* is a large, 15-foot-high boulder. In "The Geology of Long Island," Jay T. Fox mentions a glacial boulder at Whitestone Landing.
If this is indeed the White Stone, then going by Fox's description of it, the boulder measures 20 feet in height.

Two sizeable boulders can be seen on Rock Point (the blunted, arrowhead-like projection of land at Whitestone), one of which may be White Stone.

White Stone. Old photograph.

History: According to Jason D. Antos in *Whitestone: Images of America*, it was the white rock that gave Whitestone its name, but this may be a reference to the white limestone that the town is built on.

Directions: Going north on I-678/the Bronx Whitestone Expressway, get off of Exit 17. Continue north on the Whitestone Expressway (smaller road) for 0.2 mile. It ends at Francis Lewis Park (located at the junction of the Whitestone Expressway & 3rd Avenue). Park along either side of the street in front of the park.

From Francis Lewis Park (named in honor of one of the signers of the Declaration of Independence), it is possible to launch a kayak or canoe and paddle northeast for 0.4 mile (bypassing a number of private docks) to reach the rocks. You will need to apply for a permit to do so, however.

To be sure, it might also be possible to reach the rocks from nearby Powells Cove Boulevard (northwest of Francis Lewis Park), but a wall of private homes between the street and the East River presents what may be an insurmountable problem unless you happen to know one of the homeowners, or get permission to cross a resident's yard.

If you do paddle out to see the boulders at Whitestone, be sure to continue over to the automated light on a tiny island less than 0.1 mile from the shore. Its entire perimeter is lined with massive rocks, making it seem almost like a rock fortress.

Resources: Jason D. Antos, *Whitestone: Images of America* (Charleston, SC: Arcadia Publishing, 2006), 14.
qchron.com/editions/queenswide/it-s-called-a-great-place-to-live/article_4a3d2752-556e-550d-a969-ac5045dff5f8.html – This website mentions that the boulder is made of limestone, and located on the shore.
nycgovparks.org/parks/francis-lewis-park.
Paul Bailey (editor), *Long Island. A History of Two Great Counties: Nassau and Suffolks*, "The Geology of Long Island" by Jay T. Fox (NY: Lewis Historical Publishing Company, Inc., 1949), 11.

86. LONG ISLAND CITY GLACIAL ERRATIC

Type of Formation: Large Rock
WOW Factor: 2
Location: Hunters Point/Long Island City (Queens)
Tenth Edition, NYS Atlas & Gazetteer: p. 119, E4; **Earlier Edition NYS Atlas & Gazetteer**: p. 24, C4
Glacial Erratic GPS Coordinates: 40º45.024'N 73º56.888'W
Accessibility: Roadside
Degree of Difficulty: Easy

Description: This rock, said to be a glacial erratic, occupies a fair amount of space, but is not particularly high, possibly being no higher than the roof of an automobile. Personally, I would be more likely to call it a mound of bedrock than a glacial erratic.

History: This bulky rock, which for me remains nameless, partially blocks 12th Street, and yet has been obviously tolerated by the city, which has put up the street and buildings around it instead of blasting it to bits. Automobiles also give the rock a wide berth. The rock is partitioned off by two guardrails.

Long Island City Glacial Erratic.

Directions: Head east on Route 25, crossing the East River via the Ed Koch Queensboro Bridge to reach the Hunters Point section of Long Island City. The rock is at the junction of 12th Street and 43rd Road, north of where Routes 25 & 25A intersect. You will need to consult a map or MapQuest to figure out the best way to get to the rock once you are at Hunters Point.

What's unusual about this rock is that instead of being seen as a nuisance to progress, it has been integrated into the city's infrastructure.

Resources: everipedia.org/wiki/Long_Island_City—This site contains a photograph of the rock, the only photograph of the rock that I have seen.

Long Island City Glacial Erratic. A different view.

STATEN ISLAND (RICHMOND COUNTY)

Staten Island is an oval-shaped island, 14 miles long and 8 miles wide at its maximum, encompassing 64 square miles of land. It is the southwestern-most of the five boroughs of New York City. The island is separated from the rest of New York City by New York Bay, and from New Jersey by the Arthur Kill, aka Staten Island Sound, and the 3.0-mile-long Kill Van Kull.

Staten Island was named by Henry Hudson in honor of the Dutch governing body that authorized his expedition. Technically, however, Native Americans had first rights on nomenclature. The Algonquian called it *Aquehonga Manachnong*, meaning "as far as the place of the bad woods" and *Eghquhous*, "the bad woods." Is it possible that they held unfriendly feelings about the woods? Interestingly, the island was known as Richmond (a name imposed on it by the British) until 1975, when it officially became Staten Island.

The landscape is elevated and fairly broken up. According to J. H. Mather and L. P. Brochett, in *A Geographical History of the State of New York* (1848), "Boulders of green-stone, sandstone, gneiss, granite & etc., appear in some sections sparingly, but on the northeast part of the island in considerable abundance."

87. MOSES MOUNTAIN

High Rock Park

Type of Formation: Rock Mound
WOW Factor: 2
Location: Richmondtown (Richmond County)
Tenth Edition, NYS Atlas & Gazetteer: p. 116, AB3; **Earlier Edition NYS Atlas & Gazetteer**: p. 24, D3
Parking GPS Coordinates: 40º34.988'N 74º07.837'W
Moses Mountain GPS Coordinates: 40º35.080'N 74º07.804'W
Accessibility: Probably less than a 0.3-mile hike
Degree of Difficulty: Moderately easy
Additional Information: Moses Mountain, 1770-1778 Manor Rd, Staten Island, NY 10306

Rock Walks

Description: What's both interesting and unique about 260-foot-high Moses Mountain, aka Mt. Moses, is that it is an artificial hill made up of rock and gravel carted away from a nearby location under excavation at the time.

In many ways, it is reminiscent of prehistoric Silbury Hill—a towering, 130-foot-high mound that was created by stone-age people— near Avebury, England.

Small-to-mid-sized rocks can be seen at the summit.

There is a lookout of sorts at the top, with a small rock that you can stand on to raise your height another two feet. From the summit you can see the Greenbelt area and New Jersey's Atlantic Highlands.

History: The history of this mountain goes back to the early 1960s when New York City Planner and Parks Commissioner Robert Moses began to construct the Richmond Parkway over Todt Hill through what has become known as the Greenbelt. Rock and gravel blasted away was piled up in a remote area that grew in height, becoming known, somewhat ironically, as Moses Mountain.

Directions: Driving east on the Staten Island Expressway, get off at Exit 8, turn right onto Victory Boulevard, and go 0.4 mile. Driving west on the Staten Island Expressway, get off at Exit 10, turn left onto Victory Boulevard and go 0.7 mile.

When you come to Richmond Avenue, turn left and head south for 0.8 mile. Then turn left onto Rockland Avenue and head southeast for ~2.0 miles.

Park on the north side of Rockland Avenue, 100 feet northwest from its junction with Manor Road. Follow a path that leads northeast to the tiny summit in what appears to be less than 0.3 mile.

Resources: sigreenbelt.org/moses-mountain.
kids.outdoors.org/index.cfm?trip=C1809A3C-ACC0-6E13-B940963610533030.
nycgovparks.org/parks/R088.

88. SUGAR LOAF ROCK
Hero Park

Type of Formation: Large Boulder
WOW Factor: 3–4
Location: Richmondtown (Richmond County)
Tenth Edition, NYS Atlas & Gazetteer: p. 116, A3; **Earlier Edition NYS Atlas & Gazetteer:** p. 24, CD3
Hero Park GPS Coordinates: 40º37.830N 74º05.278′W
Sugar Loaf Rock GPS Coordinates: 40º37.813N 74º05.249′W
Accessibility: <0.05-mile walk no matter where you begin
Degree of Difficulty: Easy
Additional Information: Hero Park is bounded by Victory Boulevard, Louis Street, and Howard Avenue

Description:
According to Ira K. Morris, in *Morris's Memorial History of Staten Island, New York. Vol. 1,* there is "a prominent boulder, the shape of a sugar loaf, near the paper factory at the corner of Prospect Street and the turnpike. It now occupies a clear field, but was once surrounded by woods, and was then a point of pilgrimage for the boys of the period."

Sugar Loaf Rock as it looked before it was engulfed by the city. Old photograph.

History: During early years, Sugar Loaf Rock served as a camping and gathering place for Native Americans. In recent times, the rock became the centerpiece of Hero Park—a small tract of land that honors 144 Staten Island soldiers who died in World War I. A plaque that listed the names of the fallen soldiers was removed in the 1970s following acts of vandalism.

Directions: From the Staten Island Expressway, get off at Exit 12 and head north on Slosson Avenue for ~0.1 mile. Turn right onto Victory Boulevard and follow it northeast for ~2.0 miles until you come to Hero Park, on your right.

This park, bounded by Victory Boulevard to the west, Louis Street to the north, and Howard Avenue to the east, is tiny and readily accessed.

Resources: Ira K. Morris, *Morris's Memorial History of Staten Island, New York. Vol. 1* (NY: Memorial Publishing Company, 1898), 372.
Charles Gilbert Hine (compiler), *History and Legend of the Howard Avenue and the Serpentine Road, Grymes Hill, Staten Island* (author, 1914). Between pages 16 and 17 is a photograph of a large rock entitled "Sugar Loaf of Druid's Rock."
nycgovparks.org/parks/hero-park.
nycgovparks.org/parks/hero-park/history.

89. STONEHENGED SHORES
Mount Loretto Unique Area Nature Preserve

Type of Formation: Art Rock
WOW Factor: 3
Location: Tottenville (Richmond County)
Tenth Edition, NYS Atlas & Gazetteer: p. 116, B2; **Earlier Edition NYS Atlas & Gazetteer**: p. 24, D2
Parking GPS Coordinates: 40º30.560'N 74º13.090'W
Stonhenged Shores GPS Coordinates: 40º30.451'N 74º12.753'W
Accessibility: 0.7-mile walk
Degree of Difficulty: Easy
Additional Information: Mount Loretto Unique Area Nature Preserve, 6450 Hylan Boulevard, Staten Island, NY
Map of preserve at dec.ny.gov/outdoor/8273.html.

Rock Walks

Description: Chris Gethard, in *Weird New York*, writes that "…one is suddenly transported to an alien landscape as hundreds of stone towers, roads, rooms, and driftwood monoliths rise from the beach" at Princess Bay.

These driftwood monoliths and sculptures are the product of the creative imagination of one man, Douglas Schwartz, who has taken rock and other materials gathered along the high-tide line to create artistic works on the beach. Others have since joined in as well.

The rocks are at the base of 75-foot-high red clay cliffs.

History: Douglas Schwartz, by profession, is a zoo-keeper, but he is also an artist. His cairn-like, stone monoliths are found along the beach between Sharrott Avenue and Page Avenue.

From the late 1800s through most of the 1900s, Mount Loretto (from whom the Mount Loretto Unique Area Nature Preserve takes its name) was the site of St. Elizabeth's Home for Girls. The property was purchased by New York State in 1999 following much advocacy from the Trust for Public Land and Protectors of Pine Oak Woods, and is now the 241-acre Mount Loretto Unique Area Nature Preserve. It is owned and managed by the New York State Department of Environmental Conservation (DEC).

Directions: From Tottenville (junction of Hylan Boulevard & Page Avenue), drive east on Hylan Boulevard for 0.7 mile and turn right into the parking area for the Mount Loretto Unique Area Nature Preserve, which is by a large, open field.

From the parking area, walk past the barrier and follow the road south for 0.4 mile, taking the Beach Loop Trail. At the beach, follow the shoreline for 0.3 mile to the start of the rock sculptures.

It may be that the years have taken their toll and none of Schwartz's works have survived, or perhaps new ones have sprung up. Such things, after all, can be transitory, especially when subjected continuously to the vicissitudes of wind, rain, snow and ice.

Resources: Chris Gethard, *Weird New York* (NY: Sterling Publishing Company, Inc., 2005), 161.

nytimes.com/1998/09/20/nyregion/neighborhood-report-st-george-the-art-that-washes-in.html.
gelfmagazine.com/archives/the_rock_artist.php.
forgotten-ny.com/2007/09/mt-lorettos-rock-sculptures.
atlasobscura.com/places/mount-loretto-beach-rock-garden.
Leslie Day, *Field Guide to the Natural World of New York City* (Baltimore, MD: The Johns Hopkins University Press, 2007). A photograph of the rock sculptures can be seen on page 99.
en.wikipedia.org/wiki/Mount_Loretto_Unique_Area.
nycaudubon.org/staten-island-birding/mount-loretto-nature-preserve.

90. FORT HILL PARK BOULDER
Fort Hill Park

Type of Formation: Large Boulder
WOW Factor: Unknown
Location: New Brighton (Richmond County)
Tenth Edition, NYS Atlas & Gazetteer: p. 116, A3–4; **Earlier Edition NYS Atlas & Gazetteer**: p. 24, CD3
Parking GPS Coordinates: Park where you can
Fort Hill Park GPS Coordinates: 40º38.449′N 74º04.893′W
Accessibility: <0.05-mile hike
Degree of Difficulty: Moderately easy

Description: In *History of Richmond County, (Staten Island) New York, from its Discovery to the Present Times*, mention is made that "One of these large boulders rests directly on top of Fort Hill, New Brighton..." The park on Fort Hill is small, occupying <0.1-acre of land. Locating the boulder, then, should not prove difficult.

History: Fort Hill was once known as Fort Knyphausen, named for Baron von Knyphausen, a Prussian general who built the fort for the British during the American Revolution. It successfully repelled the American Continental Army in 1780.

The Fort Hill of today lies in an area that is heavily populated.

Directions: Driving along the Staten Island Expressway/I-278, get off at Exit 10 if you are heading west, or Exit 8 if you are heading east.

Rock Walks

Turn onto Victory Boulevard and proceed northeast for ~4.5 miles. Then bear left onto Westervelt Avenue and go north for 0.2 mile. When you come to Benziger Avenue, turn right and, after one block, left onto Daniel Low Avenue (a one–way street). Head north and you will immediately come to the southeast corner of Fort Hill on Fort Place. Going left will take you onto Fort Place, a one-way street with parking on the right. Continuing straight will take you onto Daniel Low Avenue, a two-way street with parking on the left.

From wherever you park, head up to the top of Fort Hill for a look. The catch here is that I don't know exactly where the point of access is to the park, which seems to be surrounded by private homes.

Resources: Richard M. Bayles (editor), *History of Richmond County, (Staten Island) New York, from its Discovery to the Present Times* (NY: L. E. Preston & Co., 1887), 15. Bayles also mentions that, besides at Fort Hill, "moderately large boulders, both of trap and gneiss, abound on the moraine between the Narrows and Garretson's."
nycgovparks.org/parks/fort-hill-park/dailyplant/19146.
forgotten-ny.com/2018/02/fort-hill-new-brighton – This site contains a great deal of information about Fort Hill and the houses built around it.

LONG ISLAND

Long Island was appropriately named, for it is a very long island indeed (118 miles to be exact). It consists of a chain of low hills, remnants of a glacial, terminal moraine that divided the island into two distinctive sections. To the north, the landscape is rough and broken, its shoreline strewn with boulders. To the south, the island is a relatively flat plain.

If you look at Long Island dispassionately, it assumes the shape of a fish whose tail fins are located at the island's east end; the shorter fin being Orient Point, and the longer one, Montauk Point. Or, to use an even more colorful description borrowed from Christopher Bollen's novel, *Orient*. "This is how I first saw you, Long Island...Like the body of a woman floating in New York harbor. It still amazes me that no one else sees the shape of a woman in that island separated along the coastline, her legs the two beach-lined forks that jut out to sea when the land splits, her hips and breasts the rocky inlets of oyster coves, her skull broken in the boroughs of New York City."

SUFFOLK COUNTY

Suffolk County is the east-most county in New York State, located at the east end of Long Island, occupying 66% of Long Island's surface. The other section of Long Island belongs to Nassau County, part of which has been included in a previous part of this book.

Approaching the northern shore, the ground is hilly and broken. To the south, the landscape is level and sandy, virtually flat.

The county took its name from Suffolk, England.

91. HALESITE BOULDER

Type of Formation: Medium-sized Boulder; Historic
WOW Factor: 2–3
Location: Halesite (Suffolk County)

Tenth Edition, NYS Atlas & Gazetteer: p. 112, B1–2; **Earlier Edition NYS Atlas & Gazetteer**: p. 26, AB1
Parking GPS Coordinates: 40º53.075'N 73º25.165'W
Halesite Boulder GPS Coordinates: 40º53.036'N 73º25.163'W
Accessibility: Roadside. 250-foot walk from parking area
Degree of Difficulty: Easy

Description: The *Halesite Boulder*, more commonly known as the Nathan Hale Monument, is a 5-foot high boulder that previously overlooked Huntington Harbor.

As it turns out, the Halesite Boulder is not the only significant rock in the area. In "The Geology of Long Island," Jay T. Fox mentions a "20-foot glacial boulder, ½ mile south of Halesite," which would put the boulder somewhere halfway between Halesite and Huntington. I have not been able to locate this boulder, hardly surprising given the surface area involved.

History: Nathan Hale was a colonial patriot and spy for the Continental Army who is famous for having said at the time of his hanging in 1776 (but perhaps not quite as poetically as told by legend) that "I only regret

The boulder at its original location.

that I have but one life to lose for my country."

The Halesite Boulder originally rested on a nearby beach, where it overlooked the spot where Hale is thought to have landed while setting off to accomplish his mission. A plaque honoring Hale was subsequently installed on the rock.

Later, the boulder was moved to the south end of the bay. Due to road construction in ~2012, however, the boulder was again relocated, this time a distance of only seventy feet from its previous spot. It now rests permanently in place across from the American Legion Huntington Post 360.

Directions: From Huntington (junction of Routes 110/New York Avenue) and 25A/Main Street), drive northeast on Route 110/New York Avenue for 1.0 mile. At the second roundabout, head west on Mill Dam Road for 150 feet and turn right into the parking area for the American Legion Post.

From here, walk to the front of the American Legion Post and then south across the Mill Dam Road crosswalk. The rock is to your left.

Resources: Paul Bailey (editor), *Long Island. A History of Two Great Counties: Nassau and Suffolks,* "The Geology of Long Island" by Jay T. Fox (NY: Lewis Historical Publishing Company, Inc., 1949), 11. en.wikipedia.org/wiki/Nathan_Hale. timothymaguire.com/2012/01/01/nathanhale-an-everlasting-remembrance. thehuntingtonian.com/2012/09/17/nathan-hale-rock-moved-to-accommodate-halesite-construction.

92. STONY BROOK SOUTH ENTRANCE BOULDER

Type of Formation: Large Boulder
WOW Factor: 4–5
Location: Stony Brook University (Suffolk County)
Tenth Edition, NYS Atlas & Gazetteer: p. 112, B5; **Earlier Edition NYS Atlas & Gazetteer**: p. 26, A3–4
South Entrance Boulder GPS Coordinates: 40º54.184′N 73º06.979′W
Accessibility: Roadside
Degree of Difficulty: Easy

Description: This large boulder has been described as "big as a pickup truck."

There is also another medium-sized boulder (the size of an automobile) that is next to one of the parking lots at Stony Brook. I have not been able to find it yet, but have seen a photograph of it.

Rock Walks

History: A plaque in front of the boulder provides information about its geological history.

Directions: From north of Centereach (junction of Routes 97/Nicholls Road & 347/Nesconset Highway), drive north on Route 97/Nicholls Road for 1.5 miles. Turn left onto South Drive and then, at the soonest possible moment, turn around, and return to Route 97/Nicholls Road, this time heading south. After ~250 feet, pull over to

South Entrance Boulder.

your right at the end of the guardrails). You will see a large boulder on your right.

Another approach is to follow a short trail through the woods, if one exists, or walk along the inside of the guardrail along Nichols Road for 250 feet from South Drive to reach the boulder.

The website I consulted identifies the boulder as being located near the southwest corner of Nichols Road and Stony Brook University's south entrance. This is what I've come up with, and indeed this is a pretty good-size rock.

Resources: groupfortheeastend.org/tag/glacial-erratic.
rockclimbing.com/routes/North_America/United_States/New_York/Long _Island__NY/Stony_Brook_South_Entrance_Boulder.
file:///C:/Users/Russell/Pictures/143.%20port%20jefferson%20glacial%20 erratic.pdf – This site contains photographs of two of the Stony Brook glacial erratics.

93. PATRIOT'S ROCK

Type of Formation: Large Rock
WOW Factor: 5
Location: East Setauket (Suffolk County)
Tenth Edition, NYS Atlas & Gazetteer: p. 112, A5; **Earlier Edition NYS Atlas & Gazetteer**: p. 26, A3–4
Parking GPS Coordinates: 40º56.714N 73º06.880'W
Patriot's Rock GPS Coordinates: 40º56.697'N 73º06.822'W
Accessibility: 70-foot walk
Degree of Difficulty: Easy

Description: Patriot's Rock is located in a 3.5-acre park, and serves as the park's centerpiece. The rock is about 10 feet high and 25 feet long, according to *Three Village Guidebook: The Setaukets, Poquott, Old Field & Stony Brook. Second Edition.*

History: Patriot's Rock's name arose from its role at the "Battle of Setauket." The patriots, led by Major General Samuel Holden Parsons, used the rock for cover while they fired a canon at loyalists who had taken refuge across the village green in the nearby Presbyterian Church.

Many years later, the plaque which you see on the rock was placed there by the Daughters of the American Revolution.

According to Raymond E. Spinzia, Judith A. Spinzia & Kathryn E. Spinzia, in *Long Island: A Guide to New York's Suffolk and Nassau Counties*, the Reverend Nathaniel Brewster, who was Setauket's first ordained minister, preached his first sermon from the top of the huge rock in 1665. This is obviously a rock with significant history.

A painting of Patriot's Rock by William Sidney Mount, called "The Rock on the Green" depicts the boulder as it looked at the time of the Revolutionary War. It hangs in the Long Island Museum of Art at Stony Brook [40º54.696'N 73º08.517'W].

Directions: From Stony Brook (junction of Routes 25A & 97/Nicholls Road), head northeast on Route 25A for ~1.4 miles. Turn left onto Main Street and head northwest for 0.6 mile to reach Setauket Mill

Rock Walks

Pond. The park is located on the south side of Main Street, across from the pond. Park on either side of the road.

It is only a 75-foot walk to reach the rock, which can be easily spotted from the road.

Visitors lounging about on Patriot's Rock. Old photograph.

Resources: Three Village Historical Society, *The Setaukets, Old Field and Poquott: Images of America* (Charleston, SC: Arcadia Publishing, 2005). On page 107 is a photograph taken in 1927 of a number of women belonging to the Daughters of the Revolution standing in front of the rock.
3villagecsd.k12.ny.us/Elementary/minnesauke/3villagehist/PatriotsRock.ht m.
3villagecsd.k12.ny.us/Elementary/minnesauke/3villagehist/SetauketHome. htm -- A photograph of Patriot's Rock can be seen at this site.
en.wikipedia.org/wiki/Setauket-East_Setauket,_New_York.
foursquare.com/v/patriot-rock/4fa2c2c1e4b04db7bdfee77e/photos -- This site contains several photographs of Patriot's Rock.
Raymond E. Spinzia, Judith A. Spinzia & Kathryn E. Spinzia, *Long Island: A Guide to New York's Suffolk and Nassau Counties* (NY: Hippocrence Books, 1991), 49.

Howard Klein (author) & Patricia Windrow (illustrator), *Three Village Guidebook: The Setaukets, Poquott, Old Field & Stony Brook. Second Edition* (East Setauket, NY: Thr ee Village Historical Society, 1986), 26. threevillagecommunitytrust.org/new-page-3. Julia S. Smith, "Old Setauket," *The Long Island Historical Society Quarterly*. Vol. 2, no. 2 (April, 1940), 48. "We find within the old town one monument which stood and still stands as it did, ages before the white man settled here or even the Indian social life began: the Rock, which was recently marked by Daughters of the Revolution." Perhaps Patriot's Rock was simply called the Rock before more recent times.

94. INDIAN ROCK

Type of Formation: Medium-sized Boulder
WOW Factor: 3–4
Location: East Setauket (Suffolk County)
Tenth Edition, NYS Atlas & Gazetteer: p. 112, A5; **Earlier Edition NYS Atlas & Gazetteer**: p. 26, A3–4
Estimated Indian Rock GPS Coordinates: 40°56.407′N 73°07.002′W
Accessibility: Roadside
Degree of Difficulty: Easy

Description: In *Three Village Guidebook: The Setaukets, Poquott, Old Field & Stony Brook. Second Edition,* Indian Rock is described as being 6 feet high by 15 feet long, and made out of gneiss.

History: Indian Rock's name is hardly unique or distinctive, much like the names Split Rock, Spook Rock, Spy Rock, or Balanced Rock, which tend to be generic and common in the rock community's vernacular.

Directions: From Stony Brook (junction of Routes 25A & 97/Nicholls Road), head northeast on Route 25A for ~1.4 miles. Turn left onto Main Street and proceed northwest for 0.6 mile until you reach Setauket Mill Pond. Then bear left, following Main Street as it now heads south. Go another 0.4 mile. The boulder is on the right side of

Rock Walks

the road, between Lake Street (on your right), and Watson Lane (on your left), directly next to a resident's driveway.

Resources: Howard Klein (author) & Patricia Windrow (illustrator), *Three Village Guidebook: The Setaukets, Poquott, Old Field & Stony Brook. Second Edition* (East Setauket, NY: Three Village Historical Society, 1986), 61.

95. DAVID WELD SANCTUARY BOULDERS
David Weld Sanctuary

Type of Formation: Large Boulder; Kettle Hole
WOW Factor: 4
Location: Nissequogue (Suffolk County)
Tenth Edition, NYS Atlas & Gazetteer: p. 112, B4; **Earlier Edition NYS Atlas & Gazetteer**: p. 26, A3
Parking GPS Coordinates: 40º54.316'N 73º12.517'W
Destination GPS Coordinates: *Beach Boulder* -- 40º54.648'N 73º12.643'W; *Kettles* -- 40º54.302'N 73º12.020'W (rough estimate)
Accessibility: *Beach Boulder* -- 0.5-0.7-mile hike; *Kettles* -- ~1.0-mile hike
Degree of Difficulty: Moderate
Additional Information: Sanctuary map -- geo.sunysb.edu/esp/Science_Walks/Weld/Fig_1.jpg

Description: *Boulders* -- A number of large glacial erratics (probably in the 8–10-foot range) dot the landscape along the shore and in the woods.

Kettle Hole – This 60-foot-deep depression was formed by a block of ice that melted in place at the end of the last glaciation.

History: The 125-acre sanctuary was donated to the Nature Conservancy by Mr. and Mrs. David Weld from 1969 to 1979. The Millers and the Woodys—neighbors of the Welds—also contributed by donating additional land.

The sanctuary borders the Long Island Sound.

There are other notable water-filled kettles on Long Island that are listed by Margaret M. Voelbel in her book, *The Story of an Island:*

224

Rock Walks

The Geology and Geography of Long Island: Lake Success near Great Neck; Lake Ronkonkoma in the Town of Brookhaven; Artist Lake near Middle Island; Swan Lake near Manorville; Great Pond (Wildwood Lake) near Riverhead; Water Mill Pond in the Town of Southampton; Scuttle hole near Bridgehampton; and Poxaboque in Bridgehampton.

One of the beach boulders.

Directions: The following directions were adapted from those provided by the Nature Conservancy -- From the Long Island Expressway (I-495), get off at Exit 56 and head northeast on Route 111/Wheeler Road for 1.8 miles. At a traffic light, turn left, continuing to follow Route 111 (which now become Hauppauge Road). After another 2.3 miles you will come to the junction of Routes 25 and 25A. Go straight across Route 25 and bear immediately left onto River Road.

Follow River Road north for 3.6 miles to its end. Then turn left onto Moriches Road. Head south for 0.1 mile and follow the road to your right as it heads north and becomes Horse Race Lane. After 0.4 mile, bear left onto Boney Lane/Short Beach Road. In another 0.1 mile you will come to the sanctuary's entrance, on your right.

Shoreline Boulder -- Follow the white-diamond trail markers north for ~0.5 mile to reach the beach and boulders along the shoreline.

Large inland Boulder – Instead of proceeding north at the first junction, turn right and follow the trail east for >0.2 mile. When you come to the second junction, turn left (instead of right to reach the Kettles) and walk north until you come to a large boulder.

Kettles – Follow the white-diamond markers north for >0.2 mile. At a junction, go right and head east for >0.2 mile. At another junction, bear right, and follow the trail, now heading south, for ~0.5 mile to reach the kettles.

Resources: geo.sunysb.edu/esp/Science_Walks/Weld/Weld.htm. nature.org/ourinitiatives/regions/northamerica/unitedstates/newyork/places -preserves/long-island-david-weld-sanctuary.xml. amikewholikestohike.blogspot.com/p/david-weld-sanctuary.html. nature.org/en-us/get-involved/how-to-help/places-we-protect/long-island-david-weld-sanctuary. Margaret M. Voelbel. T*he Story of an Island: The Geology and Geography of Long Island* (Port Washington, NY: Ira J. Friedman, Inc., 1965), 41.

96. SHORT BEACH BOULDER
Short Beach Park

Type of Formation: Large Boulder
WOW Factor: 7
Location: Nissequogue (Suffolk County)
Tenth Edition, NYS Atlas & Gazetteer: p. 112, B4; **Earlier Edition NYS Atlas & Gazetteer**: p. 26, AB3
Parking GPS Coordinates: 40º54.382'N 73º13.304'W
Short Beach Boulder GPS Coordinates: 40º54.515'N 73º13.095'W
Accessibility: 0.3-mile walk
Degree of Difficulty: Easy

Description: The Short Beach Boulder is roughly 15 feet high and 20 feet long, resting on the part of the beach that faces Long Island Sound.

History: The south side of Short Beach Park faces the Nissequogue River—an 8.3-mile long stream that rises from Smithtown.

Directions: Follow the directions given to the David Weld Sanctuary [see previous chapter]. Instead of turning right into the sanctuary entrance, continue west on Short Beach Road for another 0.8 mile until you come to the parking area for Short Beach Park.

From the parking area, walk north for 0.1 mile and then bear right, following the shoreline east for 0.2 mile to reach the boulder.

I must confess that I initially spent a considerable amount of time looking for the Short Beach Boulder on Short Beach at Short Beach Island (located between Long Beach and Jones Beach State Park). It was totally the wrong area. Fortunately, I finally realized my error and reoriented myself to the correct area, which is on the north side of Long Island—not the south.

97. PORT JEFFERSON BOULDER

Type of Formation: Large Boulder
WOW Factor: 5
Location: Port Jefferson (Suffolk County)
Tenth Edition, NYS Atlas & Gazetteer: p. 113, A6; **Earlier Edition NYS Atlas & Gazetteer**: p. 26, A4
Port Jefferson Boulder GPS Coordinates: 40º56.235'N 73º03.503'W
Accessibility: Roadside
Degree of Difficulty: Easy

Description: Danielle Mulch and Gilbert N. Hanson, in their article on "Port Jefferson Geomorphology, call attention to a ".... a truck-size glacial boulder in Port Jefferson, N.Y. (a parking lot was built around it, given its size)..."

Port Jefferson Boulder.

History: What I found interesting about this rock is that instead of it being blasted to bits in order to accommodate the ceaseless advancement of urbanization, a parking lot was built around it to accommodate the boulder. High marks for civic-minded Port Jefferson.

Directions: From Port Jefferson (junction of Broadway & Main Street, near the harbor), head southeast on Main Street/Route 25A for ~0.9 mile. Look for the boulder in a parking area on the west side of Main Street (710 Main Street), between Stony Hill Road and High Street.

The rock is next to the Village Internal Medicine Group.

Resources: Port Jefferson Geomorphology, Stony Brook University website:
geo.sunysb.edu/lig/Conferences/abstracts05/abstracts/mulch/Port%20Jefferson.htm.
C:/Users/Russell/Pictures/143.%20port%20jefferson%20glacial%20erratic
.pdf – This site contains a photograph of the glacial rock.

98. ROCKY POINT BOULDER

Type of Formation: Large Rock
WOW Factor: 7
Location: Rocky Point (Suffolk County)
Tenth Edition, NYS Atlas & Gazetteer: p. 113, A7; **Earlier Edition NYS Atlas & Gazetteer**: p. 27, A5
Rocky Point Boulder Coordinates: 40º57.663'N 72º56.327'W
Accessibility: Roadside
Additional Information: Location of the Noah Hallock Homestead – 172 Hallock Landing Road, Rocky Point, NY

Description: The voluminous Rocky Point Boulder is a substantial, 3-story-high rock that is historically significant, for most likely the town was named after this unusual rock for-mation. Sources state that the rock is 50 feet long, 40 feet thick, and rises up to a height of 35 feet.

According to a recent article by the Editorial Board of *Newsday*, the boulder may be the second largest glacial erratic on Long Island.

In addition, another boulder of respectable size is reputed to be in the area. In "The Geology of Long Island," Jay T. Fox mentions a glacial boulder, 25 feet by 10 feet, in the vicinity of Hallock Landing. It is smaller than the Rocky Point Boulder, and therefore harder to find. I do not know where it is at this time.

Rocky Point Boulder. Old photograph.

History: The Rocky Point Boulder has also been known to locals as Indian Rock, a name that arose when arrowheads were found in its vicinity.

The rock is on land originally owned by Noah Hallock. The Hallock farmhouse was built in 1721 and lived in by eight generations of descendants.

Directions: From south of Sound Beach (junction of Routes 25A & 20), drive east on Route 25A for 1.0 mile. Turn left onto Hallock

Rock Walks

Landing Road and proceed north for ~1.2 miles. Then bear left onto Sams Path (a road) and head west. Within 200 feet, you will see the rock, to your right, near roadside, next to a resident's driveway.

Resources: newsday.com/opinion/editorial/giant-rock-is-a-hard-case-to-make-in-suffolk-county-1.12707896.
newsday.com/long-island/columnists/rick-brand/suffolk-lawmaker-seeks-to-preserve-island-s-second-largest-rock-1.12703056.
facebook.com/groups/RockyPointLINY/permalink/913428265458151
rockypointhistoricalsociety.org/historic-sites.
Paul Bailey (editor), *Long Island. A History of Two Great Counties: Nassau and Suffolks*, "The Geology of Long Island" by Jay T. Fox (NY: Lewis Historical Publishing Company, Inc., 1949), 11.

99. INDIAN ROCK
Miller Place Beach

Type of Formation: Large Rock
WOW Factor: 6
Location: Miller Place **(Suffolk County)**
Tenth Edition, NYS Atlas & Gazetteer: p. 113, A7; **Earlier Edition NYS Atlas & Gazetteer**: p. 27, A4–5
Parking GPS Coordinates: 40º57.713'N 73º00.264'W
Estimated Indian Rock GPS Coordinates: *Possible Rock #1* -- 40º57.967'N 73º00.154'W; *Possible Rock #2* -- 40º57.975'N 72º59.650'W; *Millers Rock* -- 40º57.996'N 73º00.177'W
Accessibility: *Possible Rock #1* -- >0.3-mile walk; *Possible Rock #2* --0.8-mile walk
Degree of Difficulty: Moderately easy

Description: Indian Rock is a sizeable boulder resting at the foot of a sloping embankment.

Millers Rock is a 20-foot island of rock that lies near the shoreline of Miller Place Beach.

History: Miller Place is located along the North Shore of Long Island and contains two miles of shoreline. In the late 1800s, Miller Place

230

became a popular summer resort; later it proved attractive to seasonal residents.

As far as I can tell, the Cordwood Landing County Park is the former Camp Francoise Barstow, a Girl Scout camp that operated until 1962.

Indian Rock. Old postcard.

Directions: The question for me was how to get to the beach without trespassing on private property. The following is what I've come up with. I believe you are allowed to access Cordwood Landing County Park without a permit as long as it's not your intention to go fishing (which, I assume, it is not).

From Port Jefferson Station (junction of Routes 25A & 347), drive east on Route 25A for 1.0 mile. Turn left onto Mt. Sinai-Carmen Road and go northwest for 0.8 mile. When you come to North Country Road, turn right, and proceed northeast for ~1.5 miles. Then bear left onto Landing Road and drive north for 0.2 mile. Finally, turn right onto Pringle Road (a dirt road) at the entrance to the Cordwood Landing County Park, which a white-colored sign announces.

The shoreline is 0.3 linear mile from the parking area.

Possible Rock #1 is located along the embankment down from the northeast corner of Cordwood Landing County Park. *Possible Rock #2* is roughly 0.5 mile farther east along the beach from the northeast corner of the park.

I wish I could be more precise about the location of Indian Rock. If neither Possible Rock #1 nor Possible Rock #2 are correct, my advice is to use the photograph accompanying this chapter to find the correct rock.

Millers Rock is close to the shoreline near the northeast end of the park, and readily accessible.

Resources: en.wikipedia.org/wiki/Miller_Place,_New_York. newsday.com/lifestyle/recreation/parks/cordwood-landing-county-park-1.2070310.

100. WILDWOOD BOULDERS
Wildwood State Park

Type of Formation: Medium-sized Boulder
WOW Factor: 4–5
Location: Wading River (Suffolk County)
Tenth Edition, NYS Atlas & Gazetteer: p. 113, A9; **Earlier Edition NYS Atlas & Gazetteer**: p. 27, A6
Parking GPS Coordinates: 40º57.865′N 72º48.127′W
Destination GPS Coordinates: *Beach Boulder #1* -- 40º57.992′N 72º47.688′W; *Beach Boulder #2* -- 40º57.990′N 72º47.573′W; *Beach Boulder #3* -- 40º57.996′N 72º47.304′W
Fee: Modest fee charged
Accessibility: 0.3–0.6-mile walk
Degree of Difficulty: Easy
Additional Information: Wildwood State Park, 790 Hulse Landing Road Wading River, NY 11792

Description: A variety of boulders are encountered along a stretch of shoreline, both on land and partially in the water. According to Jessica L. McEachern and Daniel Davis in a paper entitled "Boulder Distribution at Wildwood State Park: Implications for Glacial

Processes," "the dominant lithology of these boulders is granite and granite gneiss."

Beach and boulders. From Wildwood State Park website.

There are also other boulders in the general area. In "The Geology of Long Island," Jay T. Fox writes about "2 large glacial boulders – one mile west of Wading River Station." That would place the boulders roughly near Lilco Road. Using Google Earth, I did see what looked like a good-sized boulder at 40°56.842'N 72°51.967'W. By good fortune, an old woods road/trail goes by it.

In *New York Walk Book. Third Edition*, Raymond H. Torrey, Frank Place, Jr. and Robert L. Dickinson write that "One of the largest of these erratics in the Harbor Hill Moraine lies near the Wading River marsh; it is a mass of reddish granite, originally twenty feet high and almost as wide and thick but has split into several fragments."

History: The Wildwood Boulders are part of the 600-acre Wildwood State Park, whose north side terminates at 50-foot-high bluffs overlooking Long Island Sound.

Directions: From east of East Shoreham (junction of Routes 25A & 46/William Floyd Parkway), drive east on Route 25A for ~2.9 miles. As Route 25A veers right, continue east on Sound Avenue for ~1.1 miles. Then turn left onto Hulse Landing Road/Route 54 and head north for 0.9 mile. The park entrance is on your right. Drive east for 0.5 mile to the large parking area.

Follow a 0.1-mile-long path down to the beach. Bear right at the snack stand/restrooms, and walk east for 0.6 mile to begin encountering the boulders. Some are slightly offshore, protruding out of the sea.

Resources: Raymond H. Torrey, Frank Place, Jr. & Robert L. Dickinson, *New York Walk Book. Third Edition* (NY: The American Geographical Society, 1951), 55.
parks.ny.gov/parks/68/details.aspx.
rockclimbing.com/routes/North_America/United_States/New_York/Long _Island__NY/Wild_Wood_State_Park.
skyandstone.blogspot.com/2008/11/long-island-bouldering-wildwood-state.html.
Paul Bailey (editor), *Long Island. A History of Two Great Counties: Nassau and Suffolks,* "The Geology of Long Island" by Jay T. Fox (NY: Lewis Historical Publishing Company, Inc., 1949), 11.
geo.sunysb.edu/lig/Conferences/abstracts05/abstracts/mceachern/jmabst.ht m.

101. HULSE LANDING BEACH BOULDER
Hulse Landing Beach

Type of Formation: Large Boulder
WOW Factor: 6
Location: Wildwood (Suffolk County)
Tenth Edition, NYS Atlas & Gazetteer: p. 113, A9; **Earlier Edition NYS Atlas & Gazetteer**: p. 27, A6
Possible Parking GPS Coordinates: 40º57.966′N 72º48.677′W
Hulse Landing Beach Boulder GPS Coordinates: 40º58.065′N 72º48.685′W
Accessibility: 200-foot-walk from end of road
Degree of Difficulty: Easy

Description: The 15-foot-high boulder at Hulse Landing Beach is made of pegmatite, which is a coarse-grain igneous rock. The boulder is directly along the shoreline, which ensures that it is constantly exposed to breaking waves.

History: The Hulse Landing Beach Boulder is found along the Roanoke Point Moraine—one of several places where glacial advancement stalled, and boulders and rocks were deposited.

Directions: From east of East Shoreham (junction of Routes 25A & 46/William Floyd Parkway), drive east on Route 25A for ~2.9 miles. As Route 25A veers right, continue east on Sound Avenue for ~1.1 miles. Then turn left onto Route 54/Hulse Landing Road and head north for 1.3 miles.

The Hulse Landing Beach is located at the end of Hulse Landing Road. The beach and parking area may be private – I couldn't tell for sure.

Should parking be a big issue, another option is to walk west along the beach from Wild Wood

Hulse Landing Beach parking area.

State Park [see previous chapter], a distance of 0.5 mile.

Resources: epod.usra.edu/blog/2007/08/long-island-glacial-erratic.html.

102. BAITING HOLLOW BOULDERS

Type of Formation: Large Boulder
WOW Factor: 4–5
Location: Baiting Hollow (Suffolk County)
Tenth Edition, NYS Atlas & Gazetteer: p. 113, A10; **Earlier Edition NYS Atlas & Gazetteer**: p. 27, A6–7
Parking GPS Coordinates: 40º58.625'N 72º42.461'W
Destination GPS Coordinates: *First boulder* -- 40º58.656'N 72º42.455'W; *Second Boulder* -- 40º58.687'N 72º42.258'W; *Southwest Boulder* -- 40º58.638'N 72º42.526'W
Accessibility: >0.2-mile walk
Degree of Difficulty: Easy
Additional Information: Town of Riverhead beach permits are required to park.

Description: A number of medium-to-large-sized boulders can be seen along the beach in the Baiting Hollow area.

Directions: From east of East Shoreham (junction of Routes 46/William Floyd Parkway & 25A), drive east on Route 25A for ~2.9 miles. As Route 25A veers right, continue straight ahead east on Sound Avenue. Drive over 6.5 miles. Turn left onto Roanoke Avenue and head north for 0.8 mile to a parking area.

Walk north for 100 feet to reach the beach. You will see a medium-sized boulder immediately to your left, as well as several along the shoreline. Follow the shoreline northeast, passing by a number of boulders and reaching a fairly large rock at 0.2 mile.

Large rocks can also be seen along the beach <0.1 mile southwest of the parking area.

Three miles southwest of Roanoke Avenue are a number of pretty good-sized beach boulders at GPS readings of 40°57.960′N 72°46.027′W, 40°57.977′N 72°45.883′W, and 40°57.983′N 72°45.846′W. All are located along the beach near the end of Edwards Avenue, where the road actually comes to the open beach [40°57.930′N 72°46.179′W]. The problem here may be accessible, which is why I am not going into any further detail about these rocks.

Resources:
rockclimbing.com/routes/North_America/United_States/New_York/Long _Island__NY/Baiting_Hollow_Areas.

103. TURTLE ROCK
Long Island Pine Barrens

Type of Formation: Large Boulder
WOW Factor: 6
Location: Ridge (Suffolk County)
Tenth Edition, NYS Atlas & Gazetteer: p. 113, B8; **Earlier Edition NYS Atlas & Gazetteer**: p. 27, AB5
Parking GPS Coordinates: 40°52.503′N 72°54.373′W
Turtle Rock GPS Coordinates: 40°52.548′N 72°54.499′W

Rock Walks

Accessibility: 0.1-mile hike
Degree of Difficulty: Easy

Description: Turtle Rock is a 10–12-foot-high, stand-alone boulder that is well known to partyers. Graffiti and broken glass indicate a long history of the rock being treated with disrespect.

History: Turtle Rock is located in the Long Island Pine Barrens, aka Long Island Central Pine Barrens, a publicly-protected pine barren which covers more than 100,000 acres of land. It is considered to be Long Island's largest and last remaining natural area.

Directions: From the town of Ridge (junction of Route 25 & Route 46/William Floyd Parkway), drive southwest on Route 25 for 1.1 miles. Bear left onto Smith Road and head south for 1.1 miles. Then turn into a sandy pull-off on your right.

Graffiti-loaded Turtle Rock. From rockclimbing.com.

Follow a well-worn path west, bearing left when the trail splits. You will reach the boulder in 0.1 mile.

Resources: en.wikipedia.org/wiki/Long_Island_Central_Pine_Barrens. rockclimbing.com/routes/North_America/United_States/New_York/Long _Island__NY/Turtle_Rock.

237

104. OUR LADY OF THE ISLAND BOULDER
Shrine of Our Lady of the Island

Type of Formation: Large Boulder
WOW Factor: 5–6
Location: Manorville (Suffolk County)
Tenth Edition, NYS Atlas & Gazetteer: p. 113, B9; **Earlier Edition NYS Atlas & Gazetteer**: p. 27, AB6–7
Parking GPS Coordinates: 40º50.970′N 72º45.420′W
Our Lady of the Island Boulder GPS Coordinates: 40º50.936′N 72º45.526′W
Accessibility: 0.1-mile walk
Degree of Difficulty: Easy
Additional Information: Our Lady of the Island, 258 Eastport Manor Rd, Manorville, NY 11949

Description: This large, 20-foot-high boulder has been turned into the base of a religious shrine, topped by a statue of a woman holding a baby—a dedication to Mary, Queen of all hearts.

In "A Study of Erratics on the Ronkonkoma Moraine in Eastport, Long Island," Diane Starbuck-Ribaudo, William Corbet, and Ann Marie Fishwick write that the boulder was first described by amateur geologist Colonel Bryson in 1895, who determined that the rock measured 50 feet by 20 feet. He called it the Rock Hill Boulder. Bryson estimated that the boulder must have been more than 125 feet by 20 feet before the rock was quarried.

Several smaller boulders are also mentioned in the Ribaudo-Corbet-Fishwick paper. Most are near roadside, none being greater than 3 feet in height. You will see some of them as you drive or walk around the Our Lady of the Island grounds.

History: The Shrine of Our Lady of the Island was established by the Missionaries of the Company of Mary.

Directions: From I-495, get off at Exit 70 for Manorville. Head southeast on Captain Daniel Roe Highway/Route 111 for ~2.0 miles. Turn right onto Eastport Manor Road and follow it southeast for over 0.5 mile. Then bear right into the entrance boulevard to Our Lady of the Island and drive south for 0.5 mile to the parking area directly in front of the shrine's complex of buildings. If these parking spaces are occupied, there are many other places to park along the drive in.

From the east side of the shrine, follow a wide path east for 0.1 mile to reach the boulder and statue.

The boulder serves as the statue's pedestal.

Rock Walks

Resources: J. Bryson, "Rock Hill, Long Island, N.Y" American Geologist, (Vol 16, 1895), 228–233.
rockclimbing.com/routes/North_America/United_States/New_York/Long_Island__NY/Our_Lady_Of_The_Island_Boulder.
Diane Starbuck-Ribaudo, William Corbet, & AnnMarie Fishwick, A Study of Erratics on the Ronkonkoma Moraine in Eastport, Long Island. On page 9 of the paper is a "Map of Our Lady of the Island Shrine with locations of boulders studied." These lesser boulders appear to be about 3 feet in height. Users/Russell/Pictures/Rock%20Hill%20Boulder%20Postcard%202005.pdf.

105. FIVE BOULDER TRAIN & KISSING ROCK
Shelter Island

Type of Formation: Large Boulder
WOW Factor: *Five Boulder Train* -- 3–4; *Kissing Rock* -- 4–5
Location: Shelter Island (Suffolk County)
Tenth Edition, NYS Atlas & Gazetteer: p. 114, B4; **Earlier Edition NYS Atlas & Gazetteer**: p. 28, B3
General Parking GPS Coordinates: 41º04.289'N 72º22.853'W
Destination GPS Coordinates: *Five Boulder Train* -- 41º04.262'N 72º22.854'W; *Kissing Rock* -- 41º04.183'N 72º23.068'W
Accessibility: 0.1-mile walk
Degree of Difficulty: Easy

Description: *Five Boulder Train* consists of an alignment of five boulders, each one containing a word of inspiration. Love, Faith, Honesty, Courage, and Humility are the themes dealt with.

The word Quinipet, from which the Quinipet Camp & Retreat Center comes, is Latin for "five rocks."

The expression "boulder train" is used by geologists to describe a linear or fan-shaped distribution of boulders brought to their present location by glaciers. In *Rockachusetts: An Explorer's Guide to Amazing Boulders of Massachusetts*, Christy Butler and I were able to draw readers' attention to the Babson Boulders in Gloucester, Massachusetts, which are a perfect example of a boulder train. The one on Shelter Island is very much like the Babson Boulders, only on a much smaller scale.

240

Rock Walks

Kissing Rock is a large beach boulder located at the end of Rocky Point Avenue, northeast of the Quinipet Camp & Retreat. *911 Rock* may be another name for the boulder after it was redecorated following September 11, 2001.

Ariel view of the Five Boulder Train.

History: The 25-acre Quinipet Camp & Retreat Center was founded in 1922. It is owned and operated by the New York Conference of the United Methodist Church.

According to Kent G. Lightfoot, etc., in *Prehistoric Hunter-Gatherers of Shelter Island, New York,* Shelter Island is "...the largest of the glacially-created islands situated in the Peconic and Gardiners Bay of eastern Long Island." It formed around 18–23,000 years ago.

Directions: There is no way to reach Shelter Island without taking a ferry or arriving by boat. If you go by ferry, either take the North Ferry, which departs from Greenport, or the South Ferry, which departs from North Haven.

Route 114 is the main highway, bisecting the island as it extends north/south.

The Quinipet Camp &

Kissing Rock/911 Rock.

Retreat Center is located on the west side of the island at Jennings Point.

241

The *Five Boulder Train* is located on the property of Quinipet Camp & Retreat.

Kissing Rock/911 Rock is located at the end of Rocky Point Avenue.

If you walk north and then east from Kissing Rock, you will pass by a number of medium-sized boulders that lay strewn about along the beach on the property of the Quinipet Camp & Retreat Center.

Resources: wikitravel.org/en/Shelter_Island – Kissing Rock is briefly mentioned.
Kent G. Lightfoot, etc., *Prehistoric Hunter-Gatherers of Shelter Island, New York* (Berkley, CA: Archaeological Research Facilities, 1987).
nytimes.com/1999/02/28/nyregion/shelter-rock-facing-an-uncertain-future.html.

106. EAST MARION BOULDERS

Type of Formation: Large Boulder
WOW Factor: 6
Location: East Marion (Suffolk County)
Tenth Edition, NYS Atlas & Gazetteer: p. 114, A4; **Earlier Edition NYS Atlas & Gazetteer**: p. 28, AB3
Parking GPS Coordinates: 41º08.358'N 72º21.135'W
East Marion Boulder GPS Coordinates: *Boulder along Rocky Point Road --* 41º08.301'N 72º21.097'W; **Heading *west***: *Water Rock --* 41º08.354'N 72º21.287'W; *Second Boulder --* 41º08.351'N 72º21.285'W; **Heading east -** - 41º08.408'N 72º20.956'W
Accessibility: <1.0-mile walk in totality
Degree of Difficulty: Moderately easy
Additional Information: Parking permit required

Description: A number of large, 15-foot-high boulders can be seen along the beach and near the stairs at the end of Rocky Point Road.

In *Rockhounding New York: a guide to the state's best rockhounding sites*, Robert D. Beard writes, "The beach also has many large boulders of gneiss rock. It is continually reworked by the waves..."

History: In the 1850s, East Marion was named for General Francis Marion, the "Swamp Fox" of the Revolutionary War. The town was earlier known as Oysterponds Upper Neck.

Directions: Approaching East Marion on Route 25/Main Road along the northeast tip of Long Island, turn left onto Rocky Point Road and head northwest for 1.1 miles. Take note of a medium-sized, roadside boulder on your right at ~1.0 mile. When you come to the end of the road, park in the small area provided (permit required).

From the parking area, follow a short path north to the beach, taking note of a couple of large boulders at the end of the stairs.

West – From the stairs, turn left and walk west along the beach, coming to two large rocks

Roadside boulder along Rocky Point Road.

in >0.1 mile—one along the shore, and one out in shallow water.

East – From the stairs, turn right and walk east along the beach. One medium-sized boulder is reached after 200 feet; a second at 0.2 mile.

If you don't have a permit, there may be places to pull off to the side of the road along Rocky Point Road, but I wouldn't count on it. Quite possibly, you may have to park at a considerable distance away and walk to the beach; either that, or else have a companion who can drop you off and later pick you up.

If you have to park miles away legally, this is one time that having a bike along might be helpful.

Rock Walks

In his book, *Rockhounding New York: a guide to the state's best rockhounding sites*, Robert D. Beard, makes a worthwhile point when he states, "Keep in mind that while the beach below the high-water mark may be public, the surrounding property is private..."

Amongst the East Marion boulders. Old photograph

Resources: en.wikipedia.org/wiki/East_Marion,_New_York.
rockclimbing.com/routes/North_America/United_States/New_York/Long_Island__NY/East_Marion.
thecrag.com/climbing/united-states/new-york/area/609826710.
skyandstone.blogspot.com/2008/11/long-island-bouldering-east-marion.html.
Frederick S. Lightfoot, Linda B. Martin, & Bette S. Weidman, *Suffolk County, Long Island in Early Photographs. 1867–1931* (NY: Dover Publications, Inc., 1984). On page 52 is a 1905 photograph of fishermen standing between several medium-sized boulders by the ocean.
Robert D. Beard, *Rockhounding New York: a guide to the state's best rockhounding sites* (Guilford, CT: Falcon Guides, 2014), 25. On page 24 is a photograph of Rocky Point beach and its large boulders.

Rock Walks

107. INDIAN MEMORIAL ROCK CARVINGS

Type of Formation: Rock Carving; Medium-sized Boulder
WOW Factor: 4
Location: Orient (Suffolk County)
Tenth Edition, NYS Atlas & Gazetteer: p. 114, A5; **Earlier Edition NYS Atlas & Gazetteer**: p. 28, AB3
Parking GPS Coordinates: 41º08.921'N 72º18.260'W
Destination GPS Coordinates: *Large Boulder* -- 41º09.017'N 72º18.143'W; *Indian Memorial Rock Carvings* -- 41º09.355'N 72º17.446'W
Accessibility: 0.9-mile trek
Degree of Difficulty: Moderate
Additional Information: Parking permit required

Description: A series of nearly 25 carvings can be seen in a grouping of boulders along the Long Island Sound shoreline. Most of the etchings are of Native American faces.

History: The rock carvings were made, beginning in 1933, by Elliot A. Brooks, a local artist and resident, to commemorate the Poquatuck and Montauk Native Americans. During the time, his outdoor workshop was called the Bear Rock Studio.

Photographs of the carvings can be seen in the Oysterponds Historical Society Museum [41º08.269'N 72º18.224'W], which is located on Village Lane in Orient.

From the earliest days on, Orient was a landing point for Native Americans traveling between Connecticut and Long Island.

Directions: Driving east along Route 25/Main Road towards Orient, as you approach the northeast tip of Long Island, turn left onto Youngs Road. Drive north for 0.4 mile until you reach the end of the road (which faces out toward Long Island Sound). In order to park, you must have a beach permit (or a driver who will let you off and pick you up later).

I don't see any places to park along Young Road. However, if you were to continue east on Main Road past Young Road for another 0.2 mile, it looks like there are places where one could park. Naturally, you would then have to walk back 0.6–0.8 mile to reach

245

the beach area, but that doesn't sound too bad, all things considered; especially if you bring along a bicycle.

From the parking area, follow a 75-foot-long path down to the beach and walk east (to your right) along the shoreline for ~0.9 mile until you come to the rock carvings. Stay near the shoreline to avoid

trespassing on private property. You will pass by a large boulder at <0.2 mile. Groupings of medium-to-large-sized boulders are passed further on.

The optimal time to visit the rock carvings, obviously, is during low tide.

The boulders can also be reached by boat, assuming that you have access to one, as well as a launch site.

To be sure, there might be a more direct way to access the rock carvings, but I don't know of it.

Resources: Raymond E. Spinzia, Judith A. Spinzia & Kathryn E. Spinzia, *Long Island: A Guide to New York's Suffolk and Nassau Counties* (NY: Hippocrence Books, 1991), 259.
atlasobscura.com/places/bear-rock-studio.
jeremynative.com/onthissite/listing/elliot-a-brooks-carvings.
peconicbathtub.com/orients-treasure-on-the-edge-of-the-sea.
eastendbeacon.com/orients-treasure-on-the-edge-of-the-sea.
myfamilybusiness.org/familytrees/randall/elliotalvahbrooks.htm.

108. JACOBS POINT BOULDER

Type of Formation: Large Boulder
WOW Factor: 7
Location: Northville (Suffolk County)
Tenth Edition, NYS Atlas & Gazetteer: p. 114, C1; **Earlier Edition NYS Atlas & Gazetteer**: p. 27, A7
Iron Pier Beach parking GPS Coordinates: 40°59.243′N 72°36.949′W
Jacob's Point Boulder GPS Coordinates: 40°58.801′N 72°39.612′W
Accessibility: *By water* – 2.3 mile-trek
Degree of Difficulty: Easy
Additional Information: Permit needed to park at Iron Pier Beach

Description: In "The Geology of Long Island," Jay T. Fox describes the giant boulder at Jacobs Point as "38 feet by 20 feet," literally the size of a garage.

Iron Pier Beach parking area.

Directions: From west of Northville (junction of Routes 48/Sound Avenue & 43/Northville Turnpike), drive east on Route 48/Sound Avenue for 0.1 mile. Turn left onto Pennys Road and go northwest for 0.8 mile. At this point, Pennys Road continues straight ahead, but leads to private residences very close to where Jacobs Point Boulder is. Access, however, does not seem likely here. Turn   right   onto Sound Shore Road and drive east for ~2.3 miles. When you come to Pier Road, turn left, and then immediately right into the parking area for Iron Pier Beach. A fee is charged to park, and you may need a permit as well.

Launch your watercraft from the boat launch and head west for ~2.3 miles. You will see the Jacobs Point Boulder, just up from the beach, 60 feet in front of a private residence. That's probably as close as you can get.

Resources: Paul Bailey (editor), *Long Island. A History of Two Great Counties: Nassau and Suffolks*, "The Geology of Long Island" by Jay T. Fox (NY: Lewis Historical Publishing Company, Inc., 1949), 11.

109. HITHER HILLS SPLIT ROCK & LOST BOULDER
Hither Hills State Park
Lee Koppelman County Park

Type of Formation: Split Rock; Large Boulder
WOW Factor: 5
Location: Montauk (Suffolk County)
Tenth Edition, NYS Atlas & Gazetteer: p. 115, BC9; **Earlier Edition NYS Atlas & Gazetteer**: p. 29, B5–6
Parking GPS Coordinates: 41º00.837′N 72º00.409′W
Split Rock & Lost Boulder GPS Coordinates: Not determined
Accessibility: *Split Rock* -- > 0.8 mile; *Lost Boulder* – Not determined, but probably over 2.0 miles
Degree of Difficulty: Moderate
Additional Information: Map of Hither Hills State Park & Hither Woods -- parks.ny.gov/parks/attachments/HitherHillsTrailmap.pdf.

Description: *Split Rock* is a large boulder that has split diagonally in half, its two sections relatively close together. A third, much smaller section of the boulder lays on the ground, broken off from one of the halves. The trail goes directly past the boulder.

Lost Boulder is a 12-foot-high rock.

History: The 1,755-acre Hither Hills State Park was created in 1924 by the Long Island Park Commission, thus ensuring that the property would not be lost to future land developers.

Rock Walks

Directions: From East Hampton (junction of Routes 27 & 40/Main Street), drive west on Route 27 (Montauk Highway). Eventually, you will pass by the village of Napeague, to your right. When you come to Old Military Road (also on your right), roughly 1.7 miles from Napeague, continue west on Route 27 for another 1.0 mile and turn left into a substantial-sized parking area for the Hither Hills West Overlook. Quite honestly, I'm not sure how much of a view there is any more due to the growth of trees and high brush.

The kiosk is located on the east side of the parking area.

Split Rock -- Follow the Parkway Trail northeast as it crosses over the black-marked Serpents Back Path (SB) and Power Line Road (PLR). At 0.3 mile, turn left onto the yellow-marked Split Rock Road and head northwest for another 0.5 mile to reach Split Rock.

Lost Boulder – Although the Lost Boulder Trail is listed on the park map, and therefore provides a general clue as to the boulder's location, the fact that there is a Lost Boulder Trail is unlikely to be noticed by most readers since only the initials PP/LB (LB for "Lost Boulder") are provided. No indication is made as to where the boulder might be. What I am able to provide, then, are just general directions. From Split Rock, continue northeast on the yellow-marked Split Rock Trail. At a junction, turn left onto the red-marked Ram Level Road (RL) and head north for 0.5 mile. At a junction, turn right onto the blue-marked Foggy Hollow Road (FHR) and proceed northeast. When you come to the white-marked Paumanok Path (PP), turn right and proceed east. Somewhere along this path, you will either pass by the Lost Boulder or reach a short spur path that diverts to it. I would imagine reaching the Lost Boulder is a hike of at least several miles.

Resources: C. R. Roseberry, *From Niagara to Montauk: The Scenic Pleasures of New York State* (Albany, NY: State University of New York Press, 1982), 309–311.
montaukvacations.com/hitherwoods.htm.
gonehikin.blogspot.com/2012/03/long-island-ny-hither-hills-and-hither.html.
parks.ny.gov/parks/122/details.aspx.
nynjtc.org/hike/hither-hills-and-hither-woods-loop#dialog-hike-description.

WEST SIDE OF HUDSON RIVER

SULLIVAN COUNTY

Sullivan County covers 997 square miles and is named after Major General John Sullivan, a Revolutionary War hero.

110. OVERHANG BOULDER
Long Path

Type of Formation: Large Boulder
WOW Factor: Not determined
Location: Summitville (Sullivan County)
Tenth Edition, NYS Atlas & Gazetteer: p. 102, D1; **Earlier Edition NYS Atlas & Gazetteer:** p. 35, CD7
Parking GPS Coordinates: 41º36.665'N 74º26.095'W
Overhang Boulder GPS Coordinates: Not determined
Accessibility: 0.7-mile hike
Degree of Difficulty: Moderate

Description: The only information I have been able to obtain is taken from *The Long Path Guide. Fifth Edition,* which describes the rock as "a large overhanging boulder" with scenic views into the Roosa Gap and northwest to the Catskills.

Directions: From Summitville (junction of Route 209 & Ferguson Road/Rosa Gap-Summitville Road), drive southwest on Ferguson Road for ~1.2 miles and park in a small area to your left.

Walk across the road and follow the Long Path south for 0.7 mile to reach Overhang Boulder.

Resources: Herb Chong (editor), *The Long Path Guide. Fifth Edition* (Mahwah, NJ: New York-New Jersey Trail Conference, 2002), 79.

111. MINISINK BATTLEGROUND PARK ROCKS
Minisink Battleground Park

Type of Formation: Large Boulder; Rock-Shelter
WOW Factor: 4
Location: Barryville (Sullivan County)
Tenth Edition, NYS Atlas & Gazetteer: p. 105, A10; **Earlier Edition NYS Atlas & Gazetteer**: p. 30, A3
Parking GPS Coordinates: 41º29.224'N 74º58.193'W
Destination GPS Coordinates: *Indian Rock* -- 41º29.241'N 74º58.141'W; *Other formations* – Not determined
Accessibility: 0.9-mile-loop hike
Degree of Difficulty: Moderately easy
Additional Information: Minisink Battleground Park, Route 168, Barryville, NY 12719 (845) 807-0261

Description: The *Minisink Spring Rock-Shelter* consists of a large, overhanging ledge.
Hospital Rock is a ledge with a rock overhang.
Sentinel Rock is a 6-foot-high, 8-foot-long block of rock.
Indian Rock is a medium-sized boulder at the start of the Old Quarry Trail.

Hospital Rock.

History: It was here that the Battle of Minisink took place in 1779 when Joseph Brant, leading a band of Tories and Iroquois, vanquished nearly fifty New York and New Jersey militiamen.

The *Minisink Spring Rock-shelter* has been used by prehistoric people for as far back as 4,000 years.
Hospital Rock marks the spot where Lt. Col. Benjamin Tusten and seven-teen wounded soldiers were trapped and killed by Joseph Brant's warriors.

Rock Walks

Sentinel Rock is allegedly where one of the militiamen's guards was killed, but this account remains questionable.

An historic marker at *Indian Rock* states, "Legend has it that the Indians and Tories of Joseph Brant set this stone to honor their dead and wounded who fell before the field of fire from the nearby plateau."

The 57-acre battlefield was purchased in the early 1900s by the Minisink Valley Historical Society. Since 1955, the park has been maintained by the Sullivan County Parks and Recreation Commission.

Directions: From Barryville (junction of Routes 97 & 55), go west on Route 97 for ~4.5 miles. Turn right onto Route 168/Minisink Battleground Road and head east for over 0.5 mile. Finally, turn left at the park entrance.

From the parking area, follow the Battleground Trail northeast to reach Indian Rock. Then head northwest, turning right (east) at a junction onto the Woodland Trail. Very quickly, another trail leads off to your right and takes you up to the Minisink Spring Rock-Shelter.

Return to the Battleground Trail. Follow the trail north, then south, as it takes you on a large loop, first past Hospital Rock, and then over to Sentinel Rock. Eventually, you will return to the parking area.

If you wish to see the quarry and its rocks, follow the Old Quarry Trail, either from the Interpretive Center or from Indian Rock.

Resources: Lawrence C. Swayne, "Revolutionary War Heroism Acknowledged" *Kaatskill Life* Vol. 22, No. 1 (Spring 2007), 15–19. A photograph of Hospital Rock is shown on page 16.
gonehikin.blogspot.com/search/label/NY%20MInisink%20Battleground%20Park.
minisink.org/minisinkbattle.html – This site includes a hand-drawn map of the battlefield.
co.sullivan.ny.us/?TabId=3195.
myrevolutionarywar.com/battles/790719-minisink.
scenesfromthetrail.com/2017/10/12/minisink-battleground-park.

ROCKLAND COUNTY

112. NYACK BALANCE ROCK (Historic)

Type of Formation: Balanced Rock
WOW Factor: 6–7
Location: Blauvelt (Rockland County)
Tenth Edition, NYS Atlas & Gazetteer: p. 110, A5; **Earlier Edition NYS Atlas & Gazetteer**: p. 32, D4
Parking GPS Coordinates: 41º03.739′N 73º56.372′W
Estimated Nyack Balanced Rock GPS Coordinates: 41º04.677′N 73º55.820′W (a guess)
Accessibility: 2.0-mile hike to former site
Degree of Difficulty: Moderately difficult

Description: Postcard images of the Nayack Balance Rock show a boulder that is about 12 feet high and 20 feet long. A. Touney, in his *website patch.com/new-york/nyack/bp--local-history-like-youve-never-heard-it*, gives the boulder's dimensions as being 10 feet high, 20–22 feet long, and 10–12 feet wide at its widest, with its southern end 6 feet above the bedrock.

 Cornelia F. Bedell, in *Now and Then and Long Ago in Rockland County, New York*, writes that "Probably the most perfect example of Pleistocene glacial boulders is Balance Rock on the crest of the hill southwest of the village of Nyack. It stands perfectly balanced and securely wedged on a high outcropping of rock well isolated from other rocks of similar form... It is, however, a practically perfect example of a glacial rock ground to surprising symmetry."

 Sadly, this grand, large boulder no longer exists.

History: According to Herb Chong, in *The Long Path Guide. Fifth Edition*, the balanced rock was removed by park officials in 1966 after vandals had destabilized it.

 In *Now and Then and Long Ago in Rockland County, New York*, Cornelia F. Bedell writes that "Balance Rock is our greatest geological heritage" — words that come back to haunt us now that the rock is gone.

It's hard to believe that an historical rock of this importance, featured in numerous late nineteenth-century and early twentieth-century postcards, no longer exists because of human intervention. One can't help but wonder if more could have been done to stabilize the boulder.

Nyack Balanced Rock. Postcard c.1910.

Was there a second rock of geological note? -- Cornelia F. Bedell mentions another rock close to Balanced Rock. "Not many years ago, Rockland County lost one of its great geological relics. Strangely enough, this second page of geological history rested only a few dozen yards from Balance Rock. The specimen in question was a large boulder bearing three or more glacial potholes—the span of the hand in diameter—of varying depths. The inner surfaces of these depressions were highly polished by the action of swiftly flowing water and hard pebbles and grit. This was a rare specimen, indeed, but that did not save it, for unknown workmen on the old Tweed Road failed to recognize its value and so the relic was quickly blasted to bits."

Unless I'm misunderstanding Bedell, it sounds like South Mountain not only lost one, but two unique, natural treasures.

Rock Walks

Directions: From Central Nyack (junction of Routes 303 & 59), drive south on Route 303 for ~1.9 miles. Turn left at a fork onto South Greenbush Road and head southeast for 0.6 mile. Then turn left onto Clausland Mountain Road and drive northeast for less than 0.4 mile. Turn left into the parking area for Tackamack Town Park.

Follow the Long Path north for 2.0 miles to reach the site of the former Balanced Rock. As far as I can determine, the boulder was not very far from Tweed Boulevard (Route 5). However, unless the site has been marked for its historical significance, you will probably hike right by it without notice.

Resources: hrvh.org/cdm/ref/collection/nyacklib/id/3140.
nynjtc.org/book/2-nynj-state-line-nyack.
Cornelia F. Bedell, *Now and Then and Long Ago in Rockland County, New York* (New City, NY: The Historical Society of Rockland County, 1968), 10–11.
Herb Chong (editor), *The Long Path Guide. Fifth Edition* (Mahwah, NJ: New York-New Jersey Trail Conference, 2002), 29.
patch.com/new-york/nyack/bp--local-history-like-youve-never-heard-it –
This site gives a very detailed account of Balanced Rock's history and ultimate demise.

113. MONSEY GLEN ROCKSHELTERS
Monsey Glen County Park

Type of Formation: Rock-Shelter
WOW Factor: Not determined
Location: Monsey (Rockland County)
Tenth Edition, NYS Atlas & Gazetteer: p. 108, E1; **Earlier Edition NYS Atlas & Gazetteer:** p. 32, CD3
Parking GPS Coordinates: 41º06.378′N 74º04.223′W
Rock-shelter GPS Coordinates: Not determined
Accessibility: <0.3-mile hike
Degree of Difficulty: Moderately easy

Description: A number of rock-shelters that were used by Native Americans from ~1000 B.C. to 1600 A.D can be found in Monsey Glen. According to Patricia Edwards Clyne, in *Hudson Valley Trails*

255

and Tales, "The largest of the glen's rockshelters was 49 feet long, 6 feet high, and 6 feet deep when archeologists first measured it in 1936." The rock-shelter was even larger at one time, as evidenced by a large sandstone slab laying on the ground that fell from the roof overhang many centuries ago.

Clyne writes that in the late 1950s, construction of the New York State Thruway destroyed much of the largest rock-shelter in the group, but there are others nearby that remain preserved.

History: Monsey Glen is a 25-acre park containing sandstone overhangs that once served as shelters for early Native Americans.

The park land was acquired by the county in 1976.

The abandoned New York & Erie Railroad bed from the early 1840s is one of the sights you will see as you walk through the park.

Directions: From Spring Valley (junction of Routes 59 & 45/South Main Street), drive west on Route 59 for ~1.3 miles. Turn left onto Saddle River Road, head south for 0.1 mile, and then bear right into the parking area for Monsey Glen.

From the parking area, walk west to explore the park, which is no more than 0.3 mile in length.

The New York State Thruway is ever-present and quite audible next to the south border of Monsey Glen.

Resources: Patricia Edwards Clyne, *Hudson Valley Trails and Tales* (Woodstock, NY: The Overlook Press, 1990), 68.
nynjtc.org/park/monsey-glen-county-park.
rocklandgov.com/departments/environmental-resources/county-parks-and-dog-runs/monsey-glen-park.

114. INDIAN ROCK & SPOOK ROCK

Type of Formation: Large Rock
WOW Factor: 6–7
Location: Montebello (Rockland County)

Rock Walks

Tenth Edition, NYS Atlas & Gazetteer: p. 107, E10; **Earlier Edition NYS Atlas & Gazetteer**: p. 32, CD2–3
Destination GPS Coordinates: *Indian Rock* -- 41º06.809'N 74º07.748'W; *Spook Rock*
-- 41º07.178'N 74º05.919'W
Accessibility: Roadside
Degree of Difficulty: Easy

Description: *Indian Rock* is a large, 18-foot x 9-foot x 15-foot granite boulder with an estimated weight of 17,300 tons. Geologists believe that the boulder was transported to its present location by glaciers from the nearby Ramapo Mountains-Hudson Highlands.

Indian Rock.

Although Indian Rock may look like a conglomeration of smaller rocks that have been somehow pushed together to form a pile, geologists believe that the rock was actually one single piece when dropped in place here by glaciers. Since then, stress fractures in the boulder, exploited by the repetitive effects of freezing and thawing, have caused it to break apart.

Spook Rock – Spook Rock is a pile of rocks—a shattered boulder—much like Indian Rock.

Spook Rock.

History: *Indian Rock* was at one time part of the Native American route that led from upstate New York down to the rock, ending in Mahwah, New Jersey, where tribal meetings took place.

Rock Walks

Indian Rock was nearly destroyed when Route 59 was under construction. Engineers wanted to demolish the rock to make way for the highway. Fortunately, a "Save the Rock" movement pushed back against developers, the path of Route 59 was altered ever so slightly, and Indian Rock was spared.

Spook Rock – According to legend, human sacrifices were made on the rock altar. It is presumably the spirits of those tormented souls that remain in close proximity to the rock today.

Directions: *Indian Rock* -- From Suffern (junction of Routes 59 & 85/South Airmont Road), drive west on Route 59 for 0.8 mile and turn into the parking area for the Indian Rock Shopping Center. The rock is located near the CVS Pharmacy.

From the New York State Thruway (I-87), get off at Exit 14B and drive south on North Airmont Road for ~0.3 mile. Turn right onto Route 59, and head west for 0.8 mile to reach the Indian Rock Shopping Center.

Spook Rock – From the New York State Thruway (I-87), get off at Exit 14B and head northeast on North Airmont Road for ~0.9 mile to reach the junction of Spook Rock Road and North Airmont Road/Highview Road. Spook Rock is in view on top of a supporting stone wall at the southeast corner of the junction.

To get to Spook Rock from Indian Rock, head east on Route 59 for 0.8 mile. Turn left onto North Airmont Drive and proceed northeast for ~1.2 miles to reach the junction with Spook Rock Road.

Resources: Linda Zimmerman (editor), *Rockland County Century of History* (New City, N.Y.: The Historical Society of Rockland County, 2002), 285. An article on "Indian Rock Controversy" includes a picture of Indian Rock when it was photographed with trees around it, as well as one of the rocks in the shopping plaza.
broom03.revolvy.com/topic/Glacial%20erratics&item_type=topic.
en.wikipedia.org/wiki/Montebello,_New_York.
pirc-ny.com/local-lores-and-legends.
"Paranormal Investigations of Rockland County" recounts several stories about Spook Rock.

Rock Walks

115. HIGH TOR & LITTLE TOR ERRATICS
High Tor State Park

Type of Formation: Large Boulder
WOW Factor: 5
Location: Haverstraw (Rockland County)
Tenth Edition, NYS Atlas & Gazetteer: p. 108, D1–2; **Earlier Edition NYS Atlas & Gazetteer**: p. 32, C3–4
Parking GPS Coordinates: *High Tor State Park* -- 41º11.478'N 73º59.371'W; *Long Path* -- 41º11.528'N 74º00.271'W
Destination GPS Coordinates: *High Tor Boulders* -- Not determined; *Little Tor Erratic* -- 41º11.780'N 73º59.275'W (Google Earth)
Fee: *High Tor State Park* -- Admission charged
Accessibility: Probably ~2.0-mile hike
Degree of Difficulty: Moderately difficult
Additional Information: High Tor State Park, 415 South Mountain Road New City, NY 10956

parks.ny.gov/parks/attachments/HighTorTrailMap.pdf – park map

Description: According to John Serrao in *The Wild Palisades of the Hudson*, "…several large granite and gneiss erratics were … dropped along ridge by glaciers, and can be seen off the Long Path…"

One large erratic rests on top of Little Tor, and the GPS for it was taken off of a listing on Google Earth. Raymond H. Torrey, Frank Place, Jr. & Robert L. Dickinson, in *New York Walk Book. Third Edition*, write, "Beyond this, glimpses can be had of Little Tor, identified by the gleaming white boulder perched on its summit."

History: High Tor State Park contains two significant peaks on South Mountain—797-foot-high High Tor, and 620-foot-high Little Tor. Although these peaks may not reach the elevation of the high peaks in the Catskills and Adirondacks, they are the two highest points in the Hudson Palisades.

Little Tor has the distinction of having been used by colonists as a signal point during the American Revolutionary War. The property was acquired by the Palisades Interstate Park Commission in 1943.

The Long Path crosses through High Tor State Park, following along the ridge line for ~3.5-miles.

259

Rock Walks

I have read two possible definitions of the word Tor. One says that it is English for "rocky peak"; another, that it is Celtic for "gateway," a place to commune with the gods.

Old tower on High Tor.

Directions: *High Tor State Park Entrance* -- From east of Centenary (junction of Route 9W/Congers Avenue & South Mountain Road/Haverstraw Road/Short Clove Road), head west on South Mountain Road/Haverstraw Road/Short Clove Road for over 2.0 miles. Turn right into the High Tor State Park entrance and drive north for over 0.2 mile to arrive at the parking area. From the parking area, follow the park road northeast to Tam's Point and, from there, the <0.2-mile long Tam's Path north up to the Long Trail. From this point, you can continue north on the Small Tor Spur Path up to the summit of Little Tor.

High Tor is roughly 1.3 miles southeast of Little Tor.

Long Path Entrance – From the entrance to High Tor State Park, continue west on South Mountain Road for another 1.0 mile. Turn right onto South Central Highway (Route 33) and proceed north for ~0.8 mile. Park in a small pull-off to your right. Pick up the Long Path, which takes you east, then south, as it follows along the High Tor ridge line.

Resources: John Serrao, *The Wild Palisades of the Hudson* (Westwood, NJ: Lind Publicatio0ns, 1949), 150.
en.wikipedia.org/wiki/High_Tor_State_Park.
palisadesparksconservancy.org/park_detail.php?park_id=8.
mountainproject.com/area/112475379/high-tor.
Barbara H. Gottlock & Wesley Gottlock, *New York's Palisades Interstate Park: Images of America* (Charleston, SC: Arcadia Press, 2007), 107. A photograph shows the summit of High Tor with a tower that was once used by pilots for navigational purposes. The tower was removed in 1963.
Raymond H. Torrey, Frank Place, Jr. & Robert L. Dickinson, *New York Walk Book. Third Edition* (NY: The American Geographical Society, 1951), 146.

116. ANDRÉ THE SPY ROCK
Haverstraw Beach State Park

Type of Formation: Historic Rock
WOW Factor: 2
Location: Haverstraw (Rockland County)
Tenth Edition, NYS Atlas & Gazetteer: p. 108, D2; **Earlier Edition NYS Atlas & Gazetteer**: p. 32, C4
Parking GPS Coordinates: 41º10.753'N 73º56.739'W
Rocky Point GPS Coordinates: 41º10.583'N 73º56.344'W
Estimated André the Spy GPS Coordinates: 41º10.539'N 73º56.339'W
Accessibility: 0.4-mile hike
Degree of Difficulty: Moderately easy
Additional Information: 200 Riverside Ave., Haverstraw, NY 10927

Description: André the Spy Rock is a medium-sized, granite boulder that rests along the Hudson River shoreline. The rock supposedly marks the spot where General Benedict Arnold, turning traitor in 1780, exchanged the plans to West Point with John André, a British spy. The words "André the spy landed here Sept. 1780" have been etched into the rock.

History: Haverstraw Beach State Park is a component of Rockland Lake State Park (which lies adjacent, directly to the south). The 73-acre, undeveloped Haverstraw Beach State Park was established in 1911. Don't let the name of the park fool you, however. It is not intended to be a secluded outlet for swimming.

For those interested in obscure historical facts, there is also a Major John André Monument on Andre Hill Road in Tappan, NY (41º01.281'N 73º57.289'W), which commemorates the site of Major André's hanging.

Directions: From Haverstraw (junction of Route 9W/Conger Avenue & Westside Avenue), drive southeast on Route 9W/Conger Avenue for ~1.1 miles and turn left onto Short Clove Road. After 0.3 mile, turn left onto Riverside Avenue and head southeast for 0.9 mile, parking in an area at the end of the road.

Walk past the yellow barrier and proceed south along the continuation of Riverside Avenue for 0.3 mile. Then follow a path left for 0.1 mile to the arrowhead-shaped point of land on Haverstraw Beach.

Entrance to Haverstraw Beach State Park.

According to directions provided by Raymond H. Torrey, Frank Place, Jr. and Robert L. Dickinson, in *New York Walk Book. Third Edition*, "walk downstream a few hundred feet" from the rocky point to reach the boulder—a walk of roughly 0.1 mile southeast from the point. You will come to several mid-sized boulders, one of which should be André the Spy Rock.

Resources: Raymond H. Torrey, Frank Place, Jr. & Robert L. Dickinson, *New York Walk Book. Third Edition* (NY: The American Geographical Society, 1951), 141.
palisadesparksconservancy.org/park_detail.php?park_id=7.

ORANGE COUNTY
Orange Count is named after King William III of England, who also held the titles of Stadtholder of Holland and Prince of Orange.

117. DEVIL'S DANCE HALL (Historic)
Danskammer Point

Type of Formation: Historic Rock Protrusion
WOW Factor: 2
Location: *Danskammer Point* -- Roseton (Orange County); *Parking* – New Hamburg (Dutchess County)
Tenth Edition, NYS Atlas & Gazetteer: p. 103, E7; **Earlier Edition NYS Atlas & Gazetteer**: p. 36, D4
Danskammer Point GPS Coordinates: 41º35.171'N 73º57.025'W
White's Hudson River Marina GPS Coordinates: 41º34.424'N 73º57.805'W
Accessibility: 1.0-mile trek by water

Description: The Devil's Dance Hall, aka Danskammer Point, was a long, flat surface of bedrock that jutted out into the Hudson River. In *Handy Guide to the Hudson River and Catskill Mountains*, Ernest Ingersoll describes the point as "a *Ariel view of Danskammer Point.* rocky headland with wall-like fronts of white rock." It was accidentally destroyed or greatly altered when The Cornell, a large steamer, rammed into it one misty morning in 1890.

History: Danskammer Point was named by Henry Hudson's crew as the Half Moon sailed up the Hudson River in 1609. Much to their astonishment, they observed in the early evening a cluster of Native Americans, painted in red, whooping and hollering, and dancing wildly around a flickering fire. It was like something out of Dante's

263

Rock Walks

Inferno. The word that Hudson's crew came up with, Danskammer, is Dutch for "dance hall" or "dance chamber."

A similar account of Native Americans participating in a wild ceremony at Danskammer Point was told by Lt. Cowenhoven in 1663.

Capt. Stanley Wilcox & H. W. Van Loan, in *The Hudson from Troy to the Battery*, state that there is wide belief that Captain Kidd buried pirate treasure on the point. If so, it has never been found despite the efforts of many who have looked.

Ernest Ingersoll asserts that "this point was the boundary-line between the jurisdictions of New Amsterdam and Fort Orange (Albany).

After Danskammer Point was virtually pulverized when a ship accidentally struck it in the late nineteenth century, a lighthouse was built on the rock fragments. It too is gone, and most of the site is now occupied by the Danskammer Energy Generating Station.

Directions: *Land access* – Land access appears unlikely due to the presence of the Danskammer Energy Generating Station which now occupies much of the site.

Water Access – For those who wish to see what is left of Danskammer Point, launch your watercraft from White's Hudson River Marina on 15 Point Street in New Hamburg. Head southwest down the Hudson River for 1.0 mile to reach Danskammer Point. Bear in mind that direct landing on the point may be prohibited or, minimally, restricted.

Resources: grahamhancock.com/kreisbergg7.
brickcollecting.com/roseton.htm.
cornwall-on-hudson.com/article.cfm?page=718.
Arthur G. Adams, *The Hudson River Guidebook* (NY: Fordham University Press, 1996), 203.
Lewis Beach, *Cornwall* (Newburgh, NY: E. M. Ruttenber & Sons, 1873), 8 &9. Beach tells about the story at Danskammer Point, and mentions how the boat captain exclaimed "De Duyfel's Dans-Kammer!," meaning "The Devil's Dance Chamber."
Capt. Stanley Wilcox & H. W. Van Loan, *The Hudson from Troy to the Battery* (Philmont, NY: Riverview Publishing, 2011), 71 & 72.

264

Rock Walks

Wallace Bruce, *The Hudson: Three Centuries of History, Romance and Invention* (NY: Walking News, Inc., 1982. Centennial edition reprint), 118. Ernest Ingersoll, *Handy Guide to the Hudson River and Catskill Mountains* (Astoria, NY: J. C. & A. L. Fawcett, Inc., 1989; reprint of 1910 book), 128.

118. LIFTING ROCKS

Type of Formation: Perched Boulder
WOW Factor: 6
Location: Sparrow Bush (Orange County)
Tenth Edition, NYS Atlas & Gazetteer: p. 106, B3; **Earlier Edition NYS Atlas & Gazetteer**: p. 31, AB4–5
Parking GPS Coordinates: 41º25.234'N 74º44.021'W
Estimated Lifting Rocks GPS Coordinates: 41º25.257'N 74º43.971'W (a guess)
Accessibility: Unknown
Degree of Difficulty: Difficult

Description: In *Hudson Valley Trails and Tales*, Patricia Edwards Clyne writes about "...Lifting Rocks, a spectacular formation high above Hawk's Nest Drive (Route 97), a few miles west of Port Jervis."

In *Underground Empire: Wonders and Tales of New York Caves*, Clay Perry refers to the rocks as "a curious cavity formed by a huge flat slab supported on legs of stone," and that the "formation consists of a huge slab of rock held up by three stone legs, forming a shelf or slit into which a man might crawl sideways."

According to Michael J. Worden in his website michaeljworden.com/stones.html, three large perched rocks form a triangular pattern, with each boulder being of considerable size. He considers the boulders to be megalithic in origin.

History: Hawk's Nest probably got its name from birds of prey that nest in the area.

In her book, *Hudson Valley Trails and Tales*, Patricia Edwards Clyne tells the tale of Tom Quick, who used the Lifting Rocks high ground as a lookout, and from it killed a party of Delaware warriors advancing from below. Clay Perry also narrates a similar story in *Underground Empire: Wonders and Tales of New York Caves*.

265

Directions: From Port Jervis (junction of Routes 97/42 & 209), drive northwest on Route 97/42 for ~3.0 miles. When Route 42 veers off to the right, continue straight ahead on Route 97 for another 1.2 miles and turn left into a tiny parking area. Look for a state historic marker on top of the stone wall.

Hawk's Nest—not the easiest site to access from the road. Postcard c. 1910.

This is as far as I can take you. From here, you are on your own. I'm assuming that the Lifting Rocks are uphill rather than downhill from the pull-off. This means, then, that to reach the top of the sloping hill will require a near vertical ascent of ~175 feet, with the first 10 feet or so straight up. I don't believe the ascent is doable for anyone other than a rock-climber.

On the other hand, perhaps it's possible to bushwhack through dense woods for ~0.5 mile from Route 42 (assuming that the land isn't posted) to reach the general area where I'm guessing the Lifting Rocks can be found, but this is something that I would advise against doing unless you are very deft with a compass or GPS tracking unit.

Perhaps, then, this trek is best left undone unless an easy way to reach the rocks become evident.

Rock Walks

Still, it's a shame, because if my (hopefully) educated guess is correct, the Lifting Rocks are only a little over 0.1 linear mile upward from the parking area.

Resources: Patricia Edwards Clyne, *Hudson Valley Trails and Tales* (Woodstock, NY: The Overlook Press, 1990), 171.
Clay Perry, *Underground Empire: Wonders and Tales of New York Caves* (New York: Stephen Daye Press, 1948), 127 & 128.
michaeljworden.com/stones.html.

119. MEGALITHS & CAVES
Schunemunk Mountain

Type of Formation: Block; Crevice
WOW Factor: 6
Location: Mountainville (Orange County)
Tenth Edition, NYS Atlas & Gazetteer: p. 107, AB10; **Earlier Edition NYS Atlas & Gazetteer**: p. 32, A3
Parking GPS Coordinates: 41º24.457'N 74º04.911'W
Megaliths & Caves GPS Coordinates: Not determined
Accessibility: >3.0-mile hike (a guess); ~1,500-foot ascent
Degree of Difficulty: Difficult
Additional Information: The Schunemunk State Park trail map is available at parks.ny.gov/parks/attachments/SchunnemunckTrailMap.pdf

Description: The Megaliths consist of large blocks of bedrock that have become separated by deep crevices.

According to Peggy Turco, in *Walks and Rambles in the Western Hudson Valley*, "The Megaliths are a group of impressive conglomerate knobs that pulled away, it seems, from the main body of bedrock." Caves, or fissures, have formed in the spaces created by the separation.

A megalith, by definition, is a stone of great size. The word is typically used to describe ancient construction work, such as dolmens (which the Schunemunk Megaliths are clearly not).

267

Rock Walks

History: The 1,664-foot high Schunemunk Mountain is the highest mountain in Orange County and also dissimilar geologically from its mountainous cousins in the Hudson Highlands. Its name is Lenape for "excellent fireplace."

The mountain created some notoriety in 2002 when one of its boulders killed a hiker and injured two others below him. It was a totally freak accident. A boulder being grasped by the lead hiker broke loose, killed him and then, rebounding, seriously injured two others below.

Megaliths. Photograph by Dan Balogh.

In writing this book, I always assume that boulders are harmless and pleasant entities that Nature has created, but one always needs to be mindful of their mass and destructive power when set into motion. In other words, be careful when you are hiking amidst boulders or loose rock.

Directions: From Vails Gate (junction of Routes 32 & 94), drive southeast on Route 32 for ~4.2 miles. Turn abruptly right onto Route 79/Pleasant Hill Road. Go 0.1 mile north and then turn left onto Taylor Road. Head northwest for 0.3 mile, driving over I-87 (NYS Thruway) in the process, and pull off to either side of the road in a large, off-road parking area. A kiosk is located on the northeast side of the parking area.

From the parking area, follow the white-blazed Jessup Trail west. Soon, you will cross railroad tracks. Then, after climbing steadily, the Sweet Clover Junction is reached. Turn left, and follow the yellow/teal-blazed Jessup Trail. Continue past the Dark Hollow Junction, which comes in on your left. Eventually, you will come to two large cairns where the word MEGALITH is painted on the bedrock

in big, white letters. A large, white-colored arrow points the way to
your right. Follow the spur trail to reach the Megaliths.

Resources: Peggy Turco, *Walks and Rambles in the Western Hudson
Valley* (Woodstock, VT: Backcountry Publications, 1996), 50.
en.wikipedia.org/wiki/Schunemunk_Mountain.
hikethehudsonvalley.com/hikes/schunemunk-mountain.
nynjtc.org/hike/schunemunk-mountain-dark-hollow-jessup-trails.
Peter Kick, Barbara McMartin & James M. Long, *50 Hikes in the Hudson
Valley: From the Catskills to the Taconics, and from the Ramapos to the
Helderbergs. Second Edition* (Woodstock, VT: Backcountry Publications,
2000), 69–72.
Stella Green and H. Neil Zimmerman, *50 Hikes in the Lower Hudson Valley*
(Woodstock, VT: Backcountry Guides, 2002), 175.

120. FIFTH OF JULY ROCK, JUPITER'S BOULDER, & SPLIT ROCK
Black Rock Forest

Type of Formation: Large Boulder
WOW Factor: 3–5
Location: Mountainville (Orange County)
Tenth Edition, NYS Atlas & Gazetteer: p. 108, B1; **Earlier Edition NYS Atlas
& Gazetteer**: p. 32, AB3
Parking GPS Coordinates: 41º23.055'N 74º03.890'W
Estimated Destination GPS Coordinates: *Fifth of July Rock* -- 41º22.840'N
74º03.734'W; *Jupiter's Boulder* -- 41º23.043'N 74º02.826'W; *Split Rock* --
41º23.699'N 74º02.254'W
Accessibility: *Fifth of July Rock* – 0.3-mile hike; *Jupiter's Boulder* -- >1.3-
mile hike; *Split Rock* -- ~2.5-mile hike (a guess)
Degree of Difficulty: Moderate
Additional Information: Trail map of the Black Rock Forest is available at
blackrockforest.org/files/blackrock/content/MapNewLogo-EC.pdf.
West Hudson Trail Map #7: Black Rock Forest & Storm King State
Park

Rock Walks

Description: The *Fifth of July Rock* is near Mineral Spring Falls, but I'm not positive if it is a boulder or simply a rocky overlook. Either way, the name invites exploration.

Jupiter's Boulder is an oblong-shaped, 8–10-foot-high boulder. Perhaps it was named after Jupiter, the largest planetary body in the solar system. If so, I'm not sure that the boulder's size justifies its name.

Split Rock is a divided rock that overlooks Sutherland Pond. According to the New York-New Jersey Trail Conference's *New York Walk Book. Sixth Edition*, the rock has also been known as Echo Rock.

Along the Split Rock Trail. Photograph by Dan Balogh.

History: The Black Rock Forest encompasses 3,870 acres of land. It was owned by Harvard University until 1989, at which time William Golden (a Harvard alumni) brought the land and then donated it to the newly created Black Rock Forest Preserve.

Directions: From Mountainville (junction of Route 32 & Angola Road), drive east on Angola Road for 0.9 mile. Turn right onto Mineral Spring Road, and head south for 1.3 miles. When you come to Old Spring Road, park along the side of the road in <0.1 mile.

Proceeding on foot, follow the white-blazed Scenic Trail southeast for 0.3 mile until you reach Mineral Spring Falls. Hopefully, the Fifth of July Rock will be obvious once you are there.

From Mineral Spring Falls, continue west along the Scenic Trail for another 1.0 mile until you come to Jupiter's Boulder, to your left.

To get to Split Rock, continue northeast along the Scenic Trail. When you come to a gravel road, turn left and head north. The road soon joins with the yellow-blazed Arthur Trail and continues north.

Rock Walks

After you pass by the Sutherland Pond road to your right, you will come to a gate. Just past the gate, bear right onto the blue-blazed Compartment Trail and proceed north for >0.1 mile. Finally, turn right onto the white-blazed Split Rock Trail and follow it northeast for ~0.2 mile. Split Rock is next to the trail overlooking Sutherland Pond.

I would encourage hikers to bring along the "West Hudson Trail Map #7: Black Rock Forest & Storm King State Park" to make sure that the directions provided are visually clear.

Resources: New York-New Jersey Trail Conference, *New York Walk Book. Sixth Edition* (New York: New York-New Jersey Trail Conference, 1998), 273.
lowmileage.com/2010/10/17/return-to-black-rock-forest-orange-county-new-york – This website contains a photograph of a partially glimpsed Jupiter's Boulder.
Bill & Phyllis Thomas, *Natural New York* (New York: Holt, Rinehart and Winston, 1983), 256. The authors write, "From atop Fifth of July Rock, visitors enjoy a scenic view of Schenemuck Mountain and Woodbury Valley." This suggests that the rock may be an overlook. Another source, however, mentions an actual boulder, possibly near or at the overlook.
Peter Kick, Barbara McMartin, & James M. Long, *50 Hikes in the Hudson Valley: From the Catskills to the Taconics, and from the Ramapos to the Helderbergs. Second Edition* (Woodstock, VT: Backcountry Publications, 2000), 63.

121. CROW'S NEST BOULDER & CAPTAIN KIDD'S CAVE
Storm King State Park: Crow's Nest

Type of Formation: Large Boulder; Cave
WOW Factor: Not determined
Location: West Point (Orange County)
Tenth Edition, NYS Atlas & Gazetteer: p. 108, B2; **Earlier Edition NYS Atlas & Gazetteer**: p. 32, AB3–4
Parking GPS Coordinates: 41º24.895'N 73º59.623'W
Estimated Destination GPS Coordinates: Not determined for either rock formation

Rock Walks

Accessibility: *Large Boulder* -- 1.0-mile hike; *Captain Kidd's Cave* -- Unknown

Description: In *Walks and Rambles in the Western Hudson Valley*, Peggy Turco mentions "a large erratic" just before reaching a grassy knoll that provides the first views, looking east, of the Hudson Valley.

A boulder is also said to be at the summit of Crow's Nest.

In Patricia Edwards Clyne's *Hudson Valley Trails and Tales*, a *Captain Kidd's Cave* located on Crow's Nest is mentioned, but no specific directions

The Grotto: Crow's Nest. Old photograph.

are provided. Clyne writes, "Oddly enough, a treasure of sorts was found in the Crow's Nest cave, but it was not Captain Kidd's. In the fall of 1870, a group of explorers found several old coins, none dated earlier than 1782" — a realization that since these coins were minted nearly a century after Kidd's death, they couldn't possibly be part of his treasure stash.

Clyne's story is probably based on an account by Lewis Beach's 1873 book, *Cornwall*. "Quite a number of feet above the flow of the Hudson, in the rugged and precipitous breast-bone of 'Old Cro'-nest,' was discovered, in the fall of 1872, a huge cavern..." Beach then goes on to narrate the story of how the coins were discovered, and speculates on who might have left them.

What I found particularly interesting was how James Fenimore Cooper adapted this eighteenth century tale to his story about Enoch Crosby in his 1821 novel, *The Spy*.

In the *Hudson Highlands*, William Thompson Howell, talks about several shelter caves, which may, in fact, be one and the same. Bat Cave was found when Howell and his hiking companions left Sherwood's Rock and did an arduous climb up Crow's Nest. "We wiggled into the small mouth of the cave, and by the light of half a dozen candles explored the cavity." In another section, Lowell writes about 'The Grotto on Cro' Nest'. "The Grotto... is a long shallow cavern in the granite uplift of rocks...and beneath whose shelter quite a good many persons might take refuge from a storm."

There is also a formation on a high bluff above the western bank of the Hudson River that is known as Kidd's Plug Cliff. Most likely, this bluff is the 1,350-foot east face of Crow's Nest Mountain. In *The Hudson: From the Wilderness to the Sea,,* Benson Lossing writes, "High up on the smooth face of the rock, is a mass slightly projecting,

View of Breakneck from Crow's Nest. Photograph by Dan Balogh.

estimated to be twelve feet in diameter, and by form and position, suggesting, even to the dullest imagination, the idea of an enormous plug stopping an orifice." According to Arthur G. Adams, in *The Hudson River Guidebook*, the plug was "destroyed either by quarrying or construction of the Old Storm King Highway—or possibly by artillery practice."

History: According to E. M. Ruttenber & L. H. Clark, in *History of Orange County, New York. Vol. 1*, Cro'-Nest's "modern name preserves in substance its Algonquin title, which, in ancient records, is written *Navesing*, signifying a 'resort for birds.'"

Rock Walks

The Howell Trail is named for William Thompson Howell, a late nineteenth-century writer and photographer.

I would be remiss if I didn't mention that the mountain was used as target practice for testing Parrot guns manufactured across the river at the West Point Foundry in Cold Spring. Woe be to any hiker who was doing a bushwhack on the mountain back in those days.

Directions: From west of West Point (junctions of Routes 9W, 293, & 218) drive north on Route 9W for 2.6 miles and turn into a pull-off on your right just before a yellow "Icy pavement zone" sign. A kiosk at the back of the parking area provides helpful information about the area.

Follow the white-marked Bobcat Trail north for ~0.5 mile. When you come to a junction, bear right, now following the blue-colored Howell Trail north.

According to pjneary.com/hiking/2011/02/storm-king-sp-crows-nest-nov-13-2010, a blog, I believe, by Tim Bowen, a large glacial erratic awaits on the summit. Along the climb, you will pass by the boulder mentioned in *Walks and Rambles in the Western Hudson Valley*.

I have no idea where Captain Kidd's Cave is located on the mountain. I do know that part of the mountain is out of bounds because the West Point military academy believes that a substantial number of unexploded ordinances may still litter the landscape.

Resources: William Thompson Howell, *The Hudson Highlands. Vol. 1 & Vol. 2*.
Peggy Turco, *Walks and Rambles in the Western Hudson Valley* (Woodstock, VT: Backcountry Publications, 1996), 24.
nynjtc.org/hike/crows-nest-mountainhowell-trail-route-9w#dialog-hike-description.
pjneary.com/hiking/2011/02/storm-king-sp-crows-nest-nov-13-2010.
Patricia Edwards Clyne, *Hudson Valley Trails and Tales* (Woodstock, NY: The Overlook Press, 1990), 203 & 250.
New York-New Jersey Trail Conference, *Day Walker: 32 Hikes in the New York Metropolitan Area. Second Edition* (Mahwah, NJ: New York-New Jersey Trail Conference, 2002), 224–229.

Rock Walks

Benson Lossing, *The Hudson: From the Wilderness to the Sea* (Sommersworth, NY: New Hampshire Publishing Company, 1972; facsimile of the 1866 edition), 217 & 218. On page 217 is a line drawing of Kidd's Plugg Cliff.

Lewis Beach, *Cornwall* (Newburgh, NY: E. M. Ruttenber & Sons, 1873), 54–58.

E. M. Ruttenber & L. H. Clark, *History of Orange County, New York. Vol. 1* (Interlaken, NY: Heart Lake Publishing, 1980), 33 & 34.

Ernest Ingersoll, *Handy Guide to the Hudson River and Catskill Mountains* (Astoria, NY: J. C. & A. L. Fawcett, Inc., 1989; reprint of 1910 book), 108 & 109.

122. WALT WHITMAN ROCK
Bear Mountain State Park

Type of Formation: Large Boulder
WOW Factor: 4
Location: Bear Mountain (Rockland County)
Tenth Edition, NYS Atlas & Gazetteer: p. 108, C2; **Earlier Edition NYS Atlas & Gazetteer**: p. 32, B3–4
Parking GPS Coordinates: 41º18.736'N 73º59.327'W
Walt Whitman Rock GPS Coordinates: 41º19.009'N 73º59.318'W
Fee: Modest fee 7/days a week in the summer; modest fee on weekends-only in off-season
Accessibility: >0.3-mile walk
Degree of Difficulty: Easy
Additional Information: Bear Mountain State Park, Palisades Parkway/Route 9W North Bear Mountain, NY 10911
Northern Harriman Bear Mtn. Trails, Trail Map 4
parks.ny.gov/parks/attachments/BearMountainTrailMap.pdf.

Description: The boulder supporting the 9-foot high statue of Walt Whitman is roughly 6 feet high and 12 feet long—a respectable sized rock.

History: The statue of Walt Whitman was designed by Jo Davidson and first exhibited at the 1939 New York World's Fair before arriving at its present location in 1940. The statue was commissioned by the

Rock Walks

Harriman family to honor their mother, Mary Williamson Harriman who, thirty years earlier, had donated land and money to establish the Bear Mountain-Harriman section of the Palisades Interstate Park.

A stanza from Whitman's "Song of the Open Road" has been etched into one side of the boulder.

Interestingly, there is also a Walt Whitman Boulder on the summit of Jayne's Hill, located in the West Hills County Park on Long Island [Estimated GPS Coordinates are 40°48.918'N 73°25.517'W]. The boulder is considerably smaller (probably 2–3 feet in height) and has been vandalized. The plaque on the West Hills County Park boulder is inscribed with another one of Whitman's poem, "Paumanok," from *Leaves of Grass*.

Walt Whitman Boulder. Postcard c. 1940.

The Bear Mountain Bridge, spanning the Hudson River near the park, was opened in 1924. At the time, it was the largest single span bridge in the world.

Directions: From the Bear Mountain Bridge Traffic Circle at the west end of the Bear Mountain Bridge (junction of Routes 202, 9W, & 6), drive south on Route 202/9W for 0.4 mile and turn right at the first traffic light onto Seven Lakes Drive. Turn right into either the first or second driveway to reach parking lot one or two, respectively.

From the northeast end of the parking area, walk north for <0.3 mile and then turn east, going down a staircase and following a tunnel under Route 9W that takes you to the east side of the road. From here, it is a walk of several hundred feet to the statue and boulder as you follow signs for the Bear Mountain Zoo and Trailside Museum.

Resources: Bill Bailey, *New York State Parks: A Guide to New York State Parks* (Saginaw, MI: Glovebox Guidebooks of America, 1997), 255.

hmdb.org/marker.asp?marker=47774.
New York-New Jersey Trail Conference, *Guide to the Appalachian Trail in New York and New Jersey. Ninth Edition* (Harpers Ferry, W. VI, The Appalachian Trail Conference, 1983), 71.
Leonard M. Adkins and the Appalachian Trail Conservancy, *Along the Appalachian Trail, New Jersey, New York, and Connecticut: Images of America* (Charleston, SC: Arcadia Publishing, 2014), 75. A photograph of the Walt Whitman statue can be seen but, unfortunately, very little of the underlying boulder is visible.

123. TURLE ROCK
Warwick County Park

Type of Formation: Medium-sized Rock
WOW Factor: 3–4
Location: Warwick (Orange County)
Tenth Edition, NYS Atlas & Gazetteer: p. 107, D7–8; **Earlier Edition NYS Atlas & Gazetteer**: p. 32, BC1
Parking GPS Coordinates: 41º14.410′N 74º19.926′W
Turtle Rock GPS Coordinates: 41º14.351′N 74º19.708′W
Accessibility: ~0.5-mile hike
Degree of Difficulty: Moderate
Additional Information: Warwick County Park, 25 County Park Lane, Route 17A, Warwick, NY

Description: This unique, medium-sized rock has achieved some notoriety due to its turtle-like shape. It is not a big rock, but it is distinctive.

History: There are some folks who contend that the protrusion on the left side of Turtle Rock (which gave the rock its name) was carved out by earlier visitors, and is not naturally formed. Steve Schimmrich, the Hudson River Geologist, however, contends that the formation is entirely natural.

Directions: From south of Warwick (junction of Routes 17A East & 94/Oakland Avenue), drive east on Route 17A for ~1.3 miles and turn right onto County Park Lane where a green-colored sign says

Warwick County Park. Proceed southeast for >0.7 mile. The parking area is on your left.

From the parking area, follow a road south for 0.2 mile along the east side of the woods. Then turn left onto a trail that leads uphill into the woods, heading northeast. After negotiating a hairpin turn, you will come to the top of the hill, where Turtle Rock can be seen to your left at ~0.5 mile, slightly off the path.

Turtle Rock. Photograph by Steven Schimmrich.

Resources: Linda Zimmerman, *Mysterious Hudson Valley Stone Sites* (2016). hudsonvalleygeologist.blogspot.com/2014/11/turtle-rock-in-warwick.html.

124. DATER MOUNTAIN ERRATIC
Dater Mountain Nature Park

Type of Formation: Large Boulder
WOW Factor: 6
Location: Sloatsburg (Rockland County)
Tenth Edition, NYS Atlas & Gazetteer: p. 107, D9; **Earlier Edition NYS Atlas & Gazetteer**: p. 32, C2
Parking GPS Coordinates: 41º10.345'N 74º10.533'W
Dater Mountain Erratic GPS Coordinates: 41º10.043'N 74º11.073'W
Accessibility: ~1.0-mile hike
Degree of Difficulty: Moderate
Additional Information: Trail map of the Dater Mountain Nature Park at rocklandgov.com/files/4913/4555/8821/Parks_Dater_Mountain_Map.pdf
_

Rock Walks

Description: The Dater Mountain glacial erratic is ~10 feet high and lumpy looking. What distinguishes it is the rock's proximity to telephone poles and its overlook of the New York State Thruway.

History: The Dater Mountain Nature Park encompasses 350 acres of land that were acquired in two stages between 1981 and 2004.

During the late eighteenth century into the nineteenth century, the trees on this hilly tract of land were extensively harvested to produce charcoal for the smelting of iron ore. Many of these charcoal pits still dot the landscape.

Directions: From Sloatsburg (junction of Routes 97/Seven Lakes Drive and 17), drive northeast on Route 97/Seven Lakes Drive for 0.5 mile. As soon as you pass under I-87 (NYS Thruway), turn left onto Johnsontown Road and head northeast for 0.8 mile. Park to your right in a small pull-off.

Dater Mountain Erratic. Photograph by Dan Balogh.

Walk across the road and follow the orange-blazed trail uphill. When you come to a junction after 0.1 mile, turn left onto the blue-blazed trail and proceed southwest. After you have climbed up Sleater Hill and partially descended, look for a short path/road to your left that leads to a large glacial erratic by a set of telephone poles, not that far above the New York State Thruway.

Resources: nynjtc.org/hike/dater-mountain-nature-park. rocklandgov.com/departments/environmental-resources/county-parks-and-dog-runs/dater-mountain-park.

Rock Walks

125. DUTCHESS QUARRY CAVES

Type of Formation: Shelter Cave
WOW Factor: 5
Location: Finnegans Corners (Orange County)
Tenth Edition, NYS Atlas & Gazetteer: p. 107, B7; **Earlier Edition NYS Atlas & Gazetteer**: p. 32, AB1
Mt. Lookout GPS Coordinates: 41º21.578'N 74º21.664'W
GPS Coordinates given by Funk & Steadman: 41º21.585'N 74º21.817'W
Accessibility: Unknown

Description: The Dutchess Quarry Sites consist of a series of rock-shelters, some of respectable size. In *Early Man in Orange County, New York*, George R. Walters writes, "The Dutchess Quarry Cave is situated in the cliff at an elevation of 580 feet above sea level. The opening to the cave faces northwest…The cave is roughly cylindrical in shape, 17 feet wide at the mouth and 60 feet long, narrowing down to a small fissure…It evidently at one time carried a small subterranean stream…" I presume this description is of either Cave #1 or Cave #8, which have proven to be the most significant archaeologically of the shelter caves explored.

History: Mt. Lookout is a 660-foot-high hill that has been heavily quarried.

The Dutchess Quarry Sites National Register District contains 13 acres of land on the western slope of Mount Lookout, including the top. The Dutchess Quarry site contains four caves; the Goshen Quarry Loci, four caves. There are others still to be dug out.

Orange County has owned the Mount Lookout property since the late 1830s, leasing out part of the mountain to the Goshen Quarry, who have been extracting dolomite for gravel.

Native American artifacts were discovered at the cave site in 1964 from hunter-gatherers dating back to 12,000 years ago. At the time of this discovery, it was the oldest site east of the Mississippi.

The cave site was added to the National Register of Historic Places in 1972.

280

Rock Walks

Directions: From Finnegans Corners (junction of Routes 6/Pulaski Highway & 17A), drive southwest on Route 6/Pulaski Highway for 0.5 mile. Turn left onto Quarry Road, which puts you in the general area where the shelter caves are located, to your left.

The site, being archaeologically sensitive, is probably not open to the public I would suspect, except possibly for guided tours.

Resources: Patricia Edwards Clyne, *Hudson Valley Faces & Places* (Woodstock, NY: The Overlook Press, 2005), 227.
orangecountygov.com/DocumentCenter/View/327/Dutchess-Quarry-Sites-National-Register-District---Management-and-Conservation-Report-2012-PDF.
en.wikipedia.org/wiki/Dutchess_Quarry_Cave_Site.
ioccnysaa.blogspot.com/2011/06/2011-06-11-dutchess-quarry-cave-chapter.html.
R. E. Funk & D. W. Steadman, *Dutchess Quarry Caves, Orange County, New York* (Persimmon Press Monographs in Archaeology, 1994).
Patricia Edwards Clyne, *Hudson Valley Trails and Tales* (Woodstock, NY: The Overlook Press, 1990), 119.
George R. Walters, *Early Man in Orange County, New York* (Middletown, NY: Historical Society of Middletown and the Wallkill Precinct, Inc., 1973), 3.

Dutchess Quarry Cave area. Ariel view. Google Earth.

281

PROLOGUE TO HARRIMAN STATE PARK & THE PALISADES

I am deeply indebted to Dan Balogh and his wife, Laura Petersen Balogh, for contributing most of the spectacular photographs that accompany the Harriman/Palisades section of this

book (as well as a few other spots). The Baloghs are lifetime residents of New Jersey who have been hiking trails in New York and New Jersey for the past twenty years. Over time, they have created a photo-journal of all of their treks

Dan & Laura Balogh (Palisades).

that is simply amazing to view. In fact, you can do so right now by going on Dan's website, danbalogh.com.

In addition, dozens of Dan's photographs have appeared in books and magazines.

Dan works as a systems engineer. Laura is a corporate trainer in Manhattan and also a published author.

Never has the phrase "A picture is worth a thousand words" been more accurate than now.

HARRIMAN STATE PARK: NORTHERN SECTION

History: Harriman State Park, encompassing 47,527-acres (75 square miles), contains over two hundred miles of hiking trails, thirty-one lakes and ponds, and spills over into both Orange and Rockland Counties. It is the second largest park in New York State's park system.

Harriman State Park is named after Edward Harriman and Mary Averell Harriman, who donated the initial 10,000 acres of land out of which the park grew. The state took possession of the land in 1910, and the Palisades Interstate Park Commission, beginning in 1913, began constructing dozens of group campsites throughout the park.

There are seemingly an infinite number of glacial erratics in Harriman State Park. The ones that I describe are those that have been given, in some instances, colorful names, and have become notable destinations or stopping-off points along hikes. They also tend to be trailside.

If you are interested in knowing about all the features on the Harriman Trail maps, consult "Map Index – Harriman-Bear Mountain Trails Map Set" (nynjtc.org/content/index-harriman-bear-mountain-trails-map).

Resources:
parks.ny.gov/parks/attachments/HarrimanSuggestedHiking.pdf.
parks.ny.gov/parks/145/details.aspx.

126. STOCKBRIDGE CAVE SHELTER & HIPPO ROCK
Harriman State Park

Type of Formation: Large Boulder; Shelter Cave
WOW Factor: 5
Location: Harriman (Rockland County)
Tenth Edition, NYS Atlas & Gazetteer: p. 108, C1; **Earlier Edition NYS Atlas & Gazetteer**: p. 32, B3

283

Rock Walks

Parking GPS Coordinates: 41º18.988'N 74º03.052'W
Destination GPS Coordinates: *Stockbridge Cave Shelter* -- 41º18.092'N 74º04.620'W (estimated); *Stockbridge Shelter* -- 41º18.101'N 74º04.662'W (Google Earth); *Hippo Rock* -- 41º17.870'N 74º04.793'W (estimated)
Accessibility: *Stockbridge Cave Shelter* – 1.7-mile hike; *Hippo Rock* -- ~2.2-mile hike
Degree of Difficulty: Moderately difficult
Additional Information: Northern Harriman Bear Mtn. Trails, Trail Map 4 parks.ny.gov/parks/attachments/HarrimanTrailMap.pdf – trail map

Description: *Stockbridge Cave Shelter* is an intriguing rock-shelter that hikers have augmented, using stones to create an artificial chimney.

Stockbridge Cave Shelter. Photograph by Dan Balogh.

Hershel Friedman, in his blog, the Harriman Hiker, writes, "The Cave Shelter is a rock formation of massive boulders that are stacked and forming caves and passageways that you can actually squeeze through quite deeply."

Hippo Rock is an enormous, cantilevered rock, some 8 feet high and decidedly longer, which overhangs a ledge. It seemingly defies gravity because of its greater mass resting on solid ground.

Rock Walks

History: *Stockbridge Cave Shelter* – The Stockbridge Cave was "discovered" by J. Ashton Allis in 1922. It became known as the Stockbridge Cave Shelter in 1928 as Park authorities tried to make its interior somewhat more hospitable. Today, the shelter is allegedly used by hikers as a backup refuge when Stockbridge Shelter—a rock-and-mortar structure with a plank floor—is full. According to *The Long Path. Fifth Edition*, "The Cave Shelter is set into an overhang near the base of its rock face. It is damp and hardly an inviting place to spend the night."

The Stockbridge Shelter, passed along the way between the Stockbridge Cave Shelter and Hippo Rock, was built in 1928 and is a fairly large structure.

Hippo Rock received its name from an imaginative hiker who thought that the rock resembled a hippopotamus.

Directions: From northwest of Harriman (junction of Routes 6/Long Mountain Parkway & 293), drive west on Route 6/Long Mountain Parkway for ~1.9 miles and turn right into a parking area for the Long Path next to a kiosk.

From the parking area, follow the aqua-blazed Long Path southwest for ~1.7 miles. Look for the Cave Shelter to your left, distinguished by a stone chimney. Shortly after that, you will pass by the Stockbridge Shelter.

At ~2.2 miles, you will come to Hippo Rock on your right, just southwest of the yellow-blazed Menomine Trail crossing.

Hippo Rock can also be reached from where the Long Path crosses Arden Valley Road, roughly 0.3 mile west of Tiorati Circle. It involves a ~2.0-mile hike, heading north.

Resources: Jerome Wyckoff, *Rock Scenery of the Hudson Highlands and Palisades* (Glens Falls, NY: Adirondack Mountain Club, 1971), 85.
nynjctbotany.org/whudson/nyfngbrd.html – This site makes reference to Jerome Wyckoff's book.
parks.ny.gov/parks/attachments/HarrimanTrailMap.pdf – the location of Hippo Rock is shown on the map.
New York-New Jersey Trail Conference, *New York Walk Book. Sixth Edition* (New York: New York-New Jersey Trail Conference, 1998). Mention is made of Hippo Rock on page 39.

Rock Walks

William J. Myles, *Harriman Trails: A Guide and History* (New York: The New York-New Jersey Trail Conference, 1994), 71.

Herb Chong (editor), *The Long Path Guide. Fifth Edition* (Mahwah, NJ: New York-New Jersey Trail Conference, 2002), 52.

nynjtc.org/book/6-lake-skannatati-us-route-6.

lonehiker.blogspot.com/2009/04/stockbridge-shelter-cave-shelter-hippo.html.

Leonard M. Adkins and the Appalachian Trail Conservancy, *Along the Appalachian Trail, New Jersey, New York, and Connecticut: Images of America* (Charleston, SC: Arcadia Publishing, 2014). A photograph of the Stockbridge Cave Shelter is shown on page 52.

catskillhiker.com/2014/10/28/3977.

harrimanhiker.com/2011/05/stockbridge-mountain.html.

harrimanhiker.com/2013/12/route-6-to-stockbrige-mountain-loop.html.

Hippo Rock. Photograph by Dan Balogh.

127. THE TIMP

Type of Formation: Boulder: Rock Profile
WOW Factor: 6
Location: Jones Point (Rockland County)
Tenth Edition, NYS Atlas & Gazetteer: p. 108, C2; **Earlier Edition NYS Atlas & Gazetteer**: p. 32, BC4
1777 Trailhead Parking GPS Coordinates: 41º16.438'N 73º58.387'W
Destination GPS Coordinates: Not determined
Accessibility: 3–4-mile hike depending upon route taken
Degree of Difficulty: Difficult
Additional Information: Northern Harriman Bear Mtn. Trails, Trail Map 4
parks.ny.gov/parks/attachments/BearMountainTrailMap.pdf.

Description: In *New York Walk Book. Third Edition*, Raymond H. Torrey, Frank Place, Jr., & Robert L. Dickinson write, "Above frowns the Timp, a striking cliff with a pronounced overhang, at the west end of the Dunderberg massif."

William J. Myles, in *Harriman Trails: A Guide and History*, writes about a "large boulder sitting in the [Timp] pass" called Collar Button.

There are a number of interesting boulders encountered along the hike which, to the best of my knowledge, are nameless—here's your chance to name one.

History: The 1777 Trail follows the route taken by British soldiers under the leadership of Sir Henry Clinton as they marched from Stony Point in 1777 to attack Fort Clinton and Fort Montgomery.

The Timp is a large, 1,080-foot-high mountain with a distinctive face. Timp

Hiking the Timp-Torne Trail. Photograph by Dan Balogh.

Pass is a deep notch in between The Timp and West Mountain.

287

Timp is an obsolete Dutch word for a loaf of bread or cake. I'm not really sure how that applies to the mountain. Perhaps some early Dutch explorers thought that the shape of the mountain resembled that of a loaf of bread.

Directions: From Tompkins Cove (which is the junction of Routes 9W/202/North Liberty Drive & 118/Mott Farm Road), start driving northeast on Route 9W/202/North Liberty Drive. After 1.2 miles, turn right into a parking area.

Unique boulder on hike to The Timp. Photograph by Dan Balogh.

From the parking area, walk north along Route 9W for around 100 feet. Cross over to the west side of the road and pick up the red-blazed 1777 Trail. Proceed west for >1.3 miles. At a junction, turn left onto the blue-blazed Timp-Torne Trail and continue west for ~0.5 mile. When you come to another junction, turn left onto the red-blazed Ramapo-Dunderberg

The Timp. Photograph by Dan Balogh.

Trail, which takes you south, then north as you go through the Timp Pass.

The Collar Button Boulder is close to the junction of the Red Cross Trail (coming in from the south), the unmarked Timp Pass Road (coming in from the north), and the Ramapo-Dunderberg Trail (which you are on).

Rock Walks

To make part of the hike into a loop, follow the Timp Pass Road north for a short distance, and then continue on the blue-blazed Timp-Torne Trail as it takes you east up and over The Timp, and eventually back to the 1777 trail, and east to the parking area.

Resources: Raymond H. Torrey, Frank Place, Jr., & Robert L. Dickinson, *New York Walk Book. Third Edition* (NY: The American Geographical Society, 1951), 176. On page 156, mention is made about what the word may mean.
myharriman.com/best-hikes-in-harriman-1-the-timp-and-west-mountain.
William J. Myles, *Harriman Trails: A Guide and History* (New York: The New York-New Jersey Trail Conference, 1994), 156.
danbalogh.com/timp.html.

128. CAPE HORN ROCK

Type of Formation: Large Rock
WOW Factor: 4–5
Location: Lake Shannatati (Orange County)
Tenth Edition, NYS Atlas & Gazetteer: p. 107, D10; **Earlier Edition NYS Atlas & Gazetteer**: p. 32, BC2–3
Parking GPS Coordinates: 41º14.517′N 74º06.138′W
Cape Horn Rock GPS Coordinates: Not determined
Accessibility: 1.4-mile hike
Degree of Difficulty: Moderate
Additional Information: Northern Harriman Bear Mtn. Trails, Trail Map 4.
parks.ny.gov/parks/attachments/HarrimanTrailMap.pdf

Description: According to *The Long Path Guide. Fifth Edition*, Cape Horn Rock is an "overhanging rock" near where the trail turns right. William J. Myles, in *Harriman Trails: A Guide and History*, describes it as "a great boulder."

Myles goes on to mention that there is a cave in the rocks behind the boulder that is called "Cat's Den."

History: Lake Shannatati, from where the hike begins, is a 36-acre body of water.

Seven Lakes Drive, a main road through the park, was originally called Southfields Road.

Cape Horn Rock. Photograph by Dan Balogh.

Directions: From Sloatsburg (junction of Routes 97/Seven Lakes Drive & 17), drive northeast on 97/Seven Lakes Drive for nearly 8.0 miles (or ~0.8 mile north from the Kanawauke Circle). Turn left into the parking area for Lake Shannatati.

From the north end of the parking area, follow the aqua-blazed Long Path west, initially along the north shore of Lake Shannatati, for 1.4 miles to reach the Cape Horn Rock.

Resources: Herb Chong (editor), *The Long Path Guide. Fifth Edition* (Mahwah, NJ: New York-New Jersey Trail Conference, 2002), 50.
nynjtc.org/book/6-lake-skannatati-us-route-6.
hikingproject.com/trail/7047052/hogencamp-mountain — This site describes Cape Horn as "a giant rock formation."
William J. Myles, *Harriman Trails: A Guide and History* (New York: The New York-New Jersey Trail Conference, 1994), 69.

129. ROCK HOUSE

Type of Formation: Rock-Shelter
WOW Factor: Not determined
Location: Kanawauke Circle (Orange County)
Tenth Edition, NYS Atlas & Gazetteer: p. 108, D1; **Earlier Edition NYS Atlas & Gazetteer**: p. 32, BC2–3
Parking GPS Coordinates: 41º14.150'N 74º05.956'W
Estimated Rock House GPS Coordinates: 41º14.158'N 74º05.990'W (pretty much a crude guess)
Accessibility: 0.05-mile-hike
Degree of Difficulty: Moderate
Additional Information: Northern Harriman Bear Mtn. Trails, Trail Map 4. Southern Harriman Bear Mtn. Trails, Trail Map 3
 parks.ny.gov/parks/attachments/HarrimanTrailMap.pdf

Description: It seems inevitable that the Rock House is either a rock-shelter formed by an overhanging ledge or a grouping of rocks that have come together to form a rock-enclosed shelter. William J. Myles in *Harriman Trails: A Guide and History* simply calls it a "cave."

One of the rock houses is passed on hike up Rock House Mountain. Photograph by Dan Balogh

History: Rockhouse Mountain (1,283'), the highest point in Rockland County, was named for the Rock House on its shoulder.

 "Kanawauke" (Kanawauke Circle) comes from the Onondaga word *Kanawahkee*, which means "place of much water." The word aptly applies to Lake Kanawauke, which was formerly known as

Little Long Lake, and is a sizeable body of water. Unlike some of the other lakes in Harriman State Park, it is naturally formed.

Directions: From Kanawauke Circle (junction of Routes 106/Kanawauke Road & 97/Sevens Lake Parkway), drive east on Route 106/Kanawauke Road for 0.7 mile, and turn into a tiny pull-off located on your right, approximately 0.2 mile east of where the Long Path crosses Route 106/Kanawauke.

Walk into the woods, heading back west above the road. The Rock House should be only a couple of hundred feet away according to the Southern Harriman Bear Mtn. Trails (Trail Map 3), which clearly shows the rock's position.

Resources: William J. Myles, *Harriman Trails: A Guide and History* (New York: The New York-New Jersey Trail Conference, 1994), 295. harrimanhiker.com/2011/04/rockhouse-mountain.html.

130. BOWLING ROCKS, SHIP ROCK, TIMES SQUARE BOULDER, & POTHOLE

Type of Formation: Large Boulder
WOW Factor: 3–6
Location: Kanawauke Circle (Orange County)
Tenth Edition, NYS Atlas & Gazetteer: p. 107, D10; **Earlier Edition NYS Atlas & Gazetteer**: p. 32, BC2–3
Parking GPS Coordinates: 41º13.816'N 74º08.413'W
Estimated Destination GPS Coordinates: *Bowling Rocks* -- 41º14.647'N 74º07.572'W (Google Earth); *Ship Rock* -- 41º14.954'N 74º07.646'W (Google Earth); *Times Square Boulder* -- 41º15.113'N 74º07.204'W (Google Earth); *Plateau Rocks*: 41º14.949'N 74º07.265'W
Accessibility: *Bowling Rocks* – 1.9-mile hike; *Ship Rock* – 5.0-mile hike; *Times Square Boulder* – 5.7-mile hike; *pothole* – 5.8-mile hike
Degree of Difficulty: Difficult
Additional Information: Trail map of Harriman State Park available at parks.ny.gov/parks/attachments/HarrimanTrailMap.pdf.
Northern Harriman Bear Mtn. Trails, Map 4
Southern Harriman Bear Mtn. Trails, Map 3

Description: *Bowling Rocks* consist of a smattering of stones scattered about on top of exposed bedrock, or, as William J. Myles in *Harriman Trails: A Guide and History* writes, "...a level area of bare rock dotted by boulders..." The roundness of the rocks is what prompted some creative hiker to come up with the bowling balls analogy.

Ship Rock. Photograph by Dan Balogh.

Ship Rock is a large, fractured boulder that, to some, resembles a ship's prow, bottom up. The trail passes right in front of the rock.

Times Square Boulder probably got its name for two very good reasons: 1) The boulder sits at the very busy intersection of five trails—The Ramapo-Dunderberg Trail, the Arden-Surebridge Trail, and (75 feet away) the Long Path; and 2) Somebody painted the words "Times Square" in big, white letters on the boulder, including an arrow that presumably points the way towards New York City.

The boulder stands ~6–8 feet high, with a tiny shelter under one end. Near the rock is a stone fireplace.

The unnamed *pothole,* located on a ledge to the left of the trail, was "discovered" in 1924 by Frank Place. Peggy Turco, in *Walks and Rambles in the Western Hudson Valley*, describes it as "...a chimney-like half cylinder 4 feet wide and 8 feet deep." Turco goes on to comment that "This is a glacial pothole. Usually, potholes are formed by streams where gravel whirls for millennia scouring a round pot-like depression in the stream's bedrock. The lack of any streambed at this site precludes that typical formation. It has been postulated that a stream once ran on the Wisconsin glacier. As the meltwater coursed into a crevasse at this spot, it scoured out the pothole...."

Rock Walks

The potholes are also described by Raymond H. Torrey, Frank Place, Jr. and Robert L. Dickinson, in *New York Walk Book. Third Edition*, where the path goes "around a low cliff and beneath a glacial pothole, 6 or 7 feet high on its face."

Plateau Rocks consist of a number of small-to-medium-sized boulders scattered about on an area of exposed bedrock at the summit of Hogencamp Mountain. Also to be seen is an oblong-shaped boulder propped up on one end by a tiny rock.

Laura Balogh bides her time at Time Square. Photograph by Dan Balogh.

Directions: From the Kanawauke Circle (junction of Routes 106/Kanawauke Road & 97/Seven Lakes Drive), drive west on Route 106/Kanawauke Road for 1.6 miles. Park to your right.

Hike northeast on the red-blazed Ramapo-Dunderberg Trail for 1.5 miles. At the junction with the yellow-blazed Dunning Trail, turn right and go 0.4 mile to reach *Bowling Rocks*, on your left.

Return to the Ramapo-Dundergerg Trail and continue north. After passing by the blue-blazed Lichen Trail at 5.0 miles, you will see *Ship Rock* on your right within less than 0.05 mile from the junction.

Continue east, then north, on the Ramapo-Dunderberg Trail for another 0.7 mile. Just before the junction with the Long Path/Arden-Surebridge Trail, *Times Square* rock will be to your right.

A notable *pothole* on a ledge is visible to your left along the Ramapo- Dunderberg Trail, 0.1-mile past the Long Path/Arden-Surebridge Trail intersection.

Other Approaches to Times Square: 1) From the Lemon Squeezer [see following chapter], proceed southeast on the red-blazed Arden-Surebridge Trail/Long Path for 1.1 miles to reach the Times Square

Rock Walks

junction (or a total of 4.8 miles on the Arden-Sturbridge Trail from Elk Pen).

2) From the north end of the parking area for Lake Shannatati, follow the Long Path west, initially along the north shore of Lake Shannatati, then north, for ~2.0 miles to reach the Times Square junction.

Resources: Jerome Wyckoff, *Rock Scenery of the Hudson Highlands and Palisades* (Glens Falls, NY: Adirondack Mountain Club, 1971). Photos of some medium-sized boulders on a scoured plateau of bedrock can be seen on pages 13 and 83.
gonehikin.blogspot.com/2012/02/harriman-state-park-island-pond-and.html.
myharriman.com/bald-rocks-hogencamp-mountain-hike-harriman-state-park.—A photograph of Times Square Rock is shown.
William J. Myles, *Harriman Trails: A Guide and History* (New York: The New York-New Jersey Trail Conference, 1994), 61 & 226. A photograph of the Lemon Squeezer can be seen on page 13.
myharriman.com/bald-rocks-hogencamp-mountain-hike-harriman-state-park.
Peggy Turco, *Walks and Rambles in the Western Hudson Valley* (Woodstock, VT: Backcountry Publications, 1996), 39.
Raymond H. Torrey, Frank Place, Jr. & Robert L. Dickinson, *New York Walk Book. Third Edition* (NY: The American Geographical Society, 1951), 175.

131. LEMON SQUEEZER

Type of Formation: Narrow passageway
WOW Factor: 8
Location: Southfields (Orange County)
Tenth Edition, NYS Atlas & Gazetteer: p. 107, C10; **Earlier Edition NYS Atlas & Gazetteer**: p. 32, BC2
Parking GPS Coordinates: 41º15.887'N 74º09.260'W
Estimated Lemon Squeezer GPS Coordinates: 41º15.483'N 74º07.981'W
Accessibility: 3.4-mile hike
Degree of Difficulty: Difficult
Additional Information: Northern Harriman Bear Mtn. Trails, Trail Map 4, or at parks.ny.gov/parks/attachments/HarrimanTrailMap.pdf

295

Rock Walks

Description: The Lemon Squeezer, as suggested by its name, is a very tight passageway between two large sections of rock. In *Harriman Trails: A Guide and History*, William J. Myles describes it as where "...a narrow passage formed when a great piece of rock broke off the side of the cliff." Pictures of the Lemon Squeezer show a passageway that is around 6 feet high and 1 foot wide. It is just one part of a massive area of rock.

The Lemon Squeezer is not for the claustrophobic. Photograph by Dan Balogh.

History: The Lemon Squeezer was named by J. Ashton Allis, founder of the Palisades Interstate Conference.

The name of the parking area, Elk Pen, refers to an experiment that was tried in 1919. Sixty elk were brought over from Yellowstone National Park and kept in a wired enclosure between Arden and Southfields. The elk failed to thrive, however, and the attempt to introduce this species into the region ended in the 1940s.

Directions: From Southfields (junction of Routes 17 & 19), drive northeast on Route 17 for ~1.9 miles. Turn right onto Arden Valley Road and proceed east for 0.3 mile, crossing over the New York State Thruway in the process. Then turn right onto a short road that takes you to the Elk Pen parking area after less than 0.1 mile.

Follow the white-blazed Appalachian Trail east for ~3.4 miles. Along the way, you will cross over the outlet stream from Island Pond at 1.7 miles.

The Lemon Squeezer is near the junction of the Appalachian Trail and the red-blazed Arden Surebridge Trail. If you don't wish to go through the Lemon Squeezer, follow a sign in blue letters that shows you the "Easy Way" to bypass the rock formation.

Rock Walks

The Appalachian Trail crosses the Long Path at 4.2 miles.

Resources: Raymond H. Torrey, Frank Place, Jr. & Robert L. Dickinson, *New York Walk Book. Third Edition* (NY: The American Geographical Society, 1951), 168. The rock formation is portrayed as "a cliff and huge tumbled rock fragments..."
harrimanhikers.org/harriman-hikers-at-elk-pens-harriman-state-park-ny.
gonehikin.blogspot.com/2012/02/harriman-state-park-island-pond-and.html – A photograph of the lemon squeezer can be seen on this site.
William J. Myles, *Harriman Trails: A Guide and History* (New York: The New York-New Jersey Trail Conference, 1994), 14. A photograph of the Lemon Squeezer is shown on page 13.
hikethehudsonvalley.com/hikes/harriman-state-park-lemon-squeezer-to-lichen-trail.
rootsrated.com/a/la-sportiva-hiking-trail-guide/most-technical-trail-new-york-city.
operationalaska30.com/2017/10/28/trip-report-lemon-squeezer-and-bald-rocks-loop-via-lake-skannatati-harriman-state-park-ny-10-7-17.
Peggy Turco, *Walks and Rambles in the Western Hudson Valley* (Woodstock, VT: Backcountry Publications, 1996), 41. The Lemon Squeezer is described as a "narrow cleft in the granite cliffs..."
New York-New Jersey Trail Conference, *Guide to the Appalachian Trail in New York and New Jersey. Ninth Edition* (Harpers Ferry, W. VI, The Appalachian Trail Conference, 1983), 84. The Lemon Squeezer is depicted as "a narrow, steep passage between boulders."
Leonard M. Adkins and the Appalachian Trail Conservancy, *Along the Appalachian Trail, New Jersey, New York, and Connecticut: Images of America* (Charleston, SC: Arcadia Publishing, 2014), 54. Two photographs of the Lemon Squeezer are shown.
New York-New Jersey Trail Conference, *New York Walk Book. Sixth Edition* (New York: New York-New Jersey Trail Conference, 1998). On page 282, the Lemon Squeezer is described as "a curious rock formation."

132. IRISH POTATO

Type of Formation: Large Boulder
WOW Factor: 6
Location: Kanawauke Circle (Rockland County)
Tenth Edition, NYS Atlas & Gazetteer: p. 107, D10; **Earlier Edition NYS Atlas & Gazetteer**: p. 32, BC2–3

297

Rock Walks

Parking GPS Coordinates: *Beaver Pond Campground* -- 41º14.199'N 74º04.361'W; *Route 106* -- 41º13.807'N 74º03.652'W
Irish Potato GPS Coordinates: 41º14.151'N 74º03.643'W
Fee: *Campground* – fee charged
Accessibility: *Beaver Pond Campground* -- 0.4-mile hike; *Gate Hill Road/Kanawauke Road* – 0.6-mile hike
Degree of Difficulty: Moderate
Additional Information: Lake Welch Beach, 800 Kanawauke Road, Stony Point, NY 10980 (845) 947-2444
      Northern Harriman Bear Mtn. Trails, Trail Map 4
      Southern Harriman Bear Mtn. Trails, Trail Map 3
      parks.ny.gov/parks/attachments/HarrimanTrailMap.pdf

Description: The Irish Potato is a massive, 25-foot-high, stand-alone boulder whose shape and folds vaguely resemble that of a potato. The rock is located near the summit of Irish Mountain (1,174').

History: The Irish Potato was given its name by Bill Hoeferlin, the man who started the Hikers Region Map series.

Lake Welch was named after Major William A. Welch, General Manager of the Park. There is also a trail named after Major Welch at the Bear Mountain State Park. The body of water was created in 1928 by the impoundment of Beaver Pond Brook; then, further enlarged in 1942.

Directions: *Beaver Pond Campground* -- Driving south on the Palisades Interstate Parkway, get off at Exit 16 and head southwest on Welch Drive for ~1.8 miles. At a roundabout, get off for Lake Welch Beach and the Beaver Pond Campground.

Starting from the Beaver Pond Campground, follow an informal trail northeast for 0.4 mile to reach the Irish Potato, located next to the junction with the yellow-blazed Suffern-Bear Mtn. Trail.

Route 106/Kanawauke Road -- From the Palisades Interstate Parkway, get off at Exit 14 and drive northwest on Willow Grove Road/Route 98 for 1.5 miles. From the point where Gate Hill Road enters on your right, continue northwest on Gate Hill Road/Kanawauke Road for another 0.2 mile and park in a pull-off on your left.

Leaving the parking area behind, follow the yellow-blazed Suffern-Bear Mountain Trail north for 0.6 mile. The rock is at the junction with the informal path coming up from the Beaver Pond Campground at Lake Welch.

The larger-than-life Irish Potato. Photograph by Dan Balogh.

Resources: harrimanhiker.com/2013/03/irish-potato-harriman-state-park.html – This site, created by Hershel Friedman, aka the Harriman Hiker, shows two winter shots of the Irish Potato.

agiletrekker.blogspot.com/2013/11/irish-mountain-and-pound-swamp-mountain.html – This blog site shows a photograph of the rock with a dog next to it for size.

danbalogh.com/irish.html – A series of photographs of the Irish Potato are shown on this site.

nynjtc.org/hike/suffernbear-mountain-trailpyngyp.

Irish Potato close-up. Photograph by Dan Balogh.

Hippo Rock. Photograph by Dan Balogh.

HARRIMAN STATE PARK: SOUTHERN SECTION

There are seemingly an endless number of glacial erratics in Harriman State Park. The ones that I have described are those that have been given colorful names, have interesting histories, or have become notable destinations or stopping-off points along hikes. The rocks also tend to be trailside.

133. CLAUDIUS SMITH'S CAVE

Type of Formation: Shelter Cave
WOW Factor: 6–7
Location: Tuxedo Park (Orange County)
Tenth Edition, NYS Atlas & Gazetteer: p. 107, D9–10; **Earlier Edition NYS Atlas & Gazetteer**: p. 32, C2–3
Parking GPS Coordinates: 41º11.781'N 74º11.043'W
Claudius Smith's Cave GPS Coordinates: 41º11.867'N 74º10.078'W
Accessibility: 1.6-mile hike
Degree of Difficulty: Moderate
Additional Information: Southern Harriman Bear Mtn. Trails, Trail Map 3
      parks.ny.gov/parks/attachments/HarrimanTrailMap.pdf

Description: The Claudius Smith's Cave, aka Claudius Smith's Den, is described by Patricia Edwards Clyne in *Caves for Kids in Historic New York*. "The upper cave is formed by a horizontal crack at the base of an imposing cliff. It is 30 feet long, 8 feet deep

Scouting the terrain from the top of Claudius Smith's Cave. Photograph by Dan Balogh.

and 8 feet high at its tallest point. Part way across the entrance, Smith built a protective wall of rock, the remains of which can still be seen. From this cave a winding passageway, with an excellent observation post about a third of the way up, leads through the rocks to the top of the cliff."

The top of the cliff is commonly called Claudius Smith's Rock.

In *Rock Scenery of the Hudson Highlands and Palisades*, Jerome Wyckoff writes that the cave "...formed as slabs weathered out of the cliff. The cave's size is made possible by wide joint spacing."

In *Suffern: 200 Years 1773–1973*, additional descriptions of Claudius Smith Cave are offered. "The lower cave had once been an Indian shelter and numerous prehistoric artifacts have been found there. The Smith gang used it to shelter their animals (the Horsestable). The upper cave was partially built up in front for protection. From the rear of the overhang there was a winding passageway which led to an escape route at the top of the hill."

This was just one of several caves that Smith used for hideouts. According to Patricia Edwards Clyne, in *Hudson Valley Trails and Tales*, "A few hundred feet downhill to the east, there is another cave called Horse Stable Rock Shelter, since it was used to harbor the gang's four-footed loot."

A Horse Stable Rock was also reputedly used by Smith and his gang, roughly 0.5 mile from Route 202 near Wesley.

History: Claudius Smith was a real-life, Tory outlaw. He led a gang of lawless men, including three of his sons, who raided settlers, retreating back to the cave to avoid capture. In the end, Smith's luck ran out. He was caught and hanged on January 22, 1779.

The cave is reputed to be the largest Indian rock-shelter in southern New York State. The Minsi Native Americans used the cave while on hunting expeditions. We know this because pottery shards and arrowheads have been found nearby.

Directions: From south of Southfields (junction of Routes 17 & 17A), drive south on Route 17 for ~2.4 miles. Turn left onto East Village Road, and then immediately left into a large parking area. From here, walk south along Route 17 to the Tuxedo Train Station. Follow the tracks south for a short distance, and then cross over the Ramapo River via a steel footbridge.

Once across the river, head north along East Village Road; then immediately right onto Grove Drive, proceeding north for 0.1 mile to pick up the trailhead on your right.

Follow the red-blazed Ramapo-Dunderberg Trail east into the woods. At a junction, 1.2 miles from the Tuxedo Station, continue straight ahead on the red-blazed Tuxedo-Mt. Ivy Trail as the red-blazed Ramapo-Dunderberg Trail heads left. Pay attention at this junction, and make sure to stay on the trail leading off to your right. After another 0.4 mile, you will come to Claudius Smith's Cave, on your left. Both the upper and lower caves are worth a look.

The Blue Disk Trail, to your left, takes you to the summit above the caves, which some call Claudius Smith's Rock.

Resources: New York-New Jersey Trail Conference, *New York Walk Book. Sixth Edition* (New York: New York-New Jersey Trail Conference, 1998). A line drawing of Smith's cave is on page 305. The cave is described as "an overhanging rock formation used as a hideout during the Revolutionary War."
Patricia Edwards Clyne, *Caves for Kids in Historic New York* (Monroe, NY: Library Research Associates, 1980), 63–75.
history.com/this-day-in-history/claudius-smith-cowboy-of-the-ramapos-hangs.
en.wikipedia.org/wiki/Claudius_Smith.
Jerome Wyckoff, *Rock Scenery of the Hudson Highlands and Palisades* (Glens Falls, NY: Adirondack Mountain Club, 1971). A photograph of the rock can be seen on pages 4 and 34.
New York-New Jersey Trail Conference, *Day Walker: 32 Hikes in the New York Metropolitan Area. Second Edition* (Mahwah, NJ: New York-New Jersey Trail Conference, 2002). A photograph of the cave is shown on page 176. This is followed by a chapter on Claudius Smith, his exploits, and the cave, 177–183.
Philip H. Smith, *Legends of the Shawangunk and its Environ* (Fleischmanns, NY: Purple Mountain Press Ltd, 1967), 60–65.
Village of Suffern Bicentennial Committee, *Suffern: 200 Years 1773–1973* (Suffern, NY: Village of Suffern Bicentennial Committee, 1973), 80–84. "Bandits of the Ramapos" goes into the history of Smith and his lawless men.
Patricia Edwards Clyne, *Hudson Valley Trails and Tales* (Woodstock, NY: The Overlook Press, 1990), 174–181.

Clay Perry, *Underground Empire: Wonders and Tales of New York Caves* (New York: Stephen Daye Press, 1948), 137 & 138. nynjctbotany.org/whudson/nyclauds.html. Raymond H. Torrey, Frank Place, Jr. & Robert L. Dickinson, *New York Walk Book. Third Edition* (NY: The American Geographical Society, 1951), 132 & 133. "Here are two dens of Claudius Smith and a number of smaller shelters at intervals along the summit. The former are horizontal cracks at the foot of successive cliffs. The upper are 8 to 10 feet high and 30 feet long with a depth of 10 feet. While the lower is longer and deeper but not so high."

134. BONARA'S ROCK, ELBOW BRUSH, & LARGE, UNNAMED BOULDER

Type of Formation: Large Boulder; Tight Squeeze
WOW Factor: 5
Location: Tuxedo Park (Orange County)
Tenth Edition, NYS Atlas & Gazetteer: p. 107, D9–10; **Earlier Edition NYS Atlas & Gazetteer**: p. 32, C2–3
Parking GPS Coordinates: *Tuxedo Park* -- 41º11.781'N 74º11.043'W; *Johnsontown Road Circle* -- 41º10.803'N 74º09.822'W
Estimated Destination GPS Coordinates: *Bonara's Rock* – not determined; *Elbow Brush* -- 41º11.653'N 74º10.121'W (a guesstimate); *Large, Unnamed Boulder*—not determined; *Almost Perpendicular* -- 41º11.055'N 74º10.276'W (a guesstimate)
Accessibility: From Claudius Smith Cave: *Elbow Brush* –0.4-mile hike; *Bonara's Rock* – >0.4-mile hike; *Top of "Almost Perpendicular"* – 1.1-mile hike

From Johnsontown Circle: *Top of "Almost Perpendicular"* – 0.9-mile hike; *Bonara's Rock & Elbow Brush* -- ~1.6-mile hike; *Claudius Smith Cave* – ~2.0-mile hike
Degree of Difficulty: Moderately difficult
Additional Information: Southern Harriman Bear Mtn. Trails, Trail Map 3parks.ny.gov/parks/attachments/HarrimanTrailMap.pdf

Description: According to William J. Myles, in *Harriman Trails: A Guide and History, Bonara's Rock*, also known as Rockneath, is a very large rock. I have no specific information, however, as to the rock's exact size.

Elbow Brush is a narrow passageway so constricted that hikers must take off their backpacks in order to squeeze through this rock formation. A spur path bypasses Elbow Brush for those who are less adventurous.

Large, Unnamed Boulder – This large rock has a Native American association, but I can find no specifics about it, nor whether the rock has a name.

A prominent, trailside boulder. Photograph by Dan Balogh.

History: In 1928, *Bonara's Rock* was named after John Bonara, who was a member of the Paterson Rambler's Club. Bonara loved the site so much that he built a furnished cabin against the rock.

Large Boulder -- According to the Village of Suffern Bicentennial Committee, "...the large boulder served as an Algonquin shelter."

Directions: *Claudius Smith Cave Approach* -- From the rocky top of Claudius Smith Cave, follow the Blue Disc Trail south. After 0.3 mile, you will pass through a narrow passage called Elbow Brush. At 0.6 mile, a gas pipeline corridor is passed.

Heading up Pound Mountain, follow a short spur path that leads to *Bonara's Rock* ~0.2 mile before reaching the mountain summit.

At 1.1 miles, you will be at the top of Almost Perpendicular, getting ready to descend.

The steep descent takes you down to the white-marked Kakiat Trail at 1.5 miles, "just below a huge boulder." From here, it is another 0.5 mile along the Blue Disc Trail to reach the Johnsontown Circle.

Rock Walks

Approaching the entrance to Elbow Brush. Photograph by Dan Balogh.

Johnsontown Circle Approach – Follow the Blue Disc Trail. In 0.9 mile, you will be at the top of Almost Perpendicular (a steep climb); at ~1.2, as you come down from Pond Mountain cliff, look for a spur path to Bonara's Rock; at 1.4 miles, a gas pipline corridor is passed; at 1.7 miles, you will come to Elbow Brush; then, at 2.0 miles, Claudius Smith Cave is reached.

Resources: Village of Suffern Bicentennial Committee, *Suffern: 200 Years 1773–1973* (Suffern, NY: Village of Suffern Bicentennial Committee, 1973), 84.
William J. Myles, *Harriman Trails: A Guide and History* (New York: The New York-New Jersey Trail Conference, 1994), 29. There is also a photograph of hikers ascending the very steep, near-vertical slope of "Almost Perpendicular" on page 29.

135. LARGE BOULDER NEAR JOHNSONTOWN ROAD CUL-DE-SAC

Type of Formation: Large Boulder
WOW Factor: 5
Location: Sloatsburg (Orange County)
Tenth Edition, NYS Atlas & Gazetteer: p. 107, D9–10; **Earlier Edition NYS Atlas & Gazetteer**: p. 32, C2
Parking GPS Coordinates: 41º10.803'N 74º09.822'W
Large Boulder near Cul-de-sac GPS Coordinates: 41º10.784'N 74º09.876'W
Accessibility: 0.05-mile walk
Degree of Difficulty: Easy
Additional Information: Southern Harriman Bear Mtn. Trails, Trail Map 3
parks.ny.gov/parks/attachments/HarrimanTrailMap.pdf

Description: This large boulder is frequently seen, greeting hikers at the start of the Blue Disc Trail.

History: At an earlier time, Johnsontown Road continued farther north beyond the cul-de-sac. This section was abandoned in 1962 when Seven Lakes Drive was constructed.

Directions: From Sloatsburg (junction of Routes 97/Seven Lakes Drive and 17), drive northeast on Route 97/Seven Lakes Drive for 0.5 mile. As soon as you pass under I-87 (NYS Thruway), turn left onto Johnsontown Road and head northeast for ~1.7 miles. Park at the cul-de-sac.

From the cul-de-sac, walk back along the road for 100 feet, crossing over a tiny stream, and turn right at the start of the Blue-Disc Trail. The large rock is immediately to your left.

Large boulder near Blue Disc trailhead. Photograph by Dan Balogh.

136. HORSESTABLE ROCK

WOW Factor: 4
Location: Montebello (Rockland County)
Tenth Edition, NYS Atlas & Gazetteer: p. 107, E10; **Earlier Edition NYS Atlas & Gazetteer**: p. 32, CD2–3
Parking GPS Coordinates: 41º08.748'N 74º06.760'W
Horsestable Rock GPS Coordinates: 41º09.828'N 74º06.127'W (Google Earth)
Accessibility: ~2.2-mile hike
Degree of Difficulty: Moderate
Additional Information: Map of Kakiat County Park is available at rocklandgov.com/files/7413/4555/9420/Parks_Kakiat_Map.pdf
　　　　Southern Harriman Bear Mtn. Trails, Trail Map 3
　　　　parks.ny.gov/parks/attachments/HarrimanTrailMap.pdf

308

Rock Walks

Description: Horsestable Rock is a large boulder that sits close to the gas line corridor that runs northwest/southeast in the woods above Montebello. According to Cornelia F. Bedell, in *Now and Then and Long Ago in Rockland County, New York*, the "...rock weighs many hundreds of tons..."

The rock was named for its proximity to Horsestable Mountain.

History: The 376-acre Kakiat County Park was created in 1972, eleven years after the County Board of Supervisors bought the land.

"Kakiat" is Native American for *kackyachtaweke*, a word that means a "draw" — a place where one side of a stream is open, and the other side is bounded by a hill.

Directions: From Suffern (junction of Route 202/Wayne Avenue and Orange Avenue), take Route 202/Wayne Avenue/Haverstraw Road northeast for ~3.0 miles. Opposite the Viola Elementary School, turn left into the Kakiat County Park and park in the designated parking area.

From the parking area, cross over the bridge spanning the Mahwah River. Follow the white-blazed Kakiat Trail northwest for 0.9 mile. When you come to the gas line corridor, turn right, and follow the corridor northeast for ~1.2 miles. Horsestable Rock will be on your right, less than 35 feet from the edge of the woods.

Resources: nynjctbotany.org/whudson/nykakiat.html.
rocklandgov.com/departments/environmental-resources/county-parks-and-dog-runs/kakiat-park.
Cornelia F. Bedell, *Now and Then and Long Ago in Rockland County, New York* (New City, NY: The Historical Society of Rockland County, 1968), 10.

137. THE EGG

Type of Formation: Large Rock
WOW Factor: 5
Location: Montebello (Orange County)
Tenth Edition, NYS Atlas & Gazetteer: p. 107, D10; **Earlier Edition NYS Atlas & Gazetteer**: p. 32, A3–4
Parking GPS Coordinates: 41º08.748'N 74º06.760'W
Destination GPS Coordinates: *Rock at junction of Suffern-Bear Mtn. Trail and Conklins Crossing* -- 41º10.162'N 74º06.879'W (a guesstimate); *The Egg* -- 41º10.137'N 74º06.616'W; *Boulder near The Egg* -- 41º10.132'N 74º06.630'W
Accessibility: 2.8-mile hike
Degree of Difficulty: Moderately difficult
Additional Information: Southern Harriman Bear Mtn. Trails, Trail Map 3
parks.ny.gov/parks/attachments/HarrimanTrailMap.pdf

Description: The Egg is a massive dome of rock jutting out from the woods. Some have described it as a "great boulder."

The Egg. Photograph by Dan Balogh.

Along the way to The Egg, two large boulders are encountered at the junction of the Suffern-Bear Mtn. Trail and Conklins Crossing.

There is also a boulder of some size 80 feet southwest of The Egg.

Directions: From Suffern (junction of Routes 202/Wayne Avenue and 59/Orange Avenue), take Route 202/Wayne Avenue (Haverstraw Road) northeast for ~3.0 miles. Opposite the Viola Elementary School, turn left into the Kakiat County Park and park in the designated parking area.

From the parking area, cross over the bridge spanning the Mahwah River and follow the white-blazed Kakiat Trail northwest for 1.5 miles. At a junction, turn right onto the yellow-blazed Suffern-Bear Mtn. Trail and proceed northeast. At 1.1 miles, you will pass by the Conklins Crossing junction; in another 0.2 mile, you will come to The Egg (after a total of 2.8 miles from the start).

The Egg can also be reached from the start of the Suffern-Bear Mtn. Trail, but it involves a trek of 5.8 miles.

Resources: backpacker.com/trips/new-york-ny-southern-harriman-loop. youtube.com/watch?v=lXz4FZnXdTc – A 2:23 minute video by the Harriman Hikers of a hike up to The Egg can be viewed.

138. STONE GIANT

Type of Formation: Large Boulder; Rock-Shelter
WOW Factor: 5
Location: Sloatsburg (Orange County)
Tenth Edition, NYS Atlas & Gazetteer: p. 107, D10; **Earlier Edition NYS Atlas & Gazetteer**: p. 32, C2–3
Parking GPS Coordinates: 41º10.430'N 74º10.118'W
Destination GPS Coordinates – *Glacial Erratics* – Not determined; *Stone Giant #1*: 41º10.495'N 74º08.263'W; *Stone Giant #2*: 41º10.513'N 74º08.253'W (Google Earth)
Accessibility: *Glacial Erratics* -- ~1.0-mile hike; *Stone Giants* -- ~2.7-mile hike *
Degree of Difficulty: Moderate
Additional Information: Southern Harriman Bear Mtn. Trails, Trail Map 3 parks.ny.gov/parks/attachments/HarrimanTrailMap.pdf

Description: *Two Unnamed Glacial Erratics* -- According to Stella Green and H. Neil Zimmerman, in *50 Hikes in the Lower Hudson Valley*, "Two huge erratics frame a small waterfall on the brook…"

The *Stone Giant*, aka *Ga-Nus-Quah Rock*, is a grouping of large, 15-foot-high rocks next to Pine Meadow Brook. Google Earth shows two sites that are relatively close together.

Rock Walks

In *Suffern: 200 Years 1773–1973*, the Stone Giant site is described as "An Indian rockshelter with a huge boulder known as 'Ganusquah (Stone Giant)...'" In addition, "there is a fireplace here, and rocky cliffs to examine..."

An old photograph of the Stone Giant shows the profile of a Native American face with a broad, protruding proboscis, which is perhaps the feature that gave the rock its name.

Stone Giant. Old photograph.

Directions: From north of Sloatsburg (junction of Routes 97/Seven Lakes Drive & 17/Orange Turnpike), drive northeast on Route 97/Seven Lakes Drive for 1.5 miles and turn right into the Reeves Meadow Information Center, named for Robert Reeves who operated a farm in the area.

Starting from the parking area, follow the red-blazed Pine Meadow Trail east. Just before you reach the point where the yellow-blazed Stony Brook Path comes in on your left at 0.4 mile, take note of two large erratics that Stella Green and H. Neil Zimmerman refer to in *50 Hikes in the Lower Hudson Valley*.

At 0.6 miles, the trail crosses the Columbia Gas Transmission Company pipeline; at 1.2 miles, the Hillburn-Torne-Sebago Trail is reached and passed, as well as a footbridge, at 1.6 miles. Finally, at 1.8 miles, you will come to two sets of large rocks—the Stone

Rock Walks

Giants—which are on the right side of the trail. Look for the rock-shelter that is reported in *Suffern: 200 Years 1773–1973*.

Resources: New York-New Jersey Trail Conference, *Day Walker: 32 Hikes in the New York Metropolitan Area. Second Edition* (Mahwah, NJ: New York-New Jersey Trail Conference, 2002), 173.
backpacker.com/trips/new-york-city-pine-meadow-lake#!
Village of Suffern Bicentennial Committee, *Suffern: 200 Years 1773–1973* (Suffern, NY: Village of Suffern Bicentennial Committee, 1973), 77. A photograph of the Giant Stone can be seen on page 79.
William J. Myles, *Harriman Trails: A Guide and History* (New York: The New York-New Jersey Trail Conference, 1994). A photograph of William Myles taken at Ga-Nus-Quah Rock in 1936 is shown on page 91.
Stella Green and H. Neil Zimmerman, *50 Hikes in the Lower Hudson Valley* (Woodstock, VT: Backcountry Guides, 2002), 116.
nynjtc.org/hike/diamond-mountainstony-brook-loop#dialog-hike-description.
mountainproject.com/area/107403866/ga-nus-quah-rocks.
Leonard M. Adkins and the Appalachian Trail Conservancy, *Along the Appalachian Trail, New Jersey, New York, and Connecticut: Images of America* (Charleston, SC: Arcadia Publishing, 2014), 51. A hiker is shown leaning against the rock.
New York-New Jersey Trail Conference, *New York Walk Book. Sixth Edition* (New York: New York-New Jersey Trail Conference, 1998), 292.

139. THREE WITCHES

Type of Formation: Large Boulder
WOW Factor: 5
Location: Willow Grove (Rockland County)
Tenth Edition, NYS Atlas & Gazetteer: p. 108, D1; **Earlier Edition NYS Atlas & Gazetteer**: p. 32, C3
Parking GPS Coordinates: 41º13.786′N 74º03.619′W
Three Witches GPS Coordinates: 41º13.486′N 74º03.862′W (Google Earth)
Accessibility: 0.5-mile-long hike
Degree of Difficulty: Moderate
Additional Information: Southern Harriman Bear Mtn. Trails, Trail Map
3parks.ny.gov/parks/attachments/HarrimanTrailMap.pdf

Rock Walks

Description: The Three Witches (possibly named after the three Witches from Shakespeare's play *Macbeth*) consist of three, large glacial erratics somewhat aligned in a row. Some hikers refer to them as Moe, Larry, and Curly.

History: The Suffern-Bear Mountain Trail takes you through the former estate of George Briggs Buchanan, who was vice president of the Corn Products Refining Company, producer of KARO syrup. Buchanan named his estate ORAK, which is KARO spelled backwards. Clever, huh?

Directions: From the Palisades Interstate Parkway, get off at Exit 14, and drive northwest on Willow Grove Road for 1.5 miles. From where Gate Hill Road enters on your right, continue northwest on Gate Hill Road/Kanawauke Road for another 0.2 mile and park in a pull-off on your left.

From the parking area, follow the yellow-blazed Suffern-Bear Mountain Trail southwest. You will pass through ORAK—the ruins of the Buchanan estate at 0.4 mile. The Three Witches are encountered soon after, ~0.5 mile from the start of the hike.

Resources: New York-New Jersey Trail Conference, *New York Walk Book. Sixth Edition* (New York: New York-New Jersey Trail Conference, 1998), 300. The book describes the Three Witches as "…large glacial erratics…"

140. RACCOON BROOK HILL CAVES

Type of Formation: Talus Cave
WOW Factor: 5
Location: Sloatsburg (Rockland County)
Tenth Edition, NYS Atlas & Gazetteer: p. 107, D10; **Earlier Edition NYS Atlas & Gazetteer:** p. 32, C2–3
Parking GPS Coordinates: 41º'N 74º'W
Raccoon Brook Hill Caves GPS Coordinates: 41º10.376'N 74º08.243'W (Google Earth)
Accessibility: ~2.0-mile hike

Rock Walks

Degree of Difficulty: Difficult
Additional Information: Southern Harriman Bear Mtn. Trails, Trail Map 3
parks.ny.gov/parks/attachments/HarrimanTrailMap.pdf

Description: *Raccoon Brook Hill Caves* -- In *Suffern: 200 Years 1773–1973*, the Village of Suffern Bicentennial Committee describe the caves as a "jumble of rock boulders" that contain a number of tiny caves.

History: According to William J. Myles, in *Harriman Trails: A Guide and History*, Native American artifacts have been found at the site and are now at the Bear Mountain Museum.

Near Raccoon Brook Hill Caves. Photograph by Dan Balogh

Directions: From north of Sloatsburg (junction of Routes 97/Seven Lakes Drive & 17/Orange Turnpike), drive northeast on Route 97/Seven Lakes Drive for 1.5 miles and turn right into the Reeves Meadow Information Center.

From the Information Center, follow the red-blazed Pine Meadows Trail east for 1.6 miles, along the way passing by a gas line corridor at 0.6 mile, and the Hillburn-Torre-Sebago Trail at 1.2 miles. Be sure to stay on the south side of Pine Meadow Brook. At a junction with the Kakiat Trail, bear right and follow the Kakiak Trail southeast for 0.3 mile. Then turn left onto the black-marked Raccoon Brook Hills Trail. You will come to the caves within 0.05 mile, literally at the foot of Raccoon Hill. If you arrive at the yellow-blazed Poached Egg Trail (on your left), then you have gone almost 0.5 mile too far along the Raccoon Brook Hills Trail.

Resources: Village of Suffern Bicentennial Committee, *Suffern: 200 Years 1773–1973* (Suffern, NY: Village of Suffern Bicentennial Committee, 1973), 78.
nycdayhiking.com/hikes/raccoonbrook.htm.
nynjtc.org/hike/raccoon-brook-hills-trailcascade-slid-loop#dialog-hike-description.
scratchpad.wikia.com/wiki/Raccoon_Brook_Hills_Trail.
William J. Myles, *Harriman Trails: A Guide and History* (New York: The New York-New Jersey Trail Conference, 1994), 100.

141. THE PULPIT

Type of Formation: Large Rock
WOW Factor: Unknown
Location: Tuxedo (Orange County)
Tenth Edition, NYS Atlas & Gazetteer: p. 107, D10; **Earlier Edition NYS Atlas & Gazetteer**: p. 32, A3–4
Parking GPS Coordinates: 41º10.430'N 74º10.118'W
The Pulpit GPS Coordinates: Not determined
Accessibility: >3.0-mile hike
Degree of Difficulty: Moderately difficult
Additional Information: Southern Harriman Bear Mtn. Trails, Trail Map 3parks.ny.gov/parks/attachments/HarrimanTrailMap.pdf

Description: The Pulpit is a large rock that juts out from the cliff edge on top of a bluff.

Rock Walks

History: The Raccoon Brook Trail was blazed in 1931 by Paul Scubert. He named it "Trail of the Raccoon Hills." According to William J. Myles, in *Harriman Trails: A Guide and History*, the jutting rock was called The Pulpit by early hikers, but no credit is given to any one hiker in particular.

Standing above The Pulpit. Photograph by Dan Balogh.

Directions: From north of Sloatsburg (junction of Routes 97/Seven Lakes Drive & 17/Orange Turnpike), drive northeast on Route 97/Seven Lakes Drive for 1.5 miles and turn right into the Reeves Meadow Information Center.

From the Information Center parking area, walk 0.2 mile west on the Pine Meadow Trail. Then turn left onto the blue-blazed Seven Hills Trail and head first south, and then north, for 2.6 miles.

When you come to the junction with the Raccoon Brook Hills Trail, turn right and head east on the Raccoon Hill Brook Trail. At 0.3 mile you will pass by the Reeves Brook Trail (which enters on your left). Soon after, you will cross over a small brook and then begin climbing a steep fault scarp. Look up to see *The Pulpit*, high above you.

Resources: William J. Myles, *Harriman Trails: A Guide and History* (New York: The New York-New Jersey Trail Conference, 1994), 99 & 100. scratchpad.wikia.com/wiki/Raccoon_Brook_Hills_Trail. northjersey.com/story/sports/2017/08/30/hiking-harriman-state-park/608293001.

142. MONITOR ROCK & CRACKED DIAMOND

Type of Formation: Large Boulder
WOW Factor: 7
Location: Sloatsburg (Rockland County)
Tenth Edition, NYS Atlas & Gazetteer: p. 107, D10; **Earlier Edition NYS Atlas & Gazetteer**: p. 33, C2–3
Parking GPS Coordinates: 41º11.920'N 74º07.773'W
Destination GPS Coordinates: *Monitor Rock* -- 41º11.401'N 74º07.489'W; *Cracked Diamond* -- ~41º11.324'N 74º07.457'W (estimated); *Two other boulders* -- 41º11.368'N 74º07.499'W (100 feet on path to right from path left to Monitor Rock)
Accessibility: *Monitor Rock* -- 0.7-mile hike; *Cracked Diamond* – 0.8-mile hike
Degree of Difficulty: Moderate
Additional Information: Southern Harriman Bear Mtn. Trails, Trail Map 3 parks.ny.gov/parks/attachments/HarrimanTrailMap.pdf

Description: *Monitor Rock* -- In *Harriman Trails: A Guide and History*, William J. Myles describes the rock as a "...large quartz boulder" located on a ledge. Pictures of it show a huge overhang, and a tight squeeze between two ledges.

Raymond H. Torrey, Frank Place. Jr. and Robert L. Dickinson, in *New York Walk Book. Third Edition*, draw attention to "a ledge surmounted by a six-foot white quartz boulder."

Cracked Diamond is a very large, tilted rock that William Myles calls a "great boulder." The rock is located on a ridge on Diamond Mountain, directly to the left of the trail.

A number of other good-sized erratics are located in the general area, but I have no real descriptions of them.

History: Monitor Rock was named by the Fresh Air Club after a copy of the Christian Science Monitor was found tucked away under the rock.

During the days when Woodtown Road was drivable, the Seven Hills Trail originally started from Monitor Rock. The road is now a horse trail.

Diamond Mountain was called Halfway Mountain until 1927.

Rock Walks

Directions: From Sloatsburg (junction of Routes 97/Seven Lakes Drive & 17), drive northeast on Route 97/Seven Lakes Drive for ~4.3 miles. Turn left into a parking area for Lake Sebago (a man-made lake created in 1925 by the damming up of Stony Brook and Emmetfield Swamp).

Approaching Monitor Rock. Photograph by Dan Balogh.

Walk across Seven Lakes Drive and head south on the blue-blazed Seven Hills Trail for ~0.6 mile. Turn left (west) onto the former Woodtown Road and quickly cross Diamond Creek. After 0.1 mile, the trail leaves the old road, and then turns sharply right.

To Monitor Rock -- Follow a white-blazed spur path to the left that leads to Monitor Rock at a ledge in 300 feet.

To Cracked Diamond – Continue following the Seven Hills Trail for another 0.1 mile. You will come to the Cracked Diamond Rock 0.1 mile before the intersection with the Tuxedo-Mt. Ivy Trail.

According to Charlie Stein, in his photoblog lowmileage.com /2013/06/30/harriman-state-park-rockland-county-new-york-2, a number of large boulders can be seen along this hike, of which

Cracked Diamond Rock is just one of many. This seems to be par for the course for many sections of Harriman State Park.

Resources: William J. Myles, *Harriman Trails: A Guide and History* (New York: The New York-New Jersey Trail Conference, 1994), 126.
scenesfromthetrail.com/2017/08/15/diamond-mountain-loop-from-lake-sebago-boat-launch-harriman-state-park – This site contains excellent photographs of Monitor Rock and Cracked Diamond.
lowmileage.com/2013/06/30/harriman-state-park-rockland-county-new-york-2.
Raymond H. Torrey, Frank Place, Jr. & Robert L. Dickinson, *New York Walk Book. Third Edition* (NY: The American Geographical Society, 1951), 177.

143. HIGH HILL TRAIL BOULDER

Type of Formation: Large Boulder
WOW Factor: Unknown
Location: Sloatsburg (Rockland County)
Tenth Edition, NYS Atlas & Gazetteer: p. 107, D10; **Earlier Edition NYS Atlas & Gazetteer**: p. 32, C2–3
Parking GPS Coordinates: 41º12.637'N 74º07.289'W
Estimated Destination GPS Coordinates: 41º12.641'N 74º07.275'W
Accessibility: Roadside or near roadside
Degree of Difficulty: Easy

Description: The only reference to the High Hill Trail Boulder that I can find is taken from Raymond H. Torrey, Frank Place, Jr., and Robert L. Dickinson's book, *New York Walk Book. Third Edition*. They call it, simply, a "great rock." Of course, what constitutes a "great rock" is another matter entirely, and one without an objective answer.

History: At one time, the High Hills Trail (starting at the boulder) led uphill to the summit of ~1,200-foot-high High Hills.

Rock Walks

Directions: The following are directions from Raymond H. Torrey, Frank Place, Jr., and Robert L. Dickinson's book that I am basing my extrapolations on: "Take Johnstown Road north from Baker Camp Road (which goes off Seven Lakes Drive just north of Sebago). About 0.2 mile north, just before Old Johnstown Road ends at a high cut, scramble down and cross Seven Lakes Drive. On the opposite bank, the beginning of High Hill Trail is marked by a great boulder with a cairn on top."

Here's what I've come up with: From Sloatsburg (junction of Routes 97/Seven Lakes Drive & 17), drive northeast on 97/Seven Lakes Drive for ~4.8 miles. You will see, to your left, Camp Baker Road which, if you were to follow it north for 0.3 mile, would take you to a horseshoe turn, from where you could park and continue north on the old Johnstown Road for another 0.2 mile, and then scramble down an embankment to Seven Lakes Drive.

Knowing this, then, let's continue north on Seven Lakes Drive for 0.45 mile from the turn for Camp Baker Road. If all goes well, you should come to the approximate spot where you would be if you followed Raymond H. Torrey, Frank Place, Jr., and Robert L. Dickinson's directions. This spot is marked by a large rock or rock outcrop on your left at 41º12.640'N 74º07.307'W, which is where the northbound and southbound lanes of Seven Lakes Road begin to divide. The "great rock," I presume, must be directly across on the east side of Seven Lakes Drive, or somewhere close by.

The boulder would be a snap to find if the trail up to High Hill still existed, but I suspect it was abandoned years ago, for I do not see the trail mentioned in the current literature nor on contemporary trail maps, nor even as an outline on Google Earth.

Resources: Raymond H. Torrey, Frank Place, Jr., & Robert L. Dickinson, *New York Walk Book. Third Edition* (NY: The American Geographical Society, 1951), 288 & 419.

144. GLACIAL BOULDER, KITCHEN STAIRS, VALLEY OF DRY BONES, THE ODD COUPLE, MACILVAIN'S ROCKS, GRANDPA & GRANDMA ROCKS, LEAN-ON-ME, AND THE EGG

Type of Formation: Large Boulder
WOW Factor: 4–7
Location: Suffern (Rockland County)
Tenth Edition, NYS Atlas & Gazetteer: p. 107, E10; **Earlier Edition NYS Atlas & Gazetteer**: p. 32, CD2–3
Parking GPS Coordinates: 41º07.017'N 74º09.315'W
Trailhead GPS Coordinates: 41º07.134'N 74º09.465'W
Destination GPS Coordinates: *Glacial Boulder* -- 41º07.548'N 74º09.157'W (Google Earth); *Kitchen Stairs* -- 41º07.912'N 74º08.891'W (Google Earth); *Valley of Dry Bones* -- 41º08.963'N 74º08.022'W (Google Earth); *Odd Couple* -- 41º08.986'N 74º08.006'W (Google Earth); *MacIlvain's Rocks* and *Grandpa & Grandma Rocks* -- 41º09.558'N 74º07.304'W (Google Earth); *Lean-on-me* -- 41º09.558'N 74º07.304'W (Google Earth); *The Egg* -- 41º10.148'N 74º006.638'W (Google Earth)

Accessibility: *Glacial Boulder* – ~1.0 mile hike
Kitchen Stairs – 1.5-mile hike
Valley of Dry Bones – 3.2-mile hike
Odd Couple -- 3.3-mile hike
MacIlvain's Rocks – 4.3-mile hike
Grandpa & Grandpa Rocks – 4.4-mile hike
Lean-on-me – 4.8-mile hike
The Egg – 5.8-mile hike

Approaching the Valley of Dry Bones. Photograph by Dan Balogh.

Degree of Difficulty: Moderate to difficult
Additional Information: Southern Harriman Bear Mtn. Trails, Trail Map 3
parks.ny.gov/parks/attachments/HarrimanTrailMap.pdf

Rock Walks

Description: *Glacial Boulder* – A photograph of this unnamed boulder reveals a stand-alone, inclined rock some 6–8 feet high.

Kitchen Stairs is described as "...a broken fault face..."

Valley of Dry Bones is a field of (relatively speaking) small boulders. It was named for the way in which the rocks resemble a graveyard of animal bones; a reference, apparently, to Ezekiel, Chapter 37, in the Bible.

The *Odd Couple* are two large boulders in close proximity to

Grandpa Rock. Photograph by Dan Balogh.

one another. Apparently, they look unevenly matched size-wise.

MacIlvain's Rocks are a field of smaller rocks named after William J, MacIlvain of the Fresh Air Club who managed to lead his group through what seemed to be, in retrospect, the most difficult route possible.

Grandma Rock. Photograph by Laura Balogh.

Grandpa & Grandma Rocks are two large boulders, one particularly pointed, surrounded by a retinue of grandchildren (smaller boulders). They were named by Frank Place & Raymond Torry in 1926 while scouting the Suffern-Bear Mountain Trail.

Lean-on-me is a large, oval shaped boulder on a platform of exposed bedrock. Its front end rests on a smaller boulder.

The Egg is called "a great boulder" by William J. Myles in *Harriman Trails: A Guide and History,* undoubtedly because of its size and oval shape. To my thinking, it looks like a large dome.

Rock Walks

History: Kitchen Stairs, Valley of Dry Bones, and Grandma & Grandpa Rocks were named by Frank Place in 1925.

Directions: At Suffern (junction of Routes 59 & 202), park in the commuter parking area off Route 59 just south of the Thruway overpass. If it is still the case that hikers are only allowed to park there on weekends, then you will need to drive around Suffern to find roadside parking (at least during the week).

Regardless of where you have ended parking, walk north on Orange Avenue/Route 59. As soon as you have passed under I-87/New York State Thruway, continue north for <0.1 mile, and pick up the Suffern-Bear Mountain trailhead, which will be on your right.

Follow the Suffern-Bear Mountain Trail (SBM) northeast. At 1.4 miles, you will ascend a rock formation known as *Kitchen Stairs*. At 3.2 miles, you will come to the *Valley of Dry Bones*, where many boulders litter the woods along the trail.

In less than 0.05 mile further you will come upon the *Odd Couple*, two large glacial boulders in close proximity to one another.

After ~4.4 miles (or 0.2 mile from crossing the Columbia Gas Company pipe line corridor and passing through the MacIlvain's Rocks), you will come to the *Grandpa & Grandma Rocks*.

Within another 0.4 mile, *Lean-on-me Rock* is encountered.

At 5.8 miles, *The Egg* is reached shortly after passing by the white-blazed Conklin Crossing which enters on your left. The Egg, if nothing else, provides a high point with views.

Resources: New York-New Jersey Trail Conference, *New York Walk Book. Sixth Edition* (New York: New York-New Jersey Trail Conference, 1998), 299. Mention is made of "...an area of giant boulders" soon followed by "...two big boulders, called Grandpa and Grandma Rocks."
William J. Myles, *Harriman Trails: A Guide and History* (New York: The New York-New Jersey Trail Conference, 1994), 59, 136, & 137. The MacIlvain's Rocks are mentioned on page 138.
myharriman.com/suffern-bear-mountain-trail.
lowmileage.com/2014/09/01/harriman-state-park-rockland-county-new-york-3 – The site contains photographs of some unnamed rocks as well as the Valley of Dry Bones.
myharriman.com/suffern-bear-mountain-trail-83-years-ago-stiff-new-trail-calls-hikers.

Raymond H. Torrey, Frank Place, Jr. & Robert L. Dickinson, *New York Walk Book. Third Edition* (NY: The American Geographical Society, 1951), 179.

145. WEST POINTING ROCK

Type of Formation: Large Boulder
WOW Factor: 5
Location: Ladentown (Rockland County)
Tenth Edition, NYS Atlas & Gazetteer: p. 108, D1; **Earlier Edition NYS Atlas & Gazetteer**: p. 32, C3
Parking GPS Coordinates: 41º11.112'N 74º04.478'W
West Pointing Rock GPS Coordinates: Undetermined
Accessibility: ~3.0-mile hike
Degree of Difficulty: Moderately Difficult
Additional Information: Southern Harriman Bear Mtn. Trails, Trail Map 3
parks.ny.gov/parks/attachments/HarrimanTrailMap.pdf

Description: William J. Myles, in *Harriman Trails: A Guide and History*, describes the rock as "...a 10 x 14-foot boulder, with a sharp projection on its west side."

Directions: From the Palisades Interstate Parkway, get off at Exit 13 for Route 202/ Haverstraw/ Suffern,

West Pointing Rock. Photograph by Dan Balogh.

and drive west on Route 202 for ~1.8 miles. Turn right onto Ladentown Road and head north for 0.2 mile. Then turn left onto Mountain Road and proceed northwest for 0.2 mile. When you come to Diltzes Road, turn left and head southwest for 0.2 mile. Finally,

Rock Walks

bear right into a parking area 100 feet before coming to a power station.

From the parking area, follow the red-marked Tuxedo-Mt. Ivy Trail northwest for ~3.0 miles. Bear right onto the white-blazed Breakneck Mtn Trail and head northeast for 0.2 mile to reach West Pointing Rock.

Stella Green and H. Neil Zimmerman in *50 Hikes in the Lower Hudson Valley* describe "...an open slab with large boulders..." along the trail, which may be West Pointing Rock or another rock formation entirely.

Resources: William J. Myles, *Harriman Trails: A Guide and History* (New York: The New York-New Jersey Trail Conference, 1994), 32. harrimanhiker.com/2014/01/tmi-trailhead-breakneck-mountain-loop.html. Stella Green and H. Neil Zimmerman, *50 Hikes in the Lower Hudson Valley* (Woodstock, VT: Backcountry Guides, 2002), 119.

146. IRON MOUNTAIN ERRATIC

Type of Formation: Large Boulder
WOW Factor: 6
Location: Ladentown (Rockland County)
Tenth Edition, NYS Atlas & Gazetteer: p. 108, D1; **Earlier Edition NYS Atlas & Gazetteer**: p. 32, C3
Parking GPS Coordinates: 41º11.112'N 74º04.478'W
Iron Mountain Erratic GPS Coordinates: Not determined
Accessibility: <2.0-mile hike
Degree of Difficulty: Moderately difficult

Description: The quirky Iron Mountain Erratic is a 10-foot-high boulder standing upright. If you look at the photograph and use a little imagination, the rock seemingly turns into a human foot complete with toes.

Directions: From the Palisades Interstate Parkway, get off at Exit 13 for Route 202/ Haverstraw/Suffern, and drive west on Route 202 for ~1.8 miles. Turn right onto Ladentown Road and head north for 0.2

mile. Then turn left onto Mountain Road and proceed northwest for 0.2 mile. When you come to Diltzes Road, turn left and head southwest for 0.2 mile. Finally, bear right into a parking area 100 feet before coming to a power station.

From the parking area, follow the red-marked Tuxedo-Mt. Ivy Trail northeast along a gas-line corridor for 0.2 mile. When the Tuxedo-Mt. Ivy Trail veers off to the left, continue following the gas-line for another 0.7 mile, or roughly 1.0 mile from the parking area. The unmarked Iron Mountain Trail begins here, on the left.

When you reach the top of Iron Mountain, look for the glacial erratic along the ridge line that extends north/south.

Iron Mountain Erratic. Photograph by Dan Balogh.

Resources: harrimanhiker.com/2018/07/iron-mountain-and-lime-kiln-mountain.html.

Rock Walks

147. VALLEY OF BOULDERS, GREAT BOULDERS, INDIAN ROCK-SHELTER, & BOWLING ROCKS

Type of Formation: Large Rock; Rock-Shelter
WOW Factor: 4–5
Location: Southfields (Orange County)
Tenth Edition, NYS Atlas & Gazetteer: p. 107, D9; **Earlier Edition NYS Atlas & Gazetteer**: p. 32, BC2
Parking GPS Coordinates: 41º14.507'N 74º10.534'W
Destination GPS Coordinates: *Valley of Boulders* -- 41º14.991'N 74º09.060'W (estimated); *Great Boulders* – Not determined; *Indian Rock-Shelter* -- 41º14.844'N 74º08.988'W (estimated); *Bowling Rocks* -- 41º14.647'N 74º07.572'W (Google Earth)
Accessibility: *Valley of Boulders* – 1.0-mile hike; *Great Boulders* – 1.9-mile hike; *Indian Rock-Shelter* -- ~2.2-mile hike; *Bowling Rocks* – ~4.2-mile hike
Degree of Difficulty: Moderately difficult-Difficult
Additional Information: Southern Harriman Bear Mtn. Trails, Trail Map 3 parks.ny.gov/parks/attachments/HarrimanTrailMap.pdf

Description: *Valley of Boulders* consists of a number of large rocks that have calved off from a low-lying escarpment ridge. William J. Myles, in *Harriman Trails: A Guide and History* writes, "The ravine of the brook is known as Valley of Boulders."

Great Boulders, size-wise, are encountered along the left side of the trail.

Indian Rock-Shelter – This impressive rock-shelter overlooks Green Pond, providing a nifty place to stop and have a bite or two, or to just take a breather. According to Stella Green and H. Neil Zimmerman, in *50 Hikes in the Lower Hudson Valley*, Green Pond is slowly atrophying and it is only a matter of time until the pond becomes Green Swamp.

Bowling Rocks – According to William J. Myles, "The boulders that dot the bare rock give rise to the name 'Bowling Rocks'."

History: The Nurian Trail was named after Kerson Nurian, a Bulgarian electrical engineer who constructed the trail ~1929.

Directions: From Southfields (junction of Routes 17 & 19), drive south on Route 17 for >0.1 mile and turn left into the parking area for

328

the Southfields Post Office, making sure to park as unobtrusively as possible. Walk north up Spring Street for >0.1 mile, and then right onto Railroad Avenue, which takes you to the railroad tracks within several hundred feet.

Indian Rock-Shelter. Photograph by Dan Balogh.

Follow the railroad tracks north for 0.1 mile, and then veer right, quickly crossing over the Ramapo River via a bridge and then over the New York State Thruway via the Southfields Pedestrian Bridge, aka Nurian Bridge. By now, you will have gone roughly 0.4 mile from the parking area. Head east on the white-blazed Nurian Trail. You will cross over a paved road at 1.4 miles and then, further on, trek through the "Valley of Boulders" (a ravine). "Great boulders" are passed at 1.9 miles.

Indian Rock-Shelter -- At 2.0 miles, turn right onto the yellow-marked Dunning Trail (named for James M. Dunning, past chairman of the AMC Trails Committee), which quickly takes you to the Indian Rock-Shelter in less than 0.2 mile.

329

Rock Walks

Bowling Rocks – Continue east on the yellow-blazed Dunning Trail from the second junction with the Nurian Trail. At 1.1 miles from the start of the Dunning Trail, the White Bar Trail junction is reached. Bear right onto the White Bar Trail, continuing also on the Dunning Trail. Shortly after, the two separate. Stay right on the Dunning Trail. At 1.7 miles, the Dunning Trail is crossed by the red-blazed Ramapo-Dunderberg Trail. Just a short ways beyond, you will come to the Bowling Rocks, on your left.

Resources: William J. Myles, *Harriman Trails: A Guide and History* (New York: The New York-New Jersey Trail Conference, 1994), 41 & 85.
northjersey.com/story/sports/2017/08/02/hiking-harriman-state-park/529462001.
Stella Green and H. Neil Zimmerman, *50 Hikes in the Lower Hudson Valley* (Woodstock, VT: Backcountry Guides, 2002), 122.
New York-New Jersey Trail Conference, *New York Walk Book. Sixth Edition* (New York: New York-New Jersey Trail Conference, 1998), 286.
"…an overhanging wall of stone over a jumble of boulders."
rockclimbing.com/routes/North_America/United_States/New_York/Upsta te/Hudson_Highlands.
stavislost.com/hikes/trail/harriman-state-park-island-pond-and-valley-of-boulders-loop.
nynjtc.org/content/index-harriman-bear-mountain-trails-map – index for map.
youtube.com/watch?v=ACV4nCTOfIg – youtube tour.
harrimanhiker.com/2013/10/nurian-trail-to-boston-mine-harriman.html.

Rock Walks

BERGEN COUNTY

Bergen County occupies the northeastern corner of the state of New Jersey and borders the Hudson River across from Manhattan, the Bronx, and the southern part of Westchester County.

148. LAMONT ROCK

Rockleigh Woods Sanctuary & Lamont Reserve

Type of Formation: Large Boulder
WOW Factor: 6
Location: Rockleigh (Bergen County, NJ)
Tenth Edition, NYS Atlas & Gazetteer: p. 110, A5; **Earlier Edition NYS Atlas & Gazetteer**: p. 32, D3–4
Parking GPS Coordinates: 41º00.241'N 73º55.532'W
Lamont Rock GPS Coordinates: Not determined
Accessibility: >1.0-mile hike
Degree of Difficulty: Moderate
Additional Information: Rockleigh Municipal Building, 26 Rockleigh Road, Rockleigh, NJ 07647
   nynjtc.org/sites/default/files/RockleighLamontTrailMap_Color2015.pdf – Trail map

Description: The Lamont Rock is a 10-foot-high boulder with a pronounced lean to it.

History: Both the Rockleigh Woods Sanctuary and Lamont Reserve were once part of Camp Alpine of the Greater New York Councils, Boy Scouts of America. The 84-acre Rockleigh Woods Sanctuary was purchased in 1975; the 134-acre Lamont Reserve, in 1996.

Directions: From the Palisades Interstate Parkway, get off at Exit 4 for Route 9W and proceed north on Route 9W/Palisades Boulevard for ~1.2 miles. Turn left onto Oak Tree Road and head west for <0.2 mile. Then turn left onto Closter Road which, after 0.6 mile heading southwest and crossing under the Palisades Interstate Parkway, becomes Rockleigh Road.

Rock Walks

In another 0.3 mile, turn left into the driveway for the Rockleigh Municipal Building (opposite Willow Avenue) and park at the rear of the building.

From the rear of the playground area next to where you

Lamont Rock. Photograph by Dan Balogh.

parked, follow the blue-blazed Hutcheon Trail into the woods. At 0.05 mile, bear left at a fork and follow the yellow/blue-blazed Sneden-Harding-Lamont Trail east for 0.1 mile. When you come to the next fork, stay left (as the blue-blazed Hutcheon Trail veers off to the right), and follow the yellow-blazed Sneden-Harding-Lamont Tail as it now proceeds southeast. In another ~0.6 mile, you will pass by the red-blazed Roaring Brook Trail (to your right) and then cross over Roaring Brook.

Right after the stream crossing, you will pass by the white-blazed Lamont Rock Trail (on your right). In less than another 0.05 mile, turn left onto the white-blazed Lamont Rock Trail as it departs

332

from the yellow-blazed Sneden-Harding-Lamont Trail, and follow it to the southeast corner of the preserve. From here, round the corner and continue west on the white-blazed Lamont Rock Trail for another 0.2 mile until you come to the Lamont Rock.

Most of the hike takes place in the Lamont Preserve.

Resources: nynjtc.org/hike/rockleigh-woods-sanctuary-and-lamont -reserve-loop. northjersey.com/story/sports/recreation/2016/07/07/hiking-rockleigh-woods-sanctuary/94889786.

149. HARING ROCK
Tenafly Lost Brook Preserve and Nature Center

Type of Formation: Large Rock
WOW Factor: 6
Location: Tenafly (Bergen County, NJ)
Tenth Edition, NYS Atlas & Gazetteer: p. 110, BC5; **Earlier Edition NYS Atlas & Gazetteer**: p. 24, AB4
Estimated Parking GPS Coordinates: 40º54.476'N 73º56.649'W
Estimated Haring Rock GPS Coordinates: 40º54.495'N 73º56.613'W
Accessibility: 200-foot walk
Degree of Difficulty: Easy
Additional Information: Trail map at tenaflynaturecenter.org/Trail-Map
Trail maps can also be obtained at the Visitor Center at 313 Hudson Avenue, Tenafly, NJ 07670

Description: John Serrao, in *The Wild Palisades of the Hudson*, writes, "'Haring Rock', a huge sandstone erratic which is 10 feet tall, 10 feet around, and weighs 15 tons, is visible on a marked trail off East Clinton Avenue..." It is said to be the largest sandstone glacial erratic in the region.

A second rock formation, called *Little Rock Den*, can also be seen along the Allison Trail, 500 feet before the junction with the orange-blazed Haring Rock Trail.

History: The Haring Rock is named after John J. Haring, an early twentieth-century physician, who would on occasion stop at the rock to take a break while on his journeys.

Haring Rock. Photograph by Dan Balogh

Haring Rock has not been at its present location for very long. It was relocated in order to make room for the Jewish Community Center, now 0.3 mile south, and then cemented in place upside down to ensure that it would stay put.

Both the Haring Rock Trail and the Seely Trail start at Haring Rock.

The Lost Preserve, where the rock is located, and the Tenafly Nature Center (40º55.487'N 73º56.682'W), were founded in 1961. The preserve encompasses 382 acres of land.

Directions: From southeast of Tenafly (junction of Routes 9W and 70/East Clinton Avenue), drive northwest on East Clinton Avenue for 0.5 mile and park in a small pull-off on your right.

From the pull-off, follow the orange-marked Haring Rock Trail northeast for 250 feet. When you come to the junction with the yellow/orange-marked Seely Trail, the rock will be on your right.

Resources: John Serrao, *The Wild Palisades of the Hudson* (Westwood, NJ: Lind PublicatioOns, 1949), 10.
njurbanforest.com/category/haring-rock.
njurbanforest.com/2012/03/19/tenafly-nature-center-lost-brook-preserve –
The site contains a photograph of Haring Rock.

Close-up of Haring Rock

Portion of Palisades   Palisades Section   Palisades Interstate Park

THE PALISADES

The following section goes into detail about a number of unusual rocks to be found in the Palisades—a line of steep cliffs along the west side of the Hudson River that provide dramatic views of the Manhattan skyline. The Palisades, aka New Jersey Palisades and Hudson River Palisades, extend from Jersey City, New Jersey, north to near Nyack, New York, a distance of about twenty miles. The New Jersey portion is less than 0.8 mile in width, encompassing about 2,500 acres. The cliffs start off at around a height of 300 feet at Kings Bluffs near Weehawken and gradually increase in height heading north until reaching a maximum height of 522 feet at Indian Head before ending at Tallman Mountain.

In *The Hudson: From the Wilderness to the Sea*, Benson Lossing writes, "Between Piermont and Hoboken, these rocks present, for a considerable distance, an uninterrupted, rude, columnar front, from appearance, yet not actually so in form. They have a steep slope of debris, which has been crumbling from the cliffs above, during long centuries, by the action of frost and the elements. The ridge is narrow, being in some places not more than three-fourths of a mile in width. It is really an enormous projecting trap-dyke."

The Palisades Interstate Park was created in 1900 to help preserve and safeguard the Palisades for future generations to enjoy. Until then, companies had been free to quarry the rock, and the Palisades were ultimately in danger of disappearing.

Protecting the Palisades proved to be a fairly prodigious job, for most of the Palisade lands were in private ownership, with large summer estates and woodlands overlooking the top of the Palisades, and many riverfront villages below. As in so many cases involving eminent domain, sacrifices had to be made by individual landowners.

The word Palisades comes from the Latin word *palus*, or "stake." With a little imagination, the Palisades can be seen as a wooden palisaded fortification. The Dutch called the Palisades the Dutch equivalent of "Great Chip Rocks."

The rock that forms the Palisades is diabase, more commonly known as traprock (which comes from the Swedish word *trapp* for "stairs"). Similar basalt columns can be seen at the Devil's Tower in Wyoming.

The hamlet of Palisades was earlier known as Snedens Landing.

Resources: Benson Lossing, *The Hudson: From the Wilderness to the Sea* (Sommersworth, NY: New Hampshire Publishing Company, 1972; facsimile of the 1866 edition), 360.
Jeffrey Perls, *Paths along the Hudson: A Guide to Walking and Biking* (New Brunswick, NJ: Rutgers University Press, 2001), 152 & 153.

Rock Walks

150. STATION ROCK

Type of Formation: Large Rock
WOW Factor: 2–3
Location: Palisades (Rockland County)
Tenth Edition, NYS Atlas & Gazetteer: p. 111, B5–6; **Earlier Edition NYS Atlas & Gazetteer**: p. 25, A4
Parking GPS Coordinates: 40º59.327'N 73º54.421'W
Border between Rockland County and Bergen County, N. J.: 40°59.840'N 073°54.163'W
Estimated Station Rock GPS Coordinates: 40º59.984'N 73º54.162'W
Accessibility: 1.8-mile hike (a rough guess)
Degree of Difficulty: Moderately difficult
Additional Information: Map of the Palisades Interstate Park in New Jersey available at njpalisades.org/pdfs/bywayMap.pdf.

Description: According to Alice Munro Haagensen, in *Palisades and Snedens Landing*, "Marking the boundary [between New York and New Jersey] was a great rock near the water in the middle of which was chiseled a line and the words 'Latitude 41°North.' On the south side were marked the words 'New Jersey' and on the north, 'New York'." Haagensen continues by declaring that "Considering the many graffiti on nearby rocks, it seems wise to keep its whereabouts a little vague." It is for this reason, undoubtedly, that an incomplete GPS reading of 40°59'51.20" is given in Haagensen's book.

History: Station Rock is significant, for it marks the early attempts of surveyors to delineate the boundary line between New York and New Jersey at the Palisades. As it turned out, the true border ended up being about 900 feet farther south than the 41st parallel. However, the boundary line still passes through Station Rock, giving New York an extra ten square miles of land.

One source contends that a pole was set into place next to the rock in 1930.

I see that there is also a Station Rock at the top of the Palisade cliffs, roughly 50 feet from the main trail. According to Arthur G. Adams, in *The Hudson River Guidebook*, "Here, atop the cliffs, is a 6 foot memorial shaft erected in 1882."

338

Rock Walks

Directions: Heading north on the Palisades Interstate Parkway, 1.7 miles beyond Exit 2, turn right at a sign for the State Line Lookout. Heading south on the Palisades Interstate Parkway, go 0.4 mile past Exit 3 and then turn left onto a U-Turn that takes you onto the northbound lane of the Parkway. Go 0.4 mile, and get off at the sign for the State Line Lookout.

From either approach, drive northeast for 0.6 mile on the road that leads to the parking area for the State Line Lookout.

From the State Line Lookout parking area, follow the aqua-blazed Long Path north for ~1.1 mile as it begins to descend steeply down the Palisades. When you come to the blue/white-colored Shore Trail, follow it north initially, and then south as it does a U-turn. You will reach the bottom of the Palisades at the base of Peanut Leap Falls and the ruins of the Italian Gardens and former estate of Mary Lawrence-Tonetti in another ~0.8 mile.

Continue south on the Shore Trail. You will know that you are in the general area of Station Rock when you come to a chain-link fence delineating the boundary between Bergen County (N.J.) and Rockland County.

I would suggest that you start looking for Station Rock several hundred feet back north.

If you wish, you can also reach the general area by following the directions in the following chapter that take you across the Giant Stairs, a much more demanding hike.

Resources: Alice Munro Haagensen, *Palisades and Snedens Landing* (Tarrytown, NY: Pilgrimage Publishing, 1986), 26.
en.wikipedia.org/wiki/New_York_-_New_Jersey_Line_War – This site details the NY NJ line war that lasted for 64 years
forums.geocaching.com/GC/index.php?/topic/151312-station-rock-marking-the-east-end-of-the-ny-nj-land-boundary.
Arthur G. Adams, *The Hudson River Guidebook* (NY: Fordham University Press, 1996), 124.

151. GIANT STAIRS

Type of Formation: Huge Talus Slope
WOW Factor: 9
Location: Palisades (Rockland County)
Tenth Edition, NYS Atlas & Gazetteer: p. 111, A6; **Earlier Edition NYS Atlas & Gazetteer**: p. 25, A4–5
Parking GPS Coordinates: 40º59.327'N 73º54.421'W
Giant Stairs GPS Coordinates: 40º59.086'N 73º54.344'W
Accessibility: >1.0-mile hike to start of Giant Stairs
Degree of Difficulty: Difficult
Additional Information: Map available at njpalisades.org/pdfs/map.pdf

Description: Giant Stairs, aka "Giant's Stairs" and "Stairway to the Sun," is a >0.6-mile-long section of the Palisades Shore Trail characterized by small to enormous boulders that must be scrambled over and around. This trail lies about 100 vertical feet above the river.

According to Arthur G. Adams, in *The Hudson River Guidebook*, the Giant's Stairway is a "natural stone stairway up cliffs, used as a hiking route."

You will see many boulders and pierces of talus. Take note that many of these pieces of rock have been there for thousands of years. The ones lacking vegetation are of more recent origin.

History: The Palisades Shore Trail, which the Giant Stairs is on, has been a favorite hike for many decades. At 13.5 miles in length, it is also the single longest trail along the Hudson River's shoreline. The trail was designated a National Recreation Trail in 1971.

It should be noted that the Palisades, due to geological forces, are endlessly reshaping themselves. It was as recently as 2012 that 10,000 tons of rock broke off from the cliffs just south of the State Line, leaving behind a 520-foot scar on the cliffs.

Directions: Heading north on the Palisades Interstate Parkway at 1.7 miles beyond Exit 2, turn right at a sign for the State Line Lookout.

Heading south on the Palisades Interstate Parkway, go 0.4 mile past Exit 3 and then turn left onto a U-Turn that takes you onto the northbound lane of the Parkway. Go 0.4 mile, and get off at the sign for the State Line Lookout.

From either approach, drive northeast for 0.6 mile on the road that leads to the parking area for the State Line Lookout.

Giants Stairs. Photograph by Dan Balogh. Note hiker at center of picture.

The hike begins from the parking area. Pick up the aqua-blazed Long Path near the State Line Café and head south. Soon, the trail begins to descend the cliffs of the Palisades. When you come to the junction with the blue & white-blazed Forest View Trail after >0.6 mile, turn left, and continue your descent for another >0.3 mile.

When you reach the next junction, marked by a large boulder, turn left onto the white-blazed Shore Trail. In 0.3 mile, you will reach the beginning of the Giant Stairs. Take care as you negotiate this rocky path which lies roughly 100 vertical feet above the river.

Rock Walks

After >0.5 miles you will come to a recently formed talus field, the result of a massive rockslide that took place in May of 2012.

Giants Stairs. Pen & ink sketch by Robert L. Dickinson.

If you stay on the trail, you will trek through two more talus slopes and pass between a chain-link fence that marks the boundary between New Jersey and New York State.

If you wish to continue, you will come to the Peanut Leap Cascade at the ruins of the Mary Lawrence-Tonetti estate and former Italian Garden.

Resources: Herb Chong (editor), *The Long Path Guide. Fifth Edition* (Mahwah, NJ: New York-New Jersey Trail Conference, 2002), 32. Trail information is provided.
Cy A. Adler, *Walking the Hudson, Batt to Bear: From the Battery to Bear Mountain* (Cathedral, NY: Green Eagle Press, 1997), 72.
scenesfromthetrail.com/2017/07/19/giant-stairs-palisades-interstate-park.
mapado.com/en/united-states/giant-stairs-moderate-hike-4.
outube.com/watch?v=fCtjTFef65g.
nynjtc.org/hike/giant-stairslong-path-loop-state-line-lookout.
New York-New Jersey Trail Conference, *Day Walker: 32 Hikes in the New York Metropolitan Area. Second Edition* (Mahwah, NJ: New York-New Jersey Trail Conference, 2002), 242.
scenesfromthetrail.com/2016/07/08/giant-stairs-hike-palisades-interstate-park.
nycdayhiking.com/hikes/palisad3.htm.
Arthur G. Adams, *The Hudson River Guidebook* (NY: Fordham University Press, 1996), 124.

152. "MAN-IN-THE-ROCK" PILLAR

Type of Formation: Pillar
WOW Factor: 5
Location: Palisades (Bergen County, NJ)
Tenth Edition, NYS Atlas & Gazetteer: p. 111, B6; **Earlier Edition NYS Atlas & Gazetteer**: p. 25, A4–5
Parking GPS Coordinates: 40º59.327'N 73º54.421'W
Estimated "Man-in-the-Rock" Pillar GPS Coordinates: 40º58.084'N 73º54.700'W
Accessibility: ~1.5-mile hike
Degree of Difficulty: Moderate
Additional Information: The "Hiking at Alpine Picnic Area (North)" map shows the location of the Man in the Rock -- njpalisades.org/pdfs/hikeAlpineNorth.pdf.

Rock Walks

Description: The Man-in-the-Rock" Pillar is a towering rock column that leans against the side of the rock wall. In *The Hudson River Guidebook*, Arthur G. Adams describes it as "….the highest, most isolated and conspicuous pillar of rock in the Palisades, literally curving 70 feet high between two large slides." This same, nearly identical description is found in Raymond H. Torrey, Frank Place, Jr. and Robert L. Dickinson's *New York Walk Book. Third Edition*.

One rock climber who scaled it later admitted that it didn't look all that safe or stable when he got back down and gave it a closer look.

History: The distinctive Man-in-the-Rock Pillar is located at Bombay Hook, aka Boompes Hook and Bumpy Hook—a prominent bend in the Hudson River north of Alpine.

The pillar's name comes from the face of a man that supposedly can be seen near the base of the pillar's north side.

One of several Pulpits of Rock. Pen & ink sketch by Robert L. Dickinson.

Directions: Heading north on the Palisades Interstate Parkway at 1.7 miles beyond Exit 2, turn right at a sign for the State Line Lookout.

If you are heading south on the Palisades Interstate Parkway, go 0.4 mile past Exit 3 and then turn left onto a U-Turn that takes you onto the northbound lane of the Palisades Interstate Parkway. Go 0.4 mile, and get off at the sign for the State Line Lookout.

From either approach, drive northeast for 0.6 mile on the road that leads to the parking area for the State Line Lookout.

From the parking area, follow the aqua-blazed Long Path south for ~1.5 mile to reach the pillar.

344

Rock Walks

Interestingly, Raymond H. Torrey, Frank Place, Jr. & Robert L.
Dickinson mention that it is far easier to see the full scope of this
formation from a boat rather than when you are standing next to it,
close-up.

Resources: mountainproject.com/route/106098610/pillar.
njpalisades.org/pdfs/bywayMap.pdf.
Arthur G. Adams, *The Hudson River Guidebook* (NY: Fordham University
Press, 1996), 124.
instagram.com/p/BLjKcSXAO7b.
geocaching.com/geocache/GC2D748_palisades-bombay-hook.
New York-New Jersey Trail Conference, *New York Walk Book. Sixth
Edition* (New York: New York-New Jersey Trail Conference, 1998). Quite
possibly, Richard L. Dickinson's pen & ink sketch on page 109, titled
"Rock," is of the Man-in-the-Rock Pillar.
Raymond H. Torrey, Frank Place, Jr. & Robert L. Dickinson, *New York
Walk Book. Third Edition* (NY: The American Geographical Society, 1951).
A pen and ink drawing done by Robert L. Dickinson entitled "Cleft above
Bombay Hook: is displayed on page 30. On page 36, the writers indicate
that the Man-in-the-Rocks is the northern column of Bombay Hook.

153. GRAY CRAG

Type of Formation: Rock Pillar
WOW Factor: 5
Location: Alpine (Bergen County, NJ)
Tenth Edition, NYS Atlas & Gazetteer: p. 110, B5; **Earlier Edition NYS Atlas
& Gazetteer**: p. 25, A4
Parking GPS Coordinates: 40º57.200'N 73º55.237'W
End of Ruckman Road GPS Coordinates: 40º58.470'N 73º54.652'W
Gray Crag GPS Coordinates: Not determined
Accessibility: 1.9-mile hike
Degree of Difficulty: Moderate. Hikers should give some thought before
deciding whether to cross the old cement bridge to get onto the pillar.

Description: According to Jeffrey Perls, in *Paths along the Hudson: A
Guide to Walking and Biking*, "Gray Crag [is] is the largest isolated
section of the Palisades cliff. It is more than three-hundred feet long

345

and can be reached via a bridge that crosses the narrow ravine that separates it from the main cliff."

The concrete bridge, supported by a pair of steel I-beams, is about 30 feet long and spans a ravine that is over 20–30 feet deep.

The rock pillar may be long, but it is fairly narrow, extending 10–20 feet in width. To put things into proper proportion, it stands about 40 stories above the river!

History: In 1918, John Ringling (of Ringling Brothers fame) purchased two properties to create a 100-acre estate that he and his wife, Mable, named Gray Crag. On it they built an elegant summer home which they utilized through the 1920s. Ruins of it are still visible today.

Directions: Driving north on the Palisades Interstate Parkway, get off at Exit 2 and head south for 0.2 mile to reach the park headquarters, on your left.

Driving south on the Palisades Interstate Parkway, get off at Exit 2. Turn right onto Route 9 and head north for 0.1 mile. At the first light, turn right onto Alpine Approach Road and head southeast for >0.1 mile, going underneath two overpass bridges. At a fork, turn right and drive south for 0.1 mile to reach the park headquarters, on your left.

From the main office for the Palisades Interstate Park Commission in New Jersey, follow the Long Path north for ~1.7 miles until you come to the end of old Ruckman Road. The following directions are borrowed from Herb Chong's *The Long Path Guide*: "The Long Path turns left on Ruckman Road and, in another 50 feet, turns right on a gravel road into well-developed forest. Meet a second gravel road leading right to run along the cliff edge. This road, not part of the Long Path, ends in about 900 feet at the terminus of a great split off the main face of the Palisades."

Resources: Jeffrey Perls, *Paths along the Hudson: A Guide to Walking and Biking* (New Brunswick, NJ: Rutgers University Press, 2001), 163.
lohud.com/story/life/2017/02/28/hiking-palisades/98527566.
njpalisades.org/graycrag.html.
geocaching.com/geocache/GC2D746_palisades-john-ringlings-grey-crag.

Herb Chong (editor), *The Long Path Guide. Fifth Edition* (Mahwah, NJ: New York-New Jersey Trail Conference, 2002), 22. Raymond H. Torrey, Frank Place, Jr. & Robert L. Dickinson, *New York Walk Book. Third Edition* (NY: The American Geographical Society, 1951), 37. "Up above, there stands the largest separated section of rock in the Palisades—Gray Crag, some 300 feet long and 10 to 20 feet wide." The writers go on to mention that directly north is Bombay Hook and the Man-in-the-Rock pillar.
homes.ottcommunications.com/~dsonder/Genealogy/Gray%20Crag%20ph oto%20album%20GREAT.pdf   album of Crag Crag photographs.

154. ALPINE ROCK & HAY-KEE-POOK ROCK

Type of Formation: Large Rock
WOW Factor: 3–4
Location: Alpine, NJ (Bergen County, NJ)
Tenth Edition, NYS Atlas & Gazetteer: p. 111, B6; **Earlier Edition NYS Atlas & Gazetteer**: p. 25, A4–5
Parking GPS Coordinates: 40º56.678′N 73º55.145′W
Alpine Rock GPS Coordinates: 40º56.799′N 73º55.129′W
Accessibility: 0.1-mile walk
Degree of Difficulty: Easy
Additional Information: Palisades Interstate Park Commission/New Jersey Offices, Alpine, New Jersey 07620 (201) 768-1360
Map of the Alpine Picnic Area and Boat Basin can be found at njpalisades.org/pdfs/hikeAlpineSouth.pdf

Historic Kearney House.

Description: According to Cy A. Adler, in *Walking the Hudson, Batt to Bear: From the Battery to Bear Mountain,* "Just south and in front of the old house [Kearney House] with its peeling white paint is a large, cubical rock. This black chunk of basalt, about 8 feet high, fell off the Palisades cliffs in 1896 and rolled onto the attached kitchen which it completely demolished.

Assuming the rock is thrice the density of water, this slight chip off the Palisades weighs over 70,000 pounds."

It is rare that you get to see a rock that, after breaking off from a cliff, does such damage to a downhill structure. The Alpine Rock is roughly 50 feet southeast of the Kearney House, partially concealed by brush or a tree.

There is another rock in the general area that is called *Hay-Kee-Pook*. In their *New York Walk Book. Third Edition*, Raymond H. Torrey, Frank Place. Jr. and Robert L. Dickinson write, "South of the Landing is a path full of variety and charm, which winds up and down owing to washouts on the river edge way. The big boulder by the river is known as 'Hay-Kee-Pook', and legend has it that an Indian lover committed suicide," presumably by the rock.

History: The Kearney House, aka Blackledge-Kearney House, and Lord Charles Cornwallis' Headquarters, is very historic. The southern part of the house was constructed in the 1760s; the northern addition, around 1840.

Rocks along Alpine section of Shore Trail. Photograph by Dan Balogh.

The house was first owned by Maria Blackledge and her husband, Daniel Van Sciver, and then later by James and Rachel Kearney, who ran it as a tavern. It was from these former occupants that the house came to have two names.

The house was purchased by the Palisades Interstate Park in 1907, and was added to the National Register of Historic Places in 1984.

There is a story that Lord Cornwallis used the house as his temporary headquarters while pursuing the Continental Army in 1776, although not everyone is convinced that such an event actually occurred.

Directions: The following directions have been taken off of the Palisades Interstate Park Commission's website:

Heading north on the Palisades Interstate Parkway – Get off at Exit 2, U.S. Route 9W, Alpine, Closter. Stay straight off the exit (south), passing Park Headquarters on the left. Follow Alpine Approach Road south 1 mi. downhill. Go ¾ around the small circle, then continue north the rest of the way down the hill to the entrance to Alpine Picnic Area & Boat Launch.

Heading south on the Palisades Interstate Parkway – Get off at Exit 2, U.S. Route 9W, Alpine, Closter. Turn right (north) onto U. S. Route 9W. Immediately turn right (east) at the first light, Alpine Approach Road. Go beneath two overpass bridges, then bear right (south). Pass Park Headquarters on the left. Follow Alpine Approach Road 1 mi. downhill. Go ¾ around the small circle, then continue north the rest of the way down the hill to the entrance to Alpine Picnic Area & Boat Launch."

Alpine Rock -- From the north end of the Alpine parking area, walk north for 0.1 mile. The house is to your left, opposite the second, smaller boat basin.

The boulder is near the south side of the Kearney House, no more than 50 feet away.

The *Hay-Kee-Pook Rock* is said to be south of Alpine Landing and Boat Basin. Where exactly, I don't know.

Resources: njpalisades.org/directionsAlpine.html.

Rock Walks

Cy A. Adler, *Walking the Hudson, Batt to Bear: From the Battery to Bear Mountain* (Cathedral, NY: Green Eagle Press, 1997), 68.
en.wikipedia.org/wiki/Blackledge-Kearney.
kearneyhouse.blogspot.com.
revolutionarywarnewjersey.com/new_jersey_revolutionary_war_sites/tow ns/alpine_nj_revolutionary_war_sites.htm.
Jeffrey Perls, *Paths along the Hudson: A Guide to Walking and Biking* (New Brunswick, NJ: Rutgers University Press, 2001), 159.
njpalisades.org/pdfs/kearneyBrochure.pdf.
Raymond H. Torrey, Frank Place, Jr. & Robert L. Dickinson, *New York Walk Book. Third Edition* (NY: The American Geographical Society, 1951), 37.

155. SAMPSON'S ROCK (Historic)

Type of Formation: Large Boulder
WOW Factor: 7
Location: Englewood Cliffs (Bergen County, NJ)
Tenth Edition, NYS Atlas & Gazetteer: p. 110, C5; **Earlier Edition NYS Atlas & Gazetteer**: p. 24, AB4
Junction of Floyd Street & Palisade Avenue GPS Coordinates: 40º52.885′N 73º57.177′W
Accessibility: Roadside
Degree of Difficulty: Easy

Description: According to Raymond H. Torrey, Frank Place, Jr., and Robert L. Dickinson, in *New York Walk Book. Third Edition*, "This perched boulder, which has been carried upward at least 160 feet from the meadows by the ice sheet, measures 8 by 12 by 12 feet and is of soft red sandstone touching a few points on the hard gray trap rock beneath."

Arthur C. Mack, in *The Palisades of the Hudson*, writes, "The drift [of ice] resulted also in many rocky curiosities, conspicuous among them as an isolated block of Triassic sandstone, called Sampson's Rock, perched upon the flat trap directly east of Englewood. This huge boulder, measuring nearly twelve feet in diameter and weighing many tons, was lifted 160 feet up the western slope of the ridge by the ice (it is calculated), and finally dropped in to its present resting place. Its under surface still retains the polish it received through the attrition of that movement."

History: I can find no history on this glacial erratic, despite Torrety, Frank and Dickinson's assertion that it is the "best erratic in New Jersey."

I've read that a plaque was on the boulder, but then was vandalized and taken. I do not know what was written on the plaque.

Directions: From the Palisades Interstate Parkway, get off at Exit 1 and drive west on Palisades Avenue for either 0.1 mile or 0.3 mile (depending upon which direction you were heading when you came off from the Palisades Interstate Parkway).

You will come to the junction of Palisades Avenue and Floyd Street.

For those who wish to understand the process of trying to track down natural rock formations, take note of the following directions which I took from Torrety, Frank and Dickinson's book: "A pleasant detour can be made by turning west on Palisades Avenue one block to Floyd Street and then right past seven houses to the best erratic in New Jersey—Sampson's Rock standing in a vacant lot on the right."

Using Google Earth, I followed Floyd Street north from Palisades Avenue, counting seven houses down the right side of the street. I couldn't help but notice that the space next to the seventh house was now occupied by a house under construction. This was as of June 2017. It seems like this should be the spot where the glacial erratic is, or was.

Hopefully, the boulder has not been destroyed. On the other hand, it has been nearly seventy years since Torrety, Frank and Dickinson visited the rock and published their book. A lot of things could have changed during that time.

Resources: Raymond H. Torrey, Frank Place, Jr. & Robert L. Dickinson, *New York Walk Book. Third Edition* (NY: The American Geographical Society, 1951), 23. "The best of these 'erratics' is Sampson's Rock in Englewood Cliffs." Details about the rock are on page 36.

Rock Walks

156. WASHINGTON'S HEAD & INDIAN HEAD (Historic)

Type of Formation: Rock Profile
WOW Factor: 2–3
Location: Fort Lee (Bergen County, NJ)
Tenth Edition, NYS Atlas & Gazetteer: p. 110, C5; **Earlier Edition NYS Atlas & Gazetteer:** p. 24, B4 & p. 24, A1–2
Parking GPS Coordinates: 40º51.639'N 73º57.326'W
GPS Coordinates: Unknown

Description: Two rock profiles once existed on the Palisades bluffs until they were blasted away by quarrying. Washington's Head was demolished in 1897, and Indian Head in 1898.

In the case of Indian Head, we know exactly how the rock profile met its demise. A 5-foot-wide hole was bored a hundred feet into the rock face, with 7,000 pounds of dynamite packed in. The explosion completely destroyed the rock formation, sending down 350,000 tons of diabase to be used for construction.

In *History of Bergen County, New Jersey*, J. M. Van Valen writes, "Indian Head, one of the most historic points of the Palisades, a few years ago projected one hundred and fifty feet into the North River [Hudson River] beyond the point." The destruction of Indian Head "…was one of the most successful efforts ever made to destroy the grandeur of this part of the Hudson. It broke out an area surface of one hundred and seventy-five feet by one hundred and sixty-five-feet and a depth of about one hundred feet, constituting nearly one-third of the height of the cliff."

I assume that Washington's Head was treated in a similar fashion.

Even if these rock formations had survived, in all likelihood they would now be mere shadows of their former selves, eroded by over a century of wind, rain, snow, sleet, and ice.

Interestingly, another rock face also existed along the Palisades, but only fleetingly. In *New York's Palisades Interstate Park: Images of America*, Barbara H. Gottlock & Wesley Gottlock talk about a rock slide that occurred around 1941 that created the image of Hitler's Face. Ironically, right after World War II ended, another rock

352

slide permanently erased the image. It's hard to know what to make of a synchronistic event like this.

Palisades at Fort Lee being quarried. Old photograph.

Note Indian Head profile near upper right corner. Old photograph.

According to Raymond H. Torrey, Frank Place, Jr. and Robert L. Dickinson, in *New York Walk Book. Third Edition*, "North of Ross Dock and above the Henry Hudson Drive are several striking rock formations. An immense squat column stands on a base that gives a thrilling but false impression that it might crumble at any time."

The writers also talk about a "leaning column nearby dubbed 'Fallen Caesar,'" but this may have been a name that never really told hold beyond those who first came up with it.

History: Fort Lee Park encompasses 34 acres of land next to the Hudson River. It is the site of a former Revolutionary War fort.

353

Rock Walks

It was also at Fort Lee that Thomas Payne wrote one of his political papers, beginning with the words, "These are the times that try men's souls."

In *New York Walk Book. Third Edition*, Raymond H. Torrey, Frank Place, Jr. and Robert L. Dickinson write about another Indian Head that is the highest point in the Palisades. "Looking south from Point Lookout along the ridge, one sights the face of Indian Head — hook-nosed, low forehead and, for feathers, brushes bent backwards." The formation is said to be between Forest View and State Line.

Directions: From the town of Fort Lee (junction of Routes 12/Main Street & 67/Schlosser Street), head east on Route 12/Main Street for 0.3 mile. Coming onto Route 505/River Drive, head south for 0.2 mile. Then bear left onto Henry Hudson Drive and proceed north for 1.2 miles. Park in the area for the Ross Dock Picnic Park.

The rock formations are said to have been ~1.0 mile north of Fort Lee, with Indian Head about five hundred yards from Washington Point. This would place the rock formations in the general area of the Ross Dock Picnic Park, but if you think that the two famous rock formations still exist, it will be because they are in your imagination now (which hopefully you can rely on).

To see some of the pillar formations that Raymond H. Torrey, Frank Place. Jr. and Robert L. Dickinson mention in their book, I would recommend walking north along the Shore Trail.

Resources: C. R. Roseberry, *From Niagara to Montauk: The Scenic Pleasures of New York State* (Albany, NY: State University of New York Press, 1982), 254.
Barbara H. Gottlock & Wesley Gottlock, *New York's Palisades Interstate Park: Images of America* (Charleston, SC: Arcadia Publishing, 2007), 14. amnh.org/learn-teach/young-naturalist-awards/winning-essays2/selected-winning-essays-1998-20032/shaped-by-nature-and-man-the-geological-history-of-the-palisades.
J. M. Van Valen, *History of Bergen County, New Jersey* (NY: New Jersey Publishing and Engraving Company, 1900), 653.
Capt. Stanley Wilcox & H. W. Van Loan, *The Hudson from Troy to the Battery* (Philmont, NY: Riverview Publishing, 2011), 126.

Jeffrey Perls, *Paths along the Hudson: A Guide to Walking and Biking* (New Brunswick, NJ: Rutgers University Press, 2001), 155.
Raymond H. Torrey, Frank Place, Jr. & Robert L. Dickinson, *New York Walk Book. Third Edition* (NY: The American Geographical Society, 1951), 34 & 39.
Arthur C. Mack, *The Palisades of the Hudson* (Edgewater, NJ: The Palisade Press, 1909), 39. "The greater part of old Indian Head was blown asunder to be metamorphosed into flats and skyscrapers…"

157. MISCL

1. Lewis Beach, *Cornwall* (Newburgh, NY: E. M. Ruttenber & Son, 1873). A number of boulders and unusual rocks are mentioned in Beach's book that may no longer be hiking destinations. Several of them are along West Point Road in the Giant's Haunt, and in Idlewild. Quite possibly, many are simply gone or, minimally, gone from memory.

p. 90. *Chapel Rock* – Beach mentions a stream where "its passage through the glen is checked at intervals by huge boulders—one of which is known as Chapel Rock…"

Unnamed Staten Island Boulder.

p. 108. *Lover's Rocking Stone* — "This stone, weighing several tons, is so equipoised that a child of ten can move it from side to side. It is sufficiently low to the ground to form a convenient seat for lovers."

p. 109. *Giant's Slipper* – As the story goes, a mythical, humungous giant, "whilst descending…dropped his slipper, which, turned to stone over six feet in length, in perfect shape..." It "... is still to be seen and known as the Giant's Slipper."

p. 110. *Pic-nic Rock* – The rock is described as "...a table summit of platform rock covered with moss and lichen, and provided with numerous blocks of stone of varying size, which answers for chairs and tables."

p. 115. *Poised Rock* – This strange rock "...is a parallelogram in shape, having two sides, the upper and lower, ten feet in length, and the ends about four feet. It measures eighteen feet in circumference, and being formed of granite, will weigh about fourteen tons. This huge rock stands by itself alone, lifted entirely from the pedestal rock on which it rests, except at one point. This point of contact is not over four inches square. It is supported on the extreme westerly end by a flat stone, eight inches high—eighteen inches long and fifteen wide."

p. 172. *Natural Bridge* -- Beach mentions that a Natural Bridge "...will be found spanning the stream that flows into the southwest end of Poplopen's pond...Its breadth across the stream is fifty feet and its length up and down the stream about eighty feet. In times of drought people can pass under it."

2. Jerome Wyckoff, *Rock Scenery of the Hudson Highlands and Palisades* (Glens Falls, NY: Adirondack Mountain Club, 1971).

p. 31 – *Hogencamp Mine Boulder* -- A photograph of a huge block of talus, with three hikers next to it, lies along the Dunning Trail near Hogencamp Mine (41º14.606'N 74º07.167'W).

p. 33 – *Pine Hill Boulder* -- A photograph of large blocks of talus along a steep slope on Pine Hill can be seen. A number of rocks are also shown along a dirt road that parallels a power line.

p. 84 – *Circle Mountain Boulder* -- A photograph of a rock on Circle Mountain is very reminiscent of the balanced rock in North Salem.

3. Richard M. Lederer, Jr., *The Place-Names of Westchester County, New York: Expanded Version* (Harrison, NY: Harbor Hill Books, 1980).

p. 21. *Devil's Den* and *Buzzard's Cave* – These two formations are described as sheer cliffs on the southeast side of Byram Mountain, south of Byram Lake Road, The GPS reading for Byram Lake

Reservoir is 41º10.079'N 73º41.491'W. You will have to take it from there.

Stissing Mountain (Meteor) Boulder. Old photograph.

357

p. 49. *Finch's Rock House* – This rock is described as a large cave near Windmill Farm that was excavated in 1901 by the Museum of Natural History. The cave was named for Hiram Finch, who died in 1897 and who once owned the property. In the early 1900s, the land (as well as other properties) was acquired by Elijah Watt Sells, who improved the farm, naming it North Castle Farm. Since then, North Castle Farm has become a community of homes called Windmill Farm. The general GPS for Windmill Farm is 41°08.859′N 73°40.858′W.

In the Vol. 38, no 1 (January, February, March, 1962) issue of the *Westchester Historian. Quarterly of the Westchester County Historical Society*, a photograph of Finch's Rock House taken by Mary Andrews can be seen on the cover. It is described as being near Armonk.

Glacial erratic in Dover Plains. 1907 photograph by Sidney Benham.

p. 49. *Fishing Rock* – This rock is located on Fox Island at the mouth of the Byram River by Port Chester. I could not locate Fox Island, but I did located Hawthorne Beach by the mouth of the river (40°59.305′N 73°39.412′W). It's likely that the rock is in this area.

p. 59. *Great Stone at the Wading Place* – The stone is/was located in Port Chester. The spot, defined by the rock, is still the boundary between New York and Connecticut. Originally it was the dividing line between Rye, New York and Greenwich, Connecticut, that was set in 1673. The GPS coordinate where a bridge crosses Byram River between Port Chester, New York and Greenwich, Connecticut is 41°00.726′N 73°39.342′W. Perhaps at one time this was the old Boston Post Road. It is now Putnam Avenue.

In the website hopefarm.com/connecti.htm, the Great Stone at the Wading Place is described in greater detail. "The survey of 1684 had begun at the mouth of the Byram River, at a point 30 miles from New York, had followed that stream as far as the head of tidewater, or about a mile and a half from the Sound, to a certain "wading-place," where the common road crossed the stream at a rock known and described as "The Great Stone at the Wading-Place."

p. 122. *Rock-shelter* – This rock formation is described as a "16 meter overhanging cliff used as a permanent place of shelter for Indians." It is located in North Castle, east of Middle Patent Road near Mianus River Road.

p. 122. *Trinity Lake Balanced Stone* -- "A balanced stone which rocks but doesn't tip over" is said to be on the west shore of 116-acre Trinity Lake. It seems unlikely that such a rock so precariously balanced could have lasted into this century, but who knows. The GPS for Trinity Lake is 41°13.113'N 73°33.167'W. I can take you no further.

p. 135. *Spindle Rock* – This rock, located in New Rochelle, is reported to be between Davenport Neck and Douglas Island (probably David Island); visible from Davenport Park.

I'm giving the rock a GPS reading of 40°53.678'N 73°46.058'W. It was named for its resemblance to the shape of a spindle. Some would probably call it a tiny island.

Indian Mill (pothole). Old photograph.

p. 143. *Parson's Woods Tory Cave* – This cave acquired its name from a slave who hid out there during the American Revolutionary War. Apparently, he was a Tory. The rock formation is located in Rye at Parson's Woods southeast of Theodore Fremd Avenue and North Street. I'm giving the woods a GPS of 40°58.612'N 73°41.407'W.

Rock Walks

p. 147. *Umbrella Point Rock* is visible from Manor Park in Larchmont. Its GPS Coordinates may be 40º55.248′N 73º44.560′W or something close to that.

4. *White Stone* -- Greater Astoria Historical Society, etc., *The East River: Images of America* (Charleston, SC: Arcadia Publishing, 2005).

Shown on page 18 is a photograph of White Stone, a jumbo-sized boulder, easily 15 feet high, with two Victorians posed on its top. The rock was named for a community in Queens. Whether it is still there remains to be seen, for the authors write, "A Dutch navigational journal from 1673 recorded this now long gone landmark." Maybe this is the White Stone that gave Whitestone its name.

5. *Emmet's Cave* -- William J. Myles, *Harriman Trails: A Guide and History* (New York: The New York-New Jersey Trail Conference, 1994), 370 & 371.

The cave is said to be on the east side of Brundige Hill not far from Baker Camp. The GPS Coordinates for Baker Camp, located by Lake Sebago, is 41º12.101′N 74º08.141′W. You will have to take it from there.

The cave is named after Auntie Emmet, a witch who could transform herself into a toad, and who is said to have lived in the cave.

Around 1900, the body of a man named Conklin, who had been robbed and murdered, was discovered hidden in the cave. This tale may have some truth to it.

6. *Balancing Rocks* -- Stella Green and H. Neil Zimmerman, *50 Hikes in the Lower Hudson Valley* (Woodstock, VT: Backcountry Guides, 2002), 146.

The authors mention two different balancing rocks along the blue-blazed Timp-Torne and red-on-white Ramapo-Dunderberg Trails, as you head west. Trailhead parking is located at a GPS reading of 41º16.888′N 73º57.752′W. A couple of websites that describe this hike make no mention of either balancing rocks, which leads me to believe that either they are not all that memorable, or someone has unbalanced them.

7. *Large Boulders* -- Peter Senterman, "Discover and Explore the new Andes Rail Trail," *Kaatskill Life*. Vol. 29, no. 1 (Spring 2014).

On page 57 is a photograph of the author standing next to several large boulders which he describes as "...some interesting boulders split from the ledge." The trail starts at a GPS reading of 42°05.378'N 74°49.191'W.

8. Randall Comfort (compiler), *History of Bronx Borough. City of New York* (New York: North Side News Press, 1906).

p. 2. *Immense Rock* -- "Overlooking the new Jerome Park Reservoir, just in front of the engineer's office, stands another immense rock..." The GPS reading for the general area is 40°52.903'N 73°53.631'W. I suspect that the rock may no longer exist. The area, quite frankly, looks pretty developed.

p. 2. *Great Rock* -- Comfort mentions a "Great Rock near the southerly limit of Claremont Park." I can find no reference to a great rock on the Claremont Park websites. The GPS for the southern part of Claremont Park is 40°50.254'N 73°54.499'W.

p. 2. *Large Boulder* -- "A large boulder stands near the corner of Southern Boulevard and Homes Street." The GPS reading here is 40°49.712'N 73°53.512'W. The boulder is not visible on Google Earth. If it still exists, it is well hidden.

p. 65. *Devil's Stepping Stones* -- "Just this side of Eastchester, among the rocky fields, stands a huge boulder deeply marked with the impression of the right human foot." This rock formation will be extremely difficult to find without specific directions, of which I have none to give.

9. Anita Inman Comstock, *Wondrous Westchester: Its History, Landmarks, and Special Events* (Mount Vernon, NY: Effective Learning, Inc., 1984).

A number of interesting rocks are listed on page 43:

Jimmy-Under-the-Rock – Some fellow named Jimmy came across a long rock projecting from the mountainside in North Castle and used it as the roof for his house. The house no longer exists, but apparently remnants of the rock still do.

Man-of-War Rock (Tuxedo). Old photo.

Kettle Hole Rock – Comstock contends that this hole located in Valhalla was "...either formed by water dripping and making a small entrance at top, or by Indians chopping it."

10. *Goldens Bridge Balanced Rock --* Maureen Koehl, *Lewisboro: Images of America* (Charleston, SC: Arcadia Publishing, 1997), 21.

This balanced rock is located in a wooded area off of Route 138 in Goldens Bridge. It is found on a hillside a short distance from a stream. From the photograph in the book, the rock looks to be 3–4 feet high, and longer than its height, but it is difficult to say for sure. It seems to be resting on two mounds of rock, much like a slab between two sawhorses. The directions given are really insufficient to even know where to begin looking for this rock.

11. *Upright Rock --* Maureen Koehl, *Remembering Lewisboro,* New York (Charleston, SC: The History Press, 2008), 34–44.

On page 44 is a photograph of an "...upright rock nine feet high, that tradition bequeaths to us as the point reached by the Indians in claiming their lands as far as they could walk in a day starting from Stamford."

The rock is said to be at the south end of Elmwood Road, possibly near where Elmwood Road and Smith Ridge Road intersect. The GPS reading for the junction is 41º13.3898'N 73º31.055'W. I did notice what looked like a boulder just northwest of the junction behind a private home at a GPS of 41º13.445'N 73º31.116'W, but who knows.

12. *Stissing Mountain Meteor* -- Joyce C. Ghee & Joan Spence, *Harlem Valley Pathways through Pawling, Dover, Amenia, North East, and Pine Plains: Images of America* (Charleston, SC: Arcadia Publishing, 1998).

On page 94 is a photograph of the Stissing Mountain Meteor, which looks to be a 15–20-foot-high boulder. I have no specific information on this rock, but it would prove helpful if the boulder was contained within the 590-acre

Upright Rock. Old photo.

Stissing Mountain Multiple Use Area (41º56.4048'N 73º41.686'W), for at least, then, access would not be an issue.

13. Ira K. Morris, *Morris's Memorial History of Staten Island, New York. Vol. 1* (NY: Memorial Publishing Company, 1898), 372 & 373.

Morris's book describes a number of rocks that I have been unable to locate:

Seal Rocks – "The name of several drift boulders at Princess Bay under Light House Hill, on which seals are occasionally seen in winter." The GPS reading for Lighthouse Hill is 40º30.459'N 74º12.808'W.

Nigger-head Rock – "A large boulder at the foot of the bluff at Light House Hill, Prince's Bay, and known as a landmark among

Golden Bridge Rock. Old photo.

fishermen." The GPS reading for Lighthouse Hill, once again, is 40º30.459'N 74º12.808'W.

Strawberry Rock – "This rock received its name from the circumstance that straw-berries once grew about it before the shore had washed away." The rock is/was located off shore near the foot of Central Avenue, Tottenville. Central Avenue appears to end before the shore, which makes me wonder if the area where the rock was has been filled in.

Split Rock -- "A large split rock seen at very low tide off the shore at the foot of Hannah Street, Thompkinsville." The shoreline is built up today. There may be no rock to view. The GPS reading at the end of Hannah Street is 40º38.187N 74º04.384'W.

14. *Large Boulder* -- Margaret Lundrigan & Tova Navarra, *Staten Island: Images of America* (Charleston, SC: Arcadia Publishing, 1997.

On page 124 is a photograph by Alice Austen of a girl holding a basket next to a large boulder. No specific information is provided, so good luck to anyone trying to find this rock other than knowing that it is somewhere along the Staten Island shoreline.

15. Herbert B. Nichols, *Historic New Rochelle* (New Rochelle, NY: Board of Education, 1938).

p. 109. *Enormous Rock* -- Mention is made of "an "enormous rock" between North Avenue and Carlton Terrace. The apex of the two roads is at 40º56.121'N 73º47.536'W. That might make a good starting point.

p. 112. *Potholes* -- "fine and interesting potholes can be seen in the rocks near the sound in Larchmont Shore Park." It seems entirely within the realm of possibility that these potholes can be found since the area covered in the park next to the Long Island Sound is a relatively short one.

p. 112, *Glacial Boulder* -- A glacial boulder is located "on the Shore Road at the New Rochelle-Pelham boundary line."

16. *Indian Mill (pothole)* -- Chester A. Smith, *Peekskill, A Friendly Town, Its Historic Sites and Shrines: A Pictorial History of the City from 1654 to 1952* (Peekskill, NY: The Friendly Town Association, 1952), 380.

Two photographs are shown of an 'Indian Mill' pothole near Indian Lake. It would help to have more specific information to locate this pothole. The general GPS for Indian Lake is 41°22.438'N 73°53.218'W

17. *Saddle Rock* -- Raymond E. Spinzia, Judith A. Spinzia & Kathryn E. Spinzia, *Long Island: A Guide to New York's Suffolk and Nassau Counties* (NY: Hippocrence Books, 1991), 356 & 357.

Devah and Gil Spear (editors & compilers), *The Book of Great Neck* (Great Neck, NY: n, 1928), 68.

"Saddle Rock lies between Great Neck Estates and Kings Post, overlooking Little Neck Bay."

en.wikipedia.org/wiki/Saddle_Rock,_New_York goes on to say that "The Village of Saddle Rock is so named for an offshore boulder that gives the appearance of a saddle, first noted on a map in 1658."

Two different descriptions of Saddle Rock are given—one offshore, and one overlooking Little Neck Bay. Perhaps there are two rocks that acquired the same name.

18. *Beach Boulder* -- Geoffrey K. Fleming, *St. James: Images of America* (Charleston, SC: Arcadia Publishing, 2006), 105.

A photograph, c. 1927, entitled "A Boulder at the Beach," shows a large glacial erratic.

19. *Joshua's Rock* – Larry Penny, "Nature Notes: Glacial Erratics," *East Hampton Star* (January 18, 2012); easthamptonstar.com/Outdoors/2012118/Nature-Notes-Glacial-Erratics. Presumably this rock is located somewhere in East Hampton.

20. *Lionhead Rock* – Larry Penny, "Nature Notes: Glacial Erratics," *East Hampton Star* (January 18, 2012); easthamp tonstar.com/Outdoors/2012118/Nature-Notes-Glacial-Erratics.

The rock, possibly named after Lion Gardiner, is located in Gardiners Bay. The general GPS for Gardiners Bay is 41°06.435'N 72°12.512'W.

21. *Large Boulder* -- Randall Comfort (compiler), *History of Bronx Borough. City of New York* (New York: North Side News Press, 1906), 2.

"A large boulder stands near the corner of the Southern Boulevard and Home Street." Even in Comfort's time, there was talk about the rock being destroyed to make room for the city continuing to expand. I don't see the rock on Google Earth so, indeed, it may be gone forever.

Leatherman Cave. Kinderogen area. Old photograph.

22. *The Timp* -- New York-New Jersey Trail Conference, *New York Walk Book. Sixth Edition* (New York: New York-New Jersey Trail Conference, 1998), 296. An illustration shows the vague profile of a rock face.

"Rising above is the Timp, a striking cliff with a pronounced overhang, one of the most picturesque rock faces in the park." Trailhead GPS coordinates are 41°16.866'N 73°57.779'W

23. *A-mac-lea-sin Rock* – Wallace Bruce, *The Hudson: Three Centuries of History, Romance and Invention* (NY: Walking News, Inc., 1982. Centennial edition reprint), 58.

According to Wallace Bruce, ".....at the mouth of the Nepperhan [now called the Sawmill River] west of the creek is a large rock, called

A-mac-lea-sin, the great stone to which the Indians paid reverence as an evidence of the permanency and immutability of their deity."

24. *Fort Shinnecock Boulder* – According to Jeremy Dennis, in his website jeremynative.com/onthissite/listing/fort-shinnecock, "This sacred glacial erratic marks the location of what may have been both the Shinnecock Fort and June Meeting location in the Shinnecock Hills. There have been many references to a contact-period Shinnecock fort, but the specific location has likely been disrupted by development."

It seems pretty likely, then, that the boulder is no more, but who knows until you studiously look. The general GPS reading for Old Fort Pond is roughly 40º52.790'N 72º26.400'W.

25. John McNamara, *History in Asphalt: The Origin of Bronx Street and Place Names* (The Bronx, NY: Bronx County Historical

Siwanoy Image Stone. Old photograph.

Society, 1996), 295.

   p. 295. *Indian Rock* is described as a rocky hummock that was "still visible at the end of Blackrock Avenue near Brucker Boulevard and Soundview Avenue up to 1965." No mention is made about what happened to Indian Rock after that.

   p. 476. *Sheepspen Rocks* consisted of a cluster of rocks on Tallapossa Point that formed an enclosure which suggested to some the shape of a sheep's pen. Unfortunately, these historic rocks were buried under a landfill in 1963.

   The name, Tallapoosa comes from the Tallapoosa Club, many of whose members had fought in Tallapoosa, Georgia, during the American Civil War. Tallapossa Point early on was an island in

Eastchester Bay until it was joined to the mainland. Now, apparently, it is used as a bird habitat.

p. 440. *Pigeon Rock* – At one time, Pigeon Rock was a prominent rock along the Bronx River that was well known to West Farms and Van Nest youths. The rock disappeared ~1935 when the Bronx River was slightly diverted, and the boulder buried under a landfill.

It seems to me that if you look downstream from the East Tremont Avenue Bridge spanning the Bronx River, you will be gazing into the general area where the rock once was.

26. *Large Erratic* -- Stella Green and H. Neil Zimmerman, *50 Hikes in the Lower Hudson Valley* (Woodstock, VT: Backcountry Guides, 2002), 128.

The authors mention a "large glacial erratic to the left" while doing the Rockhouse Mountain Loop trail. The

Mianus Gorge Rocks. Photograph by Daniel Chazin.

trailhead begins across the road from a small parking area off of Tiorati Brook Road (to your right). The trailhead GPS reading here 41º15.189'N 74º03.981'W.

27. *Rock-Shelters/Talus Caves* -- Patricia Edwards Clyne, *Hudson Valley Trails and Tales* (Woodstock, NY: The Overlook Press, 1990), 162.

Clyne mentions additional rock-shelters in Westchester County, including one on the western slope of Bull's Hill (at Haines Road in Bedford Hills), and another one that is formed by fallen boulders on Hillcrest Drive, north of Briarcliff Manor.

Bull's Hill Rock-Shelter -- A general GPS reading for the area is 41º14.313'N 73º42.419'W, which takes you to the west side of Bull's Hill by Haines Road.

Talus Cave – This general GPS reading for Hillcrest Drive north of Briarcliff Manor is 41º09.838'N 73º49.188'W, where there are woods to the right, and possibly jumbles of rocks.

28. *Rock-Shelters* -- There are Rock Shelter Roads in Waccabuc and Lewisboro, both in Westchester County. It seems likely to me that the roads were named for nearby rock-shelters. That doesn't help us much in terms of the practicality of locating the caves.

Bet Helicker's Cave (Armonk). Old photograph.

29. Harry T. Cook, *The Borough of the Bronx. 1639–1913* (NY: Author, 1913), 66.

Boar's Den -- Although this shelter cave was known about in the early 1900s, I can find no reference to it in the modern literature. I presume it's located somewhere in the Bronx Park, perhaps near the Bronx River.

Indian Cave -- According to Cook on page 106, "...Perhaps the most interesting is the 'Indian' which is located a short distance east of the Hunt burying ground, and about three hundred yards north of the bridge crossing the creek." The general GPS coordinates for Hunt's Point is 40º48.705'N 73º52.892'W. On page 107 can be seen a photograph of the cave.

There may be no way to track down this cave's location. In 1899, one of the Hunt family members wrote an impassioned letter to the local newspaper imploring that a projected street railway through the Hunt Burying ground be abandoned. I've got a strong feeling that the authorities went ahead with the project anyhow.

Hunt's Point, today, is so heavily developed that little green space remains, save for a few parks (and a tiny Indian gravesite in the Joseph Rodman Drake Park).

30. *Balancing Turtle Rock* -- Graham Hancock's website, grahamhancock.com/kreisbergg7, shows a photograph of a rock called the Balancing Turtle Rock on Marlboro Mtn, located in the Turtle Rock Ridge complex.

31. *Robber Rocks* – In *Town of Pawling. 200 Years. 1788–1988*, published by the Town of Pawling 200th Anniversary Committee, mention is made that "Near a portion of the turnpike close to the top of West Mountain was the area known as 'Robber Rocks.' Here, in caves and rock piles, robbers awaited drovers return from market ready to relieve them of their money." This rock formation is along today's Route 55.

32. *Glacial Rock* -- Stanley H. Benham, Sr., *Rural Life in the Hudson River Valley. 1880–1920* (Poughkeepsie, NY: Hudson House Publishing, 2005).

A photograph taken by Sidney S. Benham of a 10–12-foot-high glacial rock in Dover Plains in shown on page 2. The author, Stanley Benham, stands next to the boulder to provide a sense of the rock's size. No directions or hints on how to get to the boulder are given.

33. *Multiple Rocks* -- E. M. Ruttenber & L. H. Clark, *History of Orange County, New York. Vol. 1* (Interlaken, NY: Heart Lake Publishing, 1980).

On page 34, the authors mention *Kidd's Pocket-book*, *Lover's Rocking Stone*, and *Poised Rock*, but give no specific information about what they are and where they can be found. I think it's safe to assume that they are all located in Orange County, but that really doesn't help all that much.

34. *Man-of-War Rock* – Seeley E. Ward, "Recollections of the Sloatsburg Area," *Orange County Historical Society Publication, no. 2.* (1972–1973).

On page 19, Ward writes, "Going on up above Tuxedo just a little bit, you all know where Tuxedo Station is, where the road starts to swing around a rock wall, or rocky faced hill—there was a great big rock and it was called 'Man-of-War Rock'." A dark picture of the rock (or bluff) is shown on page 20.

Hawk Cliff Boulder. Photograph by Laura Balogh.

35. The Patterson Historical Society, *Vignettes of Patterson's Past* (Patterson, NY: Patterson Historical Society, 2007).
Huge boulder – On page 12 is a photograph with only a fraction of the rock shown. The caption reads "Nancy Clark supports a boulder the glacier left behind on the bedrock near Route 164." It is virtually impossible to estimate the size of the boulder from the photograph. A general GPS for Route 164 in Patterson is 41º29.047'N 73º37.261'W.

36. Wallace Bruce, *The Hudson: Three Centuries of History, Romance and Invention* (NY: Walking News, Inc., 1982. Centennial edition reprint), 54.

"Among the Hudson rocks are several 'Lady's Chairs', 'Lover's Leaps', 'Devil's Toothpicks', 'Devil's Pulpit'....." No indication is given, however, as to where these natural rock formations might be found.

37. *Siwanoy Indian Image Stone* – Charles Dunlap, "The Image Stone of the Siwanoys." *The Westchester Historian. Quarterly of the Westchester County Historical Society.* Vol. 4, no. 2 (April, 1925). Dunlap writes that the rock resembles a great bird. The stone is 2 feet high and 5 feet by 35 feet in breadth at its base.

Ernest Freeland Griffin (editor), *Westchester County and its People Vol. 1* (NY: Lewis Historical Publishing Company, 1946). A photo of the Indian Image Stone is shown on page 95.

The stone is located on the grounds of the Huguenot and New Rochelle Historical Association, corner of North Avenue and Paine Avenues in New Rochelle. The GPS reading for the junction of these two avenues is 40°56.079'N 73°47.504'W.

38. *Old Poker Hole* – Howard DeVoe, "Pleasantville's Lost Cavern." *Westchester Historian. Quarterly of the Westchester County Historical Society.* Vol. 33, no. 3 (July, August, September, 1957).

Mention is made of the Old Poker Hole (a cave), but no specifics are provided.

The cave is also mentioned in an article by Randall Comfort entitled "The Old Kettle Hole," which he wrote for the *Westchester County Magazine* in June of 1914.

The entrance is described as being somewhere along the western slope of a small wooded ravine, south of Pleasantville's Banks

Bombay Hook (Palisades). Old line drawing.

Cemetery. The GPS reading for the Banks Cemetery is 41°08.263'N 73°46.605'W. The cemetery is 0.2 mile from the junction of Route

141/Broadway & Bedford Road, going south on Route 141/Broadway. From here, you are on your own!

Even in the late 1950s, a group of explorers were unable to locate the cave. I don't know if anyone has had success since then.

You may find something interesting along the way in any case. DeVoe writes about "Two interesting six foot deep potholes [that demonstrate] the existence of vigorous ground water activity at some ancient epoch."

39. *Ossining Rock Shelter* -- Leslie V. Case, "The Ossining Rock Shelter." *Quarterly Bulletin. Westchester County Historical Society.* Vol. 75 no. 4 (October, 1929), 81–85.

According to Case, "The shelter is formed by a great monolith torn by glacial action from the cliff of Fordham gneiss above it." It is 11 feet by 16 feet, and 6 feet at its highest point. The rock-shelter lies 100 feet above the Pocantico River. It is the smallest of three rock-shelters in close proximity. The larger two are said to have been frequented by the mysterious Leatherman.

The directions given, which are fairly imprecise, suggest that this rock-shelter is "½ mile south of Echo Lake; around midway between Saw Mill River Road and the Bronx Parkway Extension; near intersection of Townships of Ossining, Mt. Pleasant, and New Castle." For what it's worth as a starting point, the GPS for Echo Lake is 41º10.799′N 73º48.609′W.

Erratic Behavior. Photograph by Laura Balogh.

40. *Leatherman Cave --* Allison Albee, "The Leather Man's Cave and Washburn Mill," from the old *Westchester Historian. Quarterly of the Westchester County Historical Society* Vol. 30, no. 2 (April 1954), 70.

Albee writes, "Now partially destroyed,

it was originally a favorite habitat of the red man. Ideally, situated facing a small pond its chamber originally measured 15 x 11 x 6 feet high."

This puts the rock-shelter in the area of Kinderogen Lake [41°09.461'N 73°48.520'W], which can be reached from the Taconic Parkway by getting off at Exit 6, following Pleasantville Road for 0.1 mile, and then heading northeast on Washburn Road for ~1.0 mile. That's as far as I can get you. The rest is up to you.

41. *Spook O Hole* -- Amy Ver Nooy, "The Ghost at Fiddler's Bridge and other Spooks." *Year Book Dutchess County Historical Society* (Vo. 42, 1957), 4 & 42.

The cave, located south of Poughkeepsie, was first indicated on the Beers, Ellis & Soule Atlas in 1867. In 1870, Spook O Hole was described in the *Poughkeepsie Telegraph* as "a remarkable cavity in a rocky hill on the property of J. and I. Frost..." That was the last favorable press the cave received. In 1879, a report was made to the Poughkeepsie Society of Natural Science by J. H. Booth, A. P. Jeanarett, and Henry Booth. "This cave [*Spook O Hole*], if so insignificant a fissure may be dignified by such a title, is situated in Poughkeepsie Township, and lies near Barnegat, about 60 rods [990 feet] east from the Hudson River. It is in the Barnegat limestone, contains no stalactites, is very damp and will repay no one the trouble of a visit."

All of this is really academic today, for I believe that the cave no longer exists, having been destroyed by the enormous, nearly 2.0-mile-long, > 0.5- mile-wide Clinton Point Quarry as it expanded.

42. -- Raymond H. Torrey, Frank Place, Jr. and Robert L. Dickinson, *New York Walk Book. Third Edition* (NY: The American Geographical So-ciety, 1951), 15. *Serpentine Cave* -- Mention is made that ""the trail crosses Todt Hill Road and then follows bridle paths to a 'serpentine cave.'"

In the website 3dparks.wr.usgs.gov/nyc/parks/loc7.htm, Dorothy Valentine Smith, a Staten Island Historian, talks about a cave that she knew as Indian Cave, which I presume was/is located on Todt Hill. The general GPS for Todt Hill is 40°36.094'N 74°06.254'W.

Prop Rock – In the Black Rock Forest on a path off of the Eagle Cliff Trail is a summit called Prop Rock. "There a boulder about six feet in diameter holds up, at one end, a great slab twenty feet long." As far as I can ascertain, this rock is west of Far Spy Rock (Spy Rock), north of Jim's Pond, and south of Tamarack Pond. A GPS of 41°23.392'N 74°01.540'W will give you are general idea of the area where Prop Rock is.

Bedrock at High Tor. Photograph by Dan Balogh.

43. *Skedaddle Rock* -- Marjorie Smeltzer-Stevenot, *Footprints in the Ramapos* (Ashland, OH: Bookmasters, Inc., 1993), 97. "A few who refused to be drawn into the [Civil] war hid out in 'Skedaddle Rock,' near Green Swamp in Pine Meadows, fed and protected from authorities by their families." I have no idea where this rock is, and if it really is a boulder, but the Pine Meadow area is between Johnsontown and Ladentown.

44. *Peddlers Rock* – Malcom J. Mills, *East Fishkill: Images of America* (Charleston, SC: Arcadia Press, 2006), 46. "This massive boulder, which projects into the roadway at Shenandoah and Hortontown Roads, is known locally as Peddlers Rock." An image of the rock accompanies the caption, but unfortunately is blurred.

45. *Spring House Rock-Shelter* -- Edward J. Lenik, *Indians in the Ramapos: Survival, Persistence and Presence* (North Jersey, NJ: Highlands Historical Society, 1999), 34–37. "The Spring House

Rockshelter is an overhanging rock outcrop that protrudes from a steeply sloping hillside near the bottom of a small ravine. The shelter measures twenty feet (6 meters) in length, thirteen feet (4 meters) in depth and six and one-half feet (2 meters) in maximum height..." The shelter faces west/northwest, north of Eagle Valley Road in the village of Sloatsburg. I suspect it is an archaeologically sensitive site, having been occupied by Native Americans from c. 5,000 BC to c. 1680. Artifacts from the rock-shelter are on permanent exhibit at the Sloatsburg Public Library [41º09.361'N 74º011.615'W] on 1 Liberty Rock Road in Sloatsburg.

Boulder on top of Bear Mountain. Photograph c. 1900. Note: Park rangers have searched for and never found this rock.

46. *Hanging Boulder* – In this early c. 1900 postcard, Hanging Boulder is perched next to a one-lane road in the Mount Peter area of Greenwood Lake. Given the passage of over a century of time, it seems highly unlikely that this precariously balanced rock still exists. But who knows for sure until you go to take a look.

47. William Thompson Howell, *The Hudson Highlands. Vol. 1* (A memorial set of books published in 1933, limited to 200 copies).

p. 54. *Balanced Rock on Bear Mountain* – "This rock was fixed, but in a way that to say the least was unusual. It may have weighed, perhaps, fifty tons (estimate of G. W. P.), and it rested on three points, each of which was no larger than two good sized fists. One of these points of rest was the bed rock, and the other two were cobblestones. They raised the boulder clear of the bedrock by about six inches."

Rock Walks

Hanging Boulder. Old postcard.

48. William Thompson Howell, *The Hudson Highlands. Vol. 2* (A memorial set of books published in 1933, limited to 200 copies).

p. 9. *Bear's Den* – Howell mentions a "Bear's den, below Summit Rock on the West Point Road."

p. 17. *Balanced Rock* – "On top of the Profile, over fourteen hundred feet up, is a small boulder which formerly rocked at the touch. It has lately fallen over and is now fixed."

p. 17. *Echo Rock Ridge Balanced Rock* – "One weighing a ton or more, on top of Echo Rock Ridge, at nearly as high an elevation [1,400'], is so balanced as to rock with a swing of several inches."

p. 17. *Mine Hill Boulders* – "Behind Mine Hill and over a thousand feet up are some very large boulders for that height and locality."

49. *St. Anthony's Nose* -- William J. Blake, *History of Putnam County, New York* (NY: Baker and Scribner, 1849), 165–167.

At one time there was a rock face on Breakneck Mountain named St. Anthony's Face. Blake writes, "'St. Anthony's Face', so

377

celebrated in the history of the Hudson scenery, once peered out and over the rocky battlements below, gazing, as it were, at the eternal ebb and flood of the mighty current [Hudson River]...." Blake goes on to say that "In the summer of 1846, Capt. Deering Ayers, who was engaged in the services of Harlem High Bridge Company, by one fell blast, detached an immense block of granite weighing nearly two thousand tons" — and so, another geological formation of note in the mid-nineteenth century ceased to exist.

Bouldering at the East Marion Boulder. Photograph by Christian Prellwitz.

50. Raymond H. Torry, Frank Place, Jr., & Robert L. Dickinson, *New York Walk Book, suggestions for excursions afoot within a radius of fifty to one hundred miles of the city including Westchester County, the Highlands of the Hudson and the Ramapos, northern and central New Jersey and the New Jersey Pine Barrens, Long Island, the Shawangunk Range, the Catskills, and the Taconics* (New York: American Geological Society, 1923).

     p. 99. *Brundige Cave* – Brundige Cave is located "on the east side of the spur of Brundige Mountain, about a mile north of Burnt Saw Mill Bridge. It is a perpendicular crack of 3 or 4 feet in width and extending upward for 10 or 25 feet." A pen & ink drawing of the cave can be seen on page 120.

Brundige Cave. Pen & ink sketch by Robert L. Dickinson

p. 121. *Washington Rock* – "Washington Rock is a projecting point of the trap rock ridge 520 feet above sea level...Here, in May and June of 1777, General Washington spent many days sweeping the country through his glass for movements of the British. This has been commemorated by a tablet erected here on a stone monument."

p. 122. *Chimney Rock* – "...around Chimney Rock was the encampment of the Continental troops and General Washington during the spring of 1777...About Chimney Rock clings the shadowy romance of an Indian girl whose lover had been killed by a rival. She, seeking the rock where she had last seen him, hears her lover calling. She leaps from the rocks into his arms, as she thinks, and is killed on the rocks below." A pen & ink drawing can be seen on page 120.

ACKNOWLEDGMENT

Many thanks go to –

Richard Delaney, for performing the herculean task of proofreading this enormous book; Barbara Delaney, who not only proofread *Rock Walks*, but is a fellow author and, best of all, my wife; Dan Balogh, creator of danbalogh.com, for generously providing the majority of the photographs pertaining to hikes along the west side of the Hudson River, and for furnishing both the front and back cover photographs; Lisa Motluck for reviewing the chapter on the Walt Whitman Boulder and for her valuable input on the elusive Bear Mountain Boulder; David Beck, Park Naturalist, Dutchess County, for guiding Barbara and me to the rockledge shelter at Bowdoin Park, and for reviewing the Bowdoin Park Rockledge Shelters chapter.

Daniel Chazin, photographer, hiker, and creator of dchazin@aol.com, for his photographs of Split Rock, Bear Rock, and Mianus Gorge Rocks; Carlos Gonzalez, photographer, hiker, and creator of ScenesFromTheTrails, for his photographs of the glacial erratic at Rockefeller State Park and Split Rock; Mike Todd, creator of hikethehudsonvalley.com, for his photograph of a boulder at Nuclear Lake; Alex Smoller, creator of alexsmoller@gmail.com, for his photograph of a glacial erratic in the Betsy Sluder Preserve; Christian Prellwitz, creator of the website "Sky and Stone," for his photograph of the East Marion Boulder; and Steven Schimmrich, the Hudson Valley Geologist, for his photograph of Turtle Rock.

Brendan Murphy Director of Stewardship, Westchester Land Trust, for determining whether an accessible rock-shelter exists in the Westchester County's Rockshelter Preserve—it doesn't; Barbara Ransome, Director of Operations, Greater Port Jefferson Chamber of Commerce, without whose help I would not have located the Jefferson Boulder; Amanda Cymore, park ranger, and her fellow Park rangers who spent considerable time on the summit of Bear Mountain looking for a boulder that I believed to be there; Steve Olsen, Parks Director, Dutchess County, Betsy Biddle, Executive Director at Andrus on Hudson, and Christine Tesauro, at Port

Jefferson, for being so helpful; The New York State Library, Albany, and its kind staff, for their support.

Stockbridge Cave Shelter. Photograph by Dan Balogh.

ABOUT THE AUTHOR

Russell Dunn, a former New York State licensed hiking guide, lives in Albany, New York, is married to Barbara Delaney (a fellow writer), and is the author of three previous regional guidebooks to astounding boulders and natural rock formations: *Rockachusetts: An Explorer's Guide to Amazing Boulders of Massachusetts* (co-authored with Christy Butler); *Rambles to Remarkable Rocks: An Explorer's Hiking Guide to Amazing Boulders and Rock Formations of the Greater Capital Region, Catskills, & Shawangunks;* and *Boulders Beyond Belief: An Explorer's Hiking Guide to Amazing Boulders and Natural Rock Formations of the Adirondacks.*

Dunn has also written eight waterfall guidebooks, four paddling guidebooks, three hiking guidebooks, *Adventures Around the Great Sacandaga Lake* (his first book), *Ausable Chasm in Pictures & Story* (co-authored with John Haywood & Sean Reines), and eleven photobooks of stereographic pictures.

Dunn's hobbies, when he is not writing or exploring, are stereography, magic, songwriting, and playing the guitar.

He can be reached at rdunnwaterfalls@yahoo.com.

INDEX

A

Acksin, 107
Adams, Arthur G., 53, 264, 273, 338–340, 343–345
Adee, George Townsend, 135
Adkins, Leonard M., 277, 286, 297, 313
Adler, Cy A., 343, 347, 350
Agassiz, Louis, 14
Albany, 54, 55, 58, 93, 108, 264, 381, 382
Albee, Allison, 62, 63, 373
Algonkian, 48
Algonquian, 210, 273, 305
Allis, Jr., Ashton, 285, 296
Allison Trail, 333
Almost Perpendicular, 304–306
Alpine, 344, 345, 347–349
Aolpine, Camp, 331
Alpine Picnic Area and Boat Basin, 343, 347, 349
Alpine Rock, 347–349
Alpine Rocks (photo), 348
Amackassin Creek, 106–108
Amackassin Rock, 106–109
Amackassin Rock (photo), 107
Amackassin Stone, 107, 108
Amackassin Terrace, 106
A-Mac-lea-sin Rock, 366, 367
AMC's Best Day Hikes Near New York City, 86
Amenia, 23, 363
American Museum of Natural History, 183, 184, 358
Amtrak, 30, 175, 176
Anderson, Katherine S., 82, 85, 88
Andes Rail Trail, 361
Andre, John, 261
Andre Monument, Major John, 261
Andre the Spy, 261
Andre the Spy Rock, 261, 262
Andrews, Mary, 358
Andrus Foundation, 106, 108
Andrus-on-Hudson, 108, 380
Antoniadis, Gabrielle, 87
Antos, Jason D., 206, 207
Appalachian Trail, 36–38, 42, 296, 297
Appalachian Trail Conservancy, 277, 286, 297, 313
Appleby's Island, 158
Aquehonga Manachnong, 210
Aquehung, 128
Aquehung Boulder, 103

Aquehung Boulder (photo), 103
Archive Sleuth, 95, 96, 105
Arch Rock, 191, 193, 195
Arden-Surebridge Trail, 2, 293, 294
Armonk, 96, 98, 99, 358, 369
Army Corp of Engineers, U.S., 198
Arnold, Benedict, 261
Arthur, John, 60
Arthur Trail, 270
Artist Lake, 225
Asimov, Isaac, 171, 173
Astoria Athletic Field, 199, 360
Atlantic Highlands, 211
Atlantic Ocean, 15
Austen, Alice, 364
Avalon Green Apartments, 105
Avebury, England, 211
Ayers, Capt. Deering, 378

B

Babson Boulders, Massachusetts, 240
Bailey, Bill, 276
Bailey Brook, 60
Bailey, John, 110
Bailey, Paul, 184, 207, 219, 230, 234, 248, 276
Bailey, Ranger Teddy, 139
Baiting Hollow, 235, 236
Baiting Hollow Boulders, 235, 236
Baker Camp, 321, 360
Balanced Rock: Bear Mtn, 376
Balanced Rock: Brinton Brook Sanctuary, 50, 51
Balanced Rock: Kenwood Lake, 43, 44
Balanced Rock: Mount Peter, 376
Balanced Rock: Profile, 377
Balancing Turtle Rock, 370
Bald Rock, 28
Balogh, Dan, 2, 13, 268, 270, 273, 279, 282, 284, 287, 288, 291, 293, 294, 296, 301, 305, 310, 315, 317, 322, 323, 325, 327, 332, 375
Balogh, Laura Petersen, 282, 323, 371, 373
Banks Cemetery, 372
Baptist Church Road Rock Cave, 72
Barnegat, 374
Barryville, 251, 252
Barstow, Camp Francoise, 231
Bartow-Pell Traffic Circle, 154, 156, 159, 161, 165, 168, 171, 174, 176
Baskerville, Charles A., 139
Bass Rock, 149, 150
Batavia, 55
Bat Cave, 272
Bathgate, Alexander, 121
Battleground Trail, 252

Rock Walks

389

Rock Walks

Rock Walks

Rock Walks

Rock Walks

394

Rock Walks

Rock Walks

402

Rock Walks

Rock Walks

Rock Walks

Woodland Trail, 252
Woodtown Road/Trail, 318, 319
Woodys, 224
Worden, Michael J., 265
Work Projects Administration, 138
World's Fair, New York, 275
World War I, 65, 183, 212
World War II, 352
Woolsey Rock, 179
Worthless Rock, 191, 192, 196
Wyckoff, Jerome, 285, 295, 302, 303,
    356

Y

Yasinsac, Rob, 104

Yellow Rock, 179
Yellowstone National Park, 296
Yonkers, 103, 106–108, 192
Yonkers-Hastings Line, 106, 108
Yonkers Historical Bulletin, 108, 109,
    132
Yorktown, 72, 73
Yorktown Trailway, 74

Z

Zimmerman, H. Neil, 82, 86, 269,
    311–313, 326, 328, 330, 360, 368
Zimmerman, Linda, 258, 278
Zombie Rock, 140, 143

Made in the USA
Middletown, DE
01 November 2022

13901858R00225